ESTABLISHING A LEGACY

ESTABLISHING A LEGACY

COLONEL BERND HORN

The History of The
Royal Canadian Regiment
1883–1953

Foreword by Lieutenant-General (Retired) J.E. Vance

DUNDURN PRESS
TORONTO

Copyright © Bernd Horn, 2008

All rights reserved. No part of this publication may be reproduced, stored in a retrieval system, or transmitted in any form or by any means, electronic, mechanical, photocopying, recording, or otherwise (except for brief passages for purposes of review) without the prior permission of Dundurn Press. Permission to photocopy should be requested from Access Copyright.

Editor: Michael Carroll
Copy-editor: Nigel Heseltine
Designer: Jennifer Scott
Printer: Friesens

Library and Archives Canada Cataloguing in Publication

Horn, Bernd, 1959-
  Establishing a legacy : the history of the Royal Canadian Regiment, 1883-1953 / Bernd Horn.

Includes bibliographical references and index.
ISBN 978-1-55002-822-5 (leather bound).—ISBN 978-1-55002-821-8 (bound).—
ISBN 978-1-55002-817-1 (pbk.)

  1. Canada. Canadian Army. Royal Canadian Regiment--History. I. Title.

UA602.R55H67 2008   356'.10971   C2007-907559-2

1 2 3 4 5   12 11 10 09 08

  Conseil des Arts   Canada Council
                      du Canada   for the Arts

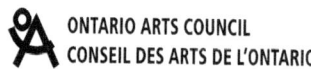 ONTARIO ARTS COUNCIL
                      CONSEIL DES ARTS DE L'ONTARIO

We acknowledge the support of the Canada Council for the Arts and the Ontario Arts Council for our publishing program. We also acknowledge the financial support of the Government of Canada through the Book Publishing Industry Development Program and The Association for the Export of Canadian Books, and the Government of Ontario through the Ontario Book Publishers Tax Credit program and the Ontario Media Development Corporation.

Care has been taken to trace the ownership of copyright material used in this book. The author and the publisher welcome any information enabling them to rectify any references or credits in subsequent editions.

J. Kirk Howard, President

Printed and bound in Canada
www.dundurn.com

Dundurn Press	Gazelle Book Services Limited	Dundurn Press
3 Church Street, Suite 500	White Cross Mills	2250 Military Road
Toronto, Ontario, Canada	High Town, Lancaster, England	Tonawanda, NY U.S.A.
M5E 1M2	LA1 4XS	14150

CONTENTS

Foreword by Lieutenant-General (Retired) J.E. Vance	7
Acknowledgements	9
Introduction	11
1 A Pressing Need: Establishing the Permanent Force and Policing the Dominion	15
2 Making Canada Proud: The "Royal Canadians" in South Africa	41
3 Service and Suffering: The Regiment in the First World War	73
4 "Fighting Men from Canada": The Regiment's Introduction to Modern War	109
5 No Soft Underbelly: The Battle for Italy	137
6 The Final Stretch: Collapsing the Third Reich	169
7 A Return to Combat: The First Regimental Tour to Korea, 1951–1952	205
8 "Spit and Polish": The Regulars in Korea, 1952–1953	227
Appendix A: Key Events Timeline	255
Appendix B: Key Appointments	319
Appendix C: Battle Honours	325
Notes	329
Glossary	385
Selected Bibliography	389
About the Author	395
Index	397

FOREWORD

I am honoured to write the foreword to this book, for it tells the story of Canada's oldest regular regiment of infantry, The Royal Canadian Regiment (RCR). I first put up the eight-pointed star in the mid-1950s, when I was commissioned into The RCR. That 50 years represent many things: For me personally it was a lifetime of soldiering for Canada; for my generation it stands for the era of the Cold War; and for The Regiment it served as the link between the war experiences that characterized the first 70 years of The RCR's existence and the demanding, uncertain, and exciting challenges facing The Regiment today.

Although two volumes covering the first 80 years of RCR history had been written previously, in the autumn of 1997 the Regimental Senate decided it was time to update those earlier editions and write the history of The Regiment since Korea. When we asked Colonel Bernd Horn to undertake these tasks in the spring of 2005, we were delighted that he willingly answered our call despite his heavy workload at the Canadian Defence Academy.

This book, *Establishing a Legacy: The History of The Royal Canadian Regiment 1883–1953*, is the first part of a two-part, updated history of The RCR, which Colonel Horn began then. At that time, The Regimental senate decided that, as well as establishing a properly organized and catalogued archives in the Regimental Museum, the project should aim to create an updated populist, yet academically sound, history of The Regiment, so that both serving and retired members of The RCR, as well as the public at large, could become more aware of The Regiment's important contribution to this great nation of ours.

This volume achieves that goal. Written in a flowing and riveting style, the book highlights the accomplishments of The Regiment attained by individual members who served together, often through hardship and horror, to establish a legacy of courage, honour, and service to the nation.

Although this is a regimental history, it is actually a story of the men and women who made up The Regiment. A regiment is a living, breathing body, as strong and as weak as its individual members and leaders — an entity comprising all those who serve its Colours. In the following pages, it is possible to trace the lineage of many of our most cherished attributes and principles, in essence, the character of The Royal Canadian Regiment. Whether following "Royals" who trekked through the rough wilderness of Canada's northwest to the Yukon, or endured the march across the harsh Transvaal, or those who "went over the top" in the slaughterhouses of Ypres, Flanders, and Passchendaele, or those who suffered the savage fighting in the challenging Italian mountains, or later in the Korean theatre of operations, what stands out is the timeless dedication to professionalism and service before self. Our history is filled with courage, honour, and tenacity. In short, this book explains how the character of The Regiment was forged.

However, this book is only part of the story. The second part, *From the Cold War into the New Millennium: The History of The Royal Canadian Regiment 1954–2008*, is currently underway. It will capture the rest of The RCR tradition of service to the nation and its people.

While these volumes are dedicated to the challenge of informing and inspiring the soldiers of The Regiment of today and tomorrow, they are also offered to the public at large. I encourage everyone to read them to better appreciate the sacrifice that the servicemen and women in The RCR, and in other regiments and branches, have performed. In so doing, they have secured the way of life Canadians now enjoy.

Pro Patria,
J.E. Vance
Lieutenant-General (Retired)
The Royal Canadian Regiment

ACKNOWLEDGEMENTS

Any work of this magnitude owes its completion to the efforts of many people. As such, I wish to thank all those who, through the contribution of materials, time, a piece of their memory, or moral support, assisted me in the completion of this volume.

As always, however, there are some whose efforts warrant special mention. In this vein I wish to thank the former and current regimental adjutants, Captain Duncan MacMillan and Captain Mike O'Leary, for their ceaseless efforts in promulgating RCR history and assisting me with this project. They are the invisible hands behind the scene that make regimental business happen.

In addition, I must thank Michel Wyczynski, both personally and on behalf of the entire Regiment for his outstanding work at bringing accuracy, discipline, and organization to the regimental archives. Because of his efforts, the RCR Museum now boasts an impressive archival collection that is accessible and user friendly to historians and The Regiment's members. I would also like to make special mention of the stellar assistance provided by William Constable, who produced most of the maps in this volume. Bill passed away 2 May 2007, and will be sadly missed.

Thanks are also due to Captain (Retired) Robert H. Mahar (and sons Donald G. and Lieutenant-Colonel (Retired) Bob Mahar), Dan Martel, Major Tom Mykytiuk, Master-Corporal V. Sellars, Dr. Emily Spencer, Craig Mantle, Claus Breede, Sabrina Shaw, Lieutenant-Colonel Mike

Pearson, Sergeant Greg Collette, H.R. Gardner, and Aileen Grant for their assistance and support. Furthermore, I wish to acknowledge the support I received from staff at the Canadian War Museum, Directorate of History and Heritage , Library and Archives Canada, the Glenbow Museum and Archives, and the Royal Military College of Canada.

I would also like to thank Michael Carroll, Nigel Heseltine, and The Dundurn Group staff for taking the rough manuscript and turning it into the polished volume that it is.

Finally, but certainly not least, I wish to thank my wife, Kim, and my daughters, Calli and Katie, for continuing to tolerate my absences and focus on historical projects.

INTRODUCTION

In many ways a regimental history is a long war story, invariably of more interest to some than others. But it is more than just the actions and achievements of a small group of individuals united through membership in a particular group or regiment. Regimental history is testimony to the feats of courage and tenacity of Canadians tested in the furnace of combat, the sometimes tedious regimen of peace, and everything between those two extremes. Regimental history speaks to our collective Canadian military heritage and legacy. It is a window on our country and ourselves.

So what exactly is a regiment? In essence it is a body of troops with a formal organization and chain of command. The word *regiment* actually derives from the Latin term *regimentum* meaning rule. Key to a regiment is the fact that it has relative administrative and tactical autonomy. Regiments first appeared in the sixteenth century, when countries began maintaining standing professional armies. They represented a dramatic change in military organization. Over time, regiments evolved to become a regular, standardized formation of a defined size that included one or more battalions, each containing a set number of companies, also of a stated size. Importantly, command is exercised by an officially prescribed number of officers with standardized ranks and functions.[1] In essence, regiments have formed the basis for the combat organization of Western armies for the last 300 years.

A key feature of a regiment is its permanency, which allows for the creation of a culture typified by regimental identity (e.g., distinctive uniforms, insignia, symbols, and traditions) and intense devotion. Not surprisingly then, it has been strongly argued that the regimental system is key to promoting cohesion, esprit de corps, and morale — all basic components of combat effectiveness. "A Regiment is one of the institutions which form character, in particular the martial habits of discipline, courage, loyalty, pride and endurance," explained Captain J.A. Johnston, a former regimental officer.[2] Similarly, Arthur Bryant professed:

> The Regiment is something more than a vehicle for orders: it is a school of military virtue. Its value to our country is that it evokes men's love, pride and loyalty and by doing so, enables them on the battlefield to transcend their own natures. This sacred and undying brotherhood, drawn from all classes and standards of education but knit together in a common pride and code, has repeatedly given [an army] a fighting strength in excess of its numbers and equipment.[3]

Within the national context, the regimental system has long been fundamental to the Canadian military experience. It has shaped, and indeed continues to shape, the attitudes and values of our military personnel, and influence the decisions and policies affecting the Canadian Forces (i.e., organization, training, administration, force generation, and employment).

However, for the soldier, senior non-commissioned officer (NCO), and officer serving in the military, the regiment takes on a meaning and significance far beyond a stiff definition. It is an emotive issue — a special bond that signifies membership in something larger than oneself — in a family with a rich history, and legacy of courage, valour, and accomplishment. This important emotional link assists, if not drives, individuals to strive to maintain and advance the regiment's name. "The record of the Regiment," asserted General Charles Foulkes, a former chair of the chiefs of staff and RCR regimental officer, "speaks for itself, and it is up to you to maintain and add to that record of achievement."[4] In sum, to members of a regiment, it is not a faceless organization, it is a vibrant living organism.

In his first book, *55 Axis*, Strome Galloway, another former regimental officer and honourary colonel of The Regiment, quoted an unknown soldier-philosopher who stated: "Men die, wars end, but the Regiment lives on!" Quite simply, a regiment is a living entity. It is a reflection of the men and women that make up its substance. As such, the history of a regiment is really the story of its members — their trials, challenges, disappointments, and achievements. It is often a story of courage and tenacity; a tale of compassion, emotion, and comradeship. For these reasons, when recounting the history of a regiment, it is necessary to tell the story of its members.

This volume describes the achievement of the members of The Royal Canadian Regiment (The RCR) in their first 70 years. The "Royal Canadians," as they were first called, later abbreviated to "Royals" during the Second World War, are Canada's oldest regular force infantry regiment. Created on 21 December 1883, The RCR has served the country with honour and distinction. From its first operational deployment to the North-West Rebellion in 1885, its members have shown courage, professionalism, and tenacity. During the Boer War, the "Royal Canadians" brought honour to The Regiment and the nation. Their victory at Paardeberg, bought at great cost in blood, was the first British victory during that conflict. The success served to raise the profile of colonial, specifically Canadian, troops in the eyes of the British, and the world.

The Regiments feats of courage and suffering, and service to the nation, continued over the next half century. In both global conflicts, the First (1914–1918) and Second (1939–1945) World Wars, as well as the Korean conflict (1950–1953), the "Royals" built on the legacy of those who came before and reinforced the great traditions of The RCR, namely chivalry, gallantry, and dash. Throughout, its members were expected to demonstrate courage, obedience, physical fitness, professional effectiveness, and pride in self and regiment. Few were found wanting. By 1953, The Regiment had earned 57 battle honours, 25 of which are emblazoned on its Colours.

Trying to capture 125 years of dramatic and dynamic history in a single volume would have been an overwhelming task. Accordingly, this volume limits itself to the major achievements, exploits, and events that shaped and forged The Royal Canadian Regiment in its first 70 years.[5] A key event summary has been included that provides additional details for those who seek such information.

Of note, this volume is the first part of a two-part history that represents the third effort to chronicle RCR regimental history.[6] Overall,

Volume 3, Part 1, *Establishing a Legacy: The History of The Royal Canadian Regiment 1883–1953*, is a modernized, populist history that captures the first 70 years of the RCR experience. Moreover, it is part of The Regiment's 125th anniversary celebrations in 2008. Most important, it is a celebration of The Regiment's greatest strength — the men and women who made it the great institution that it is. In the end, however, the essence of The RCR's efforts has always been straightforward — *Pro Patria*, or simply "For Country."

1
A Pressing Need: Establishing the Permanent Force and Policing the Dominion

Canadians have always resisted a large standing army (i.e., permanent/regular force). Politicians loathed the associated cost and the public questioned the necessity. After all, there was always a more senior partner, at first the British and later the Americans, to provide the necessary protection. As such, throughout the 1800s, Canadians deemed a citizen's militia sufficient to meet the nation's commitment to defence. Its actual effectiveness was never really an issue — as long as British regulars were stationed in Canada.

By the 1860s, however, the question of Canadian defence was reaching a climax of sorts. The British after decades of attempting to convince, cajole, and push the Canadian leadership to take on more responsibility for its own defence finally, under economic and political pressure of their own, announced the impending withdrawal of their forces from Canada, except for a small garrison at the strategic port of Halifax. Suddenly, it appeared that Canadians would be on their own.

To some this was a scary proposition. Despite the prevailing Canadian militia myth that held that military men were born and not created, and that it was the militia that successfully defended the country during the War of 1812 and would do so again when necessary, the Canadian militia was actually poorly equipped, trained, and led. However, by 1860, the British were providing instructors to train the Canadian militia in drill and musketry. Moreover, a plan to use British units and sub-units as role models and instructional cadre for the militia was also put in motion. As part of this initiative, the Canadian government was urged to establish a permanent force to serve as the training cadre for the militia once the British regulars withdrew from the continent. But as always, this advice was ignored.

Despite Confederation in 1867, the prime minister, Sir John A. Macdonald, still refused to consider the idea. Even though the dominion was a sovereign nation, he knew Canadians had no stomach for a regular army. They still believed that defence was an imperial problem. The first Militia Act of 1868 merely transformed the militia system from a provincial basis to an expanded dominion structure based on nine military districts.[1] Nonetheless, the British held true to their word and in 1869 announced that they would withdraw their forces in the following year. After an unintended delay, as a result of the Red River Rebellion in Manitoba, and the Fenian Raids in eastern and central Canada, the remaining British troops, except the Halifax garrison, left Canada in November 1871.[2]

Faced with this reality, the Canadian government relented and on 20 October 1871, established "A" and "B" Batteries to look after the artillery and stores left by the British Army at the fortresses of Quebec and Kingston, as well as to provide instruction to the militia. Initially they were commanded by British officers and manned by militiamen on temporary call-out. However, two years later the gunners were put on full-time service. Canada now had a fledgling permanent, though small, army.

The Russian war scare of 1878, as well as continued inefficiencies with the militia prompted the next major step. In June 1883, Minister of Militia and Defence Adolphe Caron proposed to cabinet the creation of infantry and cavalry schools at Toronto, Montreal, and Fredericton, with the condition that all militia officers attend the appropriate school to qualify for their appointments. This policy was implemented in the Militia Act of 1883. The permanent force, defined by the Act "as that portion of the Active Militia of Canada permanently embodied for the purpose of providing for the care and protection of forts, magazines, armaments, warlike stores, and other military service, and of securing the establishment of schools for military instruction," had now reached an important stage of its development.[3] Canada now had regular, standing units of the three principle combat arms. However, the government capped the permanent force at a maximum of a paltry 750 all ranks. Nonetheless, significantly, General Order No. 26, issued on 21 December 1883, authorized the formation of three schools of infantry, formed into one corps, known as the Infantry School Corps. The nation was at long last making a commitment to defend itself with an army that could fight. Equally important, the Infantry School Corps was the root that would develop into The Royal Canadian Regiment.

Initially, the architects of the reform envisioned that the schools would develop into instructional regiments of infantry. Under this plan, the appointed commandants would naturally become the commanding officers of their respective regiments. For that reason, no overall commander was appointed. Rather, each school reported direct to militia headquarters (HQ) in Ottawa. The obvious effect was the existence of three distinct disconnected sub-units. There existed no unifying esprit de corps or regimental ethos.

Regardless, there was a great deal of enthusiasm and energy. At each location, once authorized, a company of approximately six officers and 100 other ranks was raised. Their specific duties included the training of officers and other ranks of the volunteer militia and aid to the civil power. In addition, each company was to be so highly trained that it would serve as the "model upon which all infantry training, discipline and ceremonial should be based."[4]

Although the permanent force was largely seen by Canadians as an instructional cadre to train the volunteer militia, it was not long before they were called on to conduct actual military operations. The North-West Rebellion was the first military test of the new dominion and its fledgling permanent force. It seemed that once again, much like the crisis in 1870, the discontent of the Métis and full-blooded Natives in the West was beginning to boil over. Unsettled land claims, government policies, unfulfilled promises and a continuous influx of white settlers disillusioned and frustrated the native inhabitants of the western territories. Many felt that this was their last chance to assert their voice and ensure their interests were looked after in the development of the Canadian northwest. Action seemed the only manner to get the government's attention. Accordingly, in June 1884, they summoned Louis Riel from exile in Montana to lead them once more, as he had in 1870 during the Red River Rebellion.

On 19 March 1885, Riel and his followers declared a provisional government. Riel further promised a "war of extermination upon all those who have shown themselves hostile to our rights."[5] Any doubt of his intent disappeared seven day later, when political aspiration erupted into armed rebellion at Duck Lake. Superintendent L.N.F. Crozier of the North-West Mounted Police (NWMP) assembled 52 of his men and 43

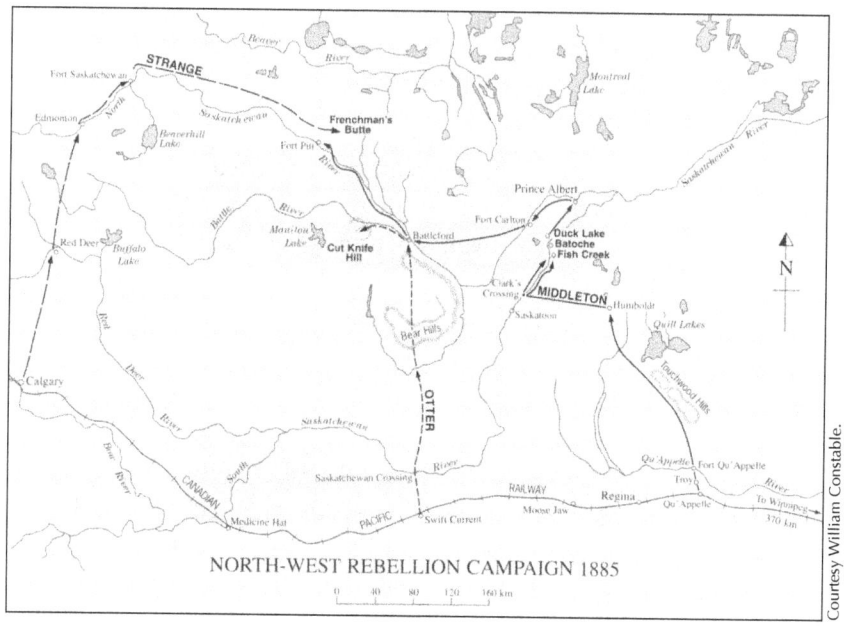

NORTH-WEST REBELLION CAMPAIGN 1885

white settlers who were sworn in as special constables to face down Riel and his followers who had earlier challenged government authority and shot at his constables. A heated discussion soon led to gunfire. Crozier quickly realized his small force was virtually surrounded and inadequate to deal with the threat. As a result, he withdrew, but not before he had sustained 23 casualties — 12 dead and 11 wounded. There was now only one possible end to the crisis.

The calamity in the West created great consternation in Ottawa. The government was rightfully concerned that the winds of discontent could sweep rapidly through the region, which, except for the thin ranks of the NWMP ("Mounties") was without a military presence West of Winnipeg. Surprisingly, the prime minister acted swiftly and decisively to authorize a force to quell the rebellion.

The government response was distinctly Canadian. Except for 59-year-old Major-General Frederick Middleton, the general officer commanding (GOC) the Canadian militia, and a few other British staff officers, the entire 6,000 man force raised to quell the revolt consisted of Canadians, and all but 363 regulars were militia.[6] On 27 March, the day after the defeat at Duck Lake, "C" Company (Coy), of the Infantry School Corps was called out for service in the Northwest. A mere three days later, under the command of Lieutenant-Colonel William D. Otter,

90 all ranks from "C" Coy, joined 250 volunteers from the 10th Royal Grenadiers and the Queen's Own Rifles of Canada (QOR of C), and boarded trains in Toronto for Winnipeg.

Raising the force was easy. Volunteers were plentiful. Equipping and supplying them, on the other hand, was a continuing problem. Equally difficult, was the task of getting them out West. The Canadian Pacific Railway was still under construction. There were gaps in the line north of Lake Superior totalling approximately 160 kilometres. At this time of year, the extreme temperatures and deep snow proved as formidable a challenge as Riel's forces. By a combination of open flat-car on rail lines, sleighs on construction roads, and marches across the ice of Lake Superior, the epic journey from Toronto to Winnipeg was completed in six days. "Of course we have had a pretty tough time," wrote Lyndhurst Wadmore to his wife, "but I wouldn't have missed it for a great deal."[7] His sentiments are representative of the soldierly understatement and thirst for adventure.

The government's swift response to the crisis paid great dividends. Many of the full-blooded Native bands, although dissatisfied with Ottawa, were holding back their support to the rebellion. The quick response and arrival of government troops only made them more hesitant to get involved. As a result, the rebellion was contained in three areas — Fort Pitt (where Chief Big Bear and his warriors were rampaging); Battleford on the North Saskatchewan River (where Chief Poundmaker was seemingly in support of the rebellion); and Batoche on the South Saskatchewan River (where Riel and 500 rebels had gathered).

Major-General Middleton was acutely aware of the need to terminate the rebellion as quickly as possible. First, he did not want it to spread, as that would make his task much more difficult. Second, he realized the effort was costing the government a great deal, therefore, the shorter the conflict the cheaper the eventual bill. He also realized that the centre of resistance and the heart of the rebellion was Batoche. Not surprisingly, Middleton wanted to focus his efforts on this objective. As a result, his campaign plan called for dividing his force into three columns. The first column under his command consisted of approximately 720 infantrymen, 150 mounted infantrymen, and 150 artillerymen with four cannon and one Gatling gun.

Middleton was greatly concerned with the potential performance of his raw, inexperienced militia troops. His own racial stereotypes of the enemy, bolstered by reports of their effectiveness, fed his unease. The Métis and Indians knew the ground, and they had a reputation as skilled marksmen as well as savage warriors. One contemporary account reflected the perception of both the public and soldiers:

> The Indians are a different class of people, and show no quarter in battle, but take every advantage to skulk behind houses or trees or stones or brush or to fight in any manner that will protect them from danger, but will be sure to inflict heavy loss on the enemy. This is their mode of warfare, and those who go to war with them know the perils and dangers to which they are subjected in meeting such a foe; and the danger they undergo of being scalped upon a sudden attack.[8]

To mitigate against this perceived threat, Middleton ensured his column included a contingent of regulars from "C" Coy. Although untried in combat, they still represented a higher level of discipline, training, and professionalism than their militia counterparts.

His column was to march from Qu'appelle to Clark's Crossing where it would be met by a column led by Lieutenant-Colonel Otter, marching from Swift Current, consisting of approximately 400 infantry (including the remainder of "C" Coy), 50 mounted men, 100 artillerymen with three cannon, and a Gatling gun. Once united, the two columns, one on each side of the Saskatchewan River, would march against Batoche to destroy the rebel stronghold. Middleton then planned to march against Poundmaker at Battleford, and continue on to Fort Pitt, where he was to link-up with his third column under Major-General Thomas Strange,[9] who marched from Calgary with his force of approximately 475 infantrymen, less than 150 mounted men, and one cannon. Once Middleton's force was completely united, he then intended to deal with Big Bear.

Although the plan seemed simple — few things in war are. Travel and supply became a nightmare. Once the rail line had to be abandoned monumental problems arose. Resupply became a major challenge. "We have had meals ... of a quality I would not serve to dogs at home," revealed one "C" Coy soldier.[10] Wagons and carts were slow, scarce, and expensive. The lack of grass at that time of year meant fodder had to be carried, but the necessity of feeding the wagon train consumed the bulk of their holdings.

The climate and environment added to the difficulties. The springtime prairie weather ranged from bitter cold to mild, creating a morass of mud as the snow melted. Rivers and creeks swelled, becoming difficult to traverse. Then there was the misery caused by mosquitoes, and periods of intense heat that made the men uncomfortable and sleep deprived. Nonetheless, the soldiers persevered and pushed on.

The environment, however, was not Middleton's only concern. News of the Frog Lake massacre and panicky reports from Battleford quickly forced the GOC to change his plan.[11] Ottawa, fearful of a massacre of the beleaguered settlers and Mounties who had taken refuge at the NWMP post in Battleford, called on Middleton for action. Although he was convinced that the reports stemming from Battleford were exaggerated, he had to do something. So, on 11 April, Middleton ordered Lieutenant-Colonel Otter to proceed to the relief of Battleford without delay and hold Poundmaker in check.

Though he had lost a substantial part of his force, Middleton still decided to march on Batoche with his own column — despite the inexperience of most of his men. He also stuck to his plan to advance up both sides of the river. With the loss of Otter and his troops, this meant he had to divide his own column and place half on each side of the Saskatchewan River. For the time being, connecting the two was a single leaky scow.

Middleton's progress was easily monitored by the rebels. Not surprisingly, Riel and his Métis, under command of the capable and wily Gabriel Dumont, were not prepared to let the government troops approach Batoche unmolested.[12] They intended to ambush the government forces while they were on the march. Dumont planned to draw Middleton's column into the ravine at Fish Creek. "I want to treat them like buffalo," shared Dumont with his men.[13] Once trapped in the narrow ravine dominated by cliffs on both sides, Dumont and his 280 men intended to slaughter the soldiers from well dug in and protected positions. Furthermore, they planned to capture the GOC and hold him hostage so that they could use him as a bargaining chip in negotiations with Ottawa.[14]

The plan failed, however. Middleton's scouts, deployed far in advance of the main party soon came upon signs of recent enemy activity. They noticed a ransacked farmstead and discovered a series of campfires with still warm embers. As they cautiously advanced the rebels were forced to open fire prematurely. The scouts reacted well and did not rush into the coulee. Rather, they dismounted and took cover as the rebels swept the position with a volley of lead. The scouts returned fire and checked any rebel intention of advancing against the main body.

ESTABLISHING A LEGACY

Ambush thwarted: the attack against the rebels at Fish Creek.

Middleton was following close behind the scouts. Alerted by the shots he immediately dispatched an aide-de-camp with orders to bring up the advance guard and the main body. He quickly extended his men, who took positions of cover on the crest and exchanged fire with the rebels. Although the phantom like enemy, hidden in the brush and their rifle pits were hard to locate, their horses, which they had tethered in the ravine, were not and 55 of them were quickly killed. Middleton's forces now attempted to dislodge the enemy but they were so well entrenched and covered that each foray elicited heavy fire and collapsed on itself with the inevitable casualties that foreshadow military failure.

At one point the rebels set fire to the prairie grass, which enveloped the right flank in smoke. Under this cover, the Métis attempted to outflank the government forces. Supported by the thick choking smoke and rifle fire that was "tremendously hot," the rebels seemed to make good progress. However, "C" Coy, Infantry School Corps and elements of the 90th Winnipeg Battalion of Rifles (now the Royal Winnipeg Rifles), rallied, took cover, and then systematically drove them back, "bluff by bluff," until the enemy "retired all together going off as hard as they could."[15] One participant boasted, "Toronto was not disgraced by her crowd of toughs ['C' Coy]."[16]

The latest reverse was enough for the rebels and by 1400 hours, firing had ceased. It became evident that the enemy had withdrawn. Middleton's

Regrouping after the battle — Major-General Frederick Middleton's two-week pause at Fish Creek.

troops collected the dead and wounded and erected a camp close to the scene of battle during the deluge from a severe thunderstorm. Middleton remained in this camp for almost two weeks while awaiting reinforcements, supplies, and the evacuation of his dead and wounded.[17]

In the interim, Lieutenant-Colonel Otter pushed hard to relieve Battleford. Marching from Swift Current, his force covered approximately 50 kilometres a day. On 24 April, the same day Middleton was fighting his action at Fish Creek, Otter marched unopposed into Battleford. He was incensed when he saw the plundered homesteads and buildings of Battleford. His anger was further fuelled by the tales of murder and depredation by the Natives, which he heard upon arrival. In view of these outrages, he decided, against the instruction of Middleton, to strike at those responsible.

Otter termed his intended attack a reconnaissance in force and based it on the requirement to force Chief Poundmaker, who was vacillating on whether to participate in the rebellion, to declare himself. Otter was especially concerned about preventing any junction between Poundmaker and Chief Big Bear.[18] As a result, he put together a small mobile force consisting of 325 of his best men, two NWMP 7-pounder cannons, a Gatling gun, and a supply train of 48 wagons.

On 1 May, his force left Battleford at 1500 hours and marched for five hours. They then halted and waited until about midnight when the moon rose. Otter then pushed on through the night intent on surprising Poundmaker and his 200 warriors. The challenge was immense. Their route ran through uneven country. Hills with dense growths of poplar and underbrush proved impenetrable to sight and passage, and an endless succession of coulees and ravines intersected their route. These obstacles made travel difficult, while giving the enemy excellent cover for ambushes.

Despite the difficult terrain, by daybreak Otter's force sighted Poundmaker's camp on the higher of two hills. It was surrounded by a wide ravine, with a large creek (Cut Knife Creek) running through it. The scouts and advance guard almost made it to the top of the first (lower) hill before the alarm was sounded in the Native camp. Apparently, an element of surprise was achieved. However, any advantage gained was soon lost.

As Otter's men reached the crest they were met by a hail of fire from the enemy coming from a myriad of densely covered ravines and gullies. The Natives, intimately familiar with the ground, now successfully began to surround the government forces. "For half an hour we had quite hot enough work and the bullets came flying about us in a not over pleasant manner," confided one participant to his diary, "We were

An artist's rendition of Poundmaker's attack on Colonel Otter's column at Cut Knife Creek, 2 May 1885.

exposed to fire from three sides and had to grin and bear it."[19] Otter later reported, "So large was their force that it required the whole of ours placed in the fighting line to meet the attack." He added, "a most vicious and determined cross fire was poured in upon our men which at first proved most destructive owing to carelessness in exposing themselves."[20] However, the government troops soon followed the example of their foe and used cover to its maximum advantage.

Otter placed his Gatling gun in the centre of the line and flanked it with his two 7-pounder cannons.[21] The troops settled into the task at hand and in the "most cool, collected and praiseworthy manner went about forcing the enemy to abandon their numerous points of advantage and cover."[22] After six hours of combat, Otter reported that his flank and rear were clear. However, to maintain this state of affairs took considerable effort. A Toronto Globe reporter who travelled with the column wrote: "The Indians were making a great fight of it, and when chased out of one position resumed fire from another."[23]

Otter was surrounded and in an untenable position. Instead of 200 enemy there were approximately 500. He could not push his attack, nor could he hold his position through the night. His cannon were useless and he had many casualties to evacuate. Believing that he had achieved his aim of a reconnaissance in force, as well as forcing Poundmaker to "declare himself," Otter ordered a withdrawal. He entrusted his regulars, "C" Coy, Infantry School Corps, to act as the rearguard.

In the end, Otter's foray was anything but successful. Luckily, Poundmaker refused to allow his warriors to give pursuit, and the government troops were able to withdraw unmolested. Even so, the engagement cost Otter eight dead and 14 wounded.[24] But, much like Fish Creek, the soldiers had acquitted themselves well. One contemporary account went so far as to state, the "C" Coy men were "admired by all for their soldiery bearing and handsome appearance."[25]

Otter now waited in Battleford to link up with Major-General Middleton's force. However, the GOC first had to capture Batoche. His two-week delay after the battle of Fish Creek had earned him much criticism. Finally, on 7 May, he broke camp and moved against the rebel stronghold. By this time reinforcements and supplies had arrived and a reconnaissance up to 10 kilometres from the rebel stronghold had been completed. He had also consolidated his column on the right side of the river, except for Major Henry Smith and his group of "C" Coy men, who were directed to board the S.S. *Northcote*, a steamboat, so they could

The confusion and unfavourable ground is clearly evident in R.L. Wadmore's contemporary drawing, *Battle of Cut Knife Creek*.

S.S. *Northcote* and "C" Coy preparing for the assault against Batoche.

proceed up the river in the steamboat and land on either bank as needed. They were also directed to cut the cable of the Batoche ferry to isolate the enemy and disrupt their communication, and support the land attack to the greatest extent possible.

Although the steamboat's approach may have been physically less strenuous then the march across land, the reception it received was much hotter. Although the boat's defences had been improved, Smith's 31 "C" Coy soldiers and one officer, as well as his augmentation of 17 other combatants, could not help but feel entrapped as they became the target for what appeared to be every hostile rifle in the Northwest. Major-General Middleton ordered Smith and the steamer to arrive at Batoche at 0900 hours on 9 May to coincide with his land attack. As they neared their destination, they returned fire in an attempt to suppress the Métis fire and create an impression of greater numbers as a ploy to draw the enemy away from Middleton's column. The effort, however, was short lived. Amid a crescendo of noise generated by bullets slamming into the boat hull and superstructure, and the loud roar of return fire from the troops aboard the *Northcote*, came a spine chilling screech and subsequent resounding crash. The rebels had raised the ferry cable at the Batoche ferry site in an attempt to capsize any government vessel that attempted to pass. As the *Northcote* fought its way past Batoche, the cable caught on the smoke stacks of the steamer and ripped them out of their sockets. The skipper, an American who now found himself involved in the thick of someone else's war continued steaming down the river. Enemy fire slackened about three kilometres later and Major Smith ordered all to cease fire.

The skipper and his civilian crew had had enough. They were unwilling to turn around and steam back to Batoche. The ship's captain cited needed repairs, the fire hazard the destroyed smoke stacks represented and the requirement for better defences as excuses for not turning back. He also argued it was too difficult to return up river safely with the two barges full of supplies they had in tow, and added that there was a pressing need to replenish the firewood supply. As a result, the *Northcote* eventually steamed for the Hudson's Bay Ferry terminal and the "C" Coy men missed the remainder of the action at Batoche.[26]

They did not, however, miss out on an epic assault. Middleton's original advance gained some advantage from the steamer's presence as some of the enemy strength was diverted. Nonetheless, it quickly stalled under the voluminous fire from a well-positioned and well-entrenched enemy.

Despite the cannons and Gatling gun, Middleton could not dislodge the Métis from their well-concealed and carefully constructed rifle pits. After an inconclusive engagement he withdrew to a temporary camp a short distance away that consisted of his circled wagons and camp equipage (i.e., a zareba).

The next day the troops advanced once again only to find they had lost ground. Without the threat of the *Northcote* and "C" Coy on the flank, the enemy had concentrated its force. Middleton scouted and attempted a flanking movement over the next two days, but the stronghold was finally taken by the initiative of his subordinates. Although not ordered to do so, Lieutenant-Colonel Arthur Williams launched his battalion at the rebels. The other flanking units joined in. "Firing as we went in rushes," wrote one senior NCO, "the whole line with a rush advanced across the open and plowed field right through and around the stores and houses and for a half mile . . . The village was ours."[27] Almost out ammunition and overwhelmed by the sight of the massed bayonet charge, the rebel line broke and melted away.

Three days later, on 15 May 1885, Riel surrendered. The rebellion was all but over. Middleton now moved his force by steamers up the

2 Company, The Royal Regiment of Canadian Infantry "marching out" at Stanley Barracks, Toronto, 1894.

North Saskatchewan River to complete his campaign plan. Poundmaker surrendered near Battleford on 26 May. Farther to the West, Big Bear fought an inconclusive engagement with Major-General Strange's troops at Frenchman's Butte on 27 May. The government forces spent the next month in a frustrating and futile pursuit in the muskeg and dense bush of Northern Saskatchewan. However, it all ended on 2 July when Chief Big Bear surrendered.

In all, the North-West Rebellion was not a stirring example of martial prowess. The government forces were bested in almost all of their engagements. Historians agree that it was numbers and resources, particularly weapons and ammunition that allowed Middleton to prevail. Moreover, Riel's interference prevented his military commander from executing a campaign that could have been more devastating to the inexperienced troops. Nonetheless, the men of "C" Coy, the Infantry School Corps, acquitted themselves well while participating in three of the four principal engagements of the conflict. The price they paid for this first foray was two killed and seven wounded, out of total losses by government forces of 26 dead and 103 wounded.

The brief conflict seemed to galvanize a recognition that militia training was in dire need of professional assistance. In the years that followed the rebellion the small contingent of regular force infantry were hard pressed to meet the demand for instructing the officers and men of the militia. In August 1887, the government authorized a fourth company — "D" Coy, to meet the expanded training requirement. It was formally established in early 1888 in London, Ontario.

Although the Infantry School Corps was expanding it still lacked a central regimental ethos and esprit de corps. As a result, in 1892 militia headquarters directed that the Corps assume regimental status, which transformed its name to the Canadian Regiment of Infantry. Concomitant with the change in status and name, the companies were redesignated using numbers instead of letters and all received the new Martini-Henry rifles. The following year, in honour of Her Majesty Queen Victoria's birthday all units of the regular force were granted the honour of a royal prefix. As such, the name changed once again to The Royal Regiment of Canadian Infantry (RRCI). Simultaneously, The Regiment was granted permission to use the imperial cipher V.R.I. (i.e., *Victoria Regina Imperatrix* — Victoria, Queen Empress) as a badge and on buttons.

The Regiment trained together for the first time in August 1894 at Lévis, Quebec, for a six-week period. Lieutenant-Colonel W. D. Otter was appointed to command the composite battalion. At long last, steps were taken to create a unified regimental spirit. This was advanced further two years later, in 1896, when Lieutenant-Colonel George J. Maunsell was appointed to command The Regiment. That same year, the first edition of Regimental Standing Orders (RSOs) was published. Notwithstanding the advancements made, the distributed companies quickly returned to conducting training for the officers and other ranks of the Canadian militia. But as a minimum, at least several important precedents had been set. First, the Regiment now had a permanently appointed commanding officer responsible for ensuring standardization and collective well-being. Second, battalion training was conducted, though it was sporadic. Third, it once again changed its name, on 31 March, 1899, becoming The Royal Canadian Regiment of Infantry (RCRI). As the Regiment neared the new millennium, its future looked promising.

The end of the century also brought a new challenge to the Regiment. The stampede for Gold in the Yukon once again turned Ottawa's attention to the Northwest. The Gold Rush that commenced in 1896, witnessed a flood of miners, speculators, and desperate individuals intent on getting rich. The ability of the Mounties to control the sudden influx of tens of thousands of people and the myriad of problems associated with a very transient and rough population, driven by greed and desperation, was severely taxed. Major J.M. Walsh, the newly appointed commissioner for the territory informed Ottawa that his new district was "in the hands of a foreign element." Police Superintendent Charles Constantine was less tactful. Dawson's engorged population of 30,000 he noted, was made up of "the sweepings of the slums and the result of a general jail delivery."[28]

The Gold Rush also intensified the fear of American encroachment fuelled by the ongoing Alaskan boundary dispute. "We would have to face the fact that 200 or 300 of our officers would be surrounded," extolled Minister of the Interior Clifton Sifton in Parliament, "by starving thousands of armed men, of alien men, not citizens of Canada, but citizens of foreign countries, and these men would have possession of the Yukon district instead of the Government of Canada."[29] More bluntly put, Lieutenant-Colonel T.D.B. Evans later wrote, "a good many of the scum of America have found their way to Dawson."[30] Within this context, on 21 March 1898, an Order-in-Council established that "a Field Force composed of volunteers from the permanent troops of the Dominion should be dispatched to Fort Selkirk."[31] And so, the Yukon Field Force was born.

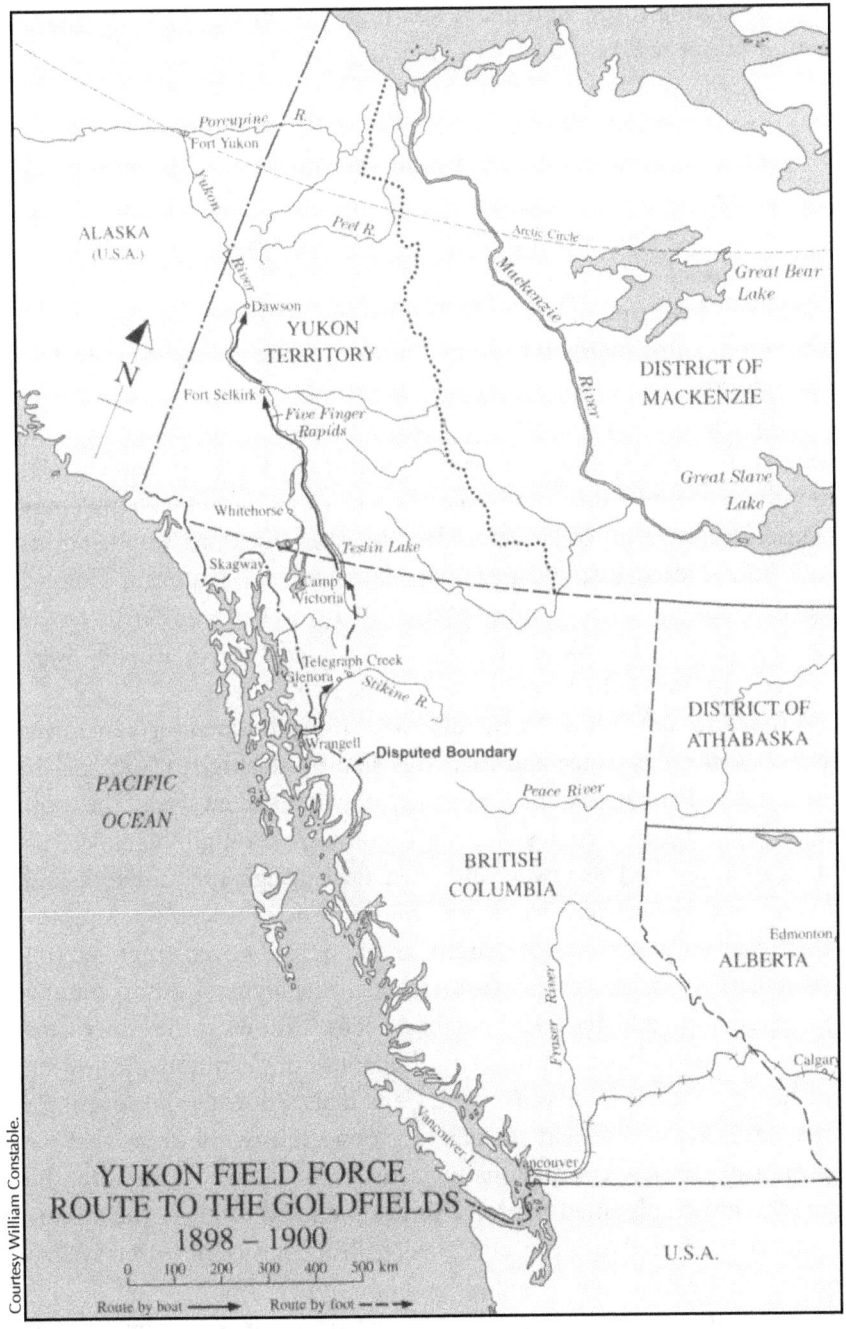

The standard for volunteers was high. "None but men absolutely sound in every way, capable of standing exceptional hardship are to be selected," insisted the militia minister.[32] In addition, any man with less than two years of service remaining was required to re-engage for a new three-year term. In all, 12 officers and 191 men, representing one-quarter of the permanent force, drawn mainly from the RRCI, but also including elements from the entirety of the Canadian Permanent Force, were called on to assist the civil authorities.[33] Once again, the Canadian government depended on its "Regulars" to help police the dominion, and equally important demonstrate its ability to protect its sovereignty.

The Yukon Field Force was specially kitted for the mission. Members were issued with special uniforms to withstand the long harsh winter months. Each individual received a heavy black pea jacket with matching trousers, fur caps, fur collars, black woollen knee stockings, woollen mitts with buckskin covers, and knee-high laced boots. Lieutenant-Colonel T.D.B. Evans, a former member of the RRCI who had transferred to the Royal Canadian Dragoons (RCD), commanded the Force. They were expected to stay in the Klondike for at least two years.

The Force left Ottawa by rail on 6 May 1898, destined for Vancouver. It arrived five days later and then travelled by steamer to Wrangell in the Alaskan Panhandle. Political reality now interjected itself. The most common and easiest routes into the Yukon were through the American ports of Dyea and Skagway, and then up through the Chilkoot and White Pass, respectively. However, Ottawa decided to avoid asking the Americans for permission to march Canadian troops over American soil, particularly since part of the reason for their deployment was to counter perceived United States (U.S.) encroachment. "Knowing the Americans as we do," boomed one minister in the House of Commons, "knowing the history of their intercourse with Canadians, knowing the advantage they have taken of Canadians at every opportunity, we know that we can not expect any concessions or favors from them."[34] Therefore, the government condemned the force to use the third route — the Stikine route often referred to as the "all Canadian Trail." It was the least travelled route into the Klondike — and for good reason.

The "all Canadian Trail" required the troops to move by steamer from Wrangell, Alaska up the Stikine River to Glenora, and then onto Telegraph Creek where the infamous Teslin Trail commenced.[35] Here their epic journey began in earnest. The Teslin Trail was a trail in name

Members of the Yukon Field Force in Telegraph Creek, British Columbia.

only. In reality it was approximately 250 kilometres of rugged bush, rock, and ridges, covered with mosquito-infested swamps and muskeg. The Field Force now had to cover the last 640 kilometres to Fort Selkirk hauling themselves and 60 tons of supplies by man pack and mule train over this inhospitable ground, or in scows and boats down fast flowing raging rivers.[36]

At Telegraph Creek the force was broken into 35-man groups. Although mules were hired from the Hudson's Bay Company (HBC) to haul the supplies on the overland trek, the sheer magnitude of the task was lost on the HBC agents and they failed to provide sufficient animals. As a result, the men were required to pack heavy loads over the appalling ground. Each mule carried 200 pounds — each man 50. An advance party of 50 men skilled with axe and saw set off early to mark the trail, and build bridges and corduroy road over the most difficult parts of the route. Their task was to do this but also reach Teslin Lake as quickly as possible so that they could complete the final leg of their trip to Fort Selkirk, the nominal capital of the Yukon at the time, by steamer

A Royal Canadian Regiment soldier on the Teslin Trail facing the soldier's timeless struggle — heavy loads and a hostile environment.

so that they could begin building the camp for the main body of the Yukon Field Force.

The trek to Fort Selkirk was easily the greatest challenge the volunteers of the Yukon Field Force had to overcome during their stay in the Yukon. It was truly a feat of endurance. The entire environment seemed to conspire against them. "The heat is overwhelming," wrote one traveller, "the thermometer reaching 29 Centigrade on the 24th of May and 38 degrees Centigrade on the 25th."[37] But the heat was only one element. The ground was another. "A weary tramp on foot for 150 miles or rather 200 miles if the actual distance in counted across a terrible country boulders & huge fallen trees," wrote Lieutenant-Colonel Evans. "The worst part, was the horrible swamps through which they had to wade up to their waists," he added, "and nothing to eat but hard biscuits, rancid strong bacon & black tea & this in midst of great heat & under perpetual attack from the biggest bloodthirstiest hordes of mosquitoes."[38]

The mosquitoes represented another major environmental obstacle. "The mosquitoes are terrible," noted one participant, "and our blood is poisoned so that our bodies are soon covered with small ulcers."[39] Private Edward Lester confided to his diary that the "mosquitoes are an awful pest & torment the life out of us; they will bite through anything, even our serge trousers."[40] Faith Fenton, the *Toronto Globe* reporter who accompanied the Force called them "these vampires among insects."[41] Georgia Powell, one of the nursing sisters wrote, "for number, size and ferocity these mosquitoes cannot be exaggerated, and despite leggings, gloves and the inevitable veil we were badly bitten."[42]

The ground to be covered was equally dismal. "The trail followed for some distance the course of the river, sometimes on the level and sometimes high above, along the face of rocky bluffs, through forests & over swamps," recorded Lester, "but everywhere there was mud." Even elevation made little difference. "We crossed one mountain (Rainy Mount), the summit of which took us an hour's hard climbing to reach," scribbled Lester in his diary, "and to make matters worse it was literally

Terrible heat, exhausting swamps, and swarms of ravenous mosquitoes were just some of the challenges for RCR soldiers en route to the Klondike.

a mountain of bog." He lamented, "The trail was something horrible, swamp, swamp, swamp, all the way along … we were floundering through bog, scrambling over tree roots & fallen logs, here & there coming across a mud hole in which the mules sank to their girths & from which they had to be hauled by main strength."[43]

To make matters worse, the men ran out of tobacco! The situation became so desperate that "some of the boys are smoking scraped willow bark."[44] The hardships soon took their toll. One member of the Force released his tension by carving his feelings, which were shared by most, into a tree. He wrote:

> Damn the journey, Damn the track,
> Damn the distance there & back,
> Damn the sunshine, Damn the weather,
> Damn the Goldfields altogether.[45]

Luckily, morale immediately improved once the groups reached Lake Teslin. The remainder of the journey from this point was by water. Lieutenant-Colonel Evans and 80 men were the first to board the steamer

Five boats and four large scows were built at Camp Victoria on Teslin Lake to transport material north. However, necessity forced this motley flotilla to be used for troop transport.

Anglian and rush off to join the advance party and assist in erecting the camp at Fort Selkirk. The remainder of the party waited at the hastily erected Camp Victoria for the steamer's return. While they waited, they built five boats and four large scows to transport their material North. However, on its return journey the *Anglian* struck a rock and the locally constructed flotilla now became the means of transport for the remainder of the force. They departed on 29 August, under the control of the second-in-command, Major D. Young.

The force finally arrived at Fort Selkirk on 11 September 1898 after a journey of approximately four months. Their camp was well under way. Around a central parade square stood a group of 12 log buildings, which were incomplete, though they all had roofs. With the additional manpower, they were completed before the early onset of the Yukon winter. The force was lodged at Fort Selkirk rather than Dawson because their primary role, in the view of Minister of Militia and Defence, Dr. Frederick Borden, was as a symbol of Canadian sovereignty. He felt that only if "necessity demanded" would the force be "ready to assist" in maintaining law and order.[46]

Notwithstanding the minister's feelings, the next month, on 1 October, two officers, 50 soldiers, and one of the two Maxim machine guns were

Yukon Field Force on parade at Fort Selkirk.

dispatched to Dawson to assist with the maintenance of law and order. The request came from the infamous Sam Steele, the superintendent of the NWMP in Dawson who needed additional personnel to ease the load of his hard-pressed Mounties. An additional 20 men were sent the following month.

The Dawson detachment of the force soon observed that Steele's men ruled Dawson with an iron fist. Although willing to overlook minor transgressions, they enforced the sanctity of life and property in accordance with Canadian law. The soldiers soon became a common sight in Dawson. They guarded their own quarters as well as the gold in the banks. They also assisted the police in guarding prisoners and enforcing law and order in general.

Throughout the long dreary winter of 1898–1899, the Force maintained a presence in both Fort Selkirk and Dawson. To relieve the boredom and the isolation of the Selkirk garrison men were rotated between the two posts. More than one member considered the duty a form of exile.[47] In the end, the impact of the Yukon Field Force and the NWMP was immense. "The whole demeanor of people changed the moment they crossed the summit," wrote Sam Steele, "the pistol was packed in the valise and not used." He added, "the desperado, if there,

The Yukon Field Force changing guard at the NWMP barracks in Dawson, 1899.

had changed his ways, no one feared him."⁴⁸ In the spring of 1899, the new Yukon Commissioner, William Ogilvie declared, "it is universally conceded by all right-thinking people that there is perhaps no more peaceable and orderly town in Canada than the town of Dawson."⁴⁹

The Yukon Field Force spent over a year assisting the Mounties in guarding banks and gold shipments, fighting fires, building hospitals, and maintaining law and order. In July 1899, the Field Force was reduced to half strength.⁵⁰ Major-General Edward Hutton, the GOC, was unhappy with the use of regular troops in such a civil function. Moreover, their absence substantially reduced the ability to train the militia. "I am urging the necessity of the withdrawal of your force as early as possible in the summer," wrote Hutton to Evans, "as your men and yourself can ill be spared from our all insufficient instructional corps."⁵¹ But there were tensions at play. More important, there were storm clouds on the horizon and trained military men would be needed elsewhere. In the end, the remainder of the Force was eventually withdrawn in June 1900.

And so, the Royal Canadian Regiment of Infantry, often unofficially and incorrectly abbreviated to the Royal Canadian Regiment, finished off the century with an enviable record of service in its first 17 years. "Royals" of all ranks began a tradition of duty and honour, highlighted by professionalism, tenacity, and endurance. This foundation would soon be tested. The next millennium would provide greater challenges, as well as opportunities for the Regiment and its members.

2
Making Canada Proud:
The "Royal Canadians" in South Africa

As members of the Yukon Field Force whiled away long hours of boredom and tedium in the Canadian far North, the GOC of the Canadian militia was actively working for their return. Their absence adversely impacted the ability to deliver necessary training to the militia. More important, there were storm clouds gathering in South Africa and Major-General E.T.H. Hutton wanted the few regular force soldiers the Dominion of Canada possessed to be ready should they be required. To Hutton, as well as many Canadians, it was important that the dominion support the "Mother Country" in the event of war in the Transvaal.

Conflict in South Africa was long in brewing. By the summer of 1899, the relationship between the British and the Boers had deteriorated dramatically, ostensibly over the denial of civic and social rights of the Uitlanders (non-residents) in the Boer republics of Transvaal and the Orange Free State. This affront to the fair treatment and democratic freedom of British subjects was too much for some to bear. The fact that large deposits of precious minerals were recently discovered in the breakaway territories did not help ease the tension.[1]

For Prime Minister Wilfrid Laurier the entire issue was troublesome. He did not want to participate in Britain's latest imperial adventure. Laurier realized that supporting an overseas military venture was costly — in money, blood, and national unity. There were large segments of Canadian society that were adamantly opposed to providing military

ESTABLISHING A LEGACY

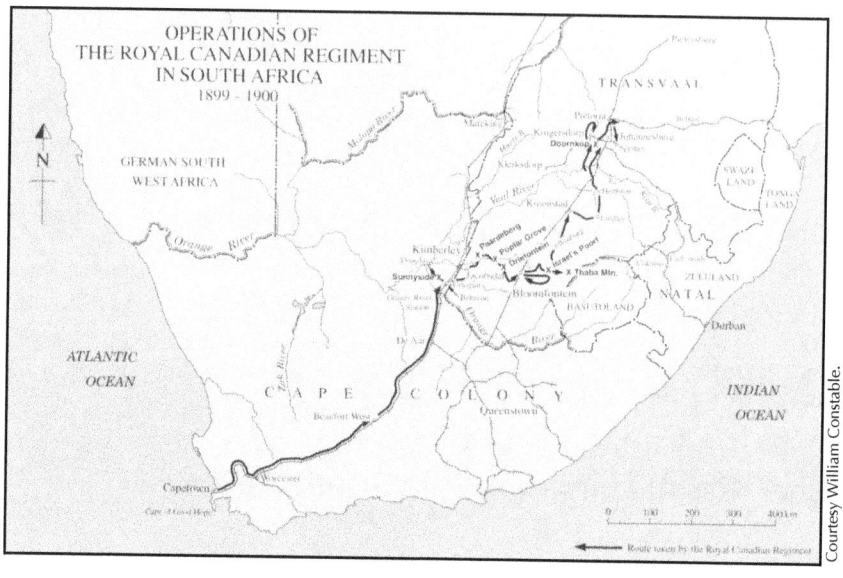

forces to support the British Empire, most notably, but not exclusively, francophones in Quebec.[2]

However, Laurier's attempts at keeping the dominion out of the war proved futile. Most of English Canada clamoured to support Britain. This swell of loyalty to England was further fuelled by the behind the scenes machinations of the GOC, Major-General Hutton, and the governor general, the Earl of Minto.[3] As such, when war was declared on 11 October 1899, Laurier was compelled, unless he wished to jeopardize the Liberal Party's chances at re-election, to commit Canadian forces to the war effort. Consequently, after two days of heated cabinet discussion, the government announced, on 14 October, that it would send a contingent to South Africa.[4] The details, however, were still to be worked out.

Joseph Chamberlain, the British colonial secretary, immediately accepted the Canadian offer to dispatch troops to South Africa. He cabled the governor general and directed that the contribution, preferably infantry, should be organized into units of approximately 125 men, with one captain and no more than three subalterns for each respective unit, and the whole force could be commanded by an officer of the rank no higher than major. The cost of mounting and equipping, as well as transport to South Africa was to be paid for by Canada. Once they disembarked they would become imperial troops, and receive pay, rations, clothing, supplie, and ammunition from the British government.[5]

Lieutenant-Colonel Otter, commander First Canadian Contingent, the 2nd (Special Service) Battalion, The RCR.

Quite simply, the intent was for the Canadian contingent, as with all colonial contingents, to be absorbed into British units and formations. This meant that Canadian and other colonial troops would be used largely for garrison, picket, and rear area security tasks, since British regulars had little faith in the martial prowess of militiamen, and thought even less of colonials. After all, the British government wanted colonial contingents for political reasons for a show of imperial unity, not for their military application or worth. "We do not want the men," wrote Chamberlain to the Canadian governor general, "the whole point of the offer would be lost unless it was endorsed by the Government of the Colony."[6]

The British intent, however, was quickly dashed. Nationalist sentiment pushed the idea of a strong unified Canadian contingent. Surprisingly, it was Governor General Minto who pressed Laurier to acknowledge the popular will and push Britain to accept a Canadian contribution worthy of Canada's position in the empire. "You will see from the cable that it is evidently intended that the Canadian troops on arriving in South Africa should be attached to the different units which they represent, and that they should not remain constituted as a Canadian contingent," warned Minto. "I think," he proffered, "it would be better if troops are to be offered at all, that they should be offered as a Canadian contingent to act as such."[7] As a result, on 18 October Laurier and his cabinet approved the establishment and deployment of a regiment of infantry, namely the 2nd (Special Service) Battalion, The Royal Canadian Regiment (RCR) — 1,000 strong commanded by Lieutenant-Colonel William D. Otter. It was to deploy as a distinct, integral Canadian unit.

With Minto's urging, the British government and the War Office accepted the Canadian contribution. They also agreed to the official request to keep the Canadian contingent together as much as possible. However, the commander-in-chief in South Africa cautioned that he "cannot guarantee that the Contingent shall always be kept together during operations." He added, the "General must be free to dispose of the force to the best advantage."[8] The Canadian government acknowledged and accepted the caveat.

Nonetheless, the overall solution once again demonstrated Laurier's political savvy. He had offered an official Canadian contribution and by doing so placated the British. But, importantly, the Canadian contingent was based on a special volunteer force that would be created especially for the conflict. Moreover, the Canadian government would only finance the raising and shipping of the force. Once in South Africa, the British government would be financially responsible for its upkeep and support. This way Laurier appeased the pro-war faction by committing Canadian troops, while at the same time restricting the Canadian involvement to volunteers and limiting financial responsibility. Thus, he could argue that the composition of the force, as well as the overall financial arrangements, was a direct response to the concerns of the anti-war factions.[9]

In the end, the 2nd Battalion, The RCR, consisted of only 100 permanent force members, the rest being volunteers. Although largely a volunteer force, the Battalion was nonetheless established as a permanent force unit because of the overwhelming nationalist sentiment, as well as the overseas deployment and nature of the mission. This tact was also taken to underline the fact that the Canadian troops did not simply represent a levy of British army recruits.

The actual mobilization of the 2nd Battalion was astonishingly rapid. This was particularly surprising since the unit consisted of eight companies that were drawn from across Canada:

"A" Coy raised in British Columbia and Manitoba;
"B" Coy raised in London;
"C" Coy raised in Toronto;
"D" Coy raised in Ottawa and Kingston;
"E" Coy raised in Montreal;
"F" Coy raised in Quebec;
"G" Coy raised in New Brunswick and Prince Edward Island; and
"H" Coy raised in Nova Scotia.

On 23 October 1899, the different companies were ordered to assemble in Quebec City. Four days later the Battalion was formally established. Incredibly, the entire unit numbering 41 officers and 998 enlisted ranks for a total of 1039, was then embarked on the S.S. *Sardinian* on 30 October. So it was that the entire force was recruited, equipped, and embarked for deployment to South Africa in less than two weeks.[10]

The S.S. *Sardinian* derogatorily dubbed the "Sardine" by the troops because of its inadequate size and facilities.

The troop transport was quickly dubbed the "Sardine." It was anything but adequate. The converted cattle ship, reported Otter, "proved to be a very slow ship, and greatly lacking in room and accommodation for the numbers on board." He added, "sanitary arrangements were particularly bad, and so crowded was the ship that parades or drills were matters of extreme difficulty."[11]

The troops were more discerning. Private Frederick Ramsay revealed, "we are packed like sardines in our bunks and hammocks."[12] "This boat is the greatest old tub to roll that was every built," wrote Arthur Bennett in a letter, "she rolls around like an intoxicated man if there is the slightest swell." He added, "Some of the fellows had it [sea sickness] pretty badly, and for the first day thought they would die, and the next more afraid than ever in case they wouldn't."[13]

Although the rapid mobilization of the battalion was an impressive feat it came at a cost. The vast majority of volunteers had little to no military experience. Although the original intention was to enlist the best members of Canada's militia regiments the necessity for speed resulted in less than ideal screening procedures. "With the exception of the permanent corps, and a few others," lamented Otter, "none had much idea of duties, interior economy or discipline." He conceded, "I was astonished to find a very large number of the men ignorant of the first principles."[14] The cramped quarters on the *Sardinian* made training next to impossible. Therefore, most training would have to wait until the troops landed in South Africa.

On arrival in Cape Town it became clear to the Canadians that the war was not progressing well. Originally, the British political and military leadership were confident that the conflict would be quickly terminated. The Boers, after all, were viewed as little more than "the levies of two insignificant Republics whose forces were but loose gatherings of armed farmers."[15] However, reality soon crushed the British optimism and arrogance. As the war progressed in the Autumn of 1899, British soldiers and politicians alike were shocked at the fighting prowess of the Boers who on one occasion after another inflicted humiliating and costly defeats on the British Field Force. These unexpected "drubbings" showed that the imperial army was woefully inadequate to meet the challenges of modern warfare. The humiliating climax came during the week of 10–15 December when three separate British formations were decisively beaten at Stormberg, Magersfontein, and Colenso. These fateful seven days were appropriately labelled "Black Week."[16]

RCR troops doing rifle drill onboard the S.S. *Sardinian* en route to South Africa.

The impact in South Africa was enormous. During "Black Week" the high commissioner in Cape Town, Alfred, Lord Milner despondently cabled Chamberlain in London, "This is the worst blow we have sustained yet during the war." He added, " The impression it has created here is simply deplorable, and this is sure to be the case throughout the Colony." Milner's alarming entry in his diary the next day had more than a hint of panic:

> December 12th [1899] — The news to-day is again extremely bad. There can be no doubt that General Gatacre's defeat on Sunday [Stormberg] was a very severe one, and the effect of a large number of British prisoners being taken through a rebel district of the Colony into the Orange Free State cannot but be most injurious. One

consequence is that, as reported by various magistrates, armed men are leaving their homes in various parts of the eastern districts, and going to join the enemy.[17]

Two days later, he acknowledged that there existed a "deep depression in loyal circles in consequence of the three disasters of the past week." He lamented, "General Buller's defeat on the Tugela [River], coming on the top of Stormberg and Magersfontein, has been rather too much for the bravest." By Christmas, he informed Chamberlain "The effects of the reverses at Stormberg, Magersfontein, and Colenso is cumulative." He warned, "Even in the remotest country districts it is now known that the enemy have had great successes." He ominously added, "the spirit of rebellion has received an enormous impetus — even in districts hitherto comparatively quiet."[18]

The effect elsewhere in the empire was similarly dramatic. "The military situation is without doubt at this moment most grave and critical," reported Winston Churchill, a future prime minister of Britain, who was a correspondent at the onset of the conflict. "We have been at war three weeks," he explained, "[and] the army that was to have defended Natal, and was indeed expected to repulse the invaders with terrible loss, is blockaded and bombarded in its fortified camp." He added, "at nearly every point along the circle of the frontiers the Boers have advanced and the British retreated. Wherever we have stood we have been surrounded … All this is mainly the result of being unready … It is also due to an extraordinary under-estimation of the strength of the Boers."[19] England now turned to their former colonies in a desperate plea for troops, no longer for political impact, but for fighting men.

And so, the largely inexperienced Canadian volunteers entered what appeared to be a desperate struggle against a wily and capable enemy. Nonetheless, the "green" Canadian soldiers were eager to get to the fight. Despite their inexperience — the raw material was there. "Of the physique and high intelligence of all ranks of the Battalion," wrote Otter, "I could not but form the very highest opinion, and it was in a great measure due to these qualities that ultimate success accrued."[20] Alas, the disappointment of the men when their expectations of battle were not immediately met.

The Battalion disembarked at Cape Town on 30 November, but it was not allowed to linger long. The desperate situation in the field necessitated its presence at the front. Therefore, the men entrained the

Members of "D" Coy on parade.

next day for Belmont.[21] However, contrary to their expectations and desires, they were not deployed to battle. Rather, they spent the next two hot and monotonous months securing the lines of communication. Their battles were more with boredom, hunger, and the harsh environment than the Boers. These conditions, exacerbated by a rigid, uncompromising and dispassionate commanding officer (CO), quickly created morale problems.

Outpost duty was both demanding and tedious. "Our present duties has I think," penned Otter in the Battalion report, "a depressing effect upon the men — these duties consist of outpost fatigues and working parties and are very heavy."[22] Private Ramsay explained, "we sleep in our tents with most of our clothes on and our accoutrements at our side." He added, "I haven't had my boots off for nearly two weeks and have forgotten what a bath is like."[23]

The harsh environment also tested the troops. Their indoctrination came immediately. The first day introduced the "Royal Canadians" to conditions they would soon come only too familiar with. "Little or nothing to eat, stinking slushy water to drink, no tents for shelter on a hot summer day in Africa and a terrible rain storm," reported one participant.[24] And when it was not raining, there was the other constant irritant: "There is nothing but sand, sand, sand and a few little tufts of

Rail move to the "Front." Note how the soldiers were packed into open rail cars.

sage brush here and there and then there are sand storms," complained Private Jesse Briggs, "They are dense, choking, blinding and penetrate every crevice."[25]

The South African environment was also hard on the clothing. "The wear and tear upon clothing and boots," reflected a Battalion report, "is excessive and Canadian made clothing (Khaki) is very much inferior to the English."[26] Both of these issues would become problematic in short order.

The shortage of food was another major dissatisfier. "Things are going from bad to worse here in the way of grub," complained Private Bennett, "we are on poor rations and we are even on water rations."[27] On a number of occasions Bennett, like others, passed on advice to those who may have been considering volunteering for the Second Contingent. "Well if the boys took my advice they would stay at home," he counselled, "for there is nothing here but a burning sun and desert storm." He added, "this is the most forsaken country I have ever seen."[28]

Lieutenant-Colonel Otter was another major aggravation. "How the boys dislike that man," revealed Private J.A. Perkins.[29] Although experienced and a skilled trainer, he was dour and uninspiring. The men found him rigid and uncompromising. They chaffed at his discipline and endless drill. One letter home revealed a common complaint:

> The Colonel, who commands this regiment has lately taken it into his head that a march every day would do us some good and harden our feet, so at 4.30 p.m. every day we are paraded and marched off under the burning sun, over rocks and sand for about 10 miles, getting back about 8 o'clock, which gives us exactly half an hour to get our supper and fix our blankets before the bugle sounds "lights-out." We are, of course, wet to the skin with perspiration and have no time to change, so sleep in our wet things, and as it gets cold as the deuce at night, the boys are all getting colds.[30]

In addition, they resented his refusal to allow a dry canteen, such as existed in all other regimental bivouacs. More odious yet, he would not even allow the YMCA (Young Men's Christian Association) to provide such a service. In addition, they felt he did not push his British superiors for better more active employment. "I don't think much of Colonel Otter.... The boys call him the Old Woman and many other pretty stiff names," confided one soldier in a letter home, "He is too fond I think of giving the men too much marching, and that at a time when it interferes with a fellow's grub time."[31]

The fact that Otter was the interim commandant of Belmont station did not help matters. His apparent preoccupation with garrison duties and mundane training created resentment. The eventual arrival of the British appointed commandant, Lieutenant-Colonel Thomas Pilcher just enflamed the problem. Within his first week, he organized a flying column that included "C" Coy, The RCR, and launched a highly successful strike against a group of Boers who were conducting operations near the town of Douglas.

On 1 January 1900, his flying column surprised the Boers at Sunnyside Kopje.[32] As the artillery shelled the unprepared enemy, The

RCR camp at De Aar, South Africa, 1900.

Royal Canadians seized a small kopje 1,200 metres from the enemy position and opened fire on the Boers. As the other British forces closed the noose on the Boers, the Canadians advanced on the enemy position closing to approximately 200 metres and awaited the order to charge. However, after four hours of fighting the almost totally surrounded Boers fled towards Douglas. Overall, the fight had been a great success. The small British force had killed six enemy, wounded 12, and captured 34.[33]

This engagement represented the first experience under fire for the Canadians, yet it seemed they conducted themselves well. "Although the fire of the Boers was apparently very hot for a time," reported Otter, "LCol Pilcher who commanded the flying column ... speaks highly of the steadiness under fire and general good conduct of the Royal Canadians during this special service."[34] Nonetheless, the attack at Sunnyside simply increased the grousing. First, the cry of favouritism arose — the other companies felt that "C" Coy was chosen because of their Toronto lineage. Moreover, it was not lost on the RCR soldiers that Pilcher, even though newly arrived as commandant of Belmont Station, spent his time planning and conducting offensive operations instead of miring himself in administration. Not surprisingly, the criticisms of Otter continued and grew.

But the expectations of the soldiers were somewhat misguided as well. Their inexperience was a substantial limitation. Otter's memories of the fight at Ridgeway in 1866 against the Fenians and later combat in the North-West Rebellion in 1885, taught him the importance of drill, discipline, and fitness. His emphasis on marching and battle drill, specifically the new "rushing tactics" that stemmed from the lessons of the defeats of "Black Week" were instrumental in preparing the "Royal Canadians" for their upcoming campaign. So too were the occasional forays into the outlying areas on reconnaissance. In all, these activities improved the physical endurance of the troops and gave them experience in operating in the harsh environment, as well as a better knowledge of the country and terrain. As late as 11 February, Otter noted, "I confess to being somewhat disappointed in the condition of many of the men ... I find that there are many who it is unsafe to put upon any extra strain for the reason that they are constitutionally unable to meet it."[35] As monotonous as this initial period may have seemed, it was instrumental in preparing the men for what lay ahead.

It was often difficult to determine which was the greatest enemy — the Boers or the African veldt. "Royal Canadians" on the march, February 1900.

The adage, be careful of what you ask for, never rang more true. The Battalion clamoured for action and they would soon get their wish. On 12 February 1900, the Battalion moved to Gras-Pan and joined the 19th Brigade under Major-General Horrace Smith-Dorrien.[36] The Battalion now began an epic campaign. Lord Robert's army of 35,000 men was set to march to Bloemfontein, which would effectively relieve the siege of Kimberley and Ladysmith, since it would force the besieging Boer armies to withdraw from their positions of vantage in Natal and Cape Colony or risk being cut-off and surrounded. The march, however, would be done without railway support. This meant a bare minimum of supplies could be carried. Tents, extra equipment, and all other superfluous materials were left behind.[37]

The march for The RCR, which numbered 31 officers and 865 other ranks, commenced on 13 February 1900. The first three days were exceedingly difficult. Although only marching an average of 19 kilometres a day, the hot climate, difficult terrain, and supplemental fatigue duties, such as assisting heavy naval guns cross rivers, took its toll. The capture of a convoy of 200 British supply wagons by the Boers on the morning of 15 February also had a significant impact. It meant that all, despite the arduous conditions, would be on short rations for some time to come.

The next day the Battalion moved into Jacobsdal and remained there during the day. Because of the excessive heat, the advance was resumed at night. That evening at 2100 hours, the Battalion departed for Klip Drift on the Modder River. Seven hours later they arrived at their objective and rested until 1800 hours, when they set off once again for Paardeberg Drift. At 0600 hours, on 18 February, the "Royal Canadians" arrived at their destination, extremely fatigued and famished. Immediately, arrangements were made for a much anticipated breakfast, despite the meager rations available.

The meal was barely started, when shots rang out in the distance. The British field force had caught General Piet Cronje's army of 5,000 on the Modder River. The hunter had become the hunted. The Boer army that had just recently besieged Kimberley was now itself trapped. The RCR were ordered to dislodge or capture them. By 0720 hours, the "Royal Canadians," most without a meal, deployed from their lines.

The troops were not impressed. "The state of many of the men was now pitiable," reported one embedded journalist. "The short rations, want of water, lack of sleep, and long, tedious and irregular marches

RCR soldiers crossing the swift-flowing Modder River at Paardeberg Drift, 18 February 1900.

had told on them," he wrote. "Others were chafed and bleeding with the sand," he added, "we threw ourselves down half-dead and were just in the act of getting breakfast, when the order came that we were to form for the attack."[38]

The perspective of the soldiers was not much different. "We were pretty well fatigued as we had not slept or ate or even had a drink of water since yesterday," scribbled Lance-Corporal John Kennedy Hill in his diary.[39] Another account reinforced the state of exhaustion. "On the night of the 17th we made a forced march (about 23 miles) arriving on the scene at daybreak," recorded Private F. Dunham in his diary. "We thought that before we went into action we should receive some food to fill our shrunken stomachs but no, we had hardly halted when we were ordered to wade the Modder [river] & attack the N[orth] side," he wrote acidly.[40]

The river proved to be a formidable obstacle. It was five feet deep and the current ran at approximately 14.5 kilometres an hour. Ropes were strung from bank to bank to assist with the crossing, but to speed up the process, groups of four men linked arms and struck for the opposite side. "We did wade across that swiftly flowing river right up to our necks,

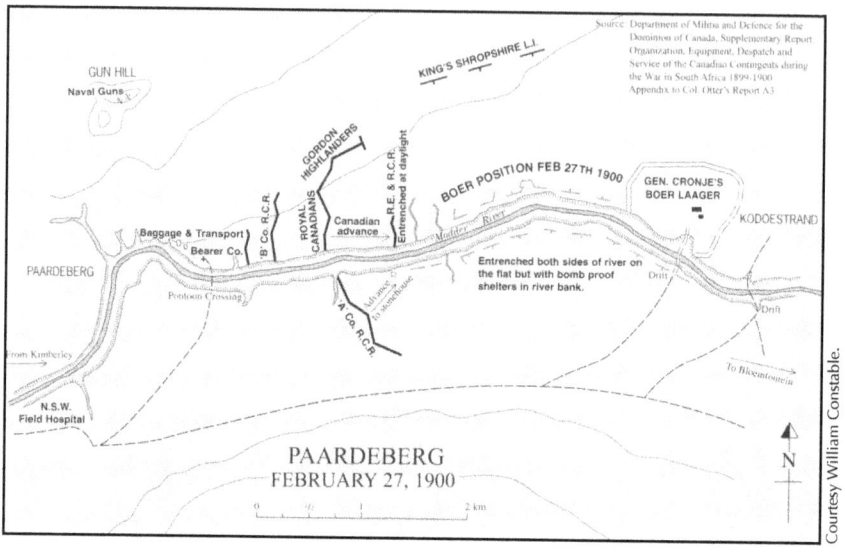

PAARDEBERG
FEBRUARY 27, 1900

four abreast," explained Dunham, "If one slipped he was supported by his comrades. Thus we gained the opposite bank."⁴¹ Lance-Corporal Kennedy Hill with a timeless understatement recounted, "we had quite a time crossing as water was up to our chins and current very strong."⁴²

Once on the other side, the men were immediately deployed into extended order in the direction of the Boer positions. By 0930 hours, the Battalion was firm on the other bank and began what would be nine days of fighting for Paardeberg drift.⁴³ Their baptism of fire was a true test of their mettle. "This was the first time [18 February] our Regiment as a whole were engaged," wrote Dunham. "Within 1800 yards of their position the bullets began to hum around … But nothing daunted us as we kept steadily marching forward," he described in his journal. He explained further:

> A sort of wild excitement to be at them came upon us so we hastened forward…. Within 800 yards we supported the front or firing line. Things began to be rather hot so we adopted the rushing tactics, that is running fifty yards then lying down for a few minutes for breath and again pushing on. This we kept up to within 450 yards for the fire was too hot and their aim too sure. Here we lay for several hours keeping up a hot fire all the time. The sun showed no mercy on us. Instead it seemed to

shine with greater fierceness so that the sweat rolled from us as it never rolled before.[44]

The Battalion had advanced with "A," "B," and "C" Coys in the forward firing line under Lieutenant-Colonel Lawrence Buchan, the Battalion second-in-command (2IC). "D" and "E" Coys were in support and the remainder in reserve. They were flanked by the Duke of Cornwall's Light Infantry (Cornwalls) on the right (but on the other side of the river) and the King's Own Shropshire Light Infantry (Shropshires) and Gordon Highlanders on the left.

Not surprisingly, the confusion on the battlefield was great. "The bullets were whizzing past us, and throwing little sprays of sand in all directions as they struck the ground," recalled Sergeant W. Hart-McHarg, "in a very few minutes we were well in the fire zone, and were ordered to lie down."[45] He quickly observed that all around them were men of the other British regiments. The advance continued until the "Royal Canadians" reached the forward firing line where they intermingled with the British regulars. "All our Battalion was to supposed to form the support," explained Captain W.J. Green, "[but] the wild Indians kept on going till they got right into the firing line." He added, "Here the bullets flew thick as hail all day."[46] Often men could not fire at the Boers for fear of hitting their comrades who were in the line fire.

Nonetheless, once the Canadians reached the firing line the advance came to a grinding halt. The Boer fire was simply overwhelming. Their accurate and smooth firing bolt action Mauser rifles cracked ceaselessly at any target that showed itself. "We lay in the burning sun, under the cover of small bushes or anthills, or lying flat on the open, jamming ourselves into the very ground to escape the peppering hail of bullets which ripped, whirred, and whinged a continual chorus of malignant warning," recounted one participant.[47]

The "Royal Canadians" were now strung out in front of the Boer positions from approximately 400 metres on the right to 700 metres on the left, the difference owing to the terrain that allowed the troops on the right more cover. Many, overcome with fatigue and feeling the affects of the relentless burning sun, fell asleep clinging to the ground or behind whatever scanty cover they could find. Some died this way — the target of Boer marksmen who continued to shoot at any target they could locate. The official Battalion report noted, "the enemy's fire was … delivered when the least exposure was made by our men." The report added, "on our part the fire discipline was excellent, the men being cool and collected, but they laboured under the difficulty of fighting an invisible enemy."[48]

At 1530 hours a brief thunderstorm drenched the pinned down soldiers providing some relief. But the storm seemed almost an omen for the tempest that would shortly engulf the "Royal Canadians." Approximately 30 minutes later the Commanding Officer of the Cornwalls, Lieutenant-Colonel William Aldworth, who had been ordered by Lord Kitchener to "finish this thing," arrived on the battlefield.[49] After a brief and unpleasant discussion with Otter he "proposed going in with bayonet." He then ordered three of his companies across the river and moved them forward to the firing line. Then, at approximately 1715 hours, after "offering five pounds to the first man in the enemy's trenches," Aldworth ordered his men to charge and "invited" all others from the wide array of gathered regiments to join them.[50] The effect was electric. Along the whole line, the intermingled soldiers of the various regiments who had been paralyzed by inactivity were seized by the sudden excitement. The "Royal Canadians" were no different and immediately rose and joined the charge.

"It was about 4.30 in the afternoon that the order passed along the line like a thunderbolt to 'fix bayonets,'" recalled Private Dunham. He elaborated, "never for a moment did we flinch, so when the order came to prepare to charge we jumped to our feet with a stifled cheer & charged."[51] Excitement and enthusiasm, however, were not enough. "And, oh! That wild, mad charge against an invisible enemy," explained Reverend O'Leary, "Hell let loose would give but a faint idea of it."[52] Lawrence Buchan, the second in command later reminisced, "the ping of passing bullet began to sing through the air, then as we got closer the ping turned into a sound like the crack of a whip or a pistol shot close to one's ear." He clarified, "nothing of the enemy was to be seen."[53]

Had those on the ground been questioned, to a man, they would have answered that a charge was a foolish idea. "When we started to move," recalled Lieutenant J.C. Mason, "the bullets fell like a perfect hailstorm."[54] Private Charles Tweddell recalled, "the bullets fell like hail all around us ... it was a fearful carnage."[55] One journalist present wrote, "the men tumbled like skittles on every side."[56] Private Dunham explained, "it was too hot for us; we were compelled to stop."[57] Another participant observed the enemy "opened a fearful fire on us which compelled us to lie down again and take cover as to advance ... would have been mere madness and could have done no good."[58]

Both Mason and Dunham agreed it was a needless act. Mason felt that "it was a hopeless undertaking to cover 600 yards of open ground when the enemy had the exact range," and Dunham wrote resignedly that "the order to charge was another of those blunderings which cost our army so dear."[59] They were representative of most. The brigade commander, Major-General Smith-Dorrien, later told his troops he had not ordered the charge — which was the truth.[60]

The charge occurred nonetheless. Lieutenant-Colonel Aldworth was one of the first to fall in the ill-fated assault. In the end, the charge netted only another 200 yards.[61] At that point the soldiers once again were forced to fling themselves to the ground and desperately attempt to melt into any available crack and crevice to avoid the deadly reach of the Mauser bullets. Darkness now became their only hope and salvation. At about 1900 hours, once the battlefield was cloaked in obscurity, Otter gave the order to withdraw. "Within a few hundred yards of the enemy we lay till night closed around us, then quietly retired," scribbled Dunham in his diary, "It was a sad moment for us, to leave the ground we had so dearly won."[62] The day's action cost the Battalion, 21 killed and 60 wounded.

Amid the death and despair, however, were also heroics. One such case was Private Richard Rowland Thompson, a 22-year-old medical student from Ottawa, who served in "D" Coy. Seeing a friend, Private J.L. Bradshaw, gravely wounded by a bullet in the neck, he crawled over to him. Although exposed to enemy fire, Thompson lay alongside Bradshaw for seven hours with his fingers compressing the man's jugular vein to prevent him from bleeding to death until stretcher bearers arrived using the darkness as cover. "I stayed out on the battlefield right under the Boer trenches with a poor fellow who had been shot in the throat," wrote Thompson to his brother, "it is marvellous how I escaped as my helmet was shot off my head by the Boers."[63] In the end, Thompson's selfless actions saved his friend's life.

At day's end, even the most inexperienced soldier realized that the Battalion had been severely blooded. Moreover, its young adventurers who had sought "action" now realized war's grim side. "We all agree," wrote one young soldier, "that we have had all the fighting we want, and will be glad to get back to the line of communication as soon as possible."[64]

Despite the unsuccessful assault, the British had achieved some success. At nightfall the Boers withdrew to a better defensive position, though Cronje's large army was now completely surrounded by an overwhelming British force. Moreover, the trap was sufficiently strong that he could not break out, nor could Boer reinforcements relieve the pressure or save him. As such, the siege progressed with antagonists manning entrenchments and continuing a constant harassing fire using artillery and small arms.

The "Royal Canadians" took their turn manning both outposts and the main entrenchment facing the Boers. The next day, 19 February, the Battalion buried its dead and manned a series of outposts five kilometres up river and approximately 3,500 metres from the Boer laager. Two days later the Battalion was sent to Artillery Hill to support the naval guns that were shelling the Boers with lyddite, as well as man a series of outposts during the night. On 22 February they were relieved but the arrival of a large Boer force that intended to break the siege meant that they were reassigned with the remainder of 19th Brigade to man a line of kopjes to the West as a blocking force. After three days, during which time there was an incessant heavy rain, the Battalion was sent back to Paardeberg Drift for a rest. This proved to be of little value as the torrential rains continued throughout the night turning their bivouac into a quagmire.

The mud, however, was the least of their concerns. The heavy rains caused the river, which ran through their bivouac and served as the only source of drinking water, to flood. The swift current also ran through the Boer laager, and now carried the debris of the besieged camp — specifically its dead and its waste. Otter reported that the greater part of their "rest day" was spent pulling dead men and animals from the banks of their bivouac to prevent them creating a dam. In the brief 24 hour period spent in the camp, Otter estimated that a minimum of 720 bodies and carcasses drifted down from the Boer laager. This fouling of the drinking supply would later create grave problems in the form of enteric and typhoid fever that eventually affected 350 men in the Battalion, 10 percent of who actually died from disease.[65]

On the morning of 26 February, the Battalion was ordered into the trenches to relieve the Cornwalls. The entrenchments were gradually being pushed towards the enemy position. When the "Royal Canadians" arrived they found themselves approximately 600 metres from the Boer lines. For the remainder of the day the Canadians engaged the Boers with small arms fire. All hoped for a conclusion to the siege and most felt that the end was near. "At present we are surrounding Cronje and his force, and now have them cooped up like rats in a hole, though it has been at a great cost," wrote one participant, "We are shelling them continually with shrapnel and lyddite, and they are readily famished, as we have learned from prisoners and almost ready to surrender."[66]

With such a turn of events the British commanders decided to put additional pressure on the Boers. In the afternoon, the Battalion received word that a night attack, at 0200 hours, would be conducted. Preparations were undertaken and the Battalion braced for its second major engagement of the war. However, the soldiers were not all overly enthusiastic. "Nothing is so trying on the nerves as a night attack," confided Private Dunham to is diary, "and we had lots of time to ponder on it."[67]

The plan of attack was for six RCR companies in the main trench (i.e., "C," "D," "E," "F," "G," and "H" companies) to advance on the Boer trenches at the assigned hour. In support, in the main trench to the right of the RCRs, were 200 Gordon Highlanders. To the left at approximately 1,500 metres were the Shropshire Light Infantry. These battalions were to provide covering fire if required. For the assaulting "Royal Canadians," the front rank of each company was to move with fixed bayonets and they were not to fire until fired upon by the enemy. The rear rank, with engineer support, was to sling their rifles and carry shovels and picks with which to entrench. Once the advance ground to a halt and could go no further, the rear rank, supported by the fire of the front rank and adjacent units, was to dig-in.[68]

At 0215 hours, in the inky Transvaal darkness, the "Royal Canadians" crept out of their entrenchments and moved forward. "It was so dark," explained Buchan, "that it was necessary for each one to grasp the arm or sleeve of his next comrade to enable us to kep touch at all."[69] They attempted to maintain an interval of one pace between men and a distance of 15 paces between ranks. Initially, the advance seemed too good to be true. The front rank moved forward without interruption for about 400 metres. Then suddenly a few stray shots rang out, followed by a terrific burst of fire that split the darkness. Luckily the initial shots served as a warning and many of the soldiers threw themselves down to the ground before the fire erupted. "Silently we advanced for several hundred yards, then the order came to ease off to the left," explained Private Dunham, "We hardly had moved two steps when a wall of fire opened up in front of us, not fifty yards away and a hail of bullets whizzed past us, sending death with it." He added, "We all dropped as flat as pancakes and lay there while the fusillade lasted."[70]

But not all were so lucky. "Now we are in for it and no mistake," reflected Gerald Carogan, "crossfire everywhere the Boers are only 100 yards from us now but, there is a solid wall of lead between us and them — the hail of lead is pouring in on us from every side … in our ranks men are dropping on every side — hundred be dead or dying in our wake, and hundreds more must die before those trenches are reached- but no its impossible — no human being can move against that hail of lead."[71]

Another participant recalled, "The first news we had of the enemy was a sheet of flame not twenty yards away."[72] The noise of the battle impressed Private William Jeffery. "The explosive bullets," he wrote, "sounded like flying devils hissing and smacking through the air."[73] One journalist witnessing the event described it as "a brief fight, but a long half hour of deadly combat." He added, "ten minutes of triple hell and twenty minutes of an ordinary inferno."[74] The Boer volley had a disastrous effect on "F" and "G" companies which were caught in the open within 60 metres of the enemy's advanced trench. Combined they suffered six killed and 21 wounded in mere minutes.[75]

The assaulting Canadians in the front rank now hugged the ground and returned fire. They were supported by the Shropshires who unleashed volleys of fire from their distant entrenchments in a vain effort to provide covering fire and distract the Boers. The rear rank of the "Royal Canadians" began to entrench, but progress was mixed. The trench on the right, being constructed by Royal Engineers (RE) who "worked liked demons" and supported by "G" and "H" companies, made rapid progress and were approximately 100 metres from the enemy position. The trenches on the left were not faring as well.

Then suddenly, the fog of war swept over the battlefield — the friction that the great theoretician Carl von Clausewitz warned of, and the same that is a curse to all field commanders. In the murky darkness, amid the carnage, death, and fear of battle, an authoritative voice ordered all "to retire and bring back your wounded."[76] The apparent directive was enough for most — the entire left side of the line, four companies in total, collapsed in a rush to the rear, back to the main trench. "I think all records for the 100 yards," penned Private Dunham, "were broken that night."[77]

The precipitous withdrawal angered Otter. The hasty retreat put the reputation of the Canadians at risk. Conscious of the disdain that the British regulars held for colonials, Otter was concerned this would simply reinforce their perceptions. However, fate smiled on The RCR that night. Daylight found "G" and "H" Companies well entrenched with the Royal Engineers still pushing on with their work. It has never become clear whether the tenacious troops simply were oblivious to the supposed order and general withdrawal that took place in the dark, or whether strong decisive local leadership prevailed. Regardless, at 0400 hours, as the light of dawn slowly seeped onto the battlefield, the Boers rose from their trenches to investigate their night's work. Suddenly, the tables were turned as they came under fire from the newly constructed trench less than 100 metres from their position.

At the same time, in the dawn shadows, an officer spotted a wounded man in the field and called for a volunteer to assist him to bring him in. Without hesitation, Private Thompson once again went to the aid of a fellow soldier with complete disregard to the danger. He dropped his rifle and ran 300 yards under fire. He arrived just before the wounded man was killed by another bullet. Thompson was recommended for the Victoria Cross (VC) for his selfless acts of courage, but in its stead, in July 1900, he received one of seven Queen's Scarves, knitted by Queen Victoria "for most distinguished private soldiers in the Colonial Forces of Canada, Australia, New Zealand, and South Africa."[78]

The firefight continued for over an hour, when unexpectedly a white flag fluttered over the advanced enemy trench. The Boers appeared to have had enough, though the Canadians were leery since this tactic had been used before as a ruse. As a result, they kept up a well-disciplined fire until 0600 hours, when an individual carrying a white flag emerged from the enemy trenches. The firing stopped immediately. Soon, groups of Boers began to flow from their entrenchments.

The battle for Paardeberg was over. By 0615 hours, the division commander, General Sir Henry Colville arrived and dispatched an officer into the Boer laager to discuss the terms of surrender — which were unconditional. Despite the questionable night attack, the tenacity of "G" and "H" Coys had not only saved the reputation of the Battalion, but had in fact created the conditions for the first major British victory of the war. Paardeberg has also been widely recognized as the turning point of the conflict. Moreover, the date of the victory was very significant. In 1881, 19 years earlier to the day, the Boers had inflicted a humiliating defeat on the British, and thus secured their independence. That embarrassment was now avenged.

The victory was a distinctly Canadian one. "The supporting companies of the Gordon Highlanders were not engaged, although the trench which protected them was subjected to a fairly heavy fire from the enemy," reported Otter. "The battalion of the Shropshire Light Infantry on our left, fired volleys at long ranges for some time after our attack developed and materially assisted us," he added. However, he was clear in his appraisal. "That the duty entailed on The Royal Canadian Regiment was most difficult and dangerous no one will deny," he wrote, "and though the advance was not so successful at all points as was hoped for, yet the final result was a complete success, and credit can fairly be claimed by the battalion for such, as it was practically acting alone."[79]

The Battalion had made Canada proud. The effects of the battle were profound. After Paardeberg, Field Marshal Lord Roberts, the British commander-in-chief in South Africa, told survivors, that they "had done noble work, and were as good a lot of men as were in the British Army." Roberts went on to say that "Canadian now stands for bravery, dash and courage."[80] Another British general stated: "Those men [Canadians] can go into battle without a leader they have intelligence and resourcefulness enough to lead themselves."[81] Praise poured in from throughout the empire congratulating the "Royal Canadians" for their "brilliant achievement," "gallant conduct," and "distinguished gallantry."[82]

The success of the Canadian troops and the international respect they garnered soon triggered a nationalist outpouring of pride in Canadian military prowess. Even the initially reluctant prime minister, Sir Wilfrid Laurier, was not immune from exploiting the Canadians' success in the field. "Is there a man whose bosom did not swell with pride, the pride of pure patriotism, the pride of consciousness," thundered Laurier in the House of Commons, "that day [Paardeberg] the fact had been revealed to the world that a new power had arisen in the West."[83]

In light of the eventual success, Otter's anger waned over the actual conduct of the troops during the attack, specifically their unauthorized retreat. For the soldiers, however, the adulation was of little immediate value. What mattered to them was the fact that Cronje's surrender meant a brief rest. The next day the "Royal Canadians" moved eight kilometres up the Modder River to Kodoes Rand to join the remainder of the British field force in a concentration area. The Battalion rested here until 7 March.

The temporary respite was brief. Now that the momentum had shifted, British commanders wanted to push the Boers hard and drive for Pretoria — their capital. The advance commenced with an attack on the Boers at Poplar Grove. Although in reserve, the "Royal Canadians" were hard pressed. First, they were tasked to provide an escort for the artillery, which had to retire in the face of accurate enemy fire. After marching hard for several kilometres to accomplish their mission, they were immediately dispatched to join the Highland Brigade that was rapidly moving against the enemy in support of a division attack. This entailed another stiff march of 16 kilometres, after which the "Royal Canadians" were ordered to seize a series of small kopjes thought to be occupied by the Boers. Luckily the Battalion achieved its objective without engagement and from the top of Slags Kraal was able to witness the hasty retreat of the Boer force.

On the morning of 10 March 1900, the final stage of the march against Bloemfontein, the capital of the Orange Free State was begun. The advance was made in three columns with the "Royal Canadians" as part of the 9th Division in the Centre. The march was largely unopposed and the British forces entered Bloemfontein three days later. The Battalion at this juncture numbered 28 officers and 712 men.

The capture of the capital as well as the Orange Free State rail lines meant that the British army could stop to rest and refit. The campaign to date had been exceedingly difficult. "All have been called upon for extraordinary exertion, and have had to undergo forced marches, short rations, great wettings, lack of water and sleep, as well as severe and trying fighting," extolled Major-General Smith-Dorrien.[84] "The Royal Canadian Regiment," reported Otter, "had suffered equally with the others in the matter of short rations; all having been for the last three weeks upon half rations at the most and at odd times not even that." He added, "as to clothing and boots, the battalion was in a pitiable condition."[85]

The soldiers and others were exceedingly more critical. Canadian volunteers, dependent on the British for leadership and management of their basic needs, were woefully disappointed. A flood of personal observations and stories from South Africa quickly passed to Canadians through letters and by returning veterans. The picture these revealed was one of Canadian troops who were suffering for long periods of time because of inadequate food, accommodation, clothing, and medical care. During the advance on Bloemfontein, Sergeant Hart-McHarg revealed that despite the hard marching, they had been on reduced rations for almost a month. He recounted, "we were hungry all the time."[86] Private Jeffery wrote: "We have been on short rations and are still mighty hungry — mighty hungry and no mistake … have been for some time now."[87] Private Bennett confided, "I never thought I would ever come down to eat what other people had thrown away, but after Cronje's surrender I was thankful to eat the crumbs and crusts that I found in the Boer boxes while strolling through the deserted laager."[88] Private Perkins wrote: "It makes our mouths water to think of a stale crust." He revealed that their general condition deteriorated constantly — "we are still weaker and there is nothing to eat."[89] One soldier simply revealed, "I want to get over this hungry feeling."[90]

Their battle with thirst was equally debilitating. "Regarding water," observed Private Bennett, "many a time on the march have I and many others been glad to quench our thirst in the puddles which the recent rains had caused and some of it was as thick as mud with blue clay."[91] Private Dunham complained, "[we] had to drink stagnant water, muddy as you could make it.[92] One contemporary account revealed, "When they reached Ramdam they hoped for water, but here they found nothing but a green slimy pool with creeping things in it. The horses turned away in disgust sniffing at it scornfully; but the men bent over and drank."[93] The Battalion's medical officer recalled, "Men were thirsty and filled their water bottles at any source, even dirty frog ponds."[94] The trek became a feat of endurance. During a four-day period the British lost 796 mules and 3,500 oxen.[95]

Equally frustrating were the uniforms that could not be replaced, but which were by mid-campaign literally in tatters. "Most of the men," explained veteran A.S. McCormick, "were in rags."[96] It was not abnormal for shoes to be devoid of soles, pants without knees or backsides, or shirts without sleeves and buttons. "Fighting seems to be the easiest part of the campaign," lamented Private Perkins, "no soles on our shoes, no buttons on our shirts, no knees in our trousers, no seat, it is enough to make anyone yearn for civilization."[97] One newspaper clipping indignantly reported, "The Ragged Canadians … Boots out at toes, undarned stockings bursting through gaps at the side, breeches torn and mended and torn again, here and there a pair of indigo canvas — the spoils of the enemy and the last refuge of the naked."[98] Moreover, the cold nights on the veldt became intolerable, particularly when it rained, as it often did during the campaign. With inadequate clothing, a single thin substandard blanket and no tents — the exhausted soldiers found themselves cold, wet, and unable to properly sleep.[99]

But no issue drew more criticism or censure than the medical care provided the sick and wounded. A Canadian officer, a medical doctor in civilian life, who visited a military hospital was "ashamed of the professional standards."[100] Reports by journalists and soldiers soon revealed the scope of the problem. A lack of adequate accommodation, bedding and blankets, as well as a dearth of qualified caring staff to look after the soldiers (i.e., keep them clean, sanitary, and free of flies and vermin) who were too weak to look after themselves, transformed a serious problem into a tragedy. And, as if matters were not bad enough, men were treated according to rank rather than their illness or wound.[101]

In the end, the Canadians could not help but feel that the British Army placed a low priority on looking after its men, particularly colonials.

Although the harsh terrain and nature of the campaign were at fault for some of the problems, others resulted from the cultural and institutional biases of Britain's Army. The fact that British regular units received their tents and replacement clothing sooner than the colonials, may not be surprising, but it left a lingering resentment with the Canadians.[102] But most important, the fact that the British Army was so incapable of providing for their basic needs added to the loss of reverence for the British military and its generals. It also fuelled the growing realization that Canada would have to look after its own sons and daughters if it wished to ensure their well-being and fair treatment when deployed overseas. In the end, the suffering of the "Royal Canadians" laid the ground work for national decisions on command and control of Canadian forces in future overseas campaigns.

Nevertheless, for the "Royal Canadians," the future consequences of their ordeal was a moot point — they still had a war to fight. A few days after their arrival to Bloemfontein enteric and typhoid fevers made their appearance with a vengeance. Within two weeks The RCR suffered over 100 cases with fresh ones appearing daily. Despite the losses, the Battalion was deployed on 31 March in reaction to Boer attacks in the local area. After a series of strenuous marches — a portion of the Battalion occupied Boesman Kop, a commanding position approximately 29 kilometres from Bloemfontein, while the remainder engaged the enemy near Waterval Drift. The next few days were spent marching back to the original bivouacs, however, the morning after arrival the "Royal Canadians" were once again deployed. Frustratingly for the troops, the enemy was now avoiding direct engagements and the hard marching was for naught. To add to their difficulty, it once again began to rain and their bivouac area was transformed into a quagmire.

On 21 April the 19th Brigade moved to Springfield to relieve another brigade from outpost duty. Two days later the Battalion was once again on the move in what would prove to be its second series of long arduous marches and combat that would not cease until they reached Pretoria. At Israels Poort, on 25 April, the Battalion was once engaged. As the brigade's advance guard, it was ordered to seize a series of kopjes that blocked the advance. The "Royal Canadians" deployed in extended order, two companies up and four deep. As they approached a wire fence, approximately 600 metres from the central kopje a "hot fire was opened upon us," reported Otter. The soldiers took cover where they could. Otter braved the fire and remained standing so that he could direct the disposition of the troops. In the process of taking cover he was struck by a bullet on the right side of his chin, which passed through the right side of his neck. Although bleeding profusely, he remained in command for the entire engagement. After a prolonged firefight, Otter observed the Boer fire was weakening and he also heard concerted action on his flank. As a result, he reinforced his front rank and advanced eventually seizing the position.[103] The battle lasted three hours.

Although the troops disliked Otter, they respected his courage. "Colonel Otter was always very cool under fire," conceded Sergeant W. Hart-McHarg, "and inspired confidence in whatever part of the field he happened to be."[104] Otter was now evacuated for treatment and Lieutenant-Colonel Buchan assumed command. The advance continued. To the soldiers it was a repeat of the heavy marching and constant fighting. Many of the engagements were long-range small arms and artillery fire, but the Battalion experienced substantial engagements at Eden Mountain, Thaba Mountain, and Klipriviersberg. Otter returned on 26 May and was in command for the march into Pretoria on 5 June 1900. Fortuitously, 19th Brigade was the lead formation in General Sir Ian Hamilton's command, and similarly it was the Battalion's turn to be vanguard within the brigade, therefore, the "Royal Canadians" led the occupying forces into the enemy's capital city.

The honour came at a price — only 27 officers and 411 men remained of the original contingent. Their accomplishments, however, were noteworthy. As part of the 19th Brigade, the Battalion "marched 620 miles, often on half rations, seldom on full," praised Major-General Smith-Dorrien. "It has taken part in the capture of ten towns," he added, "[and] fought in ten general engagements." The brigade commander concluded by stating, "in one period of 30 days it fought on 21 of them, and marched 327 miles."[105]

Nonetheless, the 19th Brigade was not allowed to linger long in Pretoria. Two days later, they were deployed to secure the lines of communication. On 11 June, the bulk of the Battalion was sent to occupy Springs a coal mining centre approximately 30 kilometres East of Johannesburg. quickly, the British established a large supply depot in the village to support operations to the North. The task, although manpower intensive because of its defensive nature and wide area of coverage, was largely uneventful although some dilatory enemy action occurred.

Soldiers on a Kopje firing on retreating Boers during the advance on Pretoria.

Throughout the occupation, Boers numbering at times between 150–800 remained in the vicinity and menaced the outposts. On 28 June, 600 Boers attacked. However, with few exceptions, the enemy contented themselves to exchange long-range rifle and gunfire at 1,500–3,000 metres. A number of short duration operations and patrols were mounted against the enemy in the following weeks but the Boers remained elusive. On 2 August 1900, the Battalion was ordered to abandon Springs, which it did the same day and moved by train to Wolvehoek.[106]

The Battalion now joined Major-General C.P. Ridley's mounted infantry column in pursuit of General DeWet's forces in the area of Vredefort. On 10 August, the Battalion was unexplainably transferred to Major-General Fitzroy Hart's column. After many days of hard marching in pursuit of the intangible Boers, often without an adequate water supply, the column was ordered to return to Pretoria, which it did on 23 August. "I should place on record the severity of these marches and strain to which officers and men were subjected," reported Otter, "not only were the marches long, averaging seventeen miles a day, but they were continuous; the roads very dusty; water scarce and rest most irregular."[107]

The Battalion once again resumed outpost duty on the lines of communication. The war now seemed to wind down for the "Royal Canadians" and they were largely employed on garrison type duties. For many of the volunteers, it was time to go home. They had done hard service — the environment was harsh; the British Army seemed incapable or unwilling to properly support them, and their CO seemed to lack a sense of compassion. He certainly could not relate to his men. He proved this once again in spades.

On 7 September 1900, Lieutenant-Colonel Otter received a request from Lord Roberts. "I trust that as many as possible of the Royal Canadians will prolong their service until the end of the war," cabled Roberts. Otter after conferring with a number of officers at his headquarters responded the next day, "your wishes will gladly be complied with." However, he had made a large assumption. All his men were volunteers who had already been extended past their six-month term and their maximum 12-month engagement was rapidly approaching. The news that they had been "volunteered" for additional service did not go over well. Obligations to family and fear of loss of employment or business in Canada caused many to resist Otter's zealous offer on their behalf. As a result, Otter was forced to take back his offer and inform Lord Roberts that a majority of the Royal Canadians demanded their discharge in Canada, on 15 October, as was their right. "I deeply regret," wrote Otter to Roberts, "having misled you."[108] In the end, 16 officers and 413 other ranks sailed from Cape Town to Halifax on 1 October 1900. The remaining 12 officers and 250 men remained in South Africa and finished out their part of the war largely on outpost duty.

On 7 November, the remainder of the 2nd Battalion embarked in Cape Town on the troop transport *Hawarden Castle* for passage to England. They arrived approximately three weeks later in Southampton to a hero's welcome. They proceeded directly to London, where the next morning they marched to Windsor Castle amid the cheers of the citizens. At 1145 hours they were reviewed by Queen Victoria who thanked them for their service in South Africa. The Battalion was then hosted for several days in England, finally departing from Liverpool on 12 December on the *Lake Champlain*. Eleven days later, the vestiges of the 2nd Special Service Battalion, The RCR arrived in Halifax. Its remaining personnel were immediately discharged and the Battalion disbanded.

Before leaving the RCR's role in the South African War, it is imperative to mention the role of the 3rd Special Service Battalion, The RCR that was raised to relieve the 1st Battalion, Leinster Regiment from garrison duty at the Halifax Citadel. The war had strained the British Army to such an extent that they sought relief wherever possible. As a result, the 3rd Battalion was established — consisting of 29 officers and 975 other ranks under the command of Lieutenant-Colonel B.H. Vidal. They assumed duty at the Citadel on 25 March 1900. Although the Battalion conducted only garrison duties its service was greatly appreciated by the British government and military command. On 1 October 1902, the

3rd Battalion was officially disbanded when a British garrison resumed control of the Halifax Citadel.

In all, the "Royal Canadians" had done Canada proud. They served with distinction and demonstrated a martial spirit, endurance, and tenacity that rivalled the vaunted British regulars. "There are no finer troops or more gallant troops in all the world," wrote Major-General Smith-Dorrien of the "Royal Canadians."[109] He was not alone in his praise. "The men of the RCR," commented the Battalion medical officer, "were a jolly lot and saw the humor in any difficulty."[110] Even the journalists were impressed. "We have seen the First Contingent," wrote one reporter, "side by side with the bravest and the best of the Imperial regiments, taking with them the hardships met with on campaign."[111] The Daily News correspondent was equally awed. "To Canada we take off our hats," he asserted, "She has sent us a regiment of infantry that wins admiration from every soldier for marching, endurance and fighting. It can challenge comparison with any battalion in Lord Roberts army, and that is saying a great deal."[112]

This came at a cost. In total, the "Royal Canadians" suffered 39 killed and 123 wounded.[113] However, their accomplishments were impressive. After all, it was the 2nd Battalion that delivered the first major British victory in the war at Paardeberg, which became the turning point of the conflict. It also awakened a patriotism and national identity at home. The martial victory in a foreign land earned Canada, through its blood, a recognition in the international community.

In addition, the hardships endured and lessons learned became the catalyst for wide sweeping militia reforms that were instituted in the landmark Militia Act of 1904. Deficiencies in command and control, supply and services, officer education and training, military autonomy, and munitions availability were all addressed.[114] Equally important, was the dispatch of distinct Canadian contingents under Canadian commanding officers, who although answerable to British commanders, also answered to their national government, setting an important precedent. The nation rejected the concept of scattering small units throughout the British field force. Rather, it insisted on a national contingent to be employed as such. Henceforth, Canadian soldiers fighting on behalf of the British Empire would do so as distinct and independent Canadian formations responsible before all else to their sovereign government. Canada would never again blindly subordinate its sons and daughters to the absolute control of Britain or any other foreign power, nor would they automatically assume that the interests of the senior ally were always the same as those of Canada. The Boer War had set an important precedent — civil and military national command and control was a principle that Canada would never again forget.

And so, the green volunteers seeking adventure evolved into hardened professionals that earned the respect of both friend and foe. Their blood and toil earned Canada an enviable reputation and set an exemplary standard for endurance, tenacity, and military prowess for others to emulate. They established the term *Royal Canadians* as a moniker of pride and honour.

3
Service and Suffering:
The Regiment in the First World War

As the "Royal Canadians" entered the new millennium, they could look back proudly upon their first decades of service. They had already participated in three operational tours of duty. In each, they demonstrated courage, endurance, and tenacity. They had soldiered in some of the harshest conditions possible, shoulder to shoulder with British regulars, and had not been found wanting. In their short period of existence they had made their country proud.

With the country once again at peace, The RCR reverted to its role as trainer for the militia. The Regiment also underwent a reorganization in 1905 following the British government's decision to withdraw its troops from Halifax, and pass the responsibility for the garrison of this strategic citadel to the Canadian government. Not surprisingly, Canada looked to its only permanent force infantry regiment to meet the task. Consequently, The RCR was reorganized on a 10 company basis. By October, the reorganization was complete and the disposition of the Regiment was as follows:

Regimental HQ — Halifax, Nova Scotia
Nos. 1–6 Coys —Halifax, Nova Scotia
No. 7 Coy — Quebec City, Quebec
No. 8 Coy — St. Jean, Quebec
No. 9 Coy — Toronto, Ontario
No. 10 Coy — London, Ontario

During the turmoil of reorganization, command of the Regiment was in control of militia headquarters in Ottawa. However, on 15 September 1905, it was passed to Lieutenant-Colonel Lyndhurst Wadmore with the instruction to maintain standards of the highest order consistent with the Regiment's short but distinguished history.

The Regiment now proceeded with its primary duties of garrisoning Halifax; providing instruction to the militia; and ensuring its own administration, training, and professional development. In July 1909, the Regiment was also called upon to aid the civil power in response to a strike that broke out at the Dominion Coal Company in Cape Breton, Nova Scotia. The strike by the United Mine Workers of America became one of the most bitter labour confrontations in Canadian history and spread to several locations in Nova Scotia. The Regiment conducted patrols and provided guards at points of greatest danger. Despite the overwhelming potential for violence, the friendly and confident disposition and bearing of the "Royals"[1] prevented open hostility. On 4 March 1910, after approximately eight months of duty, the strike was settled and the RCR soldiers were able to return to their garrison in Halifax.[2]

"A Most Unpleasant Duty." RCR soldiers stand guard at Sable Head, New Aberdeen, Cape Breton, during the Dominion Coal Company Strike.

For the next several years the Regiment, much like the Canadian government, conducted its duties without undue alarm or trepidation in regards to the international situation. However, all that abruptly changed on 28 June 1914, when the Austrian heir to the throne, Archduke Franz Ferdinand, was assassinated by Gavrilo Princip, a member of the Serbian "Black Hand" in Sarajevo. A harsh Austrian ultimatum to Serbia ended in a declaration of war on 28 July. Complex European alliances then turned this Balkan tragedy into a world war.

When Germany, Austria's ally, invaded Belgium in its flanking movement against France, it pushed a wavering England into the fray. The British had guaranteed the neutrality of Belgium and this naked aggression was too much for the English people to tolerate. As a result, on 4 August 1914, England declared war on Germany and the Austro-Hungarian Empire.

These events in far away Europe had an immediate impact on Canada. In 1914, Canada did not have control over its foreign affairs. Therefore, when Britain was at war, Canada was at war. Despite the lack of control over the nation's decision to participate, most Canadians enthusiastically welcomed the conflict. A common concern of many volunteers and militiamen was that the war would be over before they could join the great adventure.

Canada, however, was greatly unprepared for war. With a population of approximately 7.8 million people, its army consisted of 3,000 permanent force members backed by a militia of about 60,000 men. But, "a call to arms" soon changed that. A concentration at Camp Valcartier in Quebec had assembled a total of 32,665 all ranks by 8 September. Moreover, Sam Hughes, minister of militia and defence, promised the early deployment of 25,000 men to England.[3]

Although the "Royals" were eager to partake in the great adventure, their desires were initially thwarted. Britain now desperately required its regular soldiers. As such, it recalled some of its garrison troops for front line duty. However, the requirement for trained troops to guard its strategic posts around the globe remained. As a result, The RCR, as Canada's only permanent force infantry unit, was not only the most logical, but also the only choice available. Its troops were professional and well trained. They could, on short notice, deploy and ensure both Canada's honour, as well as the security of some of England's strategic posts, such as Bermuda. Therefore, The RCR became the first regiment to serve overseas — though not in Europe.

RCR soldiers, home after duty in Bermuda, relax on parade in Halifax, 17 August 1915.

The call to duty began on 19 August 1914, when Britain asked Canada to provide replacement troops for its garrison in Bermuda, which was referred to as the "Keeper of the Western Gate" for obvious reasons stemming from its strategic position in the Atlantic Ocean.[4] The next day, the adjutant-general telegraphed the commanding officer, Lieutenant-Colonel Alfred Octave Fages and queried whether the personnel of the Regiment would volunteer for service in Bermuda. Under the *Militia Act*, since Canada's security was in no way directly affected, all regimental personnel were legally required to volunteer for such overseas duty. Although disappointed that the Regiment would not sail with the first Canadian contingent to Europe, the "Royal Canadians" did not let the call to duty go unanswered. They all agreed to serve. However, the CO stipulated that the Regiment desired, as soon as circumstances allowed, to be deployed against the enemy in Europe.

The Regiment sailed from Halifax with 938 personnel (32 officers and 906 men),[5] on 10 September 1914, and arrived in Hamilton, Bermuda three days later. Upon landing, sub-units were dispersed to various points within the Bermuda islands. Regimental headquarters (RHQ), the machine-gun section, and eight companies were stationed at Prospect. Another three companies were deployed to Boaz Island and three more garrisoned St. George's Island. Some troops were also positioned on St. David's Island.[6]

Duty, although in an idyllic setting, was monotonous, particularly with an active war in progress. The Regiment's role was twofold: garrison

Bermuda and conduct training. The first entailed sentry duty and drills (i.e., searching for German submarines), as well as patrols along the beach and in the towns. The second, included musketry, entrenching, and field manoeuvres. However, the stifling heat in the summer limited activities. In addition, the split of the Regiment into three distinct detachments limited its ability to train as a cohesive unit.

In the end, the Regiment remained in Bermuda for 11 months. It was relieved by the 38th Battalion, Canadian Expeditionary Force (CEF), on 13 August 1915, and embarked on the S.S. *Caledonian* the same day. The Regiment returned to Halifax four days later but was warned off immediately to proceed overseas. All that had to be done was return stores from Bermuda, draw war equipment, exchange arms, equip a large draft, and re-attest the entire Regiment for war service.

Finally, on 25 August, the newly equipped and reorganized Regiment re-embarked on the S.S. *Caledonian* and set sail the next day. Almost two weeks later, on 6 September, the Regiment arrived in Plymouth, England. The following day it deployed to Quested Farm Camp near Shorncliffe where training began for service in France. Much had transpired during the Regiment's hiatus in Bermuda. Although the Regiment had conducted training, splitting it up among the islands, coupled with limitations in activity because of heat, location, and the lack of experienced instructors with up-to-date knowledge of developments in Europe prompted the inspector general to comment, "I consider it [RCR] will need additional training in England before it will be ready to go to the front."[7]

This "additional training" was in fact necessary. The Regiment had much to catch up on. By this time, the war had become a bitter war of attrition. The German advance at the start of the war had failed to break through the Allied line, and a series of major flanking attacks and counterattacks in 1914 and 1915 failed to provide a decisive outcome. As a result, the two opposing sides were now locked in stalemate, facing each other across a barren no man's land in entrenchments that ran from Switzerland to the English Channel. While the "Royal Canadians" were on garrison duty in Bermuda the First Canadian Division distinguished itself at Ypres, on 22 April 1915, when the Germans launched a vicious attack using gas for the first time in the war. Their tenacious defence thwarted a German breakthrough. By September, the 2nd Canadian Infantry Division had arrived in France, and so was born the Canadian Corps under the command of Lieutenant-General E.A.H. Alderson. On 5 November, the Regiment, numbering 36 officers and 1,006 other

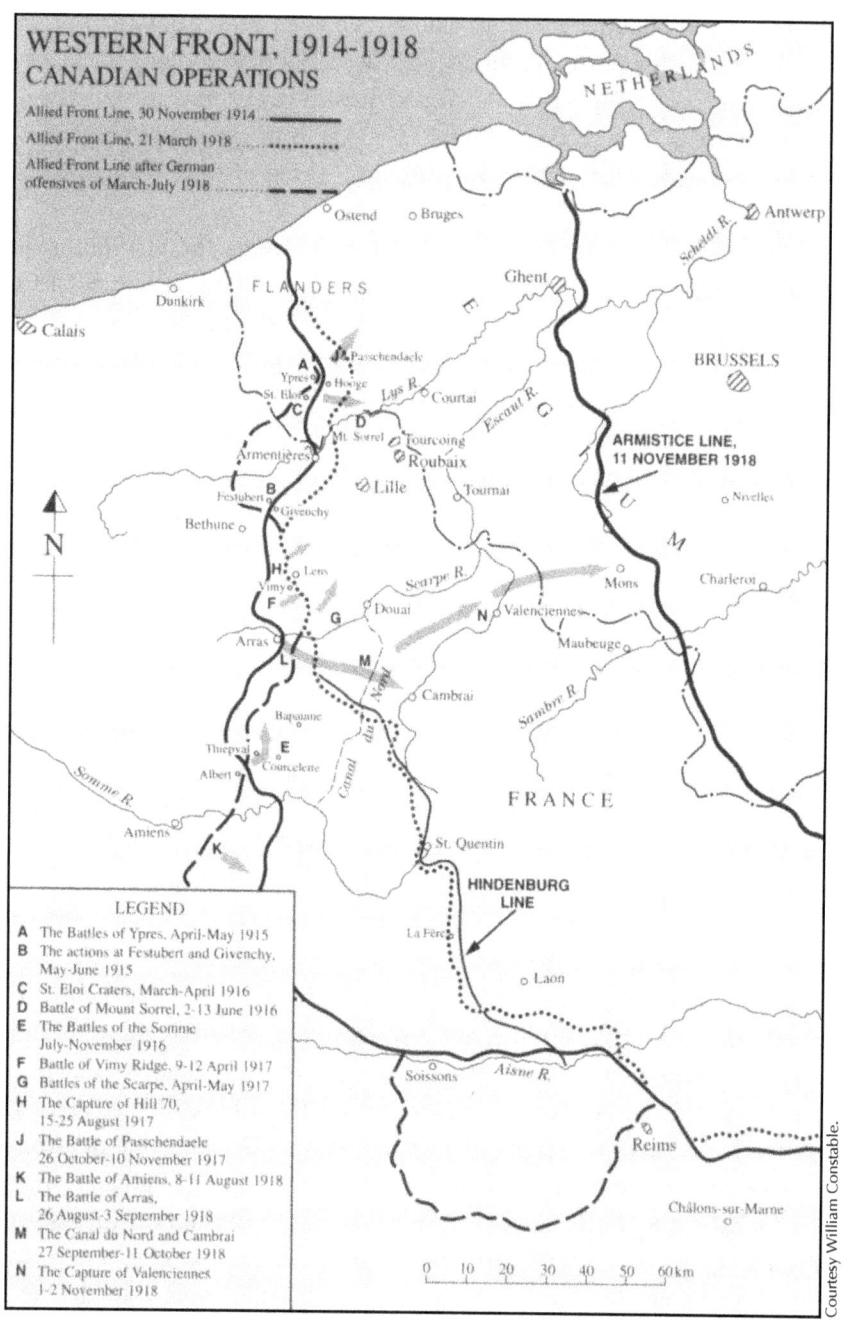

ranks, joined the formation. All ranks of The RCR who had for so long clamoured "to get into the war" could now share the suffering of trench warfare with their Canadian compatriots.

Upon arrival at the front, the "Royal Canadians" were eased into the realities of the conflict. Initially, between 10–15 November, platoons were cycled through front line duty in the trenches with a battalion from the 1st Canadian Infantry Division. This indoctrination was absolutely vital. "One week of practical experience in the trenches," conceded one soldier later, "was worth a year's training." He explained, "you learnt what you could do and what you couldn't do."[8] Four days later, the Regiment became the Corps Reserve. During this period, working parties, approximately 300 strong, were provided for service in the forward area by both day and night. And so, their apprenticeship was completed.

Finally, on 8 January 1916, the Regiment, as part of the newly formed 7th Canadian Infantry Brigade, took up its place in the front lines.[9] Here it served rotating in and out of billets and duty in the trenches. Duty at the front was both monotonous and deadly. "One loses all track of time and days here," bemoaned one soldier.[10] The troops quickly became all too familiar with the cold torrential rains, endless mud, dissolving parapets, and trenches filled knee deep with water. Even sand bags could not hold their form as their contents liquefied and seeped out into the entrenchments. In some places, trenches existed in name only — their actual form having been pounded shapeless by artillery, or they simply melted into the faceless terrain because of the incessant rain.

The troops had to deal with rats. "The trenches swarmed with them," wrote one soldier in his diary, "black rats, brown rats, all kinds and sizes of rats, rats that fed on the bodies of the dead, rats that bit sleeping men, and rats that sometimes, when cornered, would snarl and show fight."[11] The vermin were disgusting and they also carried disease.

The men were further hampered by the incessant battle against trench foot, colds, and influenza, and the discomfort of uniforms that were infested with lice. Although the Regimental War Diary records this period as "uneventful," its pages tell a different story. Day after day, aside from disease and sickness, casualties from enemy sniping, sporadic but violent bombardments, and nuisance shelling, slowly wore down the Regiment.

On 20 March 1916, the Regiment as part of the 3rd Canadian Infantry Division moved into the Ypres Salient. With the warm winds of spring came increased activity at the front. The 2nd Canadian Infantry Division was mired in a prolonged struggle for the mine craters at St. Eloi throughout April. Elsewhere, incessant rain drained morale. "Everyone is miserable," confided Sergeant Freeland to his diary. "We are soaking wet, covered with mud, and think that we have surely landed in the devil's half-acre."[12]

Moreover, constant shelling and bombardments continued to cut the ranks of the Regiment, while turning the entire battlefield into a quagmire. The effect on the entrenchments was predictable. "This section is in the most battered condition of any the Regiment has yet been in," revealed a War Diary entry, "[the] Front line is a succession of Posts, some partially connected and others not connected at all."[13]

By late May, the 3rd Division remained unbloodied. They had not yet participated in a major battle — neither in defence or offence. This was soon to change. At the end of the month the Regiment took over the Hooge sector of the front line. Their brigade (i.e., 7th Brigade) held approximately 2,000 metres of front line split between The RCR and the Princess Patricia's Canadian Light Infantry (PPCLI). The soldiers felt a premonition of dread when suddenly on the night of 31 May and the following day the enemy guns stopped and everything was " suspiciously quiet."[14]

Then, at 0830 hours, on 2 June the German shelling resumed, but with a fury and density not yet experienced by Allied troops. Canadian soldiers and their entrenchments from Mount Sorrel to Sanctuary Wood vanished in the explosions. The Germans, recalled one participant, "threw everything at us but the kitchen sink." He added, "we really got a pounding!"[15] The full ferocity fell on the neighbouring 8th Brigade and the PPCLI.[16] "All that had gone before," wrote Lord Beaverbrook, the general representative for Canada at the front, "was as nothing to this."[17]

At 1500 hours, the Germans attacked. The men in the first line had fixed bayonets, grenades, and wire cutters. The second wave carried entrenching tools, floor boards, and sandbags, so confident were they that their hailstorm of fire had subdued any resistance. And they were not far off. "At about 3 p.m. the enemy attacked and drove our front line back which had been leveled to the ground," recorded the War Diary.[18] The German attackers encountered only small, isolated pockets of resistance that were quickly overcome. Although in possession of virtually the entire front from Mount Sorrel to Tor Top, and with the road to Ypres completely open, the German troops stopped to consolidate their gains. Inexplicably, the original orders for the attack directed that they dig-in 600–700 metres west of their forward trenches. Amazingly, the Germans failed to exploit their success.

Nonetheless, the German attack was not all triumph. Although the PPCLI had suffered tremendous casualties their left still held and checked the enemy advance in their sector. Moreover, it poured a lethal fire into the right rear of the German advance. All enemy attempts at dislodging them were ineffective.

The "Royals" benefited from the stalwart efforts of the PPCLI who held their flank. "[The] PPCLI suffered tremendous losses, their right being obliged to fall back on the Reserve line, but their left still held," recorded the War Diary, "thus keeping our right in tact."[19] The Germans made repeated efforts to widen their penetration by attacking the front line held by the left company of the "Patricias" (i.e., PPCLI) and The RCR, but consistently failed. "The enemy made two attempts to come across to our trenches," wrote the regimental war diarist, "but on both occasions were driven back the men behaving splendidly."[20]

In the end, the German hesitation proved decisive. A 600-metre gap in the Canadian secondary line that they failed to exploit was eventually closed. On 3 June, local counterattacks were launched. Hasty and uncoordinated, they failed to achieve their aim, however, they did succeed in firmly closing the gap and stopping any further German penetration. Three days later, the Germans attacked into the Hooge sector once again, but The RCR had just completed a relief in place with the 28th Battalion.[21] On 13 June, the 1st Canadian Division launched a counterattack that drove the Germans back to their original front line of 2 June.

And so, the Regiment experienced its first major battle. Once again, as it had done in previous conflicts, the courage, tenacity, and skill of the "Royal Canadians" were not found wanting. The troops had conducted themselves well and upheld the honour of the Regiment.

The Regiment remained in the Ypres Salient until the beginning of September 1916. In keeping with the Canadian Corps's role of being "stationary yet aggressive" The RCR assisted in harrying the Germans through an aggressive program of raids and shelling. In September, the Regiment as part of the Canadian Corps under Lieutenant-General Sir Julian H.G. Byng, left Belgium and moved to the meat grinder of the dreaded Somme front. A few months back, on 1 July 1916, a major offensive designed to break through the German front line was launched in poorly chosen ground against a well-entrenched and well-armed enemy. The attack failed and cost the Allies approximately 60,000 casualties on the first day alone. In spite of the failure, the Allied high command decided to continue pressing forward with attacks throughout the summer. The

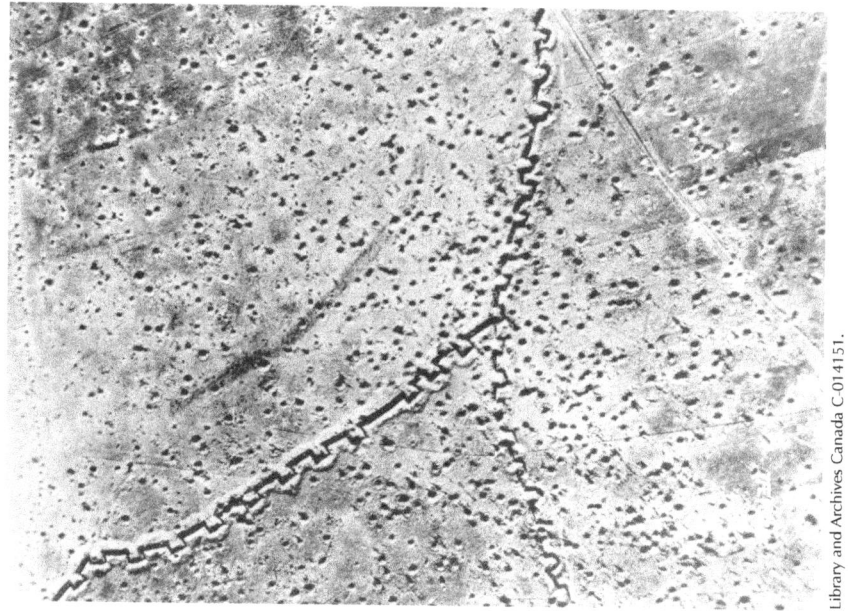

Hellish battleground — aerial photograph showing junction of Regina and Kenora trenches, during the Battle of the Somme, September-October, 1916.

focus had shifted from a breakthrough battle to a campaign of attrition intended to wear down the Germans and destroy their will to fight.[22]

On 13 September the Regiment arrived at a staging area named the "Brickfields" in preparation for its insertion into the battle. The "Royals" did not have long to wait. On 15 September, on a cool and cloudy morning, after several days of rain, 7th Brigade Headquarters ordered the Regiment to proceed to Usna Hill to act as the formation reserve. The PPCLI and 42nd Battalion, Royal Highlanders of Canada (RHC), with the 49th Battalion in support, were tasked with conducting an attack against Fabeck Graben, an objective that occupied high ground dominating the area. Corps Headquarters believed that success here would greatly assist 5th Brigade in its assault against Courcelette.

Both the 5th and 7th Brigade attacks were largely successful and the advance ground on. The next morning, at 0730 hours, The RCR received orders to continue the attack. Their objective was to seize another trench called Zollern Graben and then force their way southeast to the junction of Fabeck Graben to link up with the PPCLI who had not been able to capture their entire objective. The attack was to start at 1700 hours after a concentrated barrage, scheduled for 1645 hours, had softened up the enemy position.

"No Man's Land" in front of Canadian lines near Courcelette, France, October 1916.

The soldiers quickly developed a sense of foreboding. The storm of metal that was to precede them was ineffectual. It lacked intensity and accuracy. "The few shells that went over," bluntly stated an after-action report, "burst well in rear of the objective and caused practically no damage to the hun who was holding his line thickly."[23] The "Royal Canadians" advanced into a torrent of rifle and shellfire that cut swaths into their ranks. At approximately 150 metres from the objective, the advance finally faltered because of the enemy wall of fire and the soldiers withdrew to their jumping off point.

The brigade commander later praised his units and men, pointing out that they "went into an unknown area on four and a half hours notice, in broad daylight and under heavy shelling" and had launched an attack not from a prepared assembly area, but "a battered trench captured that morning."[24] Not surprisingly, RCR casualties were extremely heavy — 284 all ranks killed, wounded or missing.[25] At 0400 hours the next morning, the regiment was relieved from the front line and it moved to a bivouac area at Tara Hill.

The Regiment did not have long to lick its wounds. After a short rest in billets the men returned to the front. Late in the evening of 7 October, the Regiment moved through heavy enemy shelling into the front line in preparation for an attack on Regina Trench early the next morning. The attack was actually a Canadian Corps level assault. The RCR, with the 49th Battalion on their left were to lead the attack in the 7th Brigade sector.

Regina Trench was a well-sited and heavily fortified enemy position. Predictably, once the "Royals" had completed their relief in place they immediately dispatched patrols to reconnoitre the enemy wire defences. Their report was grim. Although "there were numerous gaps in the wire, through which groups of men could pass, it still formed a military obstacle."[26] The soldiers braced for the worst.

Between 0400 and 0430 hours, in a cold rain, the three assaulting companies (i.e., "A," "C," and "D") formed up in their "jumping off" position. The RCR assault was organized in three waves. The first comprised six platoons (two from each company) and the second and third wave consisted of three platoons (one from each company). At 0450 hours, an intense barrage slammed into the enemy position. High explosives shells and shrapnel filled the air for seven minutes. Then, as suddenly as it started, the barrage lifted and began to crawl forward. The

Lance-Corporal Prince posing for a portrait in his Battle Order and Lewis Gun.

"Royal Canadians" quickly advanced and clung as close to the creeping barrage as they could. Success depended on closing with the enemy before they could recover from the neutralizing effect of the artillery fire.

"With a rush, before he [enemy] had time to man his machine guns and parapet," reported one participant, "they [Royals] leapt into the trench, putting him [enemy] to flight."[27] However, the wire had proved to be a major barrier and not all got through. Nonetheless, the better parts of two companies ("A" and "C") had penetrated the enemy entrenchments and began bombing dugouts, collecting prisoners, and consolidating the position. In addition, some troops pushed beyond the trench for approximately 50 metres to screen the ongoing activities in the captured trench.

Unbeknownst to The RCR, their progress was the only success in the Canadian Corps attack. Although the creeping barrage had allowed the Canadians to reach the enemy wire relatively unmolested, once there they found the wire virtually uncut and, therefore, impassable. "Regina Trench," lamented Brigadier-General A.C. Macdonell, the 7th Canadian Infantry Brigade commander, "was not battered nor the wire cut."[28] The pre-dawn inky darkness and the rain made finding any gaps virtually impossible. As a result, the soldiers were hung up on the wire while the barrage pressed on. Then, once the storm of steel had passed them, the Germans manned their machine guns and began to sweep their wire with a deadly fire, so only small parties were able to reach their objectives, where they were easily thrown back by German counterattacks.

The RCR initially pushed out to the flanks in an attempt to close with their flanking units. However, German resistance increased. Sniping and shelling became intense. Very quickly the "Royals" realized they were alone and placed bombers and machine guns at posts to block enemy counterattacks. The situation became bleak. The RCR was now taking fire from both flanks, as well as from the front. Casualties were mounting. Supplies of bombs and other ammunition were running low and the hunters now became the hunted.

German infantry, supported by a withering flanking machine gun fire, pressed their strong bombing attacks and slowly began to roll up the left flank. "A" and "C" Coys, now "entirely surrounded, with no hope for support," hunkered down in Regina Trench and "held on with nothing on either flank and little artillery support until about 9 o'clock."[29] Private Charles Gaston, kept up a continuous fire with his Colt machine gun in spite of the heavy artillery fire and sniping he was subjected to. When his trench was completely blown in, he mounted his gun in the open and continued to lash out at the enemy.[30] Like Gaston, the few troops who remained repelled three determined counterattacks, but after four hours of resolute resistance were forced to withdraw. Singly and in small groups, the surviving "Royal Canadians" slipped into no man's land and crept from shell hole to shell hole in an attempt to make it back to friendly lines as a torrent of steel hurled through the air.

For the wounded there was no relief until darkness cloaked the battlefield. Accordingly, at dusk recovery parties were sent forward to collect the wounded and bury the dead. At approximately 2200 hours, The RHC relieved The RCR. The following day, the 140 members of the Regiment that remained moved back to bivouac at Tara Hill. Despite its lack of success, the Regiment's efforts were duly noted. "We all feel particularly proud of the splendid work of The RCR in driving through to their objective and holding it so long against odds," wrote Brigadier-General Macdonell. "No one," he added, "could have done better and few so well."[31]

The Somme had been a bleak experience for the Regiment. After only a few short months, The RCR lost approximately 671 all ranks.[32] The Regiment, now entered a period of relative calm. The Canadian Corps was allowed a period of reconstitution and training, although still required to strengthen defences and hold the line. Nonetheless, it was free from major operations. As such, The RCR spent the winter of 1916–1917, one of the coldest on record, taking its turn rotating in and out of the front line and conducting aggressive raids. But the Germans were seemingly not the greatest concern. "The only enemy we have here is the weather," lamented one soldier, "I do hope the rain is nearly all over."[33] By the Spring of 1917, change was in the air, as was a major operation.

The major operation that was planned was an attack on the formidable Vimy Ridge. This position was significant as it formed a 14 kilometre barrier across the western edge of the Douai Plain. Rising approximately 110 metres above the plain it dominated the battlefield and was arguably the most important feature on the Western Front. It was a formidable defensive position. The crest of the Ridge was anchored by two high points — Hill 135 and Hill 145. Moreover, the western slope facing the Allies rose gradually over open ground. This meant that the Canadians would advance over ground that afforded the defenders excellent fields of observation and fire.

The Ridge was the lynchpin to the German defences as it linked the Hindenburg defensive line system to the main German entrenchments

SERVICE AND SUFFERING

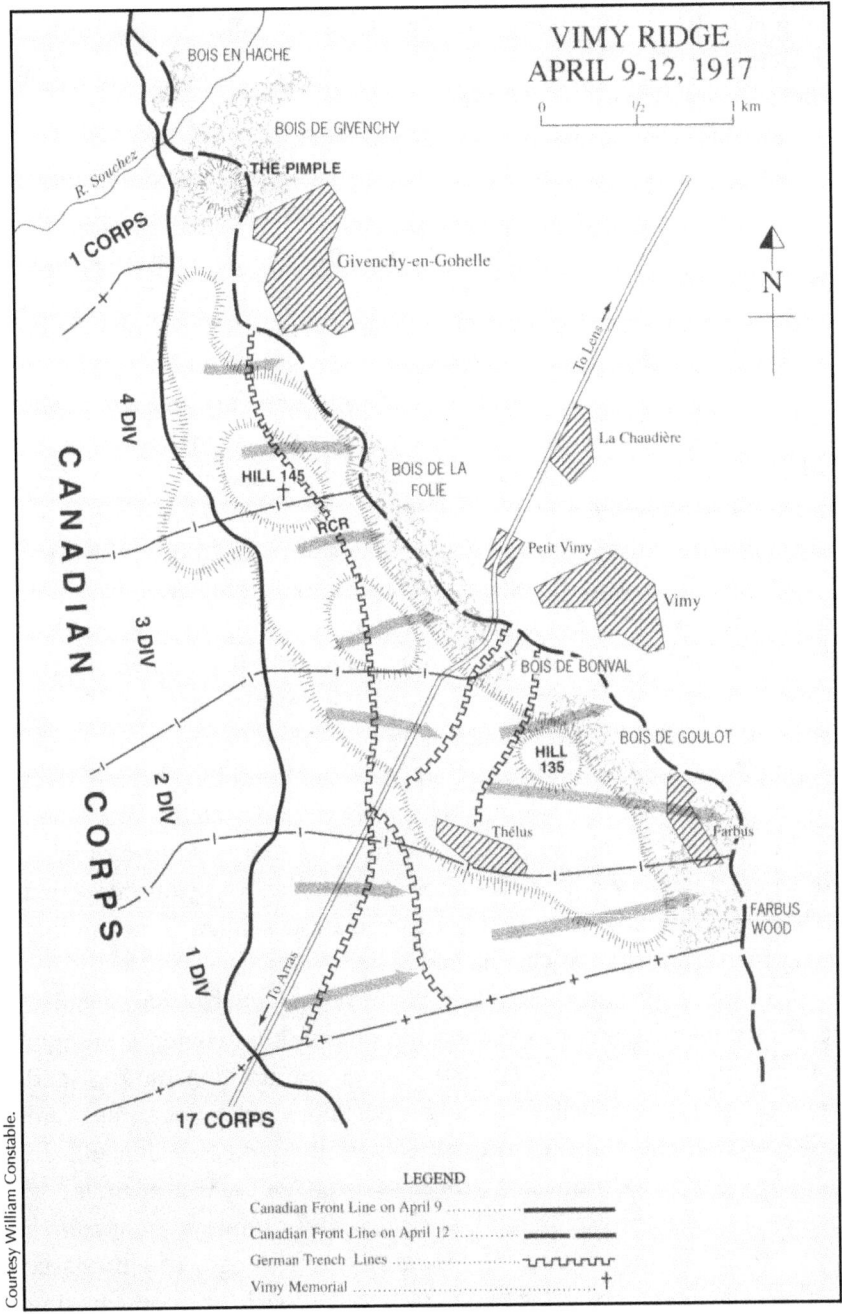

from Hill 70 to the Belgium coast. The Ridge had fallen to the Germans in October 1914 and had stayed in their control despite repeated Allied efforts to wrest it back. Soldiers on the ridge were well prepared. They had three main defensive lines, separated by as much as eight kilometres, with fortified positions between the lines, and a network of communications trenches and tunnels gouged out of the chalky terrain. Although the four-division Canadian Corps assault on the ridge was only a part of a larger British offensive (i.e., the Battles of Arras), it would become the defining event in First World War for the Canadian Corps, and the young nation of Canada. But that was still to come.

The Regiment completed its tour of front line duty and was pulled back to Bruay in mid-February. Here the "Royal Canadians," as part of 7th Brigade, conducted training and rehearsals for the attack against Vimy Ridge. Nothing was left to chance. The Corps Commander, Lieutenant-General Byng insisted on careful planning and preparation. In the rear area, the German trench system was reproduced in full scale based on aerial photographs. Tape represented trenches and flags were used to indicate strong points. Officers on horse back with flags, moving at the prescribed rate of advance, represented the creeping barrage. Troops carrying exactly what they would on the day of battle practiced rapidly exiting their jumping-off trench and following the rolling barrage over broken ground. In this manner rehearsals were repeatedly conducted. At the end of the training period, the troops had a good idea of what to expect. "If every officer was knocked out, the Non-Commissioned Officers would know what to do," explained one soldier, "It got so that every man knew exactly what he had to do."[34]

To support the attack, roads and light railway tracks were extended to ensure the necessary provisions and ammunition could be brought forward and stockpiled. Over 800 tons of ammunition, rations, and engineer stores were delivered daily.[35] Telephone, telegraph, water, and other services were also expanded to meet the increased demand. In addition, protective tunnelling proved to be one of the true engineering achievements of the war. In total, 11 electrically lit subways, eight metres or more under the ground, representing a total length of almost six-and-a-half kilometres, provided a covered approach to troops moving towards the front line.

Great consideration was also given to the fire plan. The preparatory bombardment began on 20 March. However, for the first two weeks only half the guns were fired to hide the actual scale of the artillery available.

Germans prisoners surrendering during the attack on Vimy Ridge and moving to the rear towards Canadian lines, 9 April 1917.

In total, the Canadian Corps had at its immediate disposal 245 pieces of heavy artillery and 618 field guns and howitzers. In addition, it would be supported by 280 guns of the flanking British 1st Corps.[36] Significantly, 83 percent of the German artillery had been pinpointed, so by the time the attack was to begin German artillery that could be instrumental in repulsing the Canadian assault or supporting German counter attacks, would be severely battered, if not entirely neutralized.[37] On 2 April the intensive phase of the bombardment began. More than a million artillery rounds were fired representing a weight of 50,000 tons. Much of the German defensive positions were completely obliterated. The Germans aptly titled this period "the week of suffering."[38]

On the night of 5–6 April, "D" Coy, conducted a relief in place and moved into the front line taking over the exact frontage from which the Regiment would launch its attack. Two platoons of "C" Coy occupied dugouts close by. Two nights later the remainder of the Regiment moved forward to their assembly area in Grange Tunnel guided by stakes marked with luminous paint. The wait was onerous. The cramped quarters and stress of the upcoming action was crushing on the troops. Adding to their torment on the morning of the attack was a strong driving wind that pelted all in its path with snow and sleet. Finally, exactly at 0530

ESTABLISHING A LEGACY

Defending hard-won gains — digging in the machine guns on Vimy Ridge.

hours on Easter Monday, 9 April 1917, there was a deafening roar, as 983 guns and mortars supporting the Canadian attack opened up in unison. The attack had begun.

The Canadian frontage for the attack was approximately 6,400 metres. In total, 15,000 Canadian troops stepped off as the first wave of the corps attack. These soldiers carried only their fighting equipment. However, those following in behind struggled over the crater-pocked ground with shovels, picks, large metal stakes and rolls of barbed wire.[39]

As the 16 officers and 632 soldiers and NCOs of the Regiment advanced there was a slight mist that later turned to snow and rain. "We followed the rolling, creeping artillery barrage as closely as we dared," explained one subaltern, "knowing that our only hope was to catch the enemy emerging from dug-outs" before they could man their machine guns.[40] As they pressed on over the soggy and well-churned ground they could not help but be impressed by the effectiveness of the bombardment. All that could be seen was death and destruction. "The Hun trenches and the ground," revealed one participant, "is in a terrible condition; the trenches practically cease to exist."[41] Initially there was almost no resistance — the enemy that survived was still too dazed to mount an effective defence. "It [barrage] proved to be very good indeed and our fellows pressed close on its heels carrying all before them with irresistible dash, and pinning most of the Huns in their deep dugouts," recounted 7th Brigade Headquarters' staff later.[42] In fact, the two lead companies ("C" and "D") crossed the 640 metres to their objective and captured it almost exactly in accordance with the planned timings. By 0630 hours, the Regiment had captured its initial objective, made contact with flanking units and had done so with virtually no casualties.

As the artillery barrage pounded the next set of objectives, "A" and "B" Companies used the planned pause to pass through the consolidating RCR sub-units. Once in place they waited until 0645 hours, when they pressed on in the wake of the barrage that once again resumed its forward advance. However, their progress was now hotly contested. German machine guns and snipers in La Folie Wood skilfully held up the advance and caused heavy casualties. The assaulting waves soon lost their coherence and form. Nonetheless, the "Royal Canadians" drove on where they could and by 0900 hours had reached the final objective and begun consolidating. The Germans quickly regrouped and launched a series of counterattacks, which were all successfully repulsed.

The "Royals" were not to be cheated of their prize and showed a courage and tenacity that could not be matched. For instance, Private Claude Collver and his Lewis machine gun crew were hit by an artillery shell during the advance. Collver was buried but clawed his way out. Although badly shaken and the lone survivor of his crew, he picked up the Lewis gun, collected all the ammunition he could find and continued on. At the objective he took up a post well in front of the position to cover the consolidation and was once again buried by a near miss. Stubbornly, he emerged once more, grabbed what ammunition he could find and joined a machine gun crew in another shell hole. Similarly, Private Edward Wells had two Lewis guns shot out of his hands during the assault. However, he salvaged a gun from the battlefield and was instrumental in breaking up a counter attack during the consolidation.[43] In the face of such opposition, the enemy became quickly spent, and the Regiment's sub-units were swiftly able to establish contact with their flanking units who had made similar progress.

Elsewhere the attack was almost equally successful. The 1st and 2nd Divisions on the right achieved their objectives rapidly in accordance with the planned schedule. The other units and brigades in the 3rd Division were the most successful, because of the absolute devastation wrought by the bombardment, and achieved their final objectives on time. Only the 4th Division had difficulties. Its attack on the formidable Hill 145 German strongpoint proved costly and the objective seemed unattainable. Uncut wire and heavy machine gun fire caused heavy losses. Not surprisingly, this dominant fortified island quickly slowed the progress of all adjacent units as it poured enfilading fire into the exposed flanks of advancing troops. It also proved a viable threat to the left flank of the 7th Brigade. "Owing to the Brigade on our Left being hung up, and Hill 145 being still in the possession of the enemy," noted a 7th Brigade after action report, "our Brigade was subjected to a galling fire of machine guns and snipers who took a heavy toll all along the line."[44] It was not until late in the day that the summit, after repeated attacks, was finally captured.

On the following day, 10 April, the last two German trenches remaining on Vimy Ridge in the 4th Division area were captured, and the ridge was almost entirely in Canadian hands. Much like the other Canadian units on the ridge, the Regiment spent the day digging in under sporadic shellfire and sniping. Reconnaissance patrols were dispatched to ascertain enemy intent to their front, but it soon became apparent that the Germans were not planning any counterattacks. Nonetheless, maximum effort continued to establish a viable defensive position. On 11 April, the 58th Battalion relieved The RCR, which withdrew to tents in a nearby camp.

The battle for Vimy Ridge, however, was not over. The "Pimple" on the northern edge was still in German hands. Its capture was originally designated as a British objective, but it was now passed to the Canadians. An attack on the stormy, snowy morning of 12 April wrested control from the enemy and put the ridge firmly into Canadian hands. This final turn of events prompted the Germans to withdraw to their third line of defences running through Oppy and Mericourt. This line was distant enough from the ridge to negate its strong advantages of observation and fire. The next day, the Canadian Corps conducted a general advance to pursue the Germans, but once patrols came up against stiff resistance along the new defensive line, the advance was halted. The battle for Vimy Ridge was now officially over. The five-day endeavour cost the Canadian Corps 10,602 casualties.[45] The Regiment's share was 57 killed, 155 wounded, and 65 missing — a casualty rate of approximately 43 percent.[46]

In the end, Vimy Ridge had great Canadian significance. It was a textbook example of how to plan and execute a deliberate attack and would become the template for the Corps in upcoming battles. More important, it demonstrated how effective and powerful the Canadian Corps actually was, since this was the first time the four divisions attacked together. This

SERVICE AND SUFFERING

Light railway being used to evacuate the wounded during the Battle of Vimy Ridge, 9–12 April 1917.

in turn, showed the prowess of Canada, as it was soldiers from all parts of the country, fighting shoulder to shoulder, who captured the formidable Vimy Ridge, a feat that so many others had failed to do.

The Regiment now settled into a routine in the Vimy area. Having expended so much effort capturing the ridge, the Canadians were not about to lose it. The "Royal Canadians" spent time rotating in and out of the front line, as well as providing work parties to repair defences, build strong points and repair roads. However, on 21 May the Regiment was pulled from the front to prepare for another operation.

The 7th Brigade in coordination with the 4th Division planned to conduct an extensive and rather sophisticated *raid*. This term was used only because there was no intention of holding ground. The aim was to conduct a three battalion (i.e., RCR, RHC, and 49th Battalion) night attack along 1,100 metres of German frontage in the Avion area, penetrate to a depth of 700 metres, hold the ground for approximately one and a half hours, and then conduct a controlled withdrawal. As part of the operation, all dugouts, trenches, and strong points were to be bombed and destroyed to the greatest extent possible.

Preparations for the assault followed the same level of detail and meticulous planning as the attack on Vimy Ridge. The raid was conducted

93

"Royals" receive a rum issue in the lines.

on a narrow frontage using two companies ("C" and "D") advancing astride the Vimy-Avion railway embankment. "A" Coy manned the Regiment's front lines and "B" Coy acted as the battalion reserve. At 2345 hours, the thunderous roar of the guns erupted and a savage bombardment hammered the German positions. In the cold drizzle, The RCR raiders leapt from their trenches and followed the barrage into the German lines.

Resistance was fierce. "Most of the fighting was hand-to-hand," revealed the after action report. "The bayonet and the bomb," it explained, "were the most useful weapons."[47] Despite the opposition, the "Royals" tenaciously fought their way through, bombing dugouts and destroying strong points. Blocks were strategically put into place in the trench lines to ensure they were not surprised by counterattacking elements.

One strong emplacement, which had not been affected by the bombardment, spewed out a withering fire across the German frontage and endangered the mission. However, a young subaltern, Lieutenant Milton Gregg, observed the crisis and led a party of bombers in a flanking attack that neutralized the threat. The "Royals" captured their final objective and held it until the initial withdrawal signal was given at 0115 hours on 9 June. Subsequently, the troops at the final objective withdrew through their comrades who were covering their withdrawal from intermediate positions. Thirty minutes later signal rockets once again blazed across the sky indicating the order for the final evacuation of the enemy trenches.

The raid, however, had stirred up a hornet's nest and the evacuations were conducted under very heavy fire from German artillery and trench mortars. During the withdrawal Lieutenant Gregg once again demonstrated his courage under fire. He coolly provided the necessary leadership to ensure the soldiers withdrew in good order and more impressively, ignoring a wound to himself, carried a mortally wounded fellow subaltern through the heavy fire back to friendly lines.[48]

Overall, the raid was deemed a success. Participants claimed that much damage had been done to the German positions and many enemy casualties inflicted.[49] But the cost was again substantial. Approximately 69 casualties (dead, wounded, and missing) were suffered representing a 35 percent casualty rate.[50]

The Regiment was now withdrawn from the line and underwent a period of intensive training and reconstitution. The RCR returned to the line on 21 August to begin a tour of duty in the front lines. Unfortunately for them, their tour began on the heels of the capture of Hill 70 six days earlier by other elements of the Canadian Corps. This attack had incensed the enemy and the "Royal Canadians" were submitted to savage hurricane bombardments at unexpected intervals that cut deeply into the Regiment's ranks. Each night great effort was expended to bury the dead and repair the shattered trenches. The RCR continued its wretched existence in and out of the trenches until October. However, its escape was anything but a respite.

Field Marshal, Sir Douglas Haig, the commander-in-chief of British Armies, selected the Canadian Corps to assist in successfully concluding a major offence in Flanders that had stalled. The actual Battle of Passchendaele began in mid-June. The British 5th Army had launched its attacks from a position three kilometres to the west of Ypres and advanced towards its objective, the village of Passchendaele, 10 kilometres distant. The offensive was designed to put pressure on the German Army at a time when the French Army was in complete disarray and Russia was on the verge of collapse. However, the fighting throughout the summer yielded extremely high casualties for limited returns. By mid-September the Allies were only half way to their objective. Worse yet, the high water table, incessant rains, and innumerable heavy bombardments by the artillery had turned the battlefield into a soggy, muddy swamp in which

Machine gunners "holding the line" during the Battle of Passchendaele, in Belgium, November 1917.

men and animals could drown, and any movement was an epic struggle. "It was nothing but a sea of mud," recalled one veteran.[51] It was to this nightmare that the Regiment now embarked.

The only saving grace was the fact that Lieutenant-General, Sir Arthur Currie, the newly appointed Canadian Corps commander, insisted on proper preparation and planning before he would undertake the attack.[52] Currie ensured that proper roads were built to bring up the necessary supplies and ammunition; that the ground was drained as much as possible; and most importantly that sufficient artillery and shells were positioned to support his infantry. He was a firm believer in expending shells rather than lives. He had learned quickly that carefully prepared fire support plans and massive artillery support was one of the key secrets to success.

The battle began on 26 October. During the first phase the 3rd and 4th Divisions were expected to push the front line forward by only 1,100 metres. The Regiment's role was to support the 8th and 9th Brigades by providing support, namely "carrying parties to the assaulting battalions."[53] As such, The RCR provided 250 personnel to act as stretcher-bearers and to ferry supplies. Even though theirs was a support role, enemy fire and the difficult terrain, which physically drained anyone attempting to cross it, quickly took its toll. After three days, Currie ordered a pause to the attack so that necessary supplies could be brought forward.

The second phase of the attack commenced on 30 October. The 3rd Division attacked with two brigades up (7th and 8th) each assaulting on a two battalion frontage. For the 7th Brigade, the attack was conducted by the PPCLI and the 49th Battalion. The RCR was given the task of brigade support and carrying battalion. As such, on the eve of battle the Regiment moved forward to take over the front line from the "Patricias." "C" Coy, however, was excluded as it sent two platoons to each of the assaulting battalions as a reserve. Throughout the night a nervous enemy kept up a heavy shelling, which sometimes included gas, causing a number of casualties.

The following morning, at precisely 0550 hours, the attacked began. Because of the terrible muddy terrain, the barrage crept forward at a rate of only 700 metres an hour. Predictably, the attacking force suffered heavily slogging slowly through the quagmire of mud all the while being lashed by German artillery and machine gun fire. The platoons of "C" Coy provided to the assaulting battalions suffered as well. The attack had not progressed long before additional reinforcements from "A" Coy, in the form of an additional two platoons with an ammunition resupply were sent forward both the PPCLI and the 49th Battalion.

The attack had severely depleted all units in the brigade. At 1700 hours, "D" Coy, RHC was sent from the brigade reserve to reinforce The RCR. Three-and-one-half hours later the Regiment with its augmentation was deployed to reinforce the 49th Battalion and help consolidate the new front line. The situation was still tenuous as the enemy was dug in only 200 metres away and kept up an incessant harassing fire with high explosives and gas shells. As a result, at 2200 hours, "B" Coy was dispatched to the PPCLI, which had been decimated in the attack, to assist them in consolidating their newly won position. The constant shelling continued the next day as both sides settled in. By evening the RHC took over the brigade's new front line and the widely strewn elements of the Regiment remained scattered in positions within the brigade's sector. It was not until 5 November that the Regiment was brought together once again. It then marched off to a well-deserved rest in billets at Watou.

The third phase of the attack took place the next day, but was the responsibility of the 1st and 2nd Divisions. Fighting ended on

An RCR soldier fires a trench mortar during the Battle of Passchendaele, 1917.

10 November with the capture of the now non-existent village of Passchendaele. The battle was finally over, but not before it exacted another 258 casualties from the Regiment — a 45 percent casualty rate.[54] Passchendaele, recalled one survivor, "was a horrible experience."[55]

Fortuitously, the Regiment entered a period of relative calm. The Canadian Corps was moved to the Lens area and was employed holding Vimy Ridge. During the winter of 1917-1918, the "Royal Canadians" rotated in and out of the trenches, conducted training, and assisted in fortifying the front line. The respite also allowed it to regenerate. Even the dramatic German breakthrough on 21 March 1918, when their offensive punctured the Allied line along a 80 kilometre front (at its base) and penetrated, in the first six days, to a depth of 40 kilometres, had little effect on The RCR. The Vimy front remained relatively stable. The Regiment, aside from being warned off for immediate deployment on several occasions, remained out of battle. By 28 March, the crisis had passed and the front was stabilized.

In the following months, the Regiment, along with the resto of the Canadian Corps, remained relatively inactive. Aside from holding their section of the front line on Vimy Ridge, the Canadians expended great effort in training for open warfare — specifically combined arms cooperation. Troops practiced infiltration tactics, as well as the coordinated movement of troops, tanks, and armoured cars, skilfully covered by artillery and machine gun fire. By August, they were ready once again to turn to the offensive.

On 8 August, the British Fourth Army opened the Battle of Amiens. The Canadian Corps had secretly moved to the Amiens sector almost a week prior. This was done because the Germans had long recognized the Canadians as shock troops and associated their arrival at the front as a precursor to an attack. Several additional days were used to stockpile ammunition and supplies, and by the night of 6–7 August all was ready.

The intent of the attack was to pinch off the German salient and push the front line out approximately eight to 11 kilometres. To maximize surprise there was to be no preliminary bombardment and the attack would be supported by 430 tanks. The Canadian Corps was to attack with a three division front of approximately 6,400 metres. The 3rd Division on the right had the most difficult task — it had to effect a river crossing and

Lieutenant Milton Gregg, VC.

it had to maintain contact with the French on their flank, who without tanks, would not advance without a preliminary bombardment.

At 0420 hours, on 8 August the guns erupted and pummelled the enemy position. As the barrage lifted the tanks rumbled out of the mist towards the German positions. Behind them were the assault battalions, who in turn were followed closely by the units of the reserve brigades. And so began the final "hundred days."

At the same time the Regiment moved towards the Luce River, which it crossed at 0520 hours on narrow duckboard bridges. Despite enemy shelling, casualties were light. The battalion then proceeded towards its assembly area at Heidelberg Trench. Once completely assembled, brigade headquarters ordered the "Royals" to move to their jumping off position on the edge of Harmon Wood. Then at 0820 hours, the Regiment rushed forward to attack the enemy. Progress was surprisingly rapid. The assaulting companies quickly reported, "Enemy not putting up very strong fight," to battalion headquarters (BHQ).[56]

Supported by tanks, the "Royals" quickly swept aside all opposition and advanced swiftly through the rolling terrain. Their progress was noted in the brigade report as proceeding with "something approaching the clock-like precision of a well rehearsed manoeuvre."[57] By 1030 hours, "C" Coy, the left lead sub-unit reported that it had seized its objective. Moreover, it had captured three field guns, six machine guns, and 70 prisoners. It had done so at the cost of only eight casualties. Fifteen minutes later, "A" Coy, the right lead sub-unit also announced that it had reached the final objective as well. It had captured three field guns, eight machine guns and 90 prisoners. The cost, however, was higher — it suffered 26 casualties.

Once Regimental headquarters had ensured the objectives were secure it forwarded the information on to brigade headquarters. Shortly after noon the 4th Division passed through the new front line and continued the attack. The RCR and its parent 7th Brigade now became the divisional reserve.

The first day had been a great success. The Allies had advanced 13 kilometres compared to previous years where gains were marked in mere metres. German General Erich von Ludendorff, later lamented that 8 August was the "black day of the German Army" in the war. The operation continued for the next several days and The RCR was employed in various support roles. Then, on 14 August, it was once again called on to attack. The Regiment was tasked with recapturing Parvillers. The

Germans had recovered somewhat from their initial setback and began to resist stubbornly, as well as launch vicious counterattacks.

The assault was scheduled for 2300 hours, 14 August. It was to be conducted on a two company frontage with "D" Coy on the right, and "B" Coy on the left. "C" Coy was tasked with providing two platoons to each of the lead companies and "A" Coy was in reserve. The attack had an ominous beginning. As the companies moved forward to their jumping off positions, the Germans cloaked their route in a heavy mantle of gas. "D" Coy was able to move through the obstacle and launch the attack on time. However, the gas was so dense in "B" Coy's sector that they were delayed by 27 minutes.[58]

Despite the setback the attack progressed well. The enemy was clearly exhausted and very unorganized after being subjected to the pounding of artillery and the incessant Canadian attacks over a period of a week. As a result, there seemed to be no coherent resistance. Therefore, the "Royal Canadians" made short work of the enemy pockets that showed fight and by 0110 hours, on 15 August, reported the objective secure. The following day the Regiment was relieved and moved back to Le Quesnel Wood. Amazingly, its casualties for the entire Battle of Amiens amounted to only 75 personnel.

The Regiment now enjoyed a short reprieve. Four days later, it was warned off for a move to an unknown location. The Canadian Corps had been tagged once again to participate in a new offensive against Arras. For the 3rd Division, this meant a piece of ground bordered by the Scarpe River to the north and the Arras-Cambrai Road to the south. Of great concern was the fact that the frontage widened rapidly as the formation advanced into enemy territory, necessitating the likely employment of the division's reserves to man the ever growing frontage.

The attack commenced on 26 August. The 8th Brigade punched through the German positions and captured its objectives. The 7th Brigade was now poised to push through with a two battalion advance — The RCR right forward and the PPCLI left forward. The Regiment was tasked to capture a German system of trenches and if possible drive through to attack additional enemy positions at Boiry-Notre-Dame. The Battalion employed three companies in the assault — "C" Coy right; "B" Coy centre; "A" Coy right; and "D" Coy in reserve. Immediately, the assaulting force was lashed with heavy artillery and concentrated machine gun fire from hidden positions and strong points. To add to the chaos 15 enemy fighter aircraft made a brief appearance and strafed the "Royal

Canadians." Despite the stiff opposition, the assault ground ahead. After almost seven hours of fighting, "D" Coy was sent forward to reinforce both "A" and "B" companies, and brigade headquarters deployed the RHC to fill in The RCR's flank as the frontage had widened considerably. In fact, three days into the attack the division was fighting on a frontage more than twice the length of that from which it started.

Nonetheless, the Regiment was embroiled in a vicious struggle that see-sawed back and forth. The "Royals" struggled to neutralize hidden machine gun posts and stubborn localized resistance. At one point, the enemy used camouflage and the deep grass to attempt a surprise counterattack. Discovered just in time, the German effort was violently repulsed. By early on 27 August, the brigade had established a rough frontage, though minor mopping up operations were still ongoing. The situation was stable enough that the 9th Brigade pushed through to continue the advance.

The next day, 28 August, another major attack was planned. It was a divisional assault with all three brigades in line. The 7th Brigade was to capture Pelves. Fortuitously, The RCR was the brigade reserve with the PPCLI, RHC, and 49th Battalion all in line. However, the "Royal Canadians" were quickly tapped. "B" and "D" Companies were assigned the task of protecting the left flank of the brigade and were placed under command of the PPCLI. The morning of the attack, "A" and "C" Companies were assigned to reinforce the 58th Battalion, which was severely reduced during an enemy counterattack. Notwithstanding the setback, by the end of the day the division had advanced nine kilometres, and captured a number of towns and villages. On the night of 28 August it was relieved and the Regiment withdrew to billets in the cellars of Arras.

The Regiment now spent a month rotating between the front line and billets in the rear. However, by end September it once again deployed to participate in the final great act of the war. By the now, it was clear that the German war machine was beginning to crumble. Its armies had been thrown back decisively all along the Western Front and they had fallen back on their last major fortified defensive line. Rumours of an armistice circulated, however, continued pressure was required to turn the whispers into reality. The new British offensive was designed to do just that. The Canadian Corps was tasked to crack the Canal du Nord defensive line, sweep through the system of trenches behind it, and penetrate to seize a front line consisting of the system of bridges over the Scheldt Canal north and east of Cambrai, the high ground overlooking the canal on the right front and the valley of the Sensée River on the left. This entailed manoeuvring the division, in contact, from an initial frontage of approximately 2,400 metres to 14,000 metres.

On 27 September 1918, the guns opened up once again and the 1st and 4th Divisions crossed the Canal du Nord. The 1st Division captured its objectives and penetrated the German Marcoing Line. The 4th Division also pressed on and despite heavy fighting cleared Bourlon Wood. However, its advance was checked at Fontaine-Notre-Dame. The Germans, realizing the seriousness of their situation, fought with a tenacity and stubbornness born of desperation.

That night The RCR, 611 strong moved forward in a cold driving rain and hunkered down in the ruins of Bourlon village directly behind the new front line. Just after midnight orders for the new attack arrived. The next morning at 0530 hours, supported by four tanks, the Regiment continued the advance, with "D" Coy right, "A" Coy in the centre, "C" Coy on the left, and "B" Coy in reserve. The initial push against this sector of the Marcoing Line was deceptively easy. However, upon cresting the sloping ground beyond which lay their objective, the full magnitude of the task at hand became evident. There, approximately 200 metres away, lay a formidable position protected by seemingly undisturbed belts of wire and bristling with strong points armed with machine guns. The enemy's artillery now also entered the fray with an intensity that immediately cut communications and halted the general advance. The Regimental attack quickly devolved into a struggle carried on by sub-units and smaller determined groups.

On the right flank, Lieutenant Gregg halted his company and crawled forward on his own to reconnoitre the wire and find a suitable gap. His persistent personal effort was finally rewarded when he found a passage that would allow men to singly penetrate the enemy's defensive belt. He then retraced his treacherous route, crawling and dashing back to his company. After quick instruction, he led his men to the channel in the wire and after a series of sprints and rolls found himself in the German trenches. He was quickly joined by a small group from his company. Leaving a single man to guard their flank, Gregg now took his meagre force and began to cause havoc within the enemy lines. They quickly neutralized a major strong point and took 48 prisoners. All the while, additional troops filtered through the gap in the wire and began to reinforce Gregg's small party. Their determined effort paid off as it wasn't long before half the Marcoing Line on "D" Coy's front was captured.

However, a new crisis soon developed. A German counterattack was developing from Cambrai to the front, as well as to the right. The "D" Coy force fought savagely to hold back the enemy mass, which was pressing the small force relentlessly. Catastrophically, ammunition soon ran short and it looked as if their lodgement would be lost. However, Lieutenant Gregg realizing the gravity of the situation, despite his wound, returned through the gap in the wire to gather additional bombs. His resupply turned the tables and the attacks were repulsed. Gregg, now wounded a second time, reorganized his survivors and went on to clear the remainder of the trench system along "D" Coy's frontage. Gregg would earn the Victoria Cross for his efforts.[59]

Meanwhile, "A" Coy in the centre was unfortunately of little support. As "D" Coy clawed at the enemy, "A" Coy endured a withering bombardment while hung up on uncut wire. "C" Coy on the left also ran up against an impenetrable wire obstacle and was lashed by heavy machine gun fire. Although they were able to find a shallow depression that led to the trenches, heavy fire prevented them from gaining access when they were only 50 metres away. It seemed the attack was largely stalled.

As the three sub-units continued to hammer away at the German defences, "B" Coy was thrown into the battle providing reinforcements for both "C" and "D" Companies. At 0930 hours, adding to the chaos was a lucky enemy shell that struck the Regimental headquarters and severely wounded the CO and killed several others. Major C.B. Topp, from The RHC, who had come to discuss the passage of lines he was to conduct later that night, emerged unscathed from the blast. He reported the event to the brigade commander and requested that The RCR officers left out of battle be sent forward immediately. In the interim, Topp was ordered to assume command of the Regiment. He passed command to Captain C.L. Wood at midnight.

The Regiment continued to batter at the Marcoing Line and tenaciously hang on to what it had so dearly won. Early the next morning the other battalions of the brigade passed through The RCR and continued the attack. The "Royals" now passed into reserve. The casualties were heavy and the battalion was now reorganized into three companies. Despite its losses it was thrown into battle the next day on 29 September. Once again the "Royal Canadians" took their position in the vanguard with the PPCLI and RHC, and pressed forward. After heavy fighting the brigade objectives were captured and on 1 October, 9th Brigade, passed through and continued the advance. The brief five days of fighting had cost the Regiment 37 killed, 53 missing and 204 wounded — a 48 percent casualty rate.⁶⁰

The Regiment now underwent a period of reorganization and training in the rear area. It returned to front line duty on 22 October 1918. Moving on the brigade's right flank, with the RHC on the left, 7th Brigade continued the pursuit of the German Army. The RCR advanced in the heavy rain, "C" and "D" Coys leading. Opposition was light and only minor skirmishes with enemy rear guards occurred. Belts of barbed wire and trench complexes were no longer an issue. Progress was swift. The Regiment continued chasing the Germans for next several days until relieved on the night of 27 October. The battalion then moved into billets in Aremberg.

On 7 November, the Regiment once again resumed the advance. This time The RCR were moving in support of the PPCLI. Once again, progress was rapid as the Canadians advanced in the wake of the retreating enemy. Two days later the Regiment was tasked with executing an encircling manoeuvre that would allow it to enter Mons from the north and north-east. The "Royals" crossed a canal, which proved to be the only major obstacle, using a barge and an improvised bridge they built. By early morning 10 November, the Regiment (less "A" Coy) had crossed and joined "D" Coy, which had already pushed well beyond the canal and established outposts on the Mons-Ghlin road. That night, The RCR received orders to continue the attack on Mons the next morning.

Trouble now erupted. As the early morning mist lifted, the Regiment's forward elements came under heavy and accurate fire. Directly to the front of "D" Coy's positions were large slag heaps that concealed German artillery observers and machine gun nests. Consequently, any movement was met by well-directed fire. With the war clearly nearing an end, the Canadian Corps headquarters issued strict orders to avoid heavy casualties, so the companies carefully and slowly snaked their way forward maximizing cover wherever they could.

Meanwhile, "A" Coy had moved forward from its position on the right bank of the canal near Jemappes at 0530 hours and had closed within a few hundred metres of Mons. At 1000 hours the area of the right bank was allocated to the RHC and "A" Coy was placed under command. At this time, heavy machine gun fire still spewed from the city and "A" Coy was ordered to hold fast until the enemy withdrew, as it was expected to do. Resistance continued throughout the day and night, however, at 0200 hours, on 11 November 1918, it began to tail off and RHC headquarters ordered a general advance at 0500 hours.

On the left bank, similar events occurred. All through 10 November the Regiment continued its efforts to force an entry into Mons. However, they too were met with heavy fire. Finally, at approximately midnight opposition waned. Immediately, 5 Platoon led by Lieutenant W.M. King, followed by the remainder of "B" Coy, entered Mons unopposed. The lead platoon continued its advance through the deserted streets of the city in eerie silence. However, as the troops entered the Grand Place, they were met by the chief of police who led them to the city hall where the mayor and a number of aldermen were waiting. When Lieutenant King arrived he was warmly welcomed, offered wine and was invited to sign the Golden Book of Mons to record the name and regiment of the first Allied soldier to liberate the city.[61]

At 0830 hours, Regimental headquarters received the message all had been waiting for, namely the end of the war. Hostilities were to cease at 1100 hours, and the Regiment was ordered "to stand fast on line reached at that hour." And so ended the Regiment's service and suffering in the First World War. In total, 619,000 Canadians served in the conflict.

Return to Canada: the RCR departed from Liverpool, England, on the S.S. *Adriatic*, 1 March 1919. Pictured are The RCR Colours, with the CO, Lieutenant-Colonel Hill (second from right), and his adjutant, Lieutenant Gregg, VC (far right).

Their casualties totalled 239,605, which represented a third of those who were in uniform. The Regiment suffered a total of 3,114 casualties, which included 712 killed.[62]

Once again, the "Royal Canadians" had answered the call of duty and they did so with courage, honour, and perseverance. Their suffering, much like that of all others who served throughout the war was lamentable. Conditions on the front line in the muddy morass of wasteland that was known as the Western Front was enough to drain the strongest of men. On top of that, combat which inevitably translated to casualty rates of 30–50 percent, left all participants with the understanding that their chances of coming through unscathed were limited. Yet, they served with courage and honour. As such, their service continued the relatively short but rich Regimental tradition of military professionalism and service to country.

4
"Fighting Men from Canada": The Regiment's Introduction to Modern War

Upon return to Canada, in March 1919, the Canadian Expeditionary Force battalion of The RCR was disbanded. Steps were immediately taken to rebuild the Regiment to allow it to return to its normal duties as part of the Permanent Force. The officers and men of the overseas battalion that wished to remain with the Regiment in Canada were temporarily absorbed into the unit. However, the Permanent Force was undergoing a major reconstitution that had an impact on The RCR. Both the PPCLI and the Royal 22nd Regiment (R22R) Regiments, which were formed during the First World War, were retained as units in the Permanent Force.[1] As a result, The RCR was reduced by one company.

The Regiment began recruitment immediately and quickly built up its numbers. Throughout the summer of 1919, the entire Regiment was stationed in Halifax, but in October, "D" Coy was deployed to establish a regimental station, the "Montreal Detachment," in Quebec. In the next months and years the Regiment continued its reorganization and training. Company detachments were stationed at Halifax, Montreal (later moved to St. Jean), and Toronto, as well as London. Regimental HQ also moved, settling in Tecumseh Barracks in London, Ontario.

The RCR resumed its duty of instructing the militia through the conduct of schools and summer camps. It was also called on to aid the civil power on several occasions during coal miner strikes in Nova Scotia, as well as during depression era discontent and violence in Ontario. On the whole, soldiering was difficult and far from attractive. A debt-ridden and war-weary government slashed military spending and capped the Permanent Force at 5,000, a level that, in reality, it deterred the military from ever achieving. In summary, the politicians believed that regular soldiers had a limited utility — they were only needed for instructing the militia and providing aid to the civil power. Moreover, the government felt that only limited resources were required to meet these aims.

The public was equally unsympathetic. Fatigued by the war and still lamenting the loss of so many of its men, Canadians were against military spending, if not hostile to the military itself. After all, the stories of soldiers being sent to the slaughter in knee-deep mud, against belts of razor wire, in the face of murderous machine gun fire tugged at the sensibilities of the average person. Moreover, many saw the Permanent Force as a haven for those too indolent or incapable of finding "real" employment.

As a result, Canada did little during the 1920s and 1930s to ensure that its military was capable of participating in a modern war. The economic desperation of the depression and the vacuum of peace, were barriers too great for the military leadership to overcome in their attempts to convince the government of the day to allocate scarce dollars to military spending. The consistent and destructive infighting between the different services only exacerbated the problem.

Not surprisingly, a stagnation set in. It quickly appeared that the lessons of the First World War had been completely forgotten. Although combined arms operations (i.e., the coordinated and cooperative manoeuvre of infantry, artillery, and tanks, as well as fighter aircraft) were conducted and refined during the war, in Canada, military practice reverted to pre-war standards. Motorization and mechanization were virtually ignored. In 1935, Major E.L.M. Burns, criticized the military's

RCR Carden Lloyd Machine Gun Platoon at Wolseley Barracks, London, Ontario, April 1933.

"pedestrian imagination." He observed that the military was "thinking about the operations of war in terms of mobility of the foot-soldier ... [at] 2 1/2 miles per hour," when in fact, he explained, the reality of modern war would entail "armoured fighting vehicles moving nearly a hundred miles in a day, or by aeroplanes moving a hundred miles in an hour."[2]

Although the Department of National Defence (DND) purchased 12 Carden-Lloyd machine gun carriers in 1930, which were intended for the machine gun platoons of the Permanent Force infantry battalions, they were woefully insufficient to meet the needs of a modern army. It was not until 1938, that militia headquarters in Ottawa pooled its carriers and opened the Canadian Armoured Fighting School at Camp Borden.[3] In any case, to say that Canada was unprepared for modern war in 1939 is undisputable. The Canadian Army numbered a scant 4,261 regular force personnel, with a further 51,000 non-permanent active militia members scattered across the nation. It was understrength, poorly resourced, and without even the most rudimentary equipment. In the end, it took the collapse of Europe and the imminent invasion of England in the dark spring of 1940 to focus attention on the necessity for military renewal.

It was within this context that the Regiment, spread across the country in various detachments, existed during the inter-war years. By the end of 1937, The RCR's strength stood at 34 officers and 420 other ranks, divided over the four separate garrisons. This number was only slightly over 50 percent of the Regiment's required establishment.[4] However, restrictions resulting from limited defence spending imposed severe manpower ceilings. The effect that this had on the Regiment's under-staffed and overworked personnel was dramatic. The Report of the Annual Inspection in 1932 observed, "The Permanent Force units in this District have reached the stage where they have become so reduced in numbers that they are unable to function with that high efficiency which is so desirable for instructional corps."[5] Similarly, two years later, the inspection revealed, "its small numbers give it little chance for proper training."[6] By 1938, nothing had changed. "The small numbers," echoed the annual inspection report, "make it impossible to train the personnel higher than platoon training." It added, "This is not satisfactory in an instructional corps."[7] Nonetheless, the Regiment continued its assigned tasks of teaching the militia and conducting its own training to the best of its abilities.

In 1938, growing storm clouds in Europe seemed to inject some sense of urgency into military preparedness, inadequate though it may have been. That year, the Regiment, and other permanent force units, concentrated at Niagara-on-the-Lake for the first time in nine years to conduct combined arms exercises. The years of neglect were evident. One senior participant lamented that the battalion had difficulty "to perform even the simplest operation without issuing a four-page written order...."[8] However, on a positive note, this concentration was followed by additional exercises at the brigade level in Camp Borden. Furthermore, modern equipment such as light machine guns, mortars and general purpose wheeled vehicles began to trickle into the Regiment.

Although the "Royal Canadians" benefited from the apparent change in attitudes towards military preparedness, as limited as they were, the new thinking was also indicative of the coming tempest. The rise of the German Nazi dictator Adolf Hitler, resulted in the mobilization and rearmament of Germany. Under the pretence of rebuilding the economy, spurring nationalism to strengthen a fragmented state, and righting an unjust peace, Hitler's calculated aggressiveness quickly threw the world into a series of crises. Hitler's reoccupation of the Rhineland in 1936 was summarily ignored by the European powers; similarly, the annexation of Austria, the *Anschluss,* in March 1938 was also dismissed. However, by late that year, the pattern of behaviour and aggressive rearmament of Germany began to raise some concern among the former Allied nations. Although most hoped that the September 1938 "Munich Agreement," which sacrificed portions of Czechoslovakia, would satisfy Hitler's ambitions, they were sadly mistaken. Finally, Britain drew the line across the border of Poland. Any aggression against Poland would trigger war with England.

In August 1939, more ominous signs prompted the Canadian high commissioner in London, England, to warn that war was imminent. Two days later, on 24 August, all leave was cancelled, as a state of national emergency now existed in Canada. On 30 August 1939, the Emergency Council, consisting of the prime minister, the ministers of defence, fisheries, finance, mines and resources, and the Senate government leader, was established. They now set in motion the mobilization of the nation. Two days later, on 1 September, the War Diary reveals, "Capt[ain] Foulkes telephoned [from Ottawa] to say Poland had been invaded. Mobilization ordered — 'M' day."[9]

Although Canada did not officially declare war on Germany until 10 September, this was a mere formality to the "Royal Canadians." Not a man hesitated. Every individual on parade immediately volunteered for

"Royals" scaling a cliff with their 3-inch mortar as part of their battle drill training in England, December 1942.

active service when mobilization was ordered. "When the war started, everyone was excited," recalled Tom Burnett, then a private. In a timeless explanation, he elaborated, "that's what we were training for."[10] Within the week, all Regimental detachments were directed to recruit to wartime establishment. In all, the Regiment took less than two months to achieve its required numbers.

On 10 November, the battalion was ordered to concentrate at Camp Valcartier. Here it became part of the 1st Canadian Infantry Brigade (CIB) of the 1st Canadian Division.[11] For the next month the Regiment completed its preparations for overseas duty. Then, on 17 December, The RCR departed Valcartier for Halifax. Two days later it embarked on the S.S. *Almanzora* and on 22 December actually set sail under heavy escort.

The ship vibrated with electricity. This generation of "Royal Canadians," much like those who came before, were excited at the prospect of going to war. "As we sailed up the harbour in line ahead or single file," recounted Lieutenant Daniel Spry, "the troops were all singing their heads off." He added, "It was a real moment to remember in years to come."[12] Their excitement would eventually wane. Their journey would take them through the grim realities of war and for those lucky enough to survive, last almost five-and-one-half years.

The Regiment arrived at Gourock, Scotland on 30 December and moved off immediately to Aldershot. Upon arrival the following morning, the Battalion marched off to Barossa Barracks. "Our first week here kept us extremely busy," explained then Corporal Tom Burdett, "as we not only had to get used to English methods of doing things, which are by the way delightfully vague and slow, but we also had to compete with the foulest of foul weather."[13]

The initial training in England was a throw back to an earlier era. Personnel attended courses, conducted drill on the parade square, fired range practices, and exercised fieldcraft such as digging trenches, wiring, and patrolling. For the infantry it seemed not much had changed from the last war. "Lots of tactical exercises and route marches, remembered one veteran. "We had a few more trucks, but infantry were always on their feet," he added.[14] The exercises were also dated. "Elaborate 1915-18 style trenches had been recently constructed by the Guards," recalled Major Strome Galloway, "and into these marched the RCR." He added, "Trench relief, normal trench routine and patrols were carried out."[15] The only distraction was leave and sports competitions, which were interspersed between training.

This mundane and outdated approach continued throughout the "Phony War" during the dreary winter of 1939-1940. The monotonous routine was finally shattered in the spring, when German forces invaded Norway, and then on 10 May, sliced through the Low Countries and France. The effectiveness of the assault should not have been a surprise to the Allies. The Germans had demonstrated the tactics of modern war in September 1939, when they crushed Poland. Yet, in England soldiers were still training for the last war. Undeniably, the Allies were entirely unprepared for this new form of warfare. The German Blitzkrieg unleashed on the West showcased new doctrine and tactics that they developed in the interwar years. The speed and the new multi-dimensional battlefield paralyzed the Allied forces deployed to defeat the enemy offensive. In the end, German success was because of mobility, which was achieved by a combination of concentration, firepower, surprise, and combined arms cooperation. The German inventory of fast tanks, armoured cars, and motorized infantry, supported by ground support aircraft and wireless communications simply overwhelmed Allied defence capability.

And so, as the high-pitched scream of the German *Stuka* aircraft siren, signalling yet another attack, cut through the still morning, the Allied soldiers once again cowered under cover. The situation appeared grim as their military commanders and political masters, seemingly helpless, watched as their plans for the defence of France were crushed. As the German offensive took on ominous overtones, additional troops were scrambled to help stem the enemy advance. As a result, in the early morning of 23 May 1940, The RCR was given the order to be ready to deploy to France ... by noon.

The Regiment was to be the lead unit of 1 CIB, which had been designated the lead brigade for 1 Canadian Division, for their rather vague mission to "protect the lines of communication of the British Expeditionary Force."[16] What was clear was the fact that they were on their way to France, specifically to immediately occupy Calais and Boulogne. The RCR was loaded on the S.S. *Canterbury* and ready to sail by 1100 hours. But, the ship never moved. "A period of waiting commenced at 1100 hrs," recorded the Regimental War Diary. "We were all ready to sail and yet nothing happened," wrote the Regimental diarist, "at 1900 hrs R.C.R. was ordered to disembark and move back to Barracks." He added, "It was an awful let-down. We were all keyed up for action and the Battalion had made up its mind that this was the real thing."[17]

Despite the Regiment's zeal to get into the fray, cooler heads prevailed. "I hate to see good divisions like the Canadians going to France when one feels it is like throwing snowballs into hell to keep down the temperature," wrote General Sir John Dill, vice-chief of the imperial general staff. The Canadian overseas commander, Lieutenant-General A.G.L. McNaughton agreed. The writing was on the wall. France was as good as lost. It was now necessary to save whatever possible to fight another day.

The destruction of the West took 46 days, but it was decided in only 10.[18] The Allies now came to realize that their warfighting methodology was outmoded. On the night of 2 June 1940, the remnants of the British Army were evacuated from the beaches of Dunkirk, France. However, the desperate withdrawal resulted in the loss of most their heavy equipment, weapons, and transport.[19]

A last ditch effort to save France was undertaken almost two weeks later, between 14–17 June. The British prime minister decided that a new front across the Brittany peninsula, reinforced by three divisions from England, might provide a line behind which the shattered remnants of the Allied armies still in France could withdraw and fight on. As such, the Regiment, as part of the 1st Canadian Division, was deployed with 3rd British and 52nd (Lowland) Divisions to Brest. However, once on the continent the futility of the effort quickly became evident. As a result, all were withdrawn and returned to England less than 48 hours after arriving. Britain, now braced for what seemed to be the inevitable conclusion to the German master plan — the invasion of England.

In early July, reconnaissance reports indicated barges and other vessels were being amassed in French channel ports. By August aerial attacks against shipping increased, and by mid-month had shifted to attacks against Britain proper. The "Battle of Britain," as Churchill dubbed it, was now entering its final stage. The Canadian Expeditionary Force in England, became a critical factor and was tasked with the defence of the British Isles. "Invasion was a real threat," affirmed Lieutenant-General McNaughton, and he organized his Canadians into "a mobile reserve with a 360 degree front."[20] In essence, they were prepared to operate anywhere in Great Britain to meet seaborne or airborne attacks. "In those grim days," observed Galloway, "England was almost a theatre of operations."[21]

The Regiment played its part in the defence of England against the imminent invasion. It conducted its share of sentry duty, training, patrols, and it reacted to the plethora of "stand-bys." One veteran explained, that the Regiment, as well as the other Canadians, were "poised that in the event of a German assault from the sea, [they] could be flung into battle at which ever point along the coast of South-eastern England invasion began."[22] But in the end, little of significance transpired. As the air battle played itself out, it became evident that the German Air Force could not continue to endure the enormous losses it was taking. By the third week in September the German High Command had concluded that an invasion of England was unsustainable. The invasion fleet soon dispersed and the German Air Force transitioned to less costly night attacks against England.

The immediate invasion threat passed and the Allied armies in England now focused on retraining, reorganizing, and re-equipping themselves to better fight a modern war. The remainder of 1940 was spent on individual training with a heavy emphasis on marching. The training focus transitioned to formation level training in 1941. Small anti-invasion exercises were the theme for most training schemes, which were all carried out within a divisional context. By the summer, training manoeuvres had evolved to corps level and above. However, the scenarios were still based on an anti-invasion framework. Nonetheless, the troops were becoming restless. "Morale is generally good," wrote the CO, "although the troops are still feeling the inactivity of a fighting nature at the present time."[23]

This concern was somewhat addressed by a significant evolution in training, namely "Battle Drill," which was introduced to the Canadians in England in the summer of 1941. Quite simply Battle Drill added realism and pared down military tactics to the bare essentials. It consisted of five basic elements. The first focused on developing team drills and spirit (i.e., ensuring each man knew his exact role and what was expected of him). The second element revolved around battle discipline and battle inoculation: Soldiers were taught how to act and react to the battlefield, specifically in response to the surrounding noise and confusion caused by enemy action and fire. The third component was an extension of the second. It utilized live ammunition and explosives to introduce both commanders and soldiers to a realistic battlefield where they would have to work and think under the kind of stressful conditions experienced when under fire. The fourth element consisted of developing a series of immediate action drills that could instinctively be carried out during operations. The fifth and final element was the implementation of realism and enthusiasm during every step of the Battle Drill training. Individual initiative was stressed as a key "in-theater" quality. Every man regardless of his rank was encouraged to bring forward ideas and recommendations at any time during planning or actual operations. The introduction of Battle Drill, aside from its practical benefits, was also seen as a means, "to enable us to overcome the staleness and boredom in training from which our men suffer at the present time."[24]

By late 1941, activities started to take on a more offensive overtone, and some amphibious training commenced. By the following year, combined operations training (i.e., amphibious landings) became even more important and central to training. By late 1942, the threat of an invasion of Britain had completely passed. German involvement in North Africa, as well as the costly incursions into Greece, Yugoslavia, and Crete occupied their attention. But nothing was more debilitating to them then their fatal decision to invade Russia in June 1942. This meant that Germany could not muster the resources to even contemplate an invasion of England any longer. Moreover, after the Japanese attack on Pearl Harbour on 7 December 1941, and the subsequent declaration of war by the Germans, the resource rich Americans became an official ally. Moreover, the American's "Germany first" policy meant that the Allies could now focus on taking the fight to the Germans.

The initial reaction of the United States upon entering the war was to push for a "Second Front" immediately. This was somewhat predicated by the beleaguered Russians who clamoured for Allied action against occupied Europe as a means of drawing German resources from their theatre of operations. However, the British opposed such an action. The Dieppe fiasco of 19 August 1942, had proven exactly how difficult and costly an ill-prepared return to the continent could be. Initially, the "Royal Canadians," as well as other units in the 1st Canadian Division, bridled when they discovered they were passed over for the amphibious raid in favour of the 2nd Division. However, they counted their blessings once the final tally came in. The Canadians of the 2nd Division who participated in the raid suffered a 70 percent casualty rate.[25]

In the end, Prime Minister Winston Churchill and his staff were able to convince their American counterparts that a thrust in the Mediterranean, which would attrite the Germans while the Allies built up their forces for a cross-channel invasion, was the best strategy, and agreement was reached to attack the Germans through their "soft underbelly." By the spring of 1943, the tide of the war had irrevocably changed. The Russians were now on the offensive with a seemingly endless supply of equipment and personnel. In North Africa, the Germans had been completely defeated, and in England the Allies were stockpiling unheard of quantities of men and war material.

And so, after years of preparation, the Regiment's time had come. On 13 June 1943, the "Royal Canadians" loaded onto the Dutch ship *Marnix Van St. Aldegonde* for a destination yet unknown. Four days later the ship started to work its way down river to the open sea. However, on 18 June, it halted and a large scale rehearsal with all 3,000 men representing many of the units on board was conducted. The Regiment for its part disembarked in a driving rain in the inky pre-dawn darkness, and by 0700 hours it had successfully achieved its objectives. A second dress rehearsal was conducted four days later. It was terminated early and the troops then settled in for their voyage, and changed into their tropical gear. On 28 June, the relative calm of the river was replaced by the constant swells of the sea. The Regiment was on its way to taste war first hand once again.

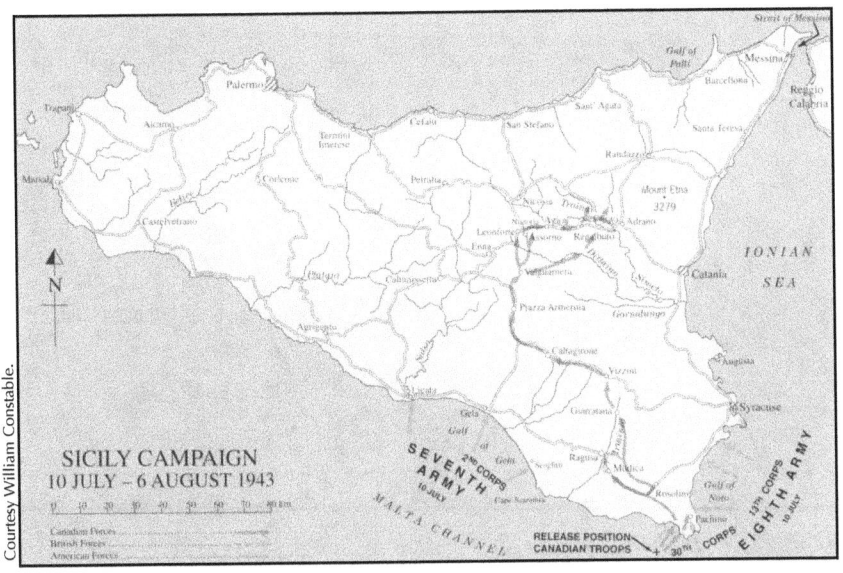

Courtesy William Constable.

SICILY CAMPAIGN
10 JULY – 6 AUGUST 1943

The following day "we woke to find ourselves riding the swells of the North Atlantic without a cloud in the sky, and a smooth sea," revealed the War Diary.[26] As the ship ploughed its way through the open ocean, the "Royal Canadians" could see they were part of something big. Transports, escort ships, and anti-aircraft cruisers were all around. The mystery of their destination was partly revealed when the senior naval officer in the convoy, Rear-Admiral Sir Philip Vian, announced by wireless radio, "We are on our way to the Mediterranean to take part in the greatest combined operation ever attempted,"[27] which narrowed the possibilities.

Finally on 1 July, the Regimental officers and men were briefed on Operation Husky, the code-name for the invasion of Sicily of which they were now part. The operation involved 180,000 Allied troops, 14,000 vehicles, 600 tanks, 1,800 guns, and 2,590 ships. The Allied plan called for two distinct thrusts. The Americans were to concentrate on the western half of the island; land at Gela and then push into central Sicily. The British and Canadian forces were to conduct the second thrust on the eastern half of the island. One British Eighth Army Corps was tasked to seize the ports of Augusta and Siracusa and then drive across the Catanian Plain. A second Eighth Army Corps, the 30th Corps, which included the 51st Highland Division and the 1st Canadian Division, was responsible for clearing the Pachino Peninsula and then pushing inland.

Lieutenant-Colonel R.M. Crowe and Major Billy Pope confirming their position near Piazza Armerina, 17 July 1943. Pope would be killed in action the following day and Crowe seven days later.

The Regiment would now, in the words of its CO, Lieutenant-Colonel R.M Crowe, "help to strike a mighty blow at the vitals of the enemy."[28]

The news was met with excitement. "And what a show," wrote Lieutenant J.R. Hunt, the Regimental intelligence officer, "The most powerful invasion force, land, sea and air, is about to strike at the first piece of home country of the Enemy, — the doomed island of Sicily."[29] The War Diary also revealed the general sentiment of the "Royal Canadians" preparing to go into battle. "Not a hole in the ground battle," it stated, "but one which will put the name of their Division and their Regiment on the lips of every Canadian at home."[30]

The commander of the Eighth Army also fuelled the pride and motivation of the Regiment when he welcomed the Canadians to the

Eighth Army. "I know well the fighting men from Canada," he proclaimed, "they are magnificent soldiers." He concluded by wishing all, "Good luck and good hunting in the home country of Italy."[31] The training and waiting was now over — the Regiment was ready to prove their worth once again.

The Regiment was assigned a challenging mission. It made up the right flank of 1 CIB and was responsible for clearing Roger Green Beach, destroying a coast defence battery and on order, capturing the Pachino airfield. The CO distilled these tasks into a three phase operation. Phase 1 would be the clearance of the landing beach. He assigned this mission to "C" and "D" Companies. Once the beach was secured, "A" and "B" Companies would launch their assault against the coast defence battery. "A" Coy would lead, seize a suspected strongpoint at Maucini and then provide a firm base from which "B" Coy could then destroy the actual coastal defence battery. After this was completed, Phase III would see the entire battalion moving forward and taking up a position on the high ground overlooking the airfield in preparation for brigade orders to attack.

The "Royal Canadians" now spent their time on ship pouring over maps, aerial photographs, and models. "The Regiment down to the humblest private," explained Galloway, "knew what phases he was to pass through and his exact job during each phase."[32] However, in war it is inevitable that changes will occur. Naval intelligence soon warned that a sand bar existed in front of the Regiment's designated beaches. Significantly, the water beyond the sand bar, which lay about 100 metres from shore, was nine feet deep. As a result, contingency plans were developed that included a change in landing vessels. Landing craft capable of carrying amphibious vehicles known as DUKWs[33] had to be found and inserted into the plan.

"The time to man craft arrived with amazing suddenness," revealed Major R.G. Liddell, "when one's serial was ordered to boat station the blower had a very final sort of sound and the ship suddenly seemed an awfully safe and comfortable sort of place to be in."[34] At 0400 hours on 10 July 1943, in inky darkness and stormy seas, the first wave of "Royal Canadians" finally pulled away from their transport ship. They were two-and-one-half hours late. The Landing Craft Troops (LCT), which carried the DUKWs, were themselves delayed. The rough seas only exacerbated the problem of transferring the troops from one vessel to the other. The second wave pulled away from the S.S. *Marnix* 15 minutes later.[35]

As the landing craft ploughed their way to shore in the half light of dawn the anxious soldiers were treated to a light show as tracers arced and stitched their way across the sky, accompanied by the loud panoply of bangs and whistles of screaming shells emanating from both the support ships and enemy defences. At 0530 hours, the first wave, "C" and "D" Coys, landed and began to clear the beach.

The Regiment's shooting war was almost a disappointment to many. It began with a fizzle. "The whole show had a sort of lavish scheme [training exercise] air and seemed less dangerous," remembered Major Liddell, "than some of the training we'd done in England." He added, "in fact it seemed hard to convince oneself that it was the serious stuff at last."[36] The enemy had virtually all but left! Only sporadic and ineffective small arms fire greeted the troops as they waded ashore. "To our surprise," wrote one participant, "our beach was NOT under fire so we pressed inland, my coy picking up 12 Wop prisoners en route — Great fun!"[37] In the end, a few prisoners were taken and the beach was quickly cleared. With the bridgehead secured, both companies quickly reorganized and took up defensive positions.

At 0600 hours, in broad daylight, "A" and "B" Coys landed and proceeded to execute their tasks. The strongpoint at Maucini was nothing more than a small barracks and was swiftly captured. It was manned by only a handful of dispirited Home Guard sentries. "Aim a rifle at them [Italians] and they would run, they didn't want to fight," explained Private George Burrows. "Once we got ashore, their hands would go up and they would volunteer to surrender," he added.[38] "B" Coy quickly moved through and overran the coastal defence battery, capturing four guns and 38 Italian prisoners, who eagerly surrendered after Sergeant Jean Bougard fired a shot into a dugout that wounded one them. The prisoners were marched back to the beachhead and the guns were destroyed by Royal Canadian Engineers (RCE). The Regiment's first combat operation seemed to be moving along splendidly.

With phase II of the plan complete, "C" and "D" Companies passed through and advanced towards the Pachino airfield taking out isolated machine gun posts and rifle positions en route. As they neared their objective the lead elements of the Regiment found that the "high ground" overlooking the airfield was not all that high. As a result, the CO was able to move forward to a vantage point scarcely 200 metres from the southern edge of the airfield. It quickly became evident that the airstrip had been ploughed to deny its use and appeared to have been abandoned.

Without waiting for orders, "C" Coy pressed on to exploit its success and moved across the eastern side of the airfield, linking up with tanks from the 51st Division who had pushed to the west. In so doing they secured their objective and captured well over a hundred enemy prisoners. Meanwhile, "A" Coy began to push onto the western half of the objective and quickly came under artillery and machine-gun fire from the northwest corner of the airfield. Assisted by flanking fire from the Hastings and Prince Edward Regiment (H&PER) on the Regiment's right, "A" Coy assaulted the barracks from where much of the small arms fire was originating. The Coy quickly seized the building and silenced any resistance. They then pressed on to take out a battery nearly 1,000 metres to the north which had been firing onto the beachhead, but had since been silenced by naval guns.

Despite the enemy's superiority in numbers, "A" Coy forced their way through the enemy wire, destroyed two machine gun strong points, and "by their aggressiveness struck terror into the hearts of the Italians."[39] When it was over they captured 130 prisoners and four 6-inch guns. The effort, however, cost the Coy five casualties, including two killed.

As "A" Coy fought the stiffest action of the day, "B" and "D" Coys pushed inland to higher ground, but ran a gauntlet of enemy machine gun fire doing so. The advance quickly turned into a series of platoon and section actions to destroy remaining enemy resistance. By 1400 hours, the entire battalion was reorganized and digging in around the objective. Everyone remained vigilant and ready to repel any enemy counter attack. Patrols were also dispatched to report on enemy activity and to prevent being unduly surprised.

The first day of the invasion had ended. The Regiment was justifiably proud as it had achieved its objectives and in so doing was the first Allied unit to capture an enemy airfield in Sicily. Within 48 hours of its capture, Allied fighters would begin flying sorties from its airstrip in support of the push inland.

The Regiment did not have long to enjoy their achievement. By early afternoon the next day, they were advancing towards Rossolini, described by one "Royal" as a "stinking little town."[40] Private Burrows complained, "the heat, lack of drinking water, dirty clothes and the walking through limestone dust, which made it hard to breathe, proved to be major hardships." He added, "the constant sweating caused the dust to seep into your eyes and pores."[41] Major Ian Hodson, recounted, "You were eating dust — breathing dust."[42] The pursuit of the enemy across the island had begun. "The next seven days," wrote Galloway, "was to see a pursuit which entailed gruelling marches along the sun-scorched dusty trails by day and in the chilly atmosphere by night."[43]

At this point of the campaign the "Royal Canadians" began to appreciate the beauty, but also the harshness, of the Sicilian landscape. "It is a mass of high hills, very rocky and covered with lovely vineyards and orchards with orange groves and apples of all sorts," wrote Captain R.G. Liddell.[44] His description belied the significance of the terrain. "Have had some terribly hard climbs in the course of our advance," explained one officer, "and in the heat of the day the tps [troops] have had to use every ounce of guts they possessed."[45] Private Burrows recalled "we called ourselves 'Monty's mountain goats!'"[46]

The Allies were making good progress and the 1 CIB commander decided to push the Regiment forward. As a result, they loaded on their motor transport, on captured enemy vehicles, and on a troop of tanks from the Three Rivers Armoured Regiment and proceeded to strike inland towards an area near Modica led by the CO personally in his carrier. The strange convoy crept along the dusty eerie Sicilian roads in the moonlit silence. The following morning, as the dawn bled into the countryside, the Regiment arrived at its position. The Battalion was immediately deployed on a hill feature commanding the road, but no enemy was in sight. At 1000 hours, a patrol mounted in a Bren gun carrier was dispatched to Ragusa to demand its surrender. A five minute barrage hammered the town to assist the occupants in making the correct decision.

The Battalion moved off two hours later and approached the town. However, the patrol had not returned and was in fact an hour late. In addition, there was no visible white flag flying to indicate that the town had surrendered. Lieutenant-Colonel Crowe, fearing these developments meant his patrol was killed or captured, prepared to lead the Regiment in an attack to take Ragusa. The lead company in the attack had just begun to deploy when Captain R.M. Dillon, the patrol leader, returned and announced the town "was ours."

The delay in Dillon's return was actually caused by the shelling. The Italian officials were so terrified by the short bombardment that they hid and it "took some persuasion [for them] to come out of hiding."[47] After a brief rest and hot meal, the Regiment fell in last in the order of march for 1 CIB to continue the advance at 2200 hours that night.

The following morning the Regiment found itself just south of Giarratana. The 1st Canadian Division had now outstripped its supply lines. Consequently, an operational pause was imposed to allow the logistical tail to catch up, as well as allow the troops to rest, most of whom had been able to accumulate only eight hours of sleep in the last four days. It also allowed General Bernard Montgomery to visit the troops. "It was an impressive ceremony and a cheering one," recorded the War Diary, "a visit much enjoyed by all ranks."[48]

The 36-hour delay was greatly appreciated and would serve the "Royal Canadians" well. To date the campaign had been quite successful. However, they had not yet met the German Army. The opposition so far consisted of Italian Coastal Defence divisions, made up of home defence battalions and batteries. The Regiment's assessment of these troops revealed that they "have neither the will nor the organization to enable them to fight a successful campaign."[49]

At midnight on 14 July 1943, the advance continued, once again with the CO leading the brigade. The Regimental objective, Vizzini was shelled and the enemy withdrew without a fight. The brigade proceeded to leap

RCR Bren gun carriers capture the rail junction north of Valguarnera, 20 July 1943.

frog battalions through a succession of objectives, namely Caltagirone, Grammichele, and Piazza Armerina. Finally, in the hills surrounding Valguarnera the "Royal Canadians" ran into the Germans. Fighting raged through the slopes and wooded knolls that separated 1 CIB from its objectives.

Communications quickly became a problem because the difficult ground with its deep ravines and gullies created havoc with the wireless radios. Quite simply the advanced companies and their 46 W/T radio sets could no longer reach the 22 W/T sets back at BHQ in the rear. It was not long before contact was completely lost. As a result, the Battalion could not count on artillery support from higher and thus, called forward its own mortar platoon. But the friction of war intervened again. As the carriers attempted to negotiate the terrain one flipped over and the other became temporarily out of action. By the time both were ready to continue to move forward contact with the forward elements of the Battalion had been irretrievably lost.[50]

The Battalion was now deployed on a razor-backed ridge overlooking the road running to Valguernera from the west. From here the "Royal Canadians" had a good view of the town. Between them and their objective were a series of small hills and knolls, covered with groves. Ominously, to their immediate front their high perch dropped about 400 metres in an even slope to a field below. Even the uninitiated realized that any advance over this ground would be costly.

At 1030 hours, the CO decided to increase the pressure on the German defenders by advancing on a one company front with "A" and "B" Coys, covered by the fire of "C" and "D" Coys so that they could seize a troublesome enemy platoon position that was holding up the advance. The attack unfolded like clock work. "It was as mad a charge as every lay upon an artist's canvas," marvelled one eyewitness' "It was a truly amazing sight to see 'A' Coy deployed like an exercise in section leading, walking down the forward slope of this high open feature, with the enemy M.G.s supplemented by a couple of mortars, kicking up dirt around them," wrote the Regimental chronicler. He added, "A few yards in their rear came the leading platoons of 'B' Coy and in between, eager to keep the action rolling, walked Lt/Col Crowe." As the attacking force neared the foot of the main feature, "B" Coy swung to the right now widening the frontage. "Spirited fighting took place," recorded the war diary, "but most of the enemy withdrew in haste when they saw the determination with which the attack was put in."[52]

At the same time as the attack was going in, Major Billy Pope, the battalion deputy commanding officer (DCO) was in the process of leading a small relieving patrol to free a body of soldiers from the H&PER who were pinned down by the enemy. His force successfully disengaged the trapped soldiers and Pope continued on foot to the "A" Coy objective. As the Battalion was reorganizing after the attack, "A" Coy observed three Mark IV German tanks commanding the western approach to the town. Pope, seizing the "A" Coy PIAT, a new anti-tank weapon, led his patrol through a covered approach to attack the tanks at close range. None of the three PIAT bombs, "due perhaps to faulty priming" were effective. However, the attack did attract the attention of the tanks who opened fire on their adversaries killing Major Pope.[53]

The remainder of the Battalion now dug in the rocky dry-grassed hillside as intermittent shelling by the German tanks, as well as heavy mortar fire, slammed into their position. As the blistering semi-tropical sun beat down on the parched, sweat dripping soldiers, all awaited the expected German counter attack. But it never came. At 2200 hours that night, the 48th Highlanders patrolled into the Valguernera and found it abandoned. By 16 July 1943, the German High Command had already come to the conclusion that they would evacuate Sicily. However, that would take time. As a result, they decided on a campaign of vicious rearguard actions that would buy them the necessary time.

The RCR spent 19 July burying their dead and resting. The advance commenced anew at midnight. The next objective was Assoro. The brigade commander assigned the Regiment the lead on the advance. The "Royal Canadians" were responsible for taking the two hill features that straddled the road into Assoro. Supported by tanks from the "Three Rivers" Regiment, the Battalion advanced with two companies on each side of the road. "A" Coy promptly warned the tanks of a minefield, "but the latter promptly drove into the field and remained there for the rest of the day — minus tracks."[54] The initial objectives were quickly seized, however, The RCR came under a fire from strong enemy positions on the hill leading up to Assoro, which was on top of a 915-metre mountaintop.

The H&PER attacked that night and successfully captured the right hand side of the Assoro feature. However, the enemy tenaciously clung to the other side and effectively cut off the bridgehead. At 1400 hours, 21 July, The RCR were ordered to send a carrying party under cover of darkness to resupply the H&PER. This was done "under the nose of the enemy positions."[55] The next morning under cover of a heavy artillery

Brigadier Chris Vokes, the commander of 2 CIB, confers with RCR Major P.R. Bingham, near Assoro, July 1943.

barrage the 48th Highlanders advanced and linked up with the H&PER and by early afternoon the enemy was cleared from Assoro.

At midnight the Regiment moved up to Assoro and positioned the unit on the high ground covering the road. Night deployments were always hard. Moving in the dark over the difficult terrain "meant continual falls, sprained ankles, sprained wrists, cuts on the forehead when they smashed their face against rock, and so it went," explained Hodson, "not a pleasant place to go."[56] Patrols were then sent out to secure the next road junction along the road to Nissoria, which would be the next Regimental objective. The brigade remained for the remainder of the next day while 2 CIB consolidated beyond their newly won prize of Leonforte. They in turn would provide the base for the next phase of the pursuit.

Upon return from orders, the brigade commander outlined the plan for the attack on Agira. It was due to commence at 1400 hours, 24 July 1943.

However, the starting line for that attack was almost five kilometres west of Nissoria. Unlike most Sicilian towns, Agira was not on a mountaintop. Rather it was in a depression astride the Leonforte-Agira highway. From a distance the town looked white and deceptively clean. At 1300 hours, under a burning sun, Lieutenant-Colonel Crowe led his reconnaissance (recce) party forward beyond the covering positions held by 2 CIB and studied the route the Battalion would follow. The ground was undulating and covered with olive orchards and grapevines. He deployed the Battalion to the right of the road with "C" and "D" Coys leading. They were responsible for clearing the town and reporting it clear. "A" and "B" Coys were then to pass through and seize the high ground east of the town and hold fast. The CO explained that the advance of 20 kilometres to the actual objective of Agira may be beyond the Battalion's capability, if it met heavy resistance and fighting at Nissoria. In that event, the H&PER, who were second in the order of march, would probably be pushed through.

The Regiment was told that they would be well supported for the attack. The entire divisional artillery was at its disposal, as well as 90 bombers and more than 100 fighter bombers in close support. In fact, according to the methodical plans of the division commander, Major-General Guy G. Simonds, the Regiment would advance behind an irresistible barrage that would advance at a rate of 100 metres every two minutes. With this overwhelming fire support, most expected a walkover.

However, at 1400 hours the Regiment was at its forming up point ready to advance, but there was no sign of any supporting aircraft. Nonetheless, for the Army, timings are important, and the advance began. At first it was almost as if they were on exercise, reminisced Major C.H. Lithgow. "The irregular line of troops moving steadily forward, shouts and hand signals from officers and N.C.O.s controlling the advance," he recalled, "the clank and whine of the Shermans [tanks] as they lifted clouds of dust and in the distance the artillery laying a smoky, metal pall over the hills."[57] The RCR encountered no enemy fire until the Battalion neared the western approach to Nissoria, when sporadic mortar and sniper fire harassed the lead elements. "C" and "D" Coys pressed on and cleared the town. All seemed to go relatively smoothly. But it was not to be. As the Coys emerged from the eastern edge of Nissoria they were met by heavy fire. Concurrently, the depth element, "A" and "B" Coys broke from cover and began their advance to pass through. Suddenly, they too were engulfed in a punishing mortar barrage. Then, as they crossed a low ridge, they were also subjected to a devastating machine gun fire. Adding to the confusion, wireless communications quickly broke down and it became difficult for BHQ, as well as the rifle coys to ascertain who was making what progress.

By 1630 hours, the CO had moved through Nissoria to its forward edge that was under direct fire. He concluded that the Battalion had firm control of the town and that the main enemy strength, of an undetermined size, was on the high ground astride the road leading to the main objective of Agira. He ordered "D" Coy to move around the left flank and clear enemy out from the area where he believed they had concentrated. This manoeuvre met with some problems. One of the assaulting platoons misunderstood the order and became lost in the town. Another of the "D" Coy platoons was designated the fire base and was therefore unavailable for the assault. As a result, a rather weakened "D" Coy now became locked in a desperate fight with the enemy on the north side of the road.

Meanwhile, the remainder of the Battalion was on the right flank, or south of the road. On this flank of the enemy-occupied hill was a large valley that led to the outskirts of Agira itself. Having been ordered to push on by Crowe, the three rifle companies bypassed the enemy position. The CO at this time took his command group of several signallers and engineers and attempted to catch up with his three rifle companies that were pushing on to Agira. As he reached the high ground to his front, he found none of his troops. He could hear firing to the front and assumed they were engaged farther on. Unfortunately wireless communication had completely broken down by this stage. Therefore, Crowe was powerless to communicate with his errant coys.

The coys were in fact to reorganize on the high ground designated as a second report line. As such, Crowe decided to move to the road and meet them on the report line itself. The ground dropped away in a series of shallow gullies and the CO continued to lead his party towards what he believed was the road. Bodies of RCR soldiers along the route seemed to confirm he was in the right direction. As they neared the top of a rise, approximately 300 metres from the road, the enemy opened up. Crowe's HQ party had been lured into a trap — they were in the centre of an enemy company position — one of three positioned on the hill feature that was creating so much trouble for the RCR. Although wounded, Crowe grabbed a signaller's rifle and tried to engage the machine gun post. Private Fred Turner, one of the signallers, attempted to crawl forward to assist the mortally wounded CO, but he too was cut down when a second machine gun supporting the first opened fire.[58]

Luckily, the remainder of the CO's party was farther back and were able to take cover. They attempted to cover the withdrawal of Crowe, Corporal W.J. Cummings and Privates F.A. Turner and Burton. However, when it became apparent that they were dead, the remainder of the group returned to Battalion HQ to report what had happened.[59]

In the interim, most the Battalion continued up the valley with no opposition until they were a few kilometres from Agira. At this point, unable to contact the CO or any other higher HQ and realizing that control had been lost, the three company commanders decided to consolidate where they were for the night. Their fortunes did not improve. The next morning as dawn seeped light onto the battlefield, the enemy, who overlooked the RCR position, inflicted yet more casualties with mortars and machine gun fire.

Importantly, however, two soldiers from "B" Coy, Privates Palmer and Johnston, who were lost, pressed on alone to the outskirts of Agira. Here they captured a prisoner, a staff car driver who was asleep in his vehicle. The information he would give would later prove invaluable in providing information that would allow 1 Canadian Division to formulate a plan to capture Agira.[60]

Meanwhile, the "D" Company attack, despite the support of the Three Rivers Regiment, who lost 10 tanks, failed. The "Royal Canadians" pulled back and with the assistance of stragglers and the remnants of Support Coy held Nissoria. However, the enemy sensed weakness, reinforced its positions, and hammered the town with intense artillery barrages. This triggered an Allied response. The artillery duel soon prompted the brigade commander to order The RCR out of Nissoria for fear of friendly fire casualties. As such, when Major T.M. Powers moved forward from the rear BHQ to assume command he found only a portion of the Battalion reorganizing in the orchards west of the town. He promptly dispatched a patrol from "D" Coy to recall the three flanking coys. And so ended, the Battalion attack. It had cost the Regiment, 17 killed and 30 wounded.

Major-General Simonds, ordered two more attacks against Agira. The H&PER and the 48th Highlanders, who both conducted separate attacks both on 25 July failed to carry the position. 1 CIB was rotated out for a rest and 2 CIB was put in the breach. The next day, the PPCLI, following a divisional artillery shoot on the enemy position on the hill, which was reportedly the heaviest since "Alamein," easily overran the position. Agira was cleared later that day.

The Regiment was able to rest and recuperate for the next few days. The three day rest was badly needed as the Regiment had completed 16 days of continuous marching, skirmishing and all out battle. However, on 30 July the brigade moved up to support 231 (Malta) Brigade in its attack on Regalbuto. The Malta Brigade had been stopped in its attempt to take the town. Strong enemy defences, which included dug-in tanks, skilfully covered every gully and avenue of approach. On the night of 31 July, the Battalion launched a night attack "but it was far too strongly held for one battalion to crack."[61]

The Battalion advanced on foot following the road as far as the town of Regalbuto and then struck out cross country south of the town. The CO deployed "D" Coy as his advance guard. The objective was a razor-backed

Soldiers of The RCR Support Coy ride mules used for transport of heavy weapons, supplies, and casualties near Regalbuto, 3 August 1943.

feature just East of Regalbuto. Predictably, wireless communications proved troublesome once again and the CO lost contact with his lead coy. Assuming the route was clear he dispatched "A" Coy to follow up. As they neared the objective they could clearly hear the ominous sound of mortars and machine guns ahead. At 0415 hours, "A" Coy reported they were held up by at least two tanks and several machine gun posts. The remaining two coys had also been dispatched in 30 minute intervals, and daylight now found the entire Battalion held up in a gully dominated by the enemy on the ridge.[62]

Throughout the day the troops suffered. For 14 hours, the "Royal Canadians" endured searing heat and lack of water, as well as the fury of German mortar, tank, and machine gun fire. The lack of success of the string of frontal attacks prompted Major-General Simonds to issue new orders. As a result, on 1 August, the brigade commander ordered

Members of The RCR Pioneer Platoon watering their mules near Regalbuto, 4 August 1943.

a withdrawal under the cover of darkness. By midnight The RCR was re-assembled in an area about four kilometres to the rear where they enjoyed their first meal in 36 hours. A divisional attack the following day dislodged the enemy from the razor-backed objective which had been used by the Germans as a rear guard position. In the interim the enemy had withdrawn from the town of Regalbuto itself.[63]

The Sicilian campaign was now all but over. The role of 1 CIB in the aftermath of Regalbuto consisted of a series of moves and consolidations towards Adrano. On 4 August after a day of rest the Regiment advanced. However it saw no more fighting. On 5 August, the 50th Division entered Catania and severed the coastal highway. The next day, the Americans from the north and west, and the British approaching from the east, began to close the ring around Mount Etna, thus cutting off the final avenue of withdrawal for the Germans. On 12 August, The RCR left its final battle

Lieutenant-General A.G.L. McNaughton addresses the "Royal Canadians" in Sicily, August 1943.

positions and moved to a rest area at Militello in Val Di Catania to await the next phase of the operation.

The move to the rest area also coincided with a change in command. Lieutenant-Colonel D.C. Spry was flown in from England to take over the Regiment. Tommy Powers reverted to the rank of major and resumed the position of DCO. The Battalion used its time in Militello to clean up, rest, and recuperate. "Everyone cleaned up," wrote Captain Liddell, "the Regiment regained all its former smartness and good sense of discipline which have always stood us in good stead." He added, "all ranks are proud of it!"[64]

The "Royal Canadians" also re-established a training regime to prepare themselves for the next battle. Sicily had proven to be a tremendous test. "It was an excellent training ground for troops," explained Private Burrow, "you could get the feeling of what it is like to face an enemy."[65] Quite simply, officers, senior NCOs, and men found the brief, but at times bitter campaign a useful experience. They tested their endurance and tenacity against a harsh, sweltering environment and an even more exigent foe in the Germans. They had learned how to fight and survive on the very demanding modern battlefield. Lessons learned would serve them well in the challenges that awaited them on the Italian mainland. And, they had not long to wait. On 26 August, regimental officers were briefed on Operation Baytown, the invasion of Italy, scheduled to start on 3 September 1943. The RCR was about to write another chapter in its distinguished history.

5
No Soft Underbelly: The Battle for Italy

The 38 day Sicilian campaign, although relatively short, provided the "Royal-Canadians" with badly needed experience. By all accounts, they, as well as all Canadians engaged, had conducted themselves well. Training in England had prepared the Regiment to a degree, but, in the end, only the actual hardships and horrors of battle could fully instil the skills and abilities needed to be successful. These hard lessons were now put into practice. Although in a supposed "rest" camp, the soldiers were given little time to relax. Normal training resumed almost immediately.

There was good reason for that. It was not lost on anyone that although Sicily had been conquered, the enemy had been anything but fully beaten. The Germans had deployed four divisions in Sicily. However, they quickly decided that defence of the island was futile and as early as 10 August decided to withdraw their forces to fight on mainland Italy.[1] As such, they executed a brilliant withdrawal and began to prepare for the Allied assault. Encounters with German forces in Sicily had demonstrated to the Allies the skill and tenacity of their enemy. Add to that the rugged terrain of Italy, and the coming contest could only be worse than what had already been experienced.

The "Royals," as newspapers now began to call the soldiers of the RCR, had not long to wait to write the next chapter of their distinguished history. On 26 August 1943, the Regimental officers were briefed on Operation Baytown, the invasion of mainland Italy. The actual landing

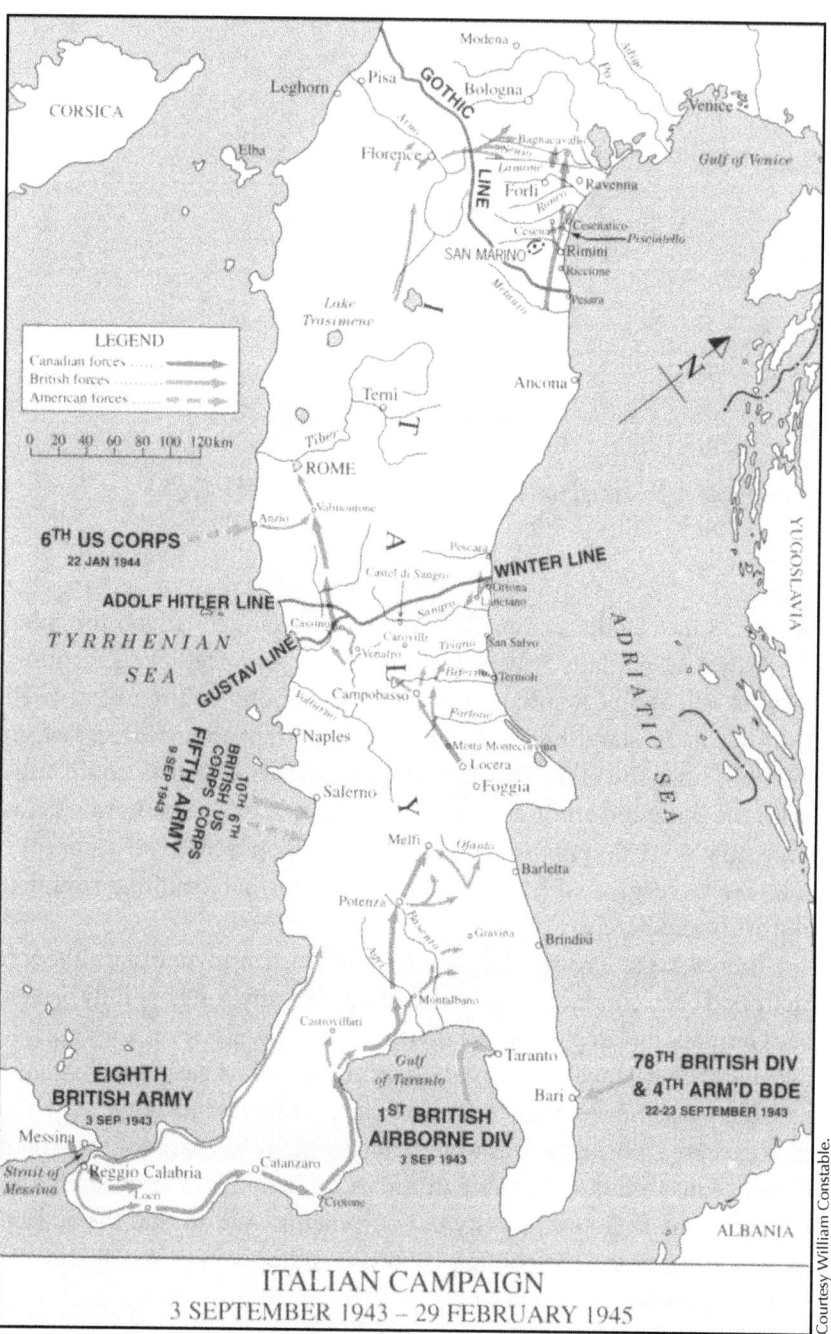

was to be made across the Straits of Messina on the shallow beaches at Reggio Di Calabria.

The plan was not overly complicated. 13th Corps, consisting of the 1st Canadian Division, 5th (British) Division, and 231 (Malta) Brigade were to make an assault on the toe of Italy by crossing the straits in landing craft. Major-General Simonds tasked 3 CIB with securing the beach just north of Reggio and clearing the immediate high ground as well as the city of Reggio itself. The divisional commander assigned 1 CIB the mission (on order) of enlarging the bridgehead area by pushing south through Reggio and securing a series of objectives that included the village of Galina, the airfield, and point 167, which consisted of the high ground overlooking the airfield. Simultaneous with the 1st Canadian Division operations, the 5th (British) Division would be making a landing to the north. The whole Corps assault was to be preceded by a tremendous heavy bombardment of the enemy beaches and coastal defences by both Allied artillery regiments, as well as ships of the Royal Navy (RN).[2]

In addition, the Royal Air Force and the U.S. Army Air Force would provide air support. They had already cut communications between the toe and the rest of the Italian mainland and were now focusing on attacking inland targets. The primary objectives of Operation Baytown were to clear the Straits of Messina for Allied shipping, and draw German divisions from central Italy down into the foot so that further Allied operations could be launched elsewhere against the mainland.[3]

For the remainder of the month the senior officers of 1 CIB studied the coastline with binoculars and maps. Finally, at 0300 hours on the morning of 1 September, the Battalion "embussed" in transport and moved off to their assembly area. The density of traffic on the narrow dusty Sicilian roads made the deployment tedious. Nonetheless, the "Royals" arrived at their new destination by late morning in the growing heat. The next day was spent pouring over the invasion plans. That afternoon the brigade commander, Brigadier H.D. Graham, inspected the Battalion. On the afternoon of 3 September 1943, after countless delays, the Battalion, specifically the three rifle companies, began to load on Landing Ships Infantry (LSI), and the Battalion's vehicles were loaded on Landing Ships Tank (LST). By 1504 hours, "A" and "B" Coys were underway, followed by "C" Coy and BHQ an hour later.[4]

The ships sailed north up the coast of Sicily to Messina and then across the Strait. If the landing at Pachino two month earlier was a

Fatigued "Royals" advancing from Reggio to Terrati, Italy, September 1943.

disappointment, the invasion of Italy was a complete letdown. It was a non-event. In fact, the sharp tidal currents in the strait, combined with the difficulty in navigating because of the great clouds of dust and smoke caused by the Allied bombardment, which obscured visibility, proved a greater challenge than any German resistance.

The beaches were totally abandoned. There were no mines, no entanglements, and no manned defences. An ineffective aerial raid by two German fighter aircraft proved to be the only enemy action encountered. German forces had withdrawn inland days earlier. "The landing was costly in ammunition," quipped Strome Galloway, "[however,] except for a stray shot or two and some bombs dropped on the beach by a couple of German planes it was a regatta."[5]

The invasion was proceeding beyond anyone's wildest expectation. The 1st Canadian Division lead element, 3 CIB, occupied their objectives as well as those assigned to 1 CIB. By 2000 hours, the Regiment was completely ashore, had passed through Reggio, which was completely evacuated by the civilian population, and was secure in its assembly area ready to resume the advance the next morning. Elsewhere, Allied units continued to expand the bridgehead and in the process collected thousands of Italian prisoners, who had begun to surrender by entire battalions.

The next morning, following brigade orders, the Regiment began its advance inland — all uphill! The march quickly became a feat of endurance. The stifling heat and steepness of the climb fatigued all. After a four hour rest on a terraced hillside, the Battalion left the road and continued up a winding mule track to the top of the densely wooded mountain. By 1930 hours, the rifle companies were in position.

The defensive posture, however, was not required. The closest Germans were approximately six kilometres away in San Stefano undertaking demolitions. The main body of the enemy was even further away — almost 100 kilometres distant. For the next several days the "Royals" held their mountain perch. Italian deserters and temperamental mules from the local surroundings were impressed to carry rations to the forward companies. The soldiers sweated out the hot days, and shivered in the pouring rain and mist on the mountain top at night. Diseases, such as yellow jaundice and malaria, as well as other sickness slowly began to appear. Although only newly arrived, the "Royals" quickly felt that their initiation to Italy was ominously foreboding.

Nonetheless, while the Regiment idled away the days in miserable conditions, events elsewhere moved forward. Finally, on 7 September 1943 the Battalion was ordered to leave its mountain position and march to Albergo da Gambarie. "The Battalion," described Galloway, "looked like quite a safari."[6] In preparation for the advance, the "Royals" had gathered up all the donkeys and mules from the surrounding area to transport their supplies, ammunition, and heavy weapons. It did not take long, however, for the mule train to disintegrate into a collection of individual and small groups of stubborn animals slowly making their own way in the wake of the marching Battalion.

The following day, the Regiment learned that Italy had formally surrendered. The news caused great excitement. The CO, Lieutenant-Colonel Dan Spry, held a parade and read out General Dwight "Ike" Eisenhower's proclamation, however, he warned "that there was to be no celebrating, as there was still a large force of Germans in Italy to contend with and we would carry on with our plans as before."[7] As was to be expected, the German military quickly filled the gaps in the Axis defences left by the Italian surrender with its own soldiers. Consequently, the Allies still faced a bitter struggle to capture the country.

The next day, on 9 September, further news was received. British airborne forces had seized Taranto on the east coast and were making their way inland. In addition, Lieutenant-General Mark Clark and his 5th Army landed at Salerno approximately 48 kilometres southeast of Naples. The Allies were determined to put pressure on the Germans.[8] Not surprisingly, the Battalion was ordered to advance. Loading into transport vehicles, the "Royals" retraced their steps through Reggio and made their way to Locri approximately 150 kilometres distant.

Clearly evident was the devastation of war. Few civilians could be seen. Buildings were transformed into rubble and often flames still played in the wreckage. Moreover, the stench of death and decay hung in the hot fetid air. The only movement to be seen was that of the countless Italian deserters who streamed past the advancing troops.

The following day, the soldiers mounted up to continue their advance. Their objective was Catanzaro. Unfortunately, a bridge demolition necessitated dismounting the vehicles approximately 29 kilometres from the objective and a gruelling march along the highway and over rough hilly ground ensued. This became the pattern for the next several weeks. The Regiment was not involved in any fighting; it was carrying out a mechanized pursuit of the enemy. "If this isn't a phoney war," grumbled Galloway, "I don't know what is!" He complained, "Ten days in a hostile country and the only shots we have fired have been at a bunch of annoying spectators!"[9]

His complaint would not go unheard for too long. Just as the fall weather began to turn, so too did the Regiment's fortunes. The temperature started to cool off, particularly at night. More trying was the persistent rain. For the soldiers, still dressed in summer khaki drill uniform, with only their oil skin gas capes for bedding, life became miserable.

More important, the enemy was preparing to fight. The Germans had pulled back across the Foggia Plain and into the Daunia Mountains, which were foothills of the Apennine Mountains. In many ways, Italy was built for defence. Its rivers ran east to west and provided natural defensive lines. The rivers, combined with the mountain ranges, created challenging terrain, which a skilled enemy could use to good effect to fight a tenaciously bitter and costly delaying action.

On 30 September "B" Coy was cut over to the vanguard of a 1 CIB force that was to lead the way to Campobasso. The vanguard force was

Private Thomas Hawkins digging in near Motta, Italy.

commanded by the CO of the 14th (Calgary) Tank Regiment and consisted of his regiment, "B" Coy, armoured cars from the Princess Louise Dragoon Guards, and detachments from other support arms. The 1 CIB lead element advanced on the axis of Highway 17 and passed through Foggia, which had been levelled by Allied air attack because of the concentration of airfields in the area. Scouts quickly reported that the enemy remained in the mountain village of Motta.

The next day, 1 October, the 1 CIB vanguard force followed the highway as it climbed serpentine-like up the escarpment towards its objective. At 1600 hours, the attack on Motta commenced with the tanks leading, supported by "B" Coy.

The narrow steep windy road proved to be a death trap. The dreaded German 88 mm anti-aircraft guns showered the tanks with a deadly welcome, and Spandau machine guns created an impenetrable wall for the infantry, causing the assault to falter. Brigadier Howard

Graham quickly turned to The RCR "B" Coy, and ordered it to capture the village.

The RCR's task was as daunting as 1 CIB's had been . The approach was open and the enemy occupied a high feature that completely dominated the valley below and afforded them observation of almost all the roads leading from Foggia to Motta.[10] Any movement in this intervening ground was immediately met with enemy fire, particularly airburst artillery shells from the versatile and deadly 88 mm guns.

By 1700 hours, the CO had assembled his Orders Group ("O" Gp) and issued orders for the attack which was to begin at dusk. Lieutenant-Colonel Spry ordered "C" and "D" Coys to seize the prominent features on the right side of the road leading into the town; "B" Coy to remain in its current position on the slope in front of the town, and "A" Coy to remain in reserve, prepared to penetrate into town on order.[11]

Private W.G. Turner grabs a quick bite to eat during a brief rest period near Motta, Italy, October 1943.

The attack started well. All companies reached their objectives without opposition and "A" Coy was ordered into the town. Its lead platoon, 7 Platoon, advanced up the narrow winding road in single file, expecting an ambush at any one of the many hairpin turns. Surprisingly, it reached the edge of town without a single shot being fired. It secured entrance and 9 Platoon was pushed through. The deadly quiet was deceiving. After the RCR had penetrated approximately 500 metres into the town in the pitch dark it "was heavily engaged by LMG [light machine gun] fire and close fighting ensued."[12] One war correspondent reported, "The Royals started up a twisting road to the little town and ran into machine-gun and shell fire as they approached the sloping cobble stoned town square."[13] The enemy fire created an impenetrable wall and the narrow built up streets made flank movement impossible.

By 2300 hours, the CO ordered "A" Coy to withdraw. He now planned to shell the town with a storm of steel and then follow up the bombardment with an attack using "A" and "B" Coys.[14] The concentrated artillery barrage began at 0250 hours, 2 October and lasted for 10 minutes. "It was the most fantastic feeling," revealed Private George Burrows, "to see and feel the shells going over your head to attack." He added, "the smell of the cordite stuck with you — you cannot replicate the smell — it was great for morale."[15]

At 0300 hours exactly, as the last shells were exploding, "B" Coy, in a torrential rain storm, led the renewed attack into Motta. "It was now well into the night," explained the commanding officer, "and a frightful wind and rain storm had broken out."[16] The attacking troops became painfully visible as they were silhouetted by bolts of lightening. Undaunted, "B" Coy pushed into the centre of town against virtually no opposition. "A" Coy attempted a right flanking but found they could not penetrate into the town because of stone walls, wire, and ground. However, it no longer mattered. The Germans had loaded onto vehicles and with lights blazing were withdrawing from the far end. As dawn started to leak onto the horizon, both companies were consolidated on the far edge of town.

The hard won fight for Motta was not yet over. "A murky dawn of a rainy Saturday," explained one journalist, "found the troops inching their way forward toward a neighboring slope which the Germans defended with machine guns, mortars and 88 millimetre all purpose guns."[17] By 0800 hours, on 2 October, the remainder of the Battalion began to reorganize. The CO sent "C" Coy forward on foot to seize some rolling ground in front of the town and within two hours, they were pinned down by heavy machine gun and artillery fire. They sustained heavy casualties and six of their supporting tanks were knocked out. "The rifle company got to within 600 yards and came under quite strong machine gun fire no movement being possible," explained Lieutenant-Colonel Spry. "The forward sections and the company commander were pinned to the ground the latter having to talk over his 18 set while lying on his side," added the CO. Although friendly artillery fire engaged the enemy throughout the day, it had little effect. Therefore, at 1630 hours, Spry gave orders for an attack on Motta Ridge.

That attack commenced three hours later with a heavy artillery bombardment. The Battalion advanced through "rolling, muddy, ploughed fields in arrow head formation," against its objective approximately 2,000 metres away. Supporting fire from tanks in hull down positions was deemed "excellent." The "Royals" achieved the road at the bottom of the ridge just after dark and luckily had not yet come under fire. After a brief reorganization the lead companies began to climb the ridge. As the troops neared the top "they were heavily engaged by enemy machine guns on fixed lines shooting down gullies and cross-fire on the top of the ridge."[18]

The fighting became confused in the dark tangle-wooded slope in a pouring rain. "The ground was wet from the rain and mud clung to the men's boots," described one war correspondent, "impeding their advance in some places the slopes were so steep they practically had to crawl."[19] The CO ordered the forward companies to dispatch platoons to clear the ridge, guard the flanks and rear, as well as patrol down the road. "Hand to hand fighting became general," revealed Spry, "and rifle butts were used freely."[20] By midnight the enemy had been pushed off the ridge. At dawn, the Regiment could finally take a breather. Dead enemy soldiers revealed that the "Royals" had battled a formidable foe, members of the 1st German Parachute Division.[21]

The Regiment received little respite, neither from the rain, nor from their chain of command. On 4 October, the 1 CIB commander ordered The RCR to conduct another attack, this time against the town of San Marco. The attack was actually part of a brigade line of advance. The RCR was responsible for the centre — San Marco, while the Hastings and Prince Edward Regiment (H&PER) were to advance over broken ground to the North, and the 48th Highlanders were to continue along the axis (an imaginary line which represents the "centre" or direction of the advance) of Highway 17. "Zero-Hour" was set for 1400 hours. The Battalion was to assault on a two company front — "C" Coy left and "B" Coy right, with "A" and "D" Coys following up respectively.

The attack was reminiscent of the First World War. In support, the Battalion had three field artillery regiments and one battery of a medium artillery regiment. A rolling barrage would cut a path of destruction approximately 400 metres wide of the centre of axis with a 100-metre lift every five minutes. There would be 11 "lifts" in all.

The RCR, "who had a very trying march straight across country lasting two hours which left them very tired at the finish" had no time to rest."[22] At 1400 hours, the first shoot of the artillery plan hammered in. "B" Coy quickly stepped off. However, unbeknownst to the officer commanding (OC), Major Strome Galloway, the CO had delayed the attack by thirty minutes because the reserve companies could not get into position in time due to the difficult terrain. As such, he ordered that the bombardment cease and recommence in 30 minutes. Tragically, the runners could not find all the forward troops because of the heavy woods and OC "B" Coy and 12 Platoon (the other two "B" Coy platoons were stopped in time) advanced only to be caught in the middle of the friendly fire. As a result, the OC was wounded and 12 Platoon became so disorganized that it was unable to participate in the attack.[23]

Notwithstanding this unfortunate incident, the assault began deceptively well. However, once the lead elements of the Battalion appeared on the slope immediately in front of the town a withering fire stopped "B" Coy in its tracks. "C" Coy was also pinned down, however, its OC attempted to use his lead platoon as a fire base and conduct a flanking with the remainder of his company, but this also failed when they were heavily engaged.

The CO quickly ordered "C" Coy, with the support of carrier platoon (dismounted), to act as a fire base and then directed "A" Coy to out flank the enemy position. They had hardly commenced their manoeuvre when they were engulfed in fire. To add to the difficulty, the other reserve force, "D" Coy also came under a heavy enfilade fire in the gully they had stumbled into.

Under a tremendous barrage and with darkness approaching Lieutenant-Colonel Spry realized the attack had failed. The enemy had fixed lines of fire and could pour a devastating fire into his troops as they attempted to negotiate the difficult ground in the dark. Moreover, the troops were now exhausted. As a result, the CO now reverted to deception. He would attempt to fool the enemy into withdrawing. "I got the impression," shared Spry, "that if the enemy received a good whack he would go."²⁴

The CO ordered his forward observation officer (FOO) to call in a Regimental artillery shoot directly in front of "C" Coy. This bombardment combined with the Regiment's close proximity and flanking movements prompted the Germans to slip out of the town. RCR patrols quickly followed up and by 0700 hours San Marco was secure. By 1100 hours, the Battalion had pushed out its control of the area to include two prominent ridge features. Later in the day, further patrols were dispatched to expand the Battalion's reach even further. However, once the brigade reached the Fortore River, 3 CIB took the lead and the Regiment now held firm at a position called Bridge Hill for several days while the 1st Canadian Division moved into position for its next major action.

As in Sicily, to date the Germans played a skilled delaying game. "You would force Jerry from a ridge, he'd fall back a mile and there would be a new ridge," lamented one veteran, "And then he'd paste the daylights out of you as you came up."²⁵ The ground was ideal for this type of battle. One officer described the challenge:

> The roads were intersected by water-courses, mountain torrents or dry river beds — serious obstacles and good defensive positions. [Field Marshal Albert] Kesselring's [German commander-in-chief in Italy] men did not mind surrendering Italian ground provided that a good price was paid. At each obstacle we found the bridge blown, mines laid, and well-armed infantry seemed to be in some strength (in reality, probably a company or less) but every man with an automatic weapon and plenty of ammunition. We would launch an attack, perhaps in battalion strength, and suffer a few casualties. As we closed on the enemy position he would withdraw ... There were few pieces of flat ground off the road where guns could be deployed or vehicles parked; these would be registered by enemy artillery and engaged when he thought we had occupied them.²⁶

Notwithstanding the difficulty, it was about to get harder. Hitler had dictated that a strong defensive line be established south of Rome on which the Allies would break their teeth. The Germans were about to stand and fight. On the Adriatic front this meant the enemy would mount a defensive system along the Sangro River into the depths of the central mountains, where the movement of mechanized armoured vehicles would be severely restricted and the superiority of air power would similarly be limited.

The next objective for 1 Canadian Division was Campobasso, approximately 80 kilometres north of Naples in the centre of the Italian peninsula. After six days at Bridge Hill, the Regiment was called forward. In a heavy rain on the evening of 11 October 1943, the "Royals" loaded onto trucks. The move was not intended to start before the next morning but because of the torrential rain, the troops were mounted on the vehicles for the night. "Sleep, though possible, was difficult in the cramped space allowed," remembered G.K. Wright. "When we awoke in the morning we felt mis-

The advance towards Campobasso grinds on, October 1943.

erable," he explained, "A shave, a shot of rum, a cup of tea and a piece of hard-tack revived us somewhat, and by noon, when we had a proper dinner, we felt somewhat more like soldiers and less like dishrags."[27]

The Battalion left the next day at 1245 hours and moved to an assembly area near Jelsi. Here they rested until midnight at which time they marched approximately 15 kilometres to Gildone. At 0830 hours, 13 October the "Royals" were on the march again advancing over a large plain that was due east of the objective. The plain was lower than its surroundings and resembled an elongated bowl. On its eastern rim, the Battalion deployed and waited for the 48th Highlanders to clear the route to its forming up point. After a brief wait, the "Royals" struck out across the bowl and were awed at the beauty of the countryside, at least, quipped one participant, "until we heard the ominous 'cra-a-ck' of a German airburst ranging shell almost directly overhead."[28] Enemy harassing fire continued during the Battalion's advance causing several casualties.

A short distance from their objective, the Battalion settled into a defensive position until their scheduled attack on Campobasso, which was to be undertaken that night. However, it was delayed until 0530 hours the next day, 14 October, to allow the assaulting troops some rest. The 1 CIB plan called for the 48th Highlanders to advance to a point within three kilometres of the city; then an attack by the H&PER on the village of Notnowna, which was south-east of the objective, followed by the assault on Campobasso itself by The RCR.

The plan began to unfold as planned. At 0530 hours, "A" Coy advanced through the 48th Highlanders and seized the dominating 'Feature 601' by 0700 hours. Surprisingly, they captured this vital piece of ground without a fight. "C" Coy quickly passed through and swarmed onto their objective, which was the near edge of town. "B" Coy had moved off at about the same time as "C" Coy on a parallel route to the right to reach the northern outskirts of the town. Both companies achieved their tasks without incident. As a result, "D" Coy was quickly pushed through "C" Coy to occupy the Castle at the western edge of the objective. Once in a position of observation, they were able to see the enemy's vehicles in the distance. The Germans had withdrawn several hours before. Once "D" Coy was established in their position, "A" and "B" Coys were also pushed to the town's forward edge. By 1600 hours, Campobasso had fallen to the Regiment without a fight.[29]

The "Royals" received a hero's welcome by the local inhabitants. The Italians' appreciated being "liberated," and expressed their joy with lots of

"Royal Canadians" pass through another Italian mountain village in pursuit of the German Army, October 1943.

hand waving and throwing of flowers. The "enthusiasm waned," however, when the town's population realized the Canadians were planning on staying for a few days. "When we began to look for billets," one veteran recalled, "it practically disappeared."[30]

The Regiment now settled into Campobasso for a "rest" period. But, it seemed as a very strange R&R centre. The "Royals" dug themselves in securely to repel any possible German counterattack. In addition, aggressive patrolling was undertaken to clear out pockets of enemy resistance and push the enemy's artillery out of range. To achieve this, a number of sub-unit actions were fought to capture the towns of Busso and Oratino. One officer remarked that the Regiment was laughingly sent to a "rest" centre but to "get the 'rest' the Regiment had to capture the town of Campobasso and several little ones." He added, "during the rest period we were under fairly constant shellfire."[31]

Nonetheless, for the Battalion, the advance had been stopped for the time being. But, not all welcomed the break. "All the common features of a rest period in The Royal Canadian Regiment began to appear," lamented one soldier, "drill parades, polishing of brass and the scrubbing of web, kit inspections, sick parades, Coy Comd's and CO's inspections [and] training."[32]

On 24 October 1943, the advance beckoned the Regiment once more. 1 CIB was tasked with striking across the Biferno River. However the far bank resembled "almost a sheer rampart" upon which stood the villages of Roccaspromonte and Castropignano approximately two kilometres apart. The only crossing point was at the site of a demolished bridge. Brigadier Graham quickly decided to send The RCR across to capture the villages that stood sentinel over the river so that the engineers could build a bridge.

The Regiment began its operations in the late afternoon of 24 October. "A" Coy crossed the river at 1705 hours followed by "C" Coy 15 minutes later. After scrambling up the steep bank they immediately struck out for Roccaspromonte. They found it abandoned. "C" Coy then pushed through and proceeded to its objective, a high feature known as Point 761, which was to the rear of Castropignano. Although it at first seemed deserted as well, as the "Royals" moved to occupy the feature they came under heavy machine gun fire that required some effort to silence.

Meanwhile, "B" Coy crossed the Biferno River at 1830 hours near the demolished bridge and cautiously made their way along the winding road that climbed the escarpment to Castropignano. Although initially heavily engaged by machine guns, the enemy hastily withdrew and ceded the town. "B" Coy reported the town clear at 0300 hours and by 1000 hours, 25 October 1943, the Battalion was consolidated within it. Five hours later the 48th Highlanders passed through to attack Torella.

The Regiment now moved into reserve and remained in Castropignano for several days. The area, however, was rich with Fascist sympathizers, causing the Battalion to mount a heavy guard against fifth columnists. Several incidents were noted: Signal wire was cut and several individuals were caught recording data on vehicle traffic. The Regiment also suffered accurate enemy shelling and suspected the reason was that its exact positions were being relayed to the Germans by Fascist elements.[33]

On 2 November 1943, The RCR relieved the H&PER in Molise. Two days later "D" Coy occupied Duronia and by 5 November the remainder of the Battalion had followed. Standing patrols were immediately dispatched

The RCR mortar platoon advancing up a mountain north of Motta Montecorvino, October 1943.

to secure the surrounding countryside. Explosions could be heard to the north — evidently the Germans conducting demolitions as they retreated in that direction. The "Royals" quickly set about cleaning up the town and arranging billets a result of Brigadier Graham informing the CO that the Regiment would hold here for some time.

The Regiment remained in Duronia until 1 December. Its stay was pleasant enough, however, heavy fall rains turned the countryside into mud and the rivers into torrents. "There are acres of deep sticky, black mud in the mountains and valleys where the Canadians now are fighting," reported one war correspondent.[34] Moreover, fighting had stiffened as the Allies closed on the German's "Winter Line."[35] The Germans now exercised a bitter scorched earth policy. Houses and buildings were burned, bridges blown, and wells poisoned. Also, booby-traps and mines were planted wherever possible. In addition, the Germans now fought to hold their positions.

The undaunted spirit of the "Royals" — Private D.B. MacDonald and his trusty Bren gun.

While the "Royals" waited in Duronia, events had moved on. General Mark Clark's 5th Army operating on the west coast of Italy due south of Rome had come to an ignominious halt. Although he had managed to break through the German defensive line at the Volturno River, terrible weather, horrendous terrain, and severe casualties teamed up against him. But a new plan was developed on 8 November. Clark would resume his offensive 10 days later, and the British General Harold Alexander would attempt another landing on the west coast just south of Rome at the same time. Key would be Monty's Eighth Army, which would also launch a new offensive on the Adriatic Coast on 20 November 1943. With Rome in his sights, General Montgomery planned to smash his way across the Sangro River, past the small towns of Ortona and Pescara and then hook westward across the Apennines to capture the Italian capital before the Americans.

As always in war, things did not go according to plan. After eight days of heavy fighting Monty's 5th Corps had crossed the Sangro and made a shallow bridgehead, however, its lead division, the 78th, was in dire need of a rest. Accordingly, on 30 November, the 1st Canadian Division was transferred to 5th Corps and fed into the battle. The Eighth Army now had to advance 50 kilometres along a coastal plain that narrowed to no more than 24 kilometres between the mountains and the sea.

On 1 December 1943, in a heavy rain, the Regiment embussed and moved to the front lines. Before departure, Montgomery promulgated a message to be read to all the troops. It stated: "[T]he Germans are in fact in the very condition in which we want them. WE WILL NOW HIT THE GERMANS A COLOSSAL CRACK."[36] These words would soon haunt Montgomery. Ironically, the latest offensive would initiate the bloodiest month of the entire Italian campaign.

The move foreshadowed the coming days. The dreary rain, razed countryside, blown bridges, and tedious traffic jams on the congested narrow Italian roads made the journey painfully slow for the troops. Just after midnight on 3 December, the Regiment had finally reached the Sangro River crossing. The Battalion debussed from their transports and began the march to their forward positions. Galloway described the crossing:

> The march across the river was terrible. Rough bridges had been thrown up and white tape was along the sides so we would not fall off. It was pitch dark. The river was not in flood but had a wide stony bed with several streams flowing in its watercourse. There was a bridge over every stream and rocky-muddy ground between. We zig-zagged our way across, stumbling and floundering, so that our single file looked like a writhing snake. When we finally got across "D" Coy took the wrong turning, and as a result, marched most of the night. The whole area is lousy with S-mines.[37]

The Battalion continued its advance to the front until 4 December when it was ordered to dig-in and occupy a defensive position just south of San Vito. Here it would await its turn to enter the battle.

Although Monty's Eighth Army had successfully punched through the Sangro River defences, the Germans decided to make their next stand a mere 14 kilometres to the north at the Moro River and at the town of Ortona just behind it. Moreover, realizing terrain dictated that the Allies approach over the narrow Adriatic plain, the Germans fed fresh reinforcements, including the 90th Panzer Grenadier Division and the reconstituted 90th Light Division of the Western Desert, into the fight.

By 5–6 December, the 1st Canadian Division, now under command of Lieutenant-General Chris Vokes,[38] was ready to cross the Moro River. Vokes planned to assault with three battalions conducting night silent attacks. He hoped that the absence of artillery support would allow them to surprise the Germans. He ordered the H&PER to cross the Moro on the right as a diversionary attack. He gave the Seaforth Highlanders of Canada the task of capturing San Leonardo in the centre, and the seizure of Villa Rogatti, approximately three kilometres upriver, was the task of the Princess Patricia's Canadian Light Infantry.

The PPCLI surprised the Germans and after a short but savage street fight captured the village. The H&PER and the Seaforths, however, were not as fortunate. Both made initial bridgeheads but were forced to withdraw in the face of fierce counterattacks. The following day the PPCLI (also known as "Patricias") fought off repeated counterattacks and the H&PER fought their own battle for survival when they re-crossed the Moro only to find themselves pinned down and subsequently cut to pieces.

So, by the end of 6 December 1943, the 1st Division had two tenuous bridgeheads across the Moro River. The "Patricias" had a reasonably firm grip of Villa Rogatti and the H&PER were barely holding on at the mouth of the River. Vokes decided to hand responsibility for Villa Rogatti over to the 8th Indian Division, while he concentrated on a more narrow front focused on San Leonardo and the Ortona-Orsogna cross-roads, which lay beyond. This would allow access to Ortona and the modern coastal Highway 16.

The next attack was a two-phased operation. It would open on 8 December with a two-pronged attack. The RCR would capture San Leonardo in a flanking attack launched through the H&PER position while the 48th Highlanders would cross the Moro River and seize La Torre just to the west. Once this was accomplished, using San Leonardo as a firm base, the 1st Armoured Brigade would push through to secure the Ortona-Orsogna crossroads.

The Regimental plan of attack was simple enough in theory. The four rifle companies would pass through one another while acquiring a succession of objectives and moving towards the town of San Leonardo.

NO SOFT UNDERBELLY

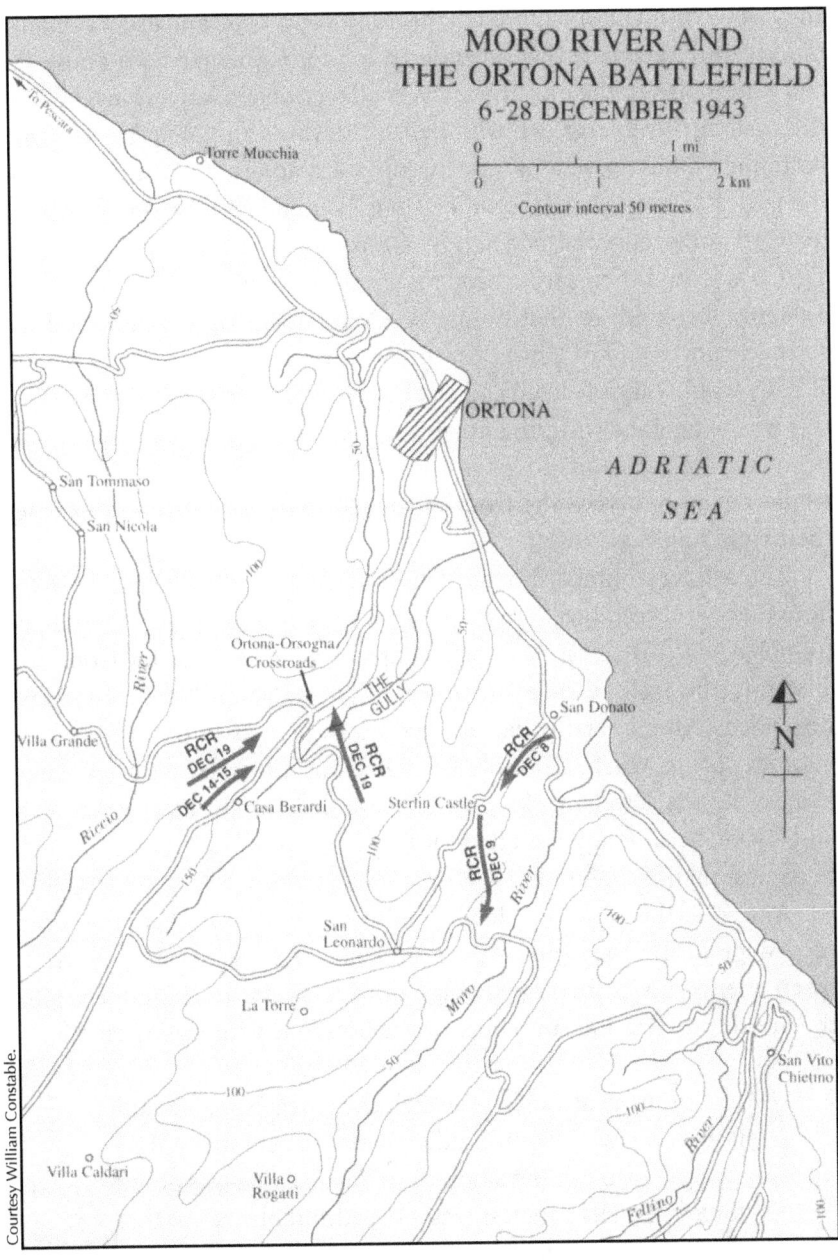

They would use a line of approach that followed a small and exceptionally muddy unnamed lane that meandered for approximately two-and-one-half kilometres to the objective. The road was on a relatively level plain that was thickly overgrown with dense vineyards and olive groves. The Battalion would move to a forming up point across the Moro River in the late afternoon on 8 December, then "A" and "B" Coys would move forward and secure the first series of report lines from which "C" and "D" Coys would then push through, continuing the advance to secure a deeper foothold. At that point, "A" Coy would leap frog forward to seize the north end of San Leonardo and cover the north roads, while "B" Coy would bound ahead and clear the southern part of the town. All this was to be done without tank or anti-tank support as vehicles could not yet cross the Moro River in this sector.[39] In addition, their attack would cut right across the front of the German positions and expose their right flank.

The artillery bombardment, delivered by 350 guns, began at 1630 hours on 8 December. "Then inferno broke loose [and] the earth trembled with cataclysmic shock," noted war artist Charles Comfort, "Instantly, the pastoral valley became a valley of death."[40] Major Mathers described, "After a terrific barrage laid down by masses of artillery and aircraft, during which the whole German front resembled a carpet being beaten, the attack went in about dark." He added, "Opposition was severe, and it soon became apparent that the Germans would defend the ground to the last man."[41]

And so, as the guns roared, "A" Coy "in the best World War I tradition" moved forward.[42] They had hardly begun when they were viciously stung by an enemy mortar barrage that annihilated an entire section. Despite the murderous fire and subsequent casualties, one witness described:

> "A" Company advanced through the barrage in splendid fashion. I saw Slim Liddell with his company HQ striding through the smoke and dust as if he was going for a stroll. His coolness was most admirable, as was that of his whole company.[43]

"B" Coy swung wide to avoid the hailstorm, however, in the growing dark and in the tangle of vineyards became temporarily lost. In the end, it took "A" Coy two hours to punch their way through, using ground and gaps in the enemy's artillery fire to reach their first report line. Meanwhile,

"B" Coy having realized their navigational error, backtracked and took up a defensive posture on "A" Coy's flank.

The CO then pushed "C" Coy through, along the winding road to the objective. The "Royals" quickly captured eight Panzer Grenadiers in a culvert. However, almost immediately the darkness erupted in flames as the enemy poured machine gun fire into the advancing troops. In concert, a German armoured car followed by a tank approached from San Leonardo. OC "C" Coy, quickly ordered his platoons to fall back, independently, onto "A" Coy's position where they were incorporated into the defence.

The situation was deteriorating. No sooner had "D" Coy crossed the start line then it came under a furious fire. With mounting casualties the troops took shelter where they could find it and the advance ground to a halt. Fortunately, its lead element, 16 Platoon, led by Lieutenant Mitch Sterlin, escaped the enemy's fire mission and was able to occupy and fortify a stone farmhouse located midway between "A" and "B" Coys. The Battalion now adopted a defensive position.

The RCR attack had failed. Ominously, as the Battalion maintained its tenuous hold on the north bank of the Moro River, the nerve-shattering rumble and ground-shaking vibrations of tanks soon assailed "A" Coy. The CO, Lieutenant-Colonel Spry, realizing his troops were in a vulnerable position with no tanks or large anti-tank weapons of their own, called in a protective wall of fire, almost on top of his forward positions, in an arc around his position. Luckily, the gunners did not let him down. Their extremely accurate and heavy concentration of high-explosive shells and shrapnel kept the prowling German tanks at bay. Moreover, the heavy concentration of fire so close to the RCR position duped the Germans into believing that the "Royals" had pulled back farther to the south, causing them to adjust their fire, which now fell safely beyond the Battalion's position.

The Battalion used the darkness to improve their situation and moved to a more defensible reverse slope position to reform into an "island of defence."[44] The CO left Sterlin and his platoon in the fortified house to hold the flank closest to the road. Before first light, brigade HQ sent word to the Battalion that a bridge over the Moro River had been completed during the night by engineers, therefore, tanks would be crossing at dawn. In addition, 2 CIB, had been ordered to attack San Leonardo. As a result, the brigade commander ordered The RCR to advance up to the town and link up and secure the right flank of 2 CIB.

"This came off in due course," recorded the War Diary, "the tks [tanks] advancing in full view, provided a very heartening sight."[45] However, looks can be deceiving. Having realized their error, the Germans now pounded the RCR position with such severity that the "Royals" now dubbed their position "Slaughterhouse Hill." Luckily, the Seaforth Highlanders attack on San Leonardo totally surprised the Germans and the Vancouver troops were able to grab a foothold. This diverted the focus of the German artillery. With the brief lapse in shelling, the CO ordered "B" and "C" Coys to advance to the town. "B" Coy took lead, while "C" Coy carried the wounded.

The lead companies had just departed from the RCR position when the German Panzer Grenadiers unleashed a violent attack that sliced between the two groups. "A" Coy and the Battalion command group were now in a fight for survival. Very quickly they were surrounded on three sides. "B" Coy, responsible for escorting the wounded being carried by "C" Coy, had no choice but to continue their move to San Leonardo. Once they reached the town, "C" Coy immediately evacuated the wounded down the road leading directly to the South bank of the Moro River. "B" Coy adopted a defensive position at the junction of the unnamed road and the main road leading from the Moro River to San Leonardo.

At the same time, "D" Coy, which had remained largely (less Sterlin's platoon) in the H&PER bridgehead, assisted the in place unit in fighting off repeated German counterattacks at that location. It seemed the Germans were intent on throwing the 1st Canadian Division back across the Moro River. The situation seemed desperate all over. "A" Coy and Spry's command group fought desperately. After approximately 20 minutes, with the noose tightening, the CO decided to withdraw to the safety of the south (friendly) side of the Moro River. He ordered "A" Coy to hold long enough to allow the command group to slip away, and then to withdraw by platoons back to the river. Lieutenant-Colonel Spry described the chaos:

> I was hitching on my equipment when suddenly the enemy was in amongst us and on three sides of us. "A" Company HQ was close by so I went across and said to the company commander that I was sorry to leave him in the lurch but the major part of the battalion was either on the move or had reached San Leonardo. The command group would therefore go with the remaining

carrier section and "A" company would stay, cover this move and then withdraw. The command group had to get out under fire and move down a terraced slope into the river valley. There was nothing dignified about this — we just ran down into the lee of the river bank.[46]

Once across the river, the CO organized the remnants of the Regiment and they dug in along the river bank. Unfortunately, in the ensuing chaos Sterlin's platoon as well as Lieutenant Jim Qualye's 8 Platoon, which was dug in beside the fortified stone house, now dubbed "Sterlin's Castle," did not receive the order to withdraw. As a result, they were left on their own and they quickly came under heavy attack. "Shell after shell after shell [fell] like an artillery conveyer belt," described Qualye, "Black plants bloomed everywhere in the field, spawned seeds of shrapnel and died."[47] Qualye quickly discovered they had been abandoned. He tried to contact Sterlin's platoon, but as he heard no answer thought they were dead, and he withdrew his platoon. This left 16 Platoon on their own to fend off the vicious German attacks. The fighting raged and the enemy actually reached the walls of the house but was thrown back. Remarkably, Sterlin's men held out and, as the cloak of night descended, they slipped away to join the Battalion.

"Sterlin's Castle" as it appears today.

Once the Battalion had consolidated, the CO planned to advance as originally ordered to San Leonardo. However, the brigade commander now ordered The RCR to cover the river and the gap between the town and the H&PER bridgehead from the south side of the Moro. As a result, "B" Coy was recalled, however, because of heavy fighting they remained in their trenches until the fire let up and then rejoined the Battalion the next morning at 0600 hours, 10 December. With the Battalion reunited, it began the laborious process of digging-in its new position. Twelve hours later, the "Royals," no doubt with many oaths, re-crossed the Moro River and began to dig-in once again, to take up their old position at "Slaughterhouse Hill" along the track between San Leonardo and the H&PER bridgehead.

Although fighting raged farther to the front, the Battalion remained in this position for several days. The pause was necessary. Regimental casualties in the three days of fighting amounted to 21 killed and 53 wounded or missing.[48]

During the pause, fighting still raged to their north. The situation was "still obscure" and the lead brigades (i.e., 2 CIB and 3 CIB) for the division were not making any progress. To the north of San Leonardo, running parallel and south of the all important Ortona-Orsogna crossroads was a natural barrier that had been respectfully dubbed the "Gully." It ran for five kilometres from the Adriatic shoreline to where it levelled out just before meeting the secondary road leading to San Leonardo. It varied in width between 200 and 300 metres and had an average depth of approximately 60 metres. Somewhat foolishly, the division commander decided to breach this obstacle directly. Unfortunately, that mistake cost countless lives as the Canadians were repeatedly repulsed as they conducted their frontal assaults.

On 14 December 1943, Brigadier Graham ordered The RCR to attack Ortona the next day. Lieutenant-Colonel Spry protested since "all points controlling the south and west approaches were still firmly held by the enemy."[49] Tentative planning continued but the order was cancelled. Two days later, on 16 December, Major-General Vokes had given up on trying to assault the "Gully" frontally and now ordered 1 CIB to seize the crossroads from the left flank.

The brigade commander now laid-out his plan. The two-phase attack would be supported by a tremendous amount of artillery — it was to be a set piece battle. The 48th Highlanders would start the operation by attacking northward from the western extremity of the Gully through

Casa Berardi as far as the road to Villa Grande. Once this had occurred, The RCR would punch east through Casa Berardi and seize the crossroads, thus, opening the way for the capture of Ortona and exploitation to the north beyond it.

The RCR, however, would not be commanded by their current CO for this operation. Brigadier Graham being severely ill with ulcers, appointed Dan Spry as the acting brigade commander, while Major W. Mathers became the acting CO. The Regiment moved out to an assembly area just outside San Leonardo on 17 December and that night orders were issued.

The next morning at 0800 hours the horizon shook as the guns roared in support of the Highlanders opening attack. The barrage was designed to hammer an area approximately 900 metres wide, for a distance of 2,000 metres. Every five minutes it would lift and advance about 100 metres with curtains of fire to seal off the flanks.[50] The shoot, which was pre-registered, was accurate and overwhelming. Not surprisingly, the 48th Highlanders' attack was successful and they seized their objective by 1030 hours. The guns now shifted to counter-battery fire.

At 1145 hours, the "Royals" launched their attack. The guns once again thundered in support. However, this time they did not pre-register and they simply fired from map coordinates, which were horrendously inaccurate.[51] Consequently, the barrage failed to suppress the enemy. The results were catastrophic. The attack on a two company front, "C" and "D" company leading, was met with such "intensive M.G. [machine gun], mortar and shell fire that the attack was completely broken up especially by M.G. fire from the many houses in the area and from across the gullies on left and right of the axis."[52] Captain V.G. Lewington explained:

> We came within 25 yards of the buildings and suddenly the whole shebang opened up. There were machine guns with a couple of Jerries each in every window. "C" Company were in the lead. "B" Company went to ground there and spread out. We were held up that night and suffered terrible casualties.[53]

Galloway, who was in reserve assessed, "Never before, either during the Sicilian or Italian campaign, had the Regiment run into such a death trap."[54] The leading elements of the Battalion, wrote Major Mathers, "were literally slaughtered where they moved."[55]

In the next hour confused fighting raged. The supporting tanks rumbled forward past the innumerable German-occupied houses that held up the forward companies as they attempted to clear them. This led to the tanks and infantry becoming separated. Adding to the confusion and friction of the battle, wireless communications between the infantry and armour also failed. The German paratroopers quickly seized on the opportunity. "The enemy MGs and snipers would allow the tks [tanks] to pass then come to life and engage the infantry."[56]

The remnants of "C" and "D" Coys fought on and "small bodies of infantry did get near to the objective but were forced to withdraw and in some cases these small bodies were cut off for the night and did not get back until the next day."[57] Major Mathers, himself wounded by a sniper in the arm, decided that to feed in his reserves would be futile so he halted the attack and consolidated his position. "Rather than throw 'good money after bad' we consolidated well within the enemy defences with what we had left," explained Mathers, "preparatory to laying on a new main effort."[58]

In essence, the assault had been smashed from the start. "C" and "D" Coys were virtually wiped out. Together they had suffered more than 100 casualties. The OCs and all six platoon commanders of the two rifle companies were all casualties, many actually killed. At the end of the attack "C" Coy was down to 15 men and was commanded by Corporal G.C. "Red" Forrest. "D" Coy was down to 14 men.

The Battalion, now commanded by Major I.A. Hodson, dug in and reorganized.[59] Its supporting tank squadron pulled back because of the onset of darkness but left one troop forward in support of the badly mauled Battalion. However, these tanks too were later withdrawn because of the close proximity of the enemy and the danger of ambush in the dark. The enemy continued to shell the Regiment heavily throughout and active patrolling by the "Royals" resulted in fire-fights throughout the night.

The next day, 19 December 1943, the Battalion was fed into the battle once again. This time the guns delivered a devastating bombardment. Supported once again by the tanks of the Three Rivers Regiment, the "Royals," with "B" Coy leading, renewed the attack at 1445 hours. With only three casualties "B" Coy quickly captured the objective. "A" Coy swiftly followed and took up a defensive posture by the railway crossing.

At this point, Major Hodson, the acting CO pushed off with the remainder of the unit, 4 Platoon leading. However, disaster struck once again. The Germans now retaliated with a heavy artillery shoot. In

A Canadian Sherman tank moves forward to support the fight at Ortona, December 1943.

addition, enemy who had remained hidden in a house also opened up on 4 Platoon as they advanced to the crossroads. The advance quickly dissolved into confusion and disorganization. Hodson decided to wait and move up after dark once the shelling lightened. "When darkness came there was still much indecision until some of the junior officers took the matter in hand and organized a move," recorded the War Diary. However, it added, "orders did not get down to some of the sections and a large number were left behind. These did not rejoin the Bn [Battalion] until next morning."[60] Once the Battalion was consolidated, Major Hodson, who was suffering from jaundice and malaria, turned unit command over to Major Strome Galloway.

The battle for the Ortona-Orsogna crossroads was over. The heavy cost in lives demonstrated its importance. Once taken, the lower "Gully" was indefensible and the enemy quickly melted away. That same day, 19 December, the Carleton and York Regiment finally broke through the impregnable "Gully" and mopped up to the outskirts of Ortona. Around midday the next day, the Loyal Edmonton Regiment passed through the Regiment on their way to Ortona.

For the Battalion, the battle for the crossroads had been horrendous. In all, it cost the Regiment 34 killed, 54 wounded, and 24 missing.[61] The "Royals" remained in position at the crossroads and conducted patrols. On 21 December, the acting brigade commander, Dan Spry, visited his former, and now decimated unit and shared with them a toast to the Regiment with what has now become the "Ortona Toast" — a glass of issue rum, brown sugar, and water.[62]

At this point, Allied commanders thought that the Germans would fall back onto their next defensive line at the Arielli River. No-one thought the enemy would fight for Ortona. They were sadly mistaken. Hitler ordered his troops to stand and fight. As a result, the Canadian infantrymen found themselves in a deadly battle. Ortona became a 2 CIB objective and the struggle became slow, tedious, and deadly. It became a battle of wills. The Germans defended each house tenaciously — forcing the Canadians to root them out at great risk and cost of life. "You'd clear an area in the daytime and they'd return by night," stated an exasperated Captain J.F. McLean, "It was not only a house-by-house battle but often a room-by-room."[63] In one day, the Loyal Edmonton Regiment advanced only 200 metres — fighting virtually for every inch of terrain in the town.

On 23 December, 1 CIB was thrown into the battle. Vokes ordered them to conduct a sweeping left hook around Ortona, which would threaten the rear of the German paratroopers holding the town. The brigade plan was for the three infantry battalions to attack in succession supported by tanks from the 11th Canadian Armoured (Ontario) Regiment in an attempt to clear the Germans from the vital high ground due west and north of Ortona, thereby cutting off the town's defenders, and hopefully force them to withdraw. This attack would also severe their supply line to Pescara. Spry, the acting brigade commander ordered the H&PER to lead the attack and advance approximately 1,000 metres and seize a key ridgeline to the north of the Tollo Road. At this point, the 48th Highlanders would push through and capture the ridge's highest point which dominated the villages of San Nicola and San Tommaso. The final phase, entailed the severely under strength RCR passing through and advancing cross-country to the coast.

The first phase of the attack was successful despite the heavy mud and tangled vineyards. However, the H&PER was forced to doggedly fight to reach and hold the ridge. The 48th Highlanders also enjoyed success after a daring and exceptionally risky attack was undertaken on a very cold, rainy dark night. Without the benefit of reconnaissance, visibility, or fire support, the Highlanders stealthily followed a narrow footpath to the top of the ridge. In the morning, they discovered they had seized their objective without firing a shot. But, the morning also brought an angry response by the Germans. They now lashed out at the two islands of Canadians planted in their midst.

It was into this hornet's nest that the "Royals" found themselves being sent. Both positions were under constant assault through shelling, infiltration attempts, and concerted counterattacks. The brigade now expected The RCR to move through both besieged positions, through contested ground, in broad daylight, with no artillery preparation, to advance to the coastal highway. The muddy ground made movement extremely difficult for the attackers. Conversely, the thick tangled vineyards provided the enemy with excellent concealment.

At first light on 24 December, the Regiment arrived in the H&PER position. One witness described the sight. "In the rain-drenched darkness of that night, the RCR moved forward," wrote Farley Mowat, a young subaltern. "Those who saw that long snake-line of men, soaked to the skin, drugged by fatigue, shorn of all desires save to drop and lie in oblivion in the yellow mud, saw the essence of what the Battle of the Bulge [salient held by H&PER] meant to all the infantry."[64] As the acting CO and his lead company commander looked over the ground they agreed on the futility of the advance — and this was just to get to their jump off position in the 48th Highlander location. However, brigade HQ had confirmed the order. As a result, "A" Coy set out in mid-morning and immediately came under a horrific barrage of mortar and artillery fire. The advance ground to a halt immediately.

Strome Galloway, the acting CO, then decided to wait until darkness before committing "B" Coy. That night in an icy drizzle another attempt was made to move forward. The mud stuck like glue and the thick vineyards, laced with stabilizing wires, were virtually impenetrable, forcing soldiers to claw and crawl their way forward. As the soldiers finally exited the vineyard they immediately came under intense machine gun fire. Unable to effectively control the battle because of the pitch dark and the morass he found himself in, Captain Tom Burdett, the acting OC, ordered a withdrawal.

With the latest failure, Spry now dropped his original plan. Instead, he ordered his former Battalion to force open a corridor between the H&PER and the 48th Highlanders. At first light on Christmas Day, "A" Coy once again stepped off and almost immediately was hammered with a devastating barrage and machine gun fire that added 20 more casualties to the 15 they had suffered the day before. Nonetheless, this time they did not fall back. Galloway pushed "B" Coy into the fray. He ordered them to outflank the machine guns that were interfering with the advance. Galloway also ordered "C" Coy to push through. As a result, although still almost a kilometre away from the 48th Highlanders, by late afternoon The RCR had pushed their perimeter out several hundred metres. They now adopted a defensive position for the night. That night a small patrol leading 60 soldiers from the Saskatchewan Light Infantry delivered rations, radio batteries, and ammunition to the beleaguered Highlanders.

As the night wore on, 1 CIB found itself straddling the ridge with three battalions tenuously linked through patrols along a narrow path. Fighting still raged as the Germans continually attempted to infiltrate the battalion perimeters. In addition, snipers, machine guns, mortars, and artillery kept up a constant harassing fire. Against this, the besieged battalions fought back and slowly began to clear the Germans from the ridge.

And then it was over. "Finally," wrote a relieved Galloway, "the enemy melted away."[65] On 28 December 1943, after suffering and inflicting grievous casualties the Germans gave up Ortona.[66] By the next day the enemy had broken contact along the entire front and was taking up new defensive positions along the Arielli River. On 30 December 1943, the Regiment moved back to positions along the Villa Grande road. It had earned a brief respite. Of the approximately 756 all ranks who had landed at Pachino almost five months prior, over 550 of these "originals" had become casualties or prisoners of war. As one veteran of the campaign observed, "It [Italy] was no soft underbelly."[67]

6
The Final Stretch: Collapsing the Third Reich

The battle for the Moro River and Ortona had drained the 1st Canadian Division and the Regiment had taken its fair share of casualties. Depleted, exhausted, and facing the harsh conditions of the Italian winter, the "Royals" braced themselves for their next task. Occupying defensive positions in the aftermath of the gruelling Ortona battle, the superstitious were somewhat unnerved when the year 1944 was ushered in by a furious Adriatic storm that brought heavy rains and colossal winds. This seemed a bad omen of what lay ahead.

The Regiment was dug in at a bivouac area just north of the Villa Grande-Ortona/Orsogna crossroads. It remained there, in relative peace conducting training, until late on 13 January when it relieved the 5th Royal West Kents in the San Nicola area. This move heralded the beginning of another period of suffering for the Regiment. "None [of the experiences of the Regiment] demanded a higher degree of courage, nor imposed greater hardship," bemoaned Major Strome Galloway, "than the four 'quiet' months spent facing the Arielli River."[1]

It was akin to a wicked time warp that hurtled the Regiment back in time to the horrors of trench warfare in the First World War. One Canadian historian described the countryside as being filled with the "desolation of shattered farmhouses and villas, burnt haystacks and shell-pocked fields, sodden with the winter rains and befouled with unburied German dead and a litter of equipment, shattered cannon, burned-out tanks and vehicles."[2] During a visit to the Regiment, Lieutenant-General

Harry Crerar, the new Canadian Corps Commander gasped, "Its just like Passchendale, just like Passchendale."[3]

Peter Stursberg, a Canadian Broadcasting Corporation (CBC) journalist, sent a similar message back home to Canadians. He reported that the mud was much like France in the last war. The soldiers, he described, "were in mud up to their knees, sometimes up to their waist." He added that they were also in "wet clothes for days."[4] The rain and mud also had a dramatic impact on mobility in the RCR area of operations. Inconsequential streams became insurmountable. Gullies became impassible because of "mud and the fast flowing stream which had swollen to proportions 20 feet wide in some places."[5]

For the RCR, the war seemed to bog down and the "Royals" settled in to a life of trench warfare. But it was not as sophisticated as that experienced by their Regimental brethren more than 30 years prior. A reporter noted that there was no continuous trench line, just forward positions and machine gun posts.[6] "Two ramshackle barricades of unconnected slit trenches and fortified farmhouses," said Galloway, represented the trench lines, "the gaps between them sometimes filled with primitive barbed wire entanglements, stretched across the torn vineyards and sodden meadows."[7] He observed, "that in this age of dispersion the soldiers in their isolated slit trenches must have found it more lonely, more terrifying … than their predecessors who huddled together in the trenches of France and Flanders."[8]

The broad gully between the two barriers was no man's land. And, control of this barren terrain would vex the soldiers of the Regiment. Lieutenant-General Crerar, harkening back to the historical legacy and reputation of Canadian soldiers as daring patrollers and raiders, directed that an active patrolling regime be implemented. Crerar decided that the he would own this desolate piece of ground that separated the Canadians and Germans. However, his decision proved hugely unpopular and costly in lives. "It's the funniest feeling going," confided Lieutenant Nelson Verge, "it's an eerie feeling going out into no-man's land not knowing whether you'll come back." He confided, "You feel the whole German army is against you [and] you're on edge all the time."[9]

Despite the trepidation and sense of futility, the patrol policy was strictly adhered to. "As soon as darkness fell," testified the War Diary, "our patrols became active."[10] Strome Galloway criticized:

> There was endless, and to most of us meaningless, patrol activity every night. In three months our battalion

carried out sixty-four patrols. The damage done to the enemy, if any, was minimal. The information gained was not worth the effort. But we were told that we must "dominate no man's land."[11]

He was not alone. Another veteran officer from the Loyal Edmonton Regiment similarly disparaged Crerar's policy. "How many good men," he lamented, "were wasted in fruitless patrolling in that dark close country, I would not hazard a guess." He added, "I do know that most of the patrolling was worthless, morale destroying and wasteful of manpower."[12] Galloway assessed, "It was largely a winter of endless patrolling, a costly and futile pastime."[13]

The conditions that prevailed during that trying winter period spoke volumes of the character and resilience of the "Royals" that held the front lines. The CO would later write:

> It was the platoon and section leaders — and above all the riflemen — who were the heroes of this period. Living in mud and water — under incessant heavy fire from every type of weapon — dog-tired — unable to light a fire to cook or even get dry — always on the alert for infiltrating enemy patrols — on patrol themselves night after night — never knowing for sure in the darkness that the chap to whom they whispered in the night was not a Hun; sometimes it was: this was their life.[14]

In January there were only two major attacks mounted on the Adriatic front. The newly arrived 11 CIB of the 5th Canadian Armoured Division passed through the RCR lines on 17 January to attempt to breach the Arielli River. Their attack failed at great cost in human life. Two weeks later, the H&PER were ordered to attack towards Tollo. Once again the attempt faltered with heavy casualties.[15] And so for most of January and February both sides fell into a routine of harassing artillery and sniper fire by day and an active patrolling agenda at night where both sides probed each others defences and attempted to dominate the terrain in no man's land. Some relief final came on the night of 10 February, when the Carleton and York Regiment relieved the RCR in San Nicola (and "B" Coy in San Tomasso). The "Royals" then deployed to a rest area south of San Vito where they undertook a period of rest, training and fatigue duties.

The relatively short rest period ended on 27 February, when the Regiment did a daylight relief in place with the Seaforth Highlanders and took over the front-line positions in front of Ortona. Although the actual front was approximately three kilometres from the seaport, life in Ortona "continued as if the war was a 100 miles away."[16] The proximity to the town allowed the "Royals" to enter the city for "eight hours of eating, sleeping, bathing and amusement."[17] As such life remained tolerable. The Regiment used this period to bring itself up to strength by absorbing reinforcements and taking care of the sick and wounded.

Throughout the months of March and April the "Royals" rotated in and out of the line as the stalemate continued. When out of the line maintenance and training were conducted in addition to the normal security posture. Continuous training was considered especially important. For instance, the GOC 1st Canadian Division ordered that nine days of training be carried out by all infantry battalions in the month of January alone. In February an entire week was dedicated solely for the purpose of "carrying out individual, section and platoon training, and re-organization of section and platoon teams."[18] Training included lessons learned, tank infantry cooperation, NCO courses, weapons (e.g., PIAT and grenade) training, fieldcraft, first aid, as well as close order drill. Drill periods were deemed important for "'smarting up' of personnel" as well as for "instilling discipline and a desire to gain an outward appearance of Regimental and personal pride as individual soldiers, and as soldiers of The Royal Canadian Regiment." The overall rationale for a robust training regime, despite the ongoing combat, was "to bring the Regiment back to the high standard of efficiency which has been seriously threatened by the heavy losses and intake of new personnel."[19]

When manning the front line positions, the "Royals," like the Germans, carried on a campaign of harassment that consisted of shelling and sniping by day and aggressive patrolling at night. Although the ceaseless hostile actions by both sides inflicted mutual casualties, little actually changed on the ground. "One day was the same as the next," lamented Major Galloway, "only worse perhaps, for it added its extra weight to the already heavy burden of discomfort and lack of achievement."[20] In this way, the wet and cold winter in Italy dragged on.

Finally, by the end of April the Regiment was pulled from the stagnant front and deployed west towards the Monte Cassino theatre of operations. There seemed to be electricity in the air. The move was cloaked in security as badges, patches, and vehicle markings were removed. Once relieved from its front line position on the Arielli Front by the Gurkhas on 21 April 1944, the "Royals" marched to Ortona, where they loaded into transport trucks and moved off to a brigade assembly area. The next morning, in a heavy rain, the trucks ploughed their way through muddy access routes to the main road. The brigade convoy then headed west driving all day until they reached the proximity of Termoli where the convoy halted on the road for the night. The next day, the Regiment arrived at its destination — a faceless, nameless track of woods near Oratino.

The Battalion now undertook a period of training in preparation for upcoming operations. For some, the first activity could be considered a distinct regimental quiff and a desire to live up to its reputation as a "spit and polish regiment" — despite the surroundings and combat operations — foot drill and saluting was conducted. Of note, either the sense of humour or the accuracy of the diarist of the Regimental War Diary comes into question. The training, he wrote, "consisted generally saluting drill and foot drill and was carried out with great enthusiasm by all concerned."[21] For those who have served the Colours, nothing more need be said!

Other than the occasional drill parade, training focused on staples such as physical conditioning, platoon attacks and patrolling, as well as lectures on mountain warfare. On 30 April the Battalion moved to a new training area near Foggia. Here the rifle companies practiced marrying-up drills and set-piece attacks with tank crews from "C" Squadron, 142nd Royal Tank Regiment (Suffolk Tanks).

On 4 May, the "Royals" moved again finally arriving at a bivouac and training site near the Volturno River. The training regime began to look more like rehearsals than continuation training. On 6 May, the RCR troops practiced construction, control, and movement of the Mark III assault boat under the watchful eye of engineer instructors. Two days later the Regiment conducted a battalion level night assault river crossing exercise. The following night a brigade level assault crossing exercise, entitled "Squile Moses" was conducted. Both exercises were extremely successfully and the Regiment was given the following day, 11 May, as a rest day. At the time, the "Royals" were not aware what tempest was brewing.

Although the momentum of the war had shifted against the Germans as early as 1942, they still proved to be a ferocious and very capable enemy. But the Allies were positioning themselves for the next big push. On the Eastern Front, a seemingly bottomless Soviet military machine was relentlessly pushing the Germans back towards their frontiers. In

England, the Allies were preparing to return to the continent and release Hitler's stranglehold on Occupied Europe. Similarly, plans to end the stalemate in Italy were in play. General Alexander, who was now GOC 15th Army Group, intended to explode up the Liri Valley by punching through the Gustav and Hitler Line defences with the American Fifth Army and the British Eighth Army. This effort was to be coordinated with a break-out from the hitherto disappointing Anzio beachhead in the rear of the German lines,[22] as well as with a concentration of Allied air power.

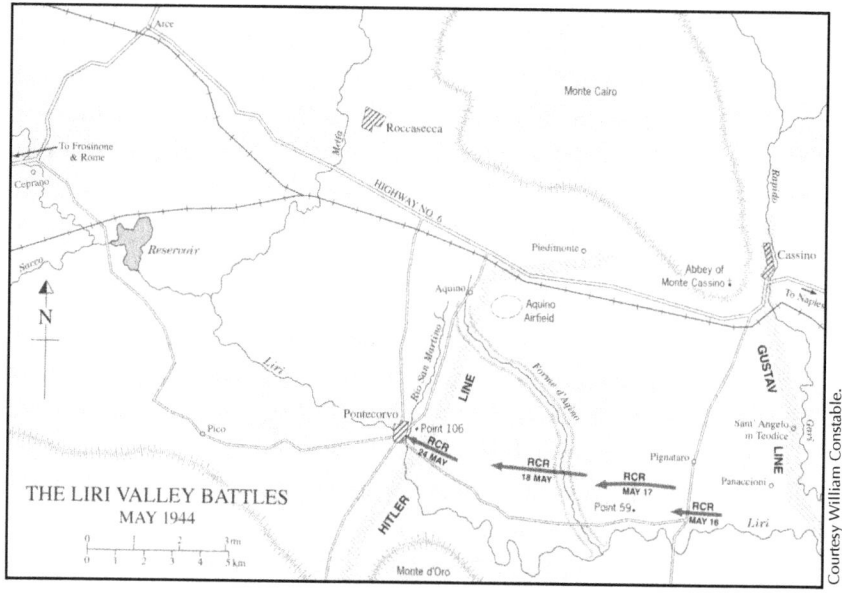

THE LIRI VALLEY BATTLES
MAY 1944

Despite the overwhelming force to be applied, the task was imposing. The Gustav Line, behind which the Germans braced for the assault, was formidable. The Germans had made expert use of the geographical features to anchor their in-depth defence. To this advantageous ground they added minefields several hundred metres deep, as well as concrete and steel pillboxes and machine-gun emplacements. In addition, anti-tank ditches were dug and anti-mobility obstacles and barriers erected. Further strengthing their defensive capability, Mark III and IV tank turrets, with their extremely deadly 75 mm guns, were embedded in concrete to assist with the destruction of Allied armoured vehicles and personnel.

The battle for the Gustav Line commenced at 2300 hours, on 11 May 1944. The Allied assessment was that the best chance of piercing the

Gustav Line and breaking the deadlock that had paralyzed the Allied advance up the Italian boot all winter lay in attacking the western end of the line where the southward flowing Liri River cut through the defensive belt before joining the Rapido River (and then becoming the Garigliano River). However, the imposing fortress of Monte Cassino, which dominated the mouth of the Liri Valley, continued to thwart the Allied drive to Rome.

The Allied breach on the first day of battle was tenuous. The Germans, though surprised, recovered quickly. As a result, only a small bridgehead across the swift Gari River was made. However, over the next two days it was slowly expanded. Elsewhere, along the Gustav Line, Algerian and Moroccan divisions began to make progress forcing the Germans on 16 May to pull back to the Hitler Line. That evening a jubilant General Alexander reported to his seniors in London, "We can now claim that we have definitely broken the Gustav Line."[23] Two days later, Polish troops captured the seemingly impregnable Monte Cassino Monastery, which had been the hinge of the enemy's defensive system, and the German position crumbled.

Initially, the RCR as part of the 1st Canadian Corps were held back as the Eighth Army Reserve. However, Alexander now wanted to exploit and chase the retreating Germans with the hope that they could bounce the Hitler Line before the enemy had a chance to regroup. Significantly, the Germans had no fresh troops with which to garrison the Hitler Line between Aquino and Pontecorvo. Alexander wished to bring the Germans to battle and destroy them, while exerting enough pressure on the flanks of the Hitler Line to make them abandon their position.[24] Alexander realized that a frontal assault against prepared positions, even against a weakened enemy, would be costly in men and equipment. With these objectives in mind, he now activated the Canadian Corps.

But, as always, the Germans had other plans. Once again they employed skilful rearguard actions to slow down the Allied onslaught. The resistance came from groups, company-sized and smaller, who were out of contact with their parent units but had orders to prevent the Allied advance catching the withdrawing German forces at any cost. The enemy fought almost entirely a small arms battle. What support they had came from "a handful of self-propelled 7.5 cm guns, one or two batteries of 105 mm guns and a few Nebelwerfers falling back on their dumps."[25]

On 14 May 1944, the 1st Canadian Division was ordered to advance and by noon the next day, its lead brigade, 1 CIB, was poised to join

Lieutenant W. Smith and Sergeant F.G. White take a moment to relax after the breaching the Hitler Line and seizing Pontecorvo, 24 May 1944.

the fight. On the night of 15 May, Lieutenant-Colonel Mathers received his orders for the next day's activities. The CO issued his orders at 0500 hours for an attack that would begin two hours later. In essence, the Battalion was to attack west along the road that ran parallel to the Liri River towards the Hitler Line. "We were to start moving," explained G.K. Wright, "and to keep moving until we made contact with the enemy or some beneficent commander kindly allowed us to stop for a rest which seemed unlikely."[26]

The attack commenced on a one company frontage with "D" Coy leading, followed by "B" Coy, "A" Coy, Tactical HQ, and "C" Coy. The advance started well enough. Wright described, "No enemy about, nothing particular to worry about except mines and the pernickety officers who kept telling us not to bunch together." He added, "the small packs seemed heavy, and the Bren gun and 2-in. [inch] Mortar numbers wondered why they had to carry so much ammunition."[27]

However, at 1030 hours, as the lead platoon descended a gentle slope leading to the foot of a large hill known as "Point 59" they came under heavy machine gun and mortar fire. The platoon commander, Lieutenant Leonard Miles attempted a left flanking but "they found the Boche [Germans] much too strong and were forced to come to a halt suffering six casualties."[28] The lead company commander dispatched another platoon to attempt a right flanking but they too were quickly pinned down by heavy fire. When his third platoon became bogged down after being ordered to attempt a deeper flanking the realization that Point 59 was heavily defended finally sank in.

With his lead company stalled and trapped in open ground, the CO decided to attack Point 59 with the entire Battalion. "B" Coy was immediately deployed to the right flank, while "A" Coy moved forward to the rear of "D" Coy. The companies immediately dug in and consolidated their positions with mortars and anti-tank guns in support. At 1300 hours a conference was held at Tactical HQ where a plan was developed.

Four hours later the attack was unleashed. "The Company had a look at their task, ground their teeth audibly, sighed and prepared for the worst," revealed one veteran.[29] "A" Company supported by three troops of the Suffolk Tank Regiment advanced across the open ground as tanks in support cloaked the oval shaped hill in smoke. "The attack went in with great dash and determination," noted the War Diary.[30] But as the tanks and "Royals" attacked up the hill they absorbed the full fury of the enemy's fire, which began to take its toll. As the lead elements clambered to the top of the formidable position they found it "occupied by objecting Germans, who promptly and thoughtlessly began throwing grenades and firing everything they had."[31]

One of the attacking platoons became disorientated and assaulted the wrong position, becoming engaged with enemy on a hill to the right of the intended objective. Their brief engagement netted them 60 prisoners. They quickly disengaged and reoriented themselves to attack their intended target while a platoon from "D" Coy moved forward and silenced the position that had caused the problem and led the assaulting platoon from "A" Coy astray.

The fighting on Point 59 was intense and "A" Coy suffered heavy casualties. Lance-Corporal R.E. Deadman found himself in a duel with a self-propelled gun and he fired his 2-inch mortar from the hip and knocked it out.³² "C" Coy attempted to reinforce "A" Coy, but heavy machine gun and mortar fire cut short their advance. Although on the objective, with mounting casualties and no easing of the enemy's intensity of fire, the CO finally ordered a withdrawal. The "Royals" had suffered 11 dead and 20 wounded in the attack.³³

The Regiment dug in below the feature and sent out patrols to the front and flanks. The following morning the 48th Highlanders attacked Point 59 at first light only to find it abandoned. The costly attack by the RCR the day prior had forced the Germans to withdraw during the night. As a result, the 48th continued the advance towards the Hitler Line following the banks of the Liri River.

The Hitler Line, although under construction for approximately five months was not yet completed. However, much like the Gustav Line, it was a formidable obstacle. Concrete and steel pillboxes were built in large numbers and the position extended to a depth of approximately 700 metres. Tank ditches had been dug across all favourable approaches and thorough mining and wiring of these obstacles made clearing lanes under fire extremely hazardous. Adding to the obstacle were belts of anti-tank and anti-personnel mines, as well as barbed-wire 20 metres deep.

The Hitler Line also included fortification types not previously encountered. Among these were the turrets of Mark V "Panther" tanks in concrete emplacements. As well, mobile and heavily armoured pillboxes that were sunk almost flush with the ground and virtually impervious to anything but a direct hit from anti-tank fire or heavy artillery fire were spread throughout the line. Finally, a series of prefabricated three-inch thick, armour-plated dugouts were buried up to 20 feet under ground to serve as nodal points for machine gun emplacements that were connected by concrete tunnels.

There was one lucky break for the Allies. The defences were built during the late fall and winter when there were no crops on the ground. The spring planting was now in progress and the plants now blinded many of the strongest emplacements and with the attack ready to be launched, the Germans had little time to clear fields of fire.³⁴

The Regiment resumed the advance at 1300 hours, 16 May 1944, moving in leap-frog fashion, company by company, until it linked up with the left flank of the 48th Highlanders. The "Royals" maintained this position until further orders were given. Throughout the late afternoon "A" Coy was subjected to heavy sniping, and later that night under cover of darkness a strong enemy force attempted to infiltrate through "C" Coy lines but were successfully repulsed. At 2300 hours, Luftwaffe bombers attacked the rear of the Battalion area and the lines of communications.

After a most unsettling night, the RCR was again ordered to advance and seize Massa Termine, which was holding up the advance of the H&PER. However, as the Battalion leap-frogged its companies forward the fluidity of the situation necessitated change. At 2330 hours on 18 May 1944, brigade HQ ordered the RCR to take up a position between the 48th Highlanders and the H&PER, who by this time had advanced onto the forward defensive lines of the Hitler Line just forward of the town of Pontecorvo — the western pivot of the line.

The next several days were used to prepare for the upcoming battle. The overall plan called for the 1st Canadian Division to punch through the enemy defences. 1 CIB was to seize Point 106, which was an enemy strong point located on a high feature that commanded the approaches to Pontecorvo. At the same time, the main effort, a more concentrated attack conducted by 2 and 3 CIBs was to be hurled at the centre of the line roughly between Pontecorvo and Aquino on Highway 6.

On 22 May, Major-General Chris Vokes convinced his corps commander, Lieutenant-General E.L.M. "Tommy" Burns, that a one brigade frontage attack to capture Point 106 and Pontecorvo may be enough to unhinge the Hitler Line. The German garrison in this sector was comprised of personnel of a reinforcement battalion who did not seem too willing to fight, leading Vokes and Burns to believe that the line might be turned from this flank by an attack directed northwards on the high ground at Point 106. If the enemy was as weak and disorganized as they believed, the Canadians could roll up the Hitler Line from Pontecorvo northwards by creating a breach that could be widened and exploited.[35]

Burns decided it would be worth a try. Subsequently, the entirety of the German position was subjected to a vicious aerial and artillery bombardment. "It was a terrible onslaught," remembered one witness. "What a confidence inspiring sight to see and hear the shells fall and the dive-bombers peel off one after another over the smoke and dust of Pontecorvo," he described, "to put a trembling fear into every German and left [sic] him with very little fighting spirit." But, he continued, "that is with the exception of the Germans charged with the defense of their own forward defended localities which were closest to our lines and escaped the main bombardment."[36] His observation would be correct.

At 1030 hours, on 22 May, with little preparation the 48th Highlanders, supported by "C" Squadron of the Suffolk Tank Regiment, were launched against the Hitler Line. As part of the plan, the RCR were to move up and occupy the 48th Highlander pre-attack position and subsequently push forward through the bridgehead established by the Highlanders and attack and capture Point 106. The first phase was accomplished with little trouble. However, the plan quickly ground to a halt.

The 48th Highlanders fought their way onto their objective but at great cost. After a hard fight, they were forced to halt because of heavy enemy resistance and the failure of the Suffolk tanks to reach them because of mines and German anti-tank guns. "C" Squadron lost 10 tanks in the process of trying to force their way forward. The Highlanders were now in a tenuous position. Alone, they now held a bridgehead approximately 600 metres wide and 400 metres deep. Moreover, they were surrounded by the enemy on three sides. "Very heavy Nebelwerfer and Arty fire was being brought down on the Bn [48th Highlanders] which was also badly enfiladed by small arms fire from the ridge to their right front (Pt 106)," captured an official report.[37]

Vokes gambit had failed and he launched the other brigades the following morning. Meanwhile, 1 CIB continued its efforts to capture Point 106 and Pontecorvo. On the morning of 23 May, the 48th Highlanders with the assistance of a fresh squadron of tanks, which were able to cross the open ground behind a massive smoke screen, pushed forward with some success. The fight was extremely bitter and the Highlanders were finally stopped half way up the hill. By 1200 hours, "D" Coy, the RCR, was able to quickly occupy a position in the bridgehead ready to push through the Highlanders on command. A little over two hours later "B" Coy took up a position to the right of "D" Coy. At 1400 hours, the H&PER launched an attack from the right flank, supported by the two RCR companies and the Highlanders. After bitter hand-to-hand to fighting the H&PER finally captured Point 106.

With the renewed onslaught German resistance began to falter. In addition, the 2nd and 3rd Canadian Infantry Brigades launched their attacks against the flanks of the Hitler Line and by end of the day, 2 CIB elements were attacking north of Pontecorvo. To add to the pressure, that morning the Americans had also begun their break-out from the Anzio beachhead. Not surprisingly, the War Diary recorded that "things had become more or less fluid"[38] and "the Hun seemed to have weakened."[39]

As a result, at 1830 hours, Lieutenant-Colonel Mathers pushed his RCR scout platoon forward to recce the approaches to Pontecorvo. As the day's light began to fade the scouts reached a prominent feature, from which they could the fleeing Germans silhouetted against the sky. Subsequently, the scouts reported the position clear and "A" Coy moved onto the objective and consolidated at 0100 hours the next morning. This now positioned the Regiment to strike into the town.

The scout platoon's work, however, was not done. They continued towards Pontecorvo on an all night patrol, capturing and killing many enemy in the process. At first light, 24 May, the scout platoon and "C" Coy entered the town. At 0630 hours, Lieutenant W. Rich, the scout platoon commander climbed into the local church tower and rang the bell to announce that Pontecorvo was secure. The remainder of the day was spent clearing the shattered and all but deserted town. "By mid-morning," explained Galloway, "prisoners were streaming in by the dozen, having been rooted out of numerous buildings and a cemetery without a fight."[40] In the end, approximately 70 prisoners were captured.

The "Royals" were now given a short period to rest and conduct maintenance. However, it did not last long. On 31 May, the Battalion spearheaded the 1st Canadian Division advance in pursuit of the withdrawing enemy. As the "Royals" had come to expect, the Germans remained a fearsome enemy, expertly deploying rearguards and artillery bombardments to delay the Allied advance. "The enemy did not withdraw until the last moment laying mines as he went and demolishing bridges," noted the War Diary.[41] "The Germans," recalled George Burrows, "were a tough enemy."[42] Nonetheless, the Regiment swept away the opposition before it and continued the pursuit.

Rome was liberated by Allied forces the next day and the Regiment was halted in the town of Anagni for rest and refit. On 9 June the RCR moved to a training area near Piedmonte. The entire 1st Canadian Division was now absorbed in training in preparation for the next push. Tank/infantry cooperation, specifically the passage of information over the armoured radio network and target indication, were the major issues to be worked out. The breaching of minefields was also stressed. After two-months, the respite came to an end.

As the Canadians trained, the Germans continued to fight a skilled delaying action. By mid-August the enemy occupied their new defensive position in the Apennine mountains, approximately 190 kilometres north of Rome, called the Gothic Line (or Pisa-Rimini Line), which stretched diagonally across Italy. On the west coast it was anchored near Pisa and on the east coast south of Rimini. It was here, on the Adriatic

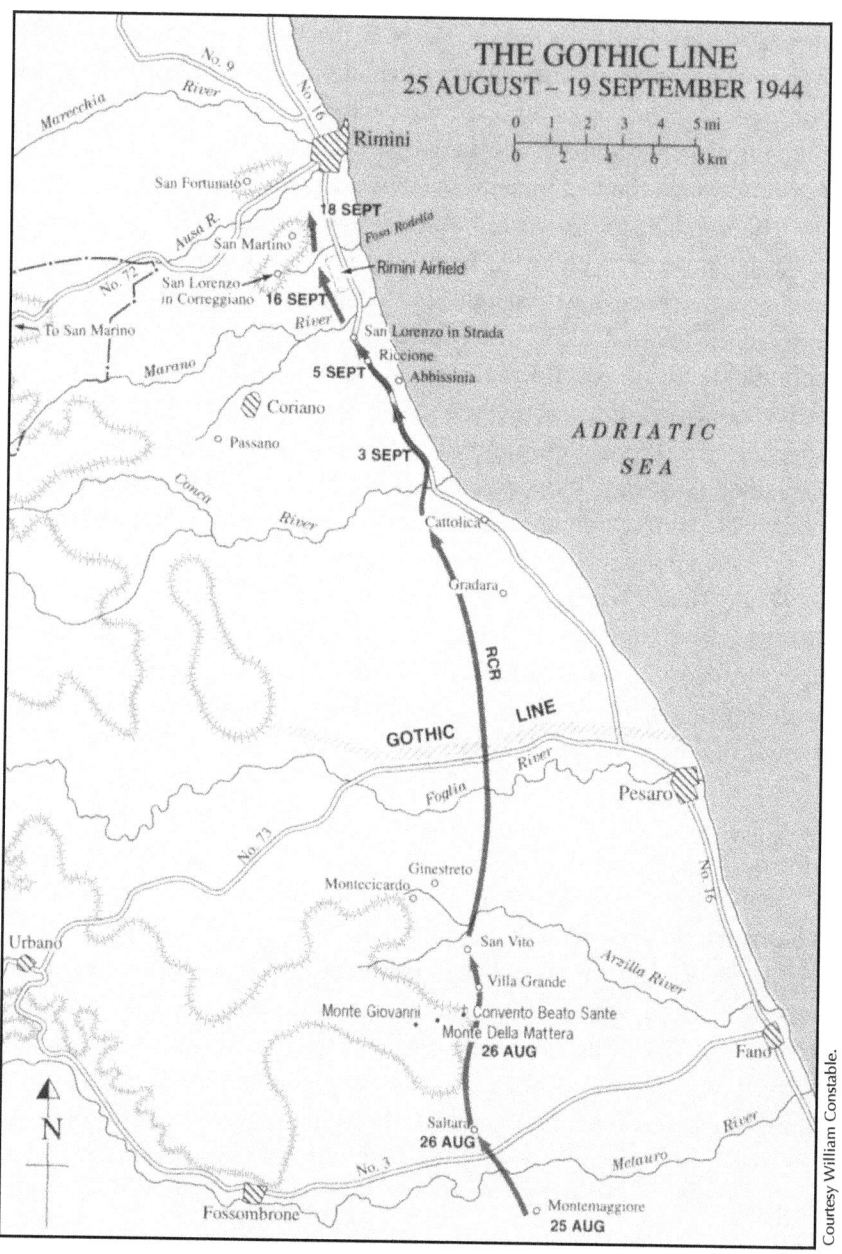

coast, that the Canadian Corps was deployed to crack the east end of the Gothic Line and open the path to Rimini and the Po Valley.

The 1st Canadian Division deployed to Florence on 5 August 1944. The brief stay in the open city was anything but peaceful. The German paratroopers facing the "Royals" engaged them with mortars and sniper fire with some success. "The enemy had his MMGs [medium machine guns] on fixed lines firing across the river and down the streets on our side and periodically the streets were swept by this MG fire," noted the War Diary.[43]

However, the elements of the civilian population also represented a threat. On 8 August 1944, "A" Coy with the support of local partisans cleared the entire company area of civilians. Approximately 150 men and women were found in possession of firearms which "included rifles, grenades, pistols, shotguns, and Schmeisers [submachine guns], and some women were found to be carrying grenades in their purses in lieu of vanity cases."[44] The subject individuals were arrested and "most of these elements were later found to be hostile to the Allies."[45]

Four days after arriving, the Canadians once again moved in secrecy to prepare for their next major offensive. By 20 August, the 1st Canadian Corps was positioned to launch their attack. The 1st Canadian Division was tasked with establishing a bridgehead across the Metauro River, which would be followed by a rapid advance past Pesaro to the Foglia River. Once these tasks had been accomplished the actual breaching of the Gothic Line would begin, and, if successful, the exploitation to capture Rimini.

On the night of 23 August 1944, the Regiment marched into its jumping off position. Unfortunately, the "new area was nearly all on forward slopes, completely overlooked by high ground occupied by the Boche on the north side of the Metauro River and as a result nearly all movement on our [RCR] part could be observed by him [Germans] from his O.P.s [observation posts]." Not surprisingly, the battalion area was shelled intermittently throughout the night. Nonetheless, once the "Royals" settled into their new position they immediately sent out recce patrols to the water line to search for crossing points and clear any mines.

A final brigade level coordination conference was held on 25 August. The RCR would attack across the river in the general direction of Saltara with the 48th Highlanders on the right with the object of establishing a bridgehead through which the H&PER would pass to continue the attack. That night at 2315 hours, in the wake of a terrific artillery barrage

"B" and "C" Coys "streaked across the river which was approximately 3 feet deep in some places and pushed forward onto their objectives, 'C' Coy arriving at the town of Saltara at 0100 hours and 'B' Coy taking up a position to the right of Saltara on the high ground."[46]

The CO quickly pushed "A" and "D" Coys through the bridgehead and they pressed forward encountering little resistance from "the rapidly retreating Huns."[47] At approximately 1630 hours, although the battalion area was still under mortar and artillery fire, and even though the forward companies were in contact only a few thousand metres to the front, the British Prime Minister Winston Churchill and the Supreme Allied Commander in Italy, General Alexander drove up in an open car to visit the engaged RCR troops. Their visit lasted approximately 20 minutes.

With the temporary distraction removed, the momentum of the advance was pressed forward. All day long the companies bounded from one high feature to the next. The ultimate objective was Convent Hill. It was believed to be strongly held, so a set piece attack was planned. A heavy artillery concentration was intended to neutralize the enemy on the hill, and tanks were moved forward to support the infantry onto the objective. However, by the time all the necessary arrangements had been made darkness began to fall and the tanks, who could not fire in the dark, withdrew to the rear. The attack seemed to fissile out.

Not to be denied, the rifle companies used their own initiative to infiltrate onto the objective by themselves. "A" Coy, followed by "B" Coy on the right and "C" Coy on the left moved onto the objective taking a number of prisoners. The remaining Germans quickly withdrew. By first light, the Regiment was consolidated on Convent Hill.

The RCR were given little time to rest. The brigade commander now ordered the "Royals" to press on towards Monteciccardo. Accordingly, "A" Coy led off. Once again the companies moved from one high feature to another, supporting each other as they moved. When the lead company bumped into a strong German position at their objective, a fortuitous change in brigade boundaries saved the RCR a stiff fight. Instead, the lead company disengaged from its contact and with the remainder of the Regiment moved off to their next objective. By first light, the Battalion moved into an assembly area near San Vito for a short but much needed rest.

By first light on 29 August, 1 CIB was in position overlooking the much vaunted Gothic Line across the Foglia River. At that point 3 CIB assumed the lead for the 1st Canadian Division. The Regiment, as part of 1 CIB, now moved back to rest in preparation for the next phase of the operation.

A resumption of combat was not long in coming. Five days later, on 2 September 1944, the "Royals" were back in the breach. The Canadians, namely 3 and 11 CIBs, had decisively breached the Gothic Line defences with the capture of the high ground at Monte Peloso and Monte Luro, which dominated the land for kilometres around. The gap that had been ripped open threatened the entire German position on the Gothic Line. As a result, the Germans rapidly pulled back their forces to the next defensible terrain approximately 13 kilometres north of the Foglia River — the Misano Ridge behind the Conca River. Although no defensive positions had been prepared here, the ground was naturally strong and well-suited for the defence. The German withdrawal was so precipitous that one veteran stated: "Jerry had pulled out so suddenly that many of the 'Minen' signs still marked the minefields."[48]

And so, the RCR moved forward towards the Conca River to lead the next phase of the pursuit. The "Royals" were to pass through the Loyal Edmonton Regiment and the Seaforth Highlanders of Canada, who were the lead Canadian elements, and cross the Conca River and establish a bridgehead. Once the bridgehead was established the 48th Highlanders were to relieve the RCR of securing the lodgement so that the "Royals" could continue the advance towards Riccione using the coastal road as their axis.

The road move to the assembly area was especially impressionable. "The whole countryside for miles around showed the retreat of the enemy," recalled Major Galloway, "for every haystack was burning and in the dark the red glow was eerie indeed." He explained, "it was though a hundred burning cigarette butts had been tossed onto the furniture in a darkened room."[49]

Brigade orders were given at 1900 hours that night and an hour-and-a-half later the Regiment drove to its final dropping off point. The CO quickly issued confirmatory orders and then "A" Coy set off. The crossing of the Conca River was uneventful, which was not surprising as it was virtually dry. By 0300 hours on 3 September 1944, the Regiment with its supporting arms was firmly established in its bridgehead. The 48th Highlanders quickly moved up and the Regiment continued its advance towards Misano Ridge.

The battalion scouts, with "C" Coy following, subsequently pushed off following the coastal road. "Just as the sun was coming up over the horizon" contact with the enemy was made. The initial fight netted five prisoners, all dreaded German paratroopers from the 1st German Parachute Division. The scouts had been moving so quickly that they penetrated the enemy's forward defensive lines and completely surprised them. However, they had now stirred up a hornet's nest.

The Regiment's lead elements had stumbled onto a major enemy strongpoint and they were now pinned down and unable to disengage from their antagonists. Here they stayed for the entire day until darkness cloaked the battlefield. In the interim, the remainder of the Regiment became embroiled in the fight in an attempt to relieve the pressure. Lieutenant-Colonel J.W. Ritchie, the new CO, directed "A" Coy to conduct a left flanking against the objective, known as the Dornier feature, to try and roll up the enemy's right flank. The leading platoons were able to infiltrate into the forward defensive lines and then the fighting "became extremely bitter as well as confused."[50] "A" Coy tenaciously fought on. As a result of their heavy casualties, the CO instructed "A" Coy to dig in and consolidate. He then ordered "D" Coy, with the support of six Churchill tanks from the 12th Royal Tank Regiment that had just arrived, to pass through "A" Coy and continue the assault. The attack progressed forward for another 600 metres when an exposed flank necessitated "C" Coy being fed into the fight to close the gap. By last light the rifle companies and tactical HQ stopped the advance and consolidated for the night.

The fight, however, was not finished. The enemy held its ground tenaciously. The following day the scouts and snipers remained busy but a planned morning attack was cancelled. That night, at 2000 hours, the battle resumed. "D" Coy led off with a flank attack supported by "A" and "C" Coys. The FOO from 2 Field Artillery Regiment commented the attack "went in with bayonets fixed in perfect extended line according to the best infantry traditions."[51] During the desperate fighting Lieutenant D. Burns, the commander of 18 Platoon, was struck in the head by machine gun fire. Falling to the ground three times, he continually struggled to his feet and stayed at the head of his platoon, personally knocking out a machine gun post and killing several enemy.[52] Inexplicably, brigade HQ ordered the attack cancelled and "D" Coy were recalled. They then took up their former position.

The next morning, 5 September, a horrific artillery barrage descended on the German positions. At 0600 hours, a deliberate attack was unleashed, however, because of the hammering the enemy had received the day before, the positions had been abandoned during the night. The

Dornier feature was now in Regimental hands. But they had little time to savour the victory.

The pursuit began immediately and a mere 400 metres away "contact had again been established with the Boche."[53] A series of bitter engagement now followed as "B" Coy assaulted another high feature. Hand-to-hand combat raged around and within the church of San Lorenzo-in-Strada, which was northwest of Riccione. "Frenzied fighting" ensued. The Germans, however, had superior numbers and it became clear the "Royals" had stumbled upon another enemy strongpoint. As a result, "B" Coy was pulled back. The CO decided to commit the entire Regiment.

Once again, at first light, the attack went in. This time a three company assault by "A," "C," and "D" Coys was launched. The advance closed to approximately 150 metres of the enemy objective when "A" Coy, the lead element, came under murderous machine gun fire. The War Diary provides the details of the engagement:

> In spite of this Capt J.B. Smith placed himself at the head of his coy and led it against strongly fortified houses and dug-in positions held by troops of the redoubtable 1 Para Div. The enemy fire inflicted many casualties but in the face of this and showing complete contempt for danger Capt Smith kept going steadily forward urging his men to within 35 yards of the enemy strongpoint determined to achieve his objective and carry out his commanding officer's intention. By this time the coy was reduced to half its strength and was coming under withering fire from three sides. Rallying the remnants and personally hurling hand grenades at the enemy Capt Smith kept leading his men forward. When last seen alive he was standing erect only a few yards from the final objective throwing the grenades in the face of point blank fire. Hit in the head by a German stick grenade he fell mortally wounded. The efforts of A Coy so employed the enemy that the remainder of the assaulting troops were saved from complete annihilation and were able to reorganize as fighting components.[54]

A group of 30 "Royals" were cut off by the fire and unable to extricate themselves. Some managed to escape back to friendly lines during the night but the others were presumed captured. "A" Coy emerged from the struggle 18 men strong. During the afternoon brigade HQ notified the RCR that the H&PER would relieve them that night. After four days of heavy fighting the Regiment would finally get some rest. It came at a heavy cost. The Regiment suffered 31 all ranks killed, 108 wounded, and 15 missing.

The relief was complete by 0230 hours, 7 September. Better yet, 3 CIB relieved 1 CIB that night, and the whole brigade moved into reserve for five days of rest and refit. It became clear that the enemy was using the intervening 19 kilometres between the current forward lines and Rimini to impose maximum delay. They used a succession of ridgelines and mountain features to their best advantage. Approximately six kilometres from Riccione stretched the Passano-Coriano ridge, which covered the crossings of the Marano River. Beyond this lay the San Lorenzo-San Martino ridge system. Behind these formidable obstacles the Germans concentrated their forces.

On 14 September 1944, the Regiment, as part of 1 CIB, moved forward once again. The next day battle was joined all along the front from the beaches along the Adriatic to 24 kilometres inland. That morning the RCR moved to their assembly area across the Marano River. 3 CIB was once again attacking the San Lorenzo-San Martino bastion and 1 CIB was responsible for covering their flank. At 1730 hours, in the midst of giving orders, Major Galloway, who was placed in command of the Regiment for the attack, was interrupted by the brigade commander who announced the RCR would have to move at 1730 hours. This left only 35 minutes to prepare!

The lead company stepped off at 1745 hours for its march to its forming up place west of the Rimini airfield. Unfortunately, once the enemy detected movement he began to shell the road and approaches. Nonetheless, by midnight the Regiment was consolidated in its jumping off position. At dawn the next morning, 16 September, 1 CIB advanced and immediately met heavy resistance. The 48th Highlanders on the left made some progress initially but quickly ground to a halt. The Greek brigade on the opposite flank was similarly pummelled as it tried to conform to the Canadian advance. The RCR stepped off at 0630 hours with "B" and "D" Coys leading. They instantly came under heavy fire. Both sub-units fought prolonged firefights with the enemy but little progress was made. A combined attack supported by heavy artillery fire was launched against the fortified gullies with some success, but at a high cost in casualties. During the advance, Corporal N.J. McMahon and his section epitomized the valiant effort put forth:

> He was in command of the foremost section of the leading platoon of the company attacking towards the Rimini airfield. When machine-gun fire from a nearby house held up his advance, on his own initiative he led his men across fire swept ground to assault the enemy post. In a hand-to-hand fight they killed twelve of the defenders, captured two and put the rest to flight. Then McMahon, who had personally accounted for five or six Germans, pushed on with his section to seize the D Company objective.[55]

Despite these efforts the advance was a slow slog. The battle dragged on to the next day. "A day [17 September] of inching forward," reported the War Diary.[56] The enemy's possession of superior terrain provided them an extraordinary advantage. Machine-gun posts set up in irrigation ditches made every "covered approach a death trap."[57] Captain Frank Rolph, a FOO with the RCR, explained:

> We didn't dare cross the ditches so we went down them. Vines were loaded with ripe grapes which obstructed our view while the land was dotted with groups of stone buildings occupied by well armed Huns. We had to take them out groups at a time. We were in one house two days firing at each other. Finally with Brens, rifles, PIATs and three-inch mortars we shifted them. We kept on advancing until a mile and a half south of Rimini ... In one position we knocked the Germans out three times but they kept replacing them only to be again mowed down.[58]

In addition, the entire Rimini airfield was lying in the Rimini Gap, which was dominated by German observation posts on the yet unconquered San Fortunato feature. In spite of these handicaps, the Regiment fought on. "Very sticky going," acknowledged the War Diary, "but our coys, by use of battle drill movements, smoke and deception managed to inflict considerable casualties on the enemy and improve their positions."⁵⁹ Major Galloway simply stated, "the flat ground makes an 'up and at 'em assault suicidal, so it is a fire fight with small arms and artillery support."⁶⁰

As the "Royals" and the other units of 1 CIB fought forward, events elsewhere were about to transform the battlefield. After heavy fighting, 4th British Division crossed the Marano River and subsequently the 4th Indian Division followed up to break the German resistance along the wall of the Apennines. At the same time the enemy's entire frontage was blasted for a 24 hour period by artillery, and air assets of the U.S. Tactical and Desert Air Forces. By the night of 18 September the flank of San Martino had been turned.

At 0300 hours the next morning, a "C" Coy patrol returned and reported no enemy contact. The Regiment quickly established a firm base east of San Marino. Without the men realizing it, the battle was over for the RCR. That night, 19 September, the Loyal Edmonton and the Royal 22nd Regiments seized the San Fortunato feature and the PPCLI and New Zealanders pushed through, crossed the Marecchia River, and isolated Rimini. The RCR remained in their positions at the Rimini airfield until 23 September 1944, when they moved to Riccione for rest and refit. The fight from the Metauro River to Rimini had cost the RCR 79 all ranks killed, 221 wounded, and 12 missing.⁶¹ It had been a hard slog.

The Regiment benefited greatly from its relatively long sojourn in Riccione. However, on 10 October 1944, in a stiff autumn wind and cold rain, the "Royals" were once again on the move. Although all could sense the war was coming to an end, it still remained a deadly endeavour. The Germans continued to fight stubbornly. This just added to the frustration — a bitter struggle for a lost cause.

Nonetheless, the 1st Canadian Division returned to the pursuit. It had been assigned a narrow front along Route 9, constrained by the Rimini-Bologna railway to the right and by mountains to the left. Major-General Chris Vokes opted to lead with a single brigade forward. In turn, 1 CIB led with the H&PER breaking trail. By 12 October they had crossed the Scolo Rigossa drainage canal, created a bridgehead, and pushed deep into enemy terrain. However, they had outstripped their flanking formations and as a result, Vokes quickly fed the RCR into the gap.

Two days later, as the advance continued, the H&PER were engaged in yet another attack to clear the enemy but were harassed by a strong pocket of Germans holed up in buildings, surrounded by a minefield in

Casa Nerri. Remarkably, "D" Coy succeeded in overrunning the objective, having traversed the minefield without a single incident. However, when they began digging in the casualties began to mount as the unsuspecting "Royals" began to step on the anti-personnel mines. It was not until the next morning that the Pioneers had managed to clear a safe lane to "D" Coy to remove the injured.

The next day, 15 October, the RCR passed through the H&PER and took over as the brigade lead. The brigadier ordered the Regiment to advance to contact on a two company frontage. Accordingly, "C" and "B" Coy as the left and right lead sub-units respectively, with a troop of tanks each in support, stepped off at 1400 hours. Enemy opposition was scattered and normally withdrew after initial contact. But resistance stiffened the following morning when the forward companies reached the banks of the Pisciatello River. Despite the initially light opposition, the going had been hard. Creeks and rivers engorged with the autumn rains spilled over their banks making the already sodden ground flooded and muddy. Moreover, the Germans had strewn the area with mines and booby-traps and their rearguard pummelled the Canadians with artillery and machine gun fire at every opportunity.

Little progress was made the next day, however, during the night of 17–18 October, the Loyal Edmonton Regiment forced a crossing of the Pisciatello River. At 0500 hours, the Regiment pushed "C" and "D" Coys across in the wake of a heavy artillery shoot. "C" Coy met fierce resistance immediately. The lead platoon and company HQ upon entering a house on its list of objectives was quickly targeted by an enemy force of 25 men with bazookas, who were also supported by a tank. This enemy force "engaged the house from 4 sides" and forced the "Royals" to pull back.[62]

In the meantime, "B" and "A" Coys were making little to no progress. The marshy ground prevented their supporting tanks from moving forward and the river line was heavily defended. In addition, "D" Coy was stalled because of intense shelling. As a result, the CO ordered the rifle companies to hold firm in their current positions.

At that point, fortune once again smiled on the RCR. The Regiment had been fighting almost continuously for a week and it was now being pulled from the line. By 0200 hours, 19 October, the relief by the Royal 22nd Regiment was complete and the RCR moved to an area, dubbed the "mudhole" near Sant'Arcangelo. The famous Italian autumn rains now "fell in torrents and the battalion rest area was a foot deep in gluey mud, with large tracts entirely inundated with water."[63] Nonetheless, the rest was welcomed. The Regiment was now down to a fighting strength of "189 rifles."[64]

Reinforcements dribbled in to the Battalion as it conducted training for its upcoming operations. Little did the "Royals" know that another period of suffering was about to transpire. On 29 November 1944, The RCR was deployed from a rest camp near Riccione and by 4 December it had closed up behind 3 CIB on the Lamone River. The Regiment's next operation would be marred with tragedy and irrevocably tied up in controversy.

With the war in its final death throes, the Allies now decided to push to Bologna. This meant that the Eighth Army had to cover 56 kilometres and storm three major river lines — the Lamone, Senio and Santerno in a dizzying period of only two weeks. The task was enormous. The official Canadian historian of the Italian campaign described the impending challenge:

> The ground ahead of the Canadians was no more promising than that over which they had fought during September and October. The major rivers which flowed north-eastward across the axis of advance all ran between high floodbanks which gave the enemy excellent observation of the intervening flats and provided him with sites for burrowed-out shelters and machine gun positions. Although numerous streams and canals drained the flats between the main watercourses with the coming of winter the ground, true to its marshy origin, was likely to become waterlogged and obstructive to movement off the main roads. As in earlier operations bridging was to be a major problem, largely because of great difficulty of developing suitable approaches across the sodden fields. The move forward between the rivers was an arduous task; to cross them, a formidable one indeed.[65]

The Eighth Army planned to advance all three divisions. The Polish Corps in the mountains, the 5th British Corps in the centre, and the Canadian Corps on the right flank. Having been assigned the Canadian Corps lead element, the 1st Canadian Division commander in turn decided that 3 CIB would lead the assault up to the Lamone River, conduct a crossing, and establish a bridgehead. At that point, 2

CIB would pass through and capture Bagnacavallo and then proceed to seize a crossing over the Senio River. The final thrust would be the responsibility of 1 CIB, who would advance beyond the Santerno River and establish a bridgehead through which 3 CIB would pass on its way to occupy Budrio, approximately 15 kilometres north-east of Bologna, where the Eighth Army would link-up with the American Fifth Army. However, as the cliché goes, the plan never survives the start line.

By the morning of 4 December after two days of fighting the commander of 3 CIB had reached the banks of the Lamone River but could not push any further. Although his brigade had suffered only a little more than a 100 casualties, he now demanded that 1 CIB take on the task of crossing the fast flowing river. The temporary acting commander of the 1st Canadian Division, Brigadier Desmond Smith, acquiesced and passed on the task. Brigadier Allan Calder, the 1 CIB commander would later regret his acceptance of this last minute mission. "If I had known then what I know now," philosophized Calder, "I would have refused the order."[66]

The eleventh hour mission was described by renowned Canadian historian Jack Granatstein: "Fighting in thick mud and cold on December 4, the 1st Brigade of the First Division launched a hastily prepared, ill-coordinated attack across the swift and 25-foot–wide Lamone River in assault boats and over temporary bridges."[67] The haste and sense of urgency would prove disastrous.

At noon, Lieutenant-Colonel Ritchie informed his company commanders that 3 CIB was unable to cross the Lamone River and that the H&PER and RCR would do so that night. Five hours later, the CO attended a brigade orders group that provided the details: a night attack with the H&PER on the right and the RCR on the left. Ritchie in turn quickly relayed his plan — a two company river assault crossing "B" Coy left, "A" right and "C" Coy in the centre rear. The CO planned to swim the companies across with the assistance of ropes.[68]

Things started to go wrong from the beginning. Intelligence reports put the river at "3–5 feet deep, and the banks fairly good and not high."[69] In actuality, the river was "10–15 feet deep, the current swift, and the water cold, and the water gap approximately 35 feet wide."[70] Additionally, the dykes on either side of the river were almost 45 feet high.[71] Scout Officer, Lieutenant J.E. Joice and Lance-Sergeant Meadows attempted to swim the icy river but in the attempt Joice cramped up and was helped back to the friendly bank by Meadows. However, both were now suffering from hypothermia, and weakened by the cold, Meadows was unable to drag Joice up the embankment so he left the officer clinging to the bank and crawled up over the dyke to get the other two scouts to help him rescue Joice. However, on return with the additional assistance, they discovered that the officer had disappeared. Weak from the cold he presumably lost his grip and was pulled into the icy current and drowned.

Upon hearing the latest news the CO aborted the original plan. Exacerbating the river conditions was the fact that the opposite bank was defended by the enemy. During the daring recce attempt the swimming party came under machine-gun fire and grenade attack. The secondary plan of using assault boats was now implemented.

The plan was amended but problems still arose. "The arty barrage came down at 0050 hrs and at 0105 hrs the coy moved out of the FUP [form up point]," recalled Major J.M. Houghton, the "A" Coy commander. "We reached the dyke wall where we were to pick up the boats and found no boats there," he added, "I spread the men out below the dyke wall and waited." Finally, at 0130 hours the boats arrived and Houghton "shoved two platoons across."[72] A short while later, at 0155 hours, 5 December 1944, "A" Coy reported it had crossed the river and had met no opposition. At 0240 hours "B" Coy had established a bridgehead with two platoons. However, its third platoon, which crossed on a partially demolished railway bridge, was caught in a mortar barrage and 18 of its 23 men became casualties.[73] By 0320 hours, "D" Coy had erected the first Olafson assault bridge and was beginning construction on the second. Fifteen minutes later "C" Coy was across and firming up in "A" Coy's area. At 0430 hours, it moved off according to plan to reach its assigned objective. "It appeared that the operation was developing into a splendid success," noted the War Diary.[74]

However, the destruction of the third "B" Coy platoon resulted in an exposed left flank. Major Eric Thorne "reported that although he was firm with two platoons he was none too happy about his position as one platoon was still unaccounted for and that a railway embankment along his left flank was approximately fifteen feet in height and obstructed his view."[75] Although he intended to use his missing platoon to dominate the dead ground once they arrived, his delay would be costly. Unfortunately, the German Reconnaissance Battalion from the 114th Jäger Division quickly discovered something was afoot and used the exposed flank to close up on "B" Coy. Approaching unseen behind the very obstacle over which Thorne voiced concern, they crept up to the crest and at 0700 hours poured a devastating fire into the unsuspecting RCR sub-unit. The Germans were later reinforced by engineers, self-propelled guns, and elements of the 356th Infantry Division.

Events quickly spiralled out of control. Fifteen minutes later, Lieutenant W.C. Watson the pioneer officer reported that the two "Littlejohn" anti-tank guns and two 6-pounder guns that had been ferried across the river were under attack. He also stated: "B" Coy HQ had been captured and the position overrun. At first, the report was dismissed as an exaggeration. However, at 0740 hours Battalion HQ received another report that indicated "a second heavier attack had been mounted against 'B' Coy and that the coy had disintegrated due to the Coy Comd having been wounded and captured" in addition to the capture and/or wounding of most of the sub-unit command elements. The only remaining platoon sergeant, Sergeant Fletcher later returned to the Battalion Tactical HQ and "told a story of overwhelming numbers of infantry and SP [self-propelled] guns being used against the coy, which at the time of the counterattack had a total fighting strength of less than forty all ranks." Fletcher painted "a picture of hand-to-hand fighting with our own troops at a disadvantage because the enemy dominated the flat ground from the railway embankment."[76]

"B" Coy was not the only crisis that morning. In the heavy mist, "C" Coy could barely discern the danger that was about to engulf them. They reported seeing tanks or SP guns but could not tell for sure because of the poor visibility. "This was the last heard from 'C' Coy until some hours later when Lieutenant L.H. Campeau arrived back at Tac HQ and told the tragic story of their decimation."[77]

The German counterattack struck "C" Coy like a rogue wave. In the darkness, "C" Coy left the bridgehead following the wrong track. This brought them into a position parallel with the railway embankment where the German counterattack had formed. Now completely cut-off and dominated by machine gun fire from the railway embankment, the trapped sub-unit was unable to dig-in. They sought the shelter of a large stone farm house from which they hoped to create a strongpoint. However, the enemy quickly moved up an SP gun into breach in the embankment and from a hull down position pulverized the building. Company Commander, Captain J.H.R. Wilkinson, seeing all was lost told those capable to make a run for "A" Coy lines. Only 13 men escaped.[78]

Meanwhile, on the right flank, the H&PER initially had difficulty. Although told not to close up to the river edge until after the preparatory bombardment the lead companies did so and were subsequently hammered by friendly artillery suffering 48 casualties in the process. The 40-odd survivors of the lead company crossed and established a bridgehead, linked up with the RCR, and dug in. At 0750 hours, the CO of the H&PER deployed his reserve companies passing them through the "A" Coy, RCR position to swing laterally to the right and reinforce his bridgehead. Remarkably, even at this time the scale of the disaster about to descend on 1 CIB was not realized.

When news of the fiasco broke, brigade headquarters ordered the RCR to hold on. At 0800 hours, Lieutenant-Colonel Ritchie directed "D" Coy to reinforce the bridgehead, as "A" Coy was the only remaining RCR element on the far bank. The enemy, however, stymied this attempt. A heavy curtain of machine-gun and artillery fire along the river line stopped them cold. Later that morning, at around 1100 hours, the H&PER, beset by rumours, pulled back to the near side of the river. Once the brigade commander learned of the withdrawal, he directed that "A" Coy, The RCR, the sole remaining lodgement on the far side of the river, be withdrawn. "The apparent success of 0630 hours," recorded the War Diary, "had turned into a ghastly failure before 1200 hours."[79] Major Houghton commented wryly, "This is an unhappy example of how a battle should not be fought."[80]

During the night the Battalion moved to the right and relieved the Royal 22nd Regiment. Here they remained for the next several days as a lull descended on the Lamone front. The Regiment reorganized the best it could and undertook a holding role along the river. It had lost 112 of the 205 men that had crossed the river.[81] It now reorganized to maintain fighting capability. "A" and "D" Coys remained intact, though under strength. "B" and "C" Coys amalgamated to form a single weak company and a fourth company, "X" Coy was generated from the scout platoon and other elements of Support Coy, as well as other personnel from "B" Echelon (e.g., shoemakers, armourers' assistants, drivers).

Finally on the night 10–11 December 1944, the Lamone River was breached by 3 CIB. The RCR crossed the river later that day in assault boats. The Regiment was now led by Lieutenant-Colonel W.W. Reid. The former CO, as well as the deputy commanding officer of the H&PER, who was in charge during the battle, along with the commander of 1 CIB, were all sacked for the failure at the Lamone River. The next few weeks the battalion engaged in bitter and confused fighting as they pressed forward in the advance. On 18 December, the RCR and H&PER attacked the

Fosso Vecchio. The attack was unsuccessful. Only "A" Coy managed to gain a foothold but they were forced to withdraw in the face of ferocious German counterattacks. "By a superhuman effort," wrote one participant, "the RCR secured a small bridgehead." Before they could be reinforced, he quickly added, "the bridgehead had already been heavily counterattacked and was disintegrating."[82] Three days later the enemy had withdrawn and the "Royals" were quickly ordered to cross the Vecchio and close up to the Naviglio Canal. By 22 December it had closed up on the Senio River with the assistance of flame throwing tanks.

The Regiment was pulled out of the line for a few days but found quickly found itself back in battle. "Most of the fighting," explained Major Galloway, the last of the original 1940-era RCR officers, "involved clearing out small pockets of enemy nestled between canals and streamlets that lay across the battlefield."[83] The fighting was unremitting. "We are all beginning to wonder why we are continuing to attack in these small piecemeal battles," questioned Galloway in his diary, "What is the aim of these puny efforts?" He added, "We are being killed off by an enemy that sits in his holes and just picks us off."[84] Some relief came on 27 December when the Regiment was relieved from the line and moved back to San Pancrazio.

The year ended with the Regiment in rest and refit. In eighteen months of war the face of the Regiment had changed greatly. Through its ranks passed four commanding officers, dozens of officers, and hundreds of men. "I fully appreciate that the going has been hard, the tempo fairly fast and tough but your determinations, skill at arms and guts has again seen the Hun off," congratulated the new 1st Canadian Corps commander, Lieutenant-General Charles Foulkes. "I am more than ever confident that you and I will see the next short stage of the operation to a successful conclusion."[85] Foulkes was correct in his optimism but not before more "Royals" would die.

The next two months became a blur of deployments, skirmishes, raids, and patrols. The Germans held the imposing banks on the far side of the Senio River and maintained an aggressive posture in both harassing fire and patrolling. On 16 February 1945, they conducted a daring raid. At 0315 hours "B" Coy reported a very heavy mortar stonk (concentration of fire) in their area. Minutes later "C" and "D" Coys were subjected to a similar stonk. Very quickly communication cables were cut and the sub-units were out of touch with each other and Tactical HQ. During this time an enemy patrol led by an English-speaking officer snuck in under their barrage and attacked a "B" Coy platoon house. "Insufficient sentries outside the house, the heavy mortar concentrations and the inky blackness of the night allowed the enemy to take our post unawares," concluded Galloway.[86] "The Boche attack was so cleverly executed that fifteen of the RCR and two arty signalers were taken prisoner," recorded the War Diary.[87]

That event marked the last major action in Italy for the Regiment. On 23 February 1945, the RCR was relieved from the front line and began its departure from Italy. On 7 March, the Regiment loaded onto two Liberty ships and four Landing Ship Tanks (LSTs) at Leghorn Harbour. Two days later they arrived at Marseille, France, and began their deployment to Belgium.

By this time the Allies were collapsing the Reich. Four Allied armies were poised to strike across the Rhine River and penetrate into Germany proper. Although the 125,000 strong German Twelfth Army in the Netherlands would have been cut-off and marginalized it could not be ignored. German authorities issued fight to the death directives and threatened to break the dykes, thus drowning much of western Holland. In response, Field Marshal Montgomery ordered the 1st Canadian Army to put an end to resistance in the Netherlands.

On 9 April 1945, the Regiment closed up about eight kilometres behind the Ijssel River. It was once again close enough to the front to hear gunfire. Two days later under the cover of smoke and a substantial artillery bombardment the PPCLI and the Seaforth Highlanders crossed the Ijssel River in amphibious armoured carriers called "Buffaloes." At 0515 hours the next morning, 12 April, the Regiment crossed the river and passed through the bridgehead. They were the left front battalion, flanked by the 48th Highlanders on their right, as part of the 1 CIB push to Apeldoorn.

The advance proceeded well. The Battalion proceeded on a two company frontage, "C" and "B" Coys right and left forward respectively. Little opposition was encountered and the operation was largely a mopping up exercise. The lead companies ploughed on through the night and into the next day. At 1900 hours on 13 April the lead companies were halted in place on the fringes of Apeldoorn. Dutch underground sources stated that the Germans were abandoning the city and the brigade commander wanted to exploit this opportunity. As a result, "C" Coy was loaded onto tanks and at 0300 hours the next morning a dash was made for the bridges of the canal blocking access into the town. The first

The RCR Band participating in the 1st Canadian Division parade to mark the liberation of Apeldoorn, 17 April 1945.

road block was simply swept aside, but the second of reinforced concrete supported by anti-tank weapons, including a formidable 88 mm gun, put an abrupt halt to the attack. "The crew of the lead tank, upon hitting the block at full speed was stunned and before the tank could be turned around it was hit by bazooka fire several times and burst into flames."[88] The Regiment now deployed for a deliberate assault.

The brigade commander decided to push into Apeldoorn on a two battalion frontage. By 2315 hours on 14 April, "B" Coy on the left and "C" Coy on the right stepped off. These two RCR sub-units represented the left front of the brigade attack, the 48th Highlanders taking up the right front. Both companies made slow progress, but stubborn resistance from German soldiers holed up in fortified houses necessitated a halt to await daylight, which would also allow for intimate tank support. At 1500 hours, 15 September, "A" Coy, supported by tanks conducted an attack on "C" Coy's right flank and broke the stiffest of the enemy resistance. The other companies were now able to push to the canal.

The canal line seemed impenetrable to direct assault and the division commander now planned an alternate scheme. The RCR would hold the entire canal frontage while 3 CIB would sweep into Apeldoorn from the South and the H&PER and 48th Highlanders would rush in from the north. This quickly changed. At 0300 hours, 17 April, two partisans contacted "C" Coy and announced that the Germans were evacuating the town. A patrol crossed the lock immediately and captured the two Germans left in charge of the demolitions. By 0430 hours, "C" Coy had crossed the canal and established a bridgehead. "A" Coy moved next and occupied the town square. The H&PER passed through the town six hours later, closely followed by the 48th Highlanders. The RCR now slipped into a reserve role and busied themselves taking control of the prisoners that began to flow in. During the day 214 prisoners were detained.

The following day the Regiment deployed to Garderen without incident. On 19 April a cross-country sweep was conducted to ensure a rumoured 600 enemy were not hiding in the woods between 1 CIB and the Zuider Zee but nothing was found. So concluded the Regiment's combat operations during the Second World War. The fighting in North-West Europe cost the Regiment 12 killed and 49 wounded.

On 4 May 1945, a BBC Newscast announced that "the Germans in N.W. Germany, Holland, Denmark, and the Frisian Islands accepted unconditional surrender, to go into effect at 0800 hours 5 May 1945."[89] Two days later the RCR and H&PER were transferred to the command of 2 CIB.[90] The task of the 1st Canadian Army now became disarming 120,000 Germans in Holland.

On 8 May, the Regiment as part of 2 CIB moved to Ijmuiden to take over the fortress and disarm the garrison. The CO and his intelligence officer went ahead to prepare the arrival of the main body. "As we crossed the front lines," recalled Lieutenant Wilf Snell, "the German troops were still sitting behind their MG 42s, ammunition belts at the ready. I said to the Colonel, 'I hope these guys got the word.'"[91] Fortuitously, they had. The remainder of the battalion arrived at 1245 hours. The War Diary noted, "It seemed very, very strange indeed to drive among Germans who were fully armed." It added, "All Germans were very smart and well disciplined and paid compliments to all Allied officers."[92] Very quickly the Regiment relieved the Germans of the various security details, namely perimeter defence and inner ammunition and supply dump guards. Then the task of disarming the enemy began.

On 19 June 1945, the Regiment handed over its commitments at the Ijmuiden Fortress and began to their return journey home. In the interim, a second battalion of the RCR was formed at Barriefield, Ontario, on 1 August 1945. It was officially designated 1 Bn (RCR), 1st Canadian Infantry Regiment, 6th Canadian Division and was organized along

Disarming German soldiers at the Ijmuiden Fortress, 11 May 1945.

American lines for employment in the Pacific theatre. However, when the war with Japan ended on 2 September 1945, the new battalion was designated the 2nd Battalion, The RCR (so as not to confuse it with the battalion of "Royals" on overseas duty) and moved to Brockville, Ontario several weeks later.

Meanwhile, on 2 September the rest of the Regiment departed Ostend for the five-hour cruise to Dover, England. The men left Southhampton on 24 September and arrived in Halifax five days later. At 1400 hours, 1 October 1945, the trip home was finally over when their train pulled

The RCR remained at the Ijmuiden for a period of almost six weeks securing the fortress and disarming German forces.

into the depot in London, Ontario. It had been a long five years and four months. The war had finally come to an end.

The Regiment's record of service during the Second World War is commendable. It earned its reputation in hard fought campaigns in Sicily,

Italy, and North-West Europe. It earned 27 battle honours,[93] and received 130 awards for gallantry and distinguished service. Its overseas service, however, came at a high cost. During the war, the Regiment suffered 370 killed and 1,207 wounded.

"We were quietly glad it was over," confided Lieutenant Wilf Snell, "and wondering what the hell we were going to do tomorrow."[94] The war seemed to have lasted a life time — for some it did. Many "Royals" demobilized and took up civilian careers. Others decided to stay with the Regiment and see what peacetime soldiering would bring. Regardless, all had shared duty and hardship and in so doing added to the Regiment's legacy of service for country.

7
A Return to Combat:
The First Regimental Tour to Korea, 1951–1952

The "Royals" had once again done their country proud. They had served during the Second World War with honour and maintained the traditions of the Regiment. They fulfilled their wartime service with fortitude and courage, and maintained, for better or worse, their reputation as a "spit and polish" regiment. The RCR now entered a period of peacetime soldiering, a state that can often be as confused and murky as combat.

Victory in Europe set the wheels of demobilization in motion for most serving members, but many, including 300 "Royals," volunteered for service in the Pacific theatre of operations. However, with the capitulation of Japan in September 1945, the Canadian Army Pacific Force was disbanded. As a result, those who had joined 1 Bn (RCR) stationed in Barriefield for preparation for what they thought would be the next phase of the conflict, found themselves without a war. As a direct result, 1 Bn (RCR) was re-designated the 2nd Battalion, RCR (2 RCR) so as not to confuse it with the expeditionary battalion that was returning home to London, Ontario, after its war service.

Upon arrival in London, the overseas battalion was quickly demobilized and the RCR was once again left with only a single battalion in Barriefield. It was responsible for assisting with the demobilization of those "Royals" who decided to return to civilian life, and recruiting members for the permanent, or active, force for peacetime duty. In November 1945, the Regiment moved from Barriefield to Brockville where it took over the infrastructure of a former officer training establishment.

"The Regiment is now home," wrote the CO, Lieutenant-Colonel W.W. Reid, "Whether or not we remain in Brockville is for someone other than I to decide. The main point is that the Regiment is home, be it in Brockville or Victoria." He pointed out that it was uncertain where the Regiment would ultimately be stationed until "we are officially recognized as the Permanent Force or Canadian Army (Active) Battalion."[1]

The future of the entire Army, not just the Regiment, was anything but clear. By late 1945, the debt-conscious Liberal government was fully aware that the war-weary public held little sympathy for continued defence expenditures or large standing military forces. The war had cost Canada $18 billion, of which $10.5 billion was added to the national debt.[2] As a result, an "Interim Force" was established for a two-year period that would allow the Department of National Defence (DND) time to carefully craft the military that the government thought was sufficient to fulfill the nation's requirements.

The post-war army was to be anything but extravagant. First, it was to consist of a representative group of all arms of the service. Second, in the view of the government, its purpose was to provide a small but highly trained and skilled professional force, which in time of war, could expand and train the citizen soldiers who "would fight that war."[3] In essence, the duty of the permanently employed "Active Force" was "to assist in the training and administration of the Reserve Force and to supply the necessary staffs, services and scientific research and development personnel, augmented by a small formation of essential field units. This field formation would be maintained as a trained field force, fully equipped and organized on war establishments, ready to meet whatever commitments might arise."[4] In essence, the strength of the post-war army was to be its mobilization potential. Brooke Claxton, the newly appointed minister of national defence (MND), announced to Parliament in 1946 that the proper role of the military, "at the present time, is as a training force for future staff officers and leaders, and for the reserve force of Canada."[5]

The RCR was eventually selected to be one of the three permanent infantry regiments. The Royal 22nd Regiment and the Princess Patricia's Canadian Light Infantry were the other two. By January 1946, the Regiment's strength had risen to 1,200 all ranks. Interim force personnel were assigned to "A" and "B" Coys. However, by midsummer reality had set in. With demobilization completed the Regiment shrunk to 300 all ranks of whom nearly half were officers and non-commissioned officers.[6]

The focus of the post-war army was not difficult to predict. As it had done in the past and would do again in the future, Canada looked to the British and Americans for guidance. The nation's generals were eager to perpetuate links with their closest allies, as well as stay abreast of the latest tactical developments in modern warfare. A 1947 National Defence Headquarters (NDHQ) study revealed that British peacetime policy was based on training and equipping all infantry formations to be air-transportable.[7] Similarly, the Americans were enhancing their air-transportability and airborne capability.

Not surprisingly, Canada quickly adopted a similar approach. But, the method also had a practical component. In consonance with the Liberal government's desire to limit defence spending, the concept of security adopted was established on smaller standing forces with greater tactical and strategic mobility. The cash-strapped Canadian political and military leadership also came to realize that such a force would provide a great political expedient. The 1946 Canada/U.S. Basic Security Plan (BSP) imposed on Canada the requirement to provide one airborne/air-transportable brigade, and its necessary airlift, as its share of the overall continental defence scheme.[8] As a result, the government had briefed Parliament, as early as 1946, that airborne training for the Active Force Brigade Group was planned. The Regiment's initial responsibility was to provide a platoon for the Canadian Special Air Service Company (Cdn SAS Coy), which was made up of one platoon from each of the three Permanent Force infantry regiments. This sub-unit was tasked to act as a training and demonstration company for the Joint Air School (JAS), which was later redesignated the Canadian Joint Air Training Centre (CJATC).[9]

The Cdn SAS Coy was a 125-man strong, specially trained company that was intended to provide an "efficient life and property saving organization capable of moving from its base to any point in Canada in ten to fifteen hours."[10] However, once the sub-unit was officially approved by the chief of the general staff (CGS) on 9 January 1948, it changed its focus more in line with its name and it began to emphasize commando operations.[11] The individuals the Regiment sent to the sub-unit fit this requirement. All were specially selected and had wartime airborne experience.[12]

Nonetheless, the Cdn SAS Coy and the Regiment's contribution to it did not last long. The sub-unit was disbanded a little over a year later. In fact, the company's number one priority fed its eventual demise. It was responsible for "providing a tactical parachute company for airborne training." The official terms of reference for the sub-unit specifically stated:

"This company is to form the nucleus for expansion for the training of the three infantry battalions as parachute battalions."[13]

However, there was a degree of lethargy in the overall scheme of things. By the summer of 1948, nothing had been done to create the vaunted airborne/air-transportable brigade group. Concrete action was now finally required. As a result, the CGS directed that training commence for one battalion of infantry for airborne/air-transported operations. This battalion represented the Canadian component necessary to meet the immediate requirements of the BSP, which had to be completed by 1 April 1949.[14]

The Basic Security Plan of two years previous had obligated the Canadian Army to be prepared for Arctic airborne and/or air-transportable operations, to counter or reduce enemy lodgements in Canada, on a prescribed schedule of availability. This program compelled the Canadian government, by 1 May 1949, to have a battalion combat team prepared to respond immediately to any actual lodgement, with a second battalion available within two months, and an entire brigade group within four months.[15]

Nothing of substance had yet been completed, except the renaming of the Active Force Brigade Group to the Mobile Striking Force (MSF). Military headquarters in Ottawa explained that the MSF would concentrate initially only for formation training. Furthermore, the Army directed that just one infantry battalion would be converted into an airborne/air-transported unit at a time. Only after the first infantry battalion (PPCLI) had completed its training would the remaining units, in a consecutive manner, undergo conversion to airborne status, until the entire brigade group was air-transportable.[16]

The RCR was officially "transformed" into an airborne unit on 1 May 1949. It was the second battalion to undergo airborne training and it began to send its personnel to Rivers, Manitoba by mid-month. Members of the Regiment were continually rotated through the necessary courses and training, and one year later, in May 1950, when three-quarters of the Battalion had earned their wings, the CO, Lieutenant-Colonel P.R. Bingham, directed that RCR personnel would now wear the distinctive maroon beret to represent their status as an airborne unit.

Another major change occurred that year when the Regiment moved from Brockville to resettle in Camp Petawawa. "At long last we have moved to what is likely to be our permanent station for a long time," commented Major C.H. Lithgow, the editor of the *Connecting File*, "To be sure Petawawa has plenty of sand, some poison ivy, and a fair number of black flies and mosquitoes at times but all things considered it is a good station."¹⁷ His optimism would not always be shared by others.

Nonetheless, as the RCR continued to train and evolve into an airborne unit, storm clouds once again began to gather threatening the relative international peace. The Second World War had changed the world in many ways. From its ashes rose many new innovations and ideas, such as new technology developed through the war (e.g., jet aircraft, rocket propulsion, atomic weapons); new societal expectations on social programs; new states, as well as a new world organization, the United Nations (UN), that carried the promise of a new peaceful world order.

However, the war also spawned two diametrically opposed superpowers that represented completely different economic, military, and political ideologies. At the end of hostilities, all the combatants but the Soviet Union swiftly demobilized their large military forces. Quickly it became evident that the taciturn ally during the war had grown into an enemy. The Soviet occupation of Eastern Europe, particularly the communist coup in Czechoslovakia in 1948, as well as revelation of Soviet spying activities in Europe and North America convinced the Europeans and North Americans that a cold war had set in and that Winston Churchill's metaphor for the chilly relations between West and East, an "iron curtain has descended across the Continent" of Europe, was correct.

The apprehension led to the creation of the North Atlantic Treaty Organisation (NATO) alliance on 4 April 1949. This commitment would see the return of Canadian troops to Europe and would impact the very fabric of the Regiment, and the Canadian Army for the next 50 years. However, before the full implications of this new alliance could even be seen a new crisis erupted on the globe.

In the inky darkness of early morning, on 25 June 1950, approximately 135,000 North Korean soldiers, supported by Soviet-supplied T-35 tanks, washed over the South Korean border like a tsunami. Against the poorly equipped and ill-trained Republic of Korea (ROK) defences and military forces, the Communist onslaught swept right up to the Korean capital of Seoul. Within three days of its initiation, the North Korean People's Army (NKPA) offensive had captured the capital.¹⁸

International condemnation was swift. On the afternoon of 25 June, the UN Security Council met and demanded an immediate halt to the aggression and the withdrawal of all NKPA forces from South Korea. Fortuitously, the Soviet Union had boycotted the Security Council

ESTABLISHING A LEGACY

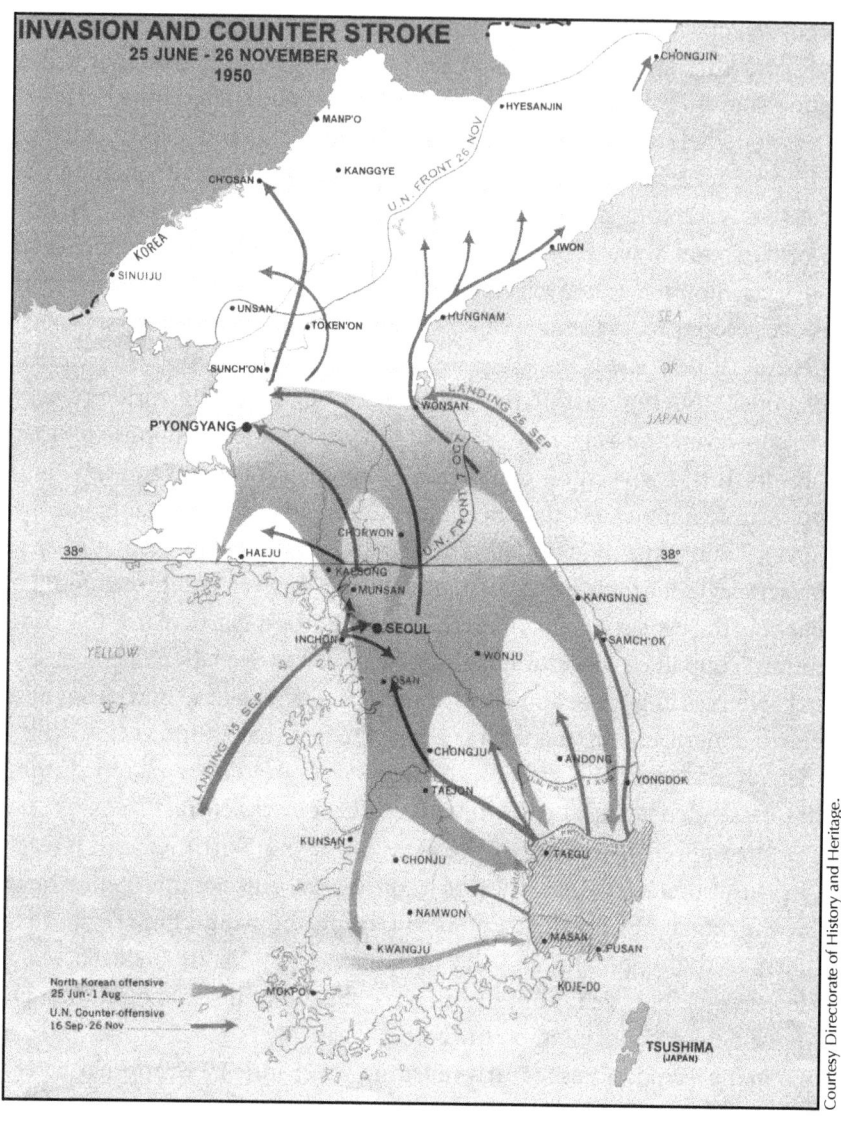

session and therefore, did not exercise its veto. This Soviet oversight allowed the UN Security Council to act. Five days later, President Harry S. Truman authorized American forces to intervene. On 5 July 1950, one U.S. division deployed from Japan and made contact with the enemy. Other nations offered assistance and two days later the Security Council recommended all forces be placed under a single commander. As a result, a UN Command was established in Tokyo under General Douglas MacArthur.

The Canadian government viewed the international environment as so volatile that it authorized the expansion of its armed forces and dramatically increased its defence expenditures.[19] This was the first time in the nation's history that the concept of large standing peacetime forces was accepted. But this was done not only to facilitate the dispatch of an expeditionary force to fight the "evils of Communism" in Korea, but also to raise a special brigade for service in Europe where most political and military leaders believed the real Communist blow would fall. As such, during the 1950–1951 period, the RCR, as well as the other two Active Force infantry regiments, expanded to provide forces not only for duty in Korea but also to man the brigade group being established for NATO.[20]

Despite the perceived threat and demands of its allies, the Canadian government was reluctant to get embroiled in another ground war. The spectre of the conscription crisis in the dying days of the Second World War still haunted the Liberal government. Initially, in July, three destroyers and a transport squadron were sent to Korea to assist in operations but this commitment was quickly dismissed by the Americans as a token effort. As a result, pressure mounted on Canada to deploy ground combat forces. On 7 August 1950, with UN forces hemmed in around the Port of Pusan, the Canadian government finally authorized the recruitment of the Canadian Army Special Force (CASF). Canada was at war once again.

Accordingly, the "Royals" were warned off for duty in Korea in the summer of 1950. "To most of us, trudging through the wilds of Algonquin Park [during Ex Beaver Dam] the name Korea didn't mean much," reminisced Major T.L.C. Pierce-Goulding, "just another trouble spot and a very remote one at that." He added, "It was very far removed from our lives ... or so we thought."[21] On return from the exercise in early August, the "Royals" discovered Korea had become very real for them. The government had authorized the expansion of all three Active Force infantry regiments, resulting in the almost immediate creation of the 2nd Battalion (2 RCR). "The ranks of the men filled very quickly," reported one officer, "and in a matter of days there were well over 1000 men to be controlled."[22]

The third battalion, 3 RCR would be officially stood-up approximately five months later, even though its embryo began to gather in Fort Lewis in November. The existing battalion in Petawawa became 1 RCR (airborne) and was tasked with training the 2nd Battalion for its tour of duty in Korea. It was also responsible for providing a nucleus of senior NCOs and officers.

Many of the new recruits were veterans of the previous war. By mid-October the initial training was complete and a month later, 2 RCR deployed to Fort Lewis, Washington to finish its preparation for war. The training focused on the staples of combat — weapons training and live fire, tactical exercises and physical fitness. On 20 April 1951, 2 RCR left for Korea, arriving in Pusan harbour on 4 May.

Their introduction to Korea was somewhat coloured. The war diarist explained:

> The portion of Pusan that we saw presented a pitiful aspect. The people are poorly clothed and live in foul smelling hovels. Every block has "home brew" or saki stills. "OFF LIMITS" signs are posted everywhere for obvious reasons. Congenital Syphillis, active Syphillis and Gonnhorea are prevalent. On reaching the rural areas the scene was more palatable. The country has a peculiar beauty, with the sides of the mountains and hills terraced for growing (every inch of arable land is tilled). The vegetation is a bright green. The people appear quite picturesque, although they smell. However, bad smells in some foods, cheese, seem to add to its lustre rather than detract from it.[23]

Nevertheless, 2 RCR joined the rest of the 25th Canadian Infantry Brigade (25 CIB), CASF, the next day.[24]

Meanwhile, the war had taken a number of dramatic turns. Initially, the UN forces had been pushed into the tiny "Pusan Perimeter" but in mid-September 1951, a daring amphibious assault was launched at Inchon, the port of Seoul. Quickly overcoming NKPA resistance, the South Korean capital was recaptured by 26 September and by the first week of October MacArthur's forces were driving a battered enemy back across the 38th Parallel. Sensing victory, the UN forces continued their advance, crossed the North Korean border and seized the capital of Pyongyang. Fatefully, MacArthur ordered his forces to advance towards the Yalu River, the boundary between North Korea and China.

With the fortunes of war apparently turned, the Canadian government cut back its commitment of an entire brigade group, 25 CIB, and dispatched only one battalion, 2 PPCLI, to Korea. After all, with the war almost won, there did not seem to be any need for additional troops. As a result, the 2 PPCLI sailed for Korea on 25 November 1950.

However, unbeknownst to the UN command, by the end of October six Chinese armies, numbering approximately 300,000 troops, had already crossed the Yalu River and were concentrating in the path of the now overconfident UN forces.[25] On 26 November the UN forces ran up against the main enemy defensive line between Pyongyang and the Yalu River. The Chinese now unleashed their ambush on MacArthur's overextended forces. The UN advance now became a rout, which was finally stopped at the Imjin River. It was into this atmosphere of crisis that 2 PPCLI arrived in December. However, the situation would worsen. The Chinese launched another crushing offensive early in the New Year and by 4 January 1951, Seoul was once again in the hands of the Communists. By 21 February 1951, the MND, Brooke Claxton, announced that the remainder of 25 CIB would be dispatched to Korea as originally intended. At about the same time, 2 PPCLI entered the line and on 24–25 April fought its famous battle of Kap'yong.[26] By 1 May the enemy offensive had come to an end and the UN forces held an irregular line some 30 kilometres south of the 38th Parallel forming an arc north of Seoul.

This was the general situation that faced the "Royals" on their arrival to Korea. The Battalion spent the first two weeks being outfitted and acclimatizing to both the weather and terrain. By 16 May 1951, 2 RCR, moved to the front lines arriving in a concentration area near the Han River two days later. For the next two weeks, the Battalion conducted operations in the rugged mountains making contact from time to time with a seemingly very elusive enemy. By 28 May, 2 RCR reached the 38th Parallel and joined up with an American armoured task force. "You have far exceeded the high expectations I had of your ability in operations," praised Brigadier J. M. Rockingham, the 25 CIB Commander, "The determination, thoroughness and speed you have shown in your first operations over the last three days, have been magnificent."[27]

A mere two days later, in a steady drizzle of rain, 2 RCR fought its first decisive battle. The brigade recommenced its advance — slow, plodding work, particularly as they approached the infamous "Iron Triangle" an area filled with peaks and crests that resembled a natural fortress. This was also the area from where the Chinese launched their earlier offensives. At present, Chinese rearguards made expert use of the ground, digging holes under large boulders from which they could fire on UN troops with relative safety from artillery or air strikes. On this day,

2 RCR was tasked with capturing Kakhul-bong (also known as Hill 467). This craggy twin-peaked feature dominated the valley through which 25 CIB was required to pass.

The brigade had already outstripped their flanking formations. As such, Rockingham was reluctant to push forward because he would expose his flanks and become vulnerable to a counterattack. Nonetheless, higher headquarters ordered him to push his brigade northwards. As a result, in the overcast dawn, Lieutenant-Colonel Robert A. Keane, the CO of 2 RCR, deployed three of his rifle companies in a complicated sweeping movement to outflank Hill 467 so that he could then seize it with a direct assault by his fourth manoeuvre company. "A" Coy, mounted in half-tracks and supported by a troop of Sherman tanks, was tasked as a cut-off and was responsible for driving rapidly to the village of Chail-li, approximately 2.5 kilometres north of Hill 467 and occupying it. "B" Coy, was to follow "A" Coy across the start line and then veer off and secure a small knoll known as Hill 162, which was 2.5 kilometres of Hill 467. Finally, "C" Coy was responsible for seizing Hill 269, midway between Chail-li and Hill 467. Once these sub-units were deployed and in a position to support the assault or destroy withdrawing Chinese forces, the scene would be set for "D" Coy to assault the main objective — the twin peaks of Kakhul-bong.

At 0600 hours, "A," "B," and "C" Coys, as well as carrier platoon crossed the start line. An artillery shoot by two regiments of medium and one regiment of field guns laid down a preliminary barrage intended to blast suspected Chinese positions. It lasted 20 minutes and then moved on to pound the village of Chail-li for another 15 minutes. The rifle companies attained their initial objectives with a minimum of resistance. By 0730 hours, "D" Coy was half way to their objective, Hill 467, when they began to receive some mortar fire. When they began to climb the rain soaked feature, the Chinese brought concentrated machine-gun fire to bear as well. By 0840 hours, "their ["D" Coy] position seemed impossible as they were pinned down from above by many LMGs [light machine guns]."[28] Lieutenant John Woods recalled, "they had a machine gun position at the top of the hill that was cleverly sited." He explained, "you couldn't move without getting a burst. I tried using my bazooka man but it didn't do any good." The problem lay in the fact that the Chinese had allowed them to advance close enough so that artillery could no longer be used safely without fear of hitting friendly forces.[29] Tucked close to the assaulting troops, the Chinese now poured a devastating fire into the "Royals."

A RETURN TO COMBAT

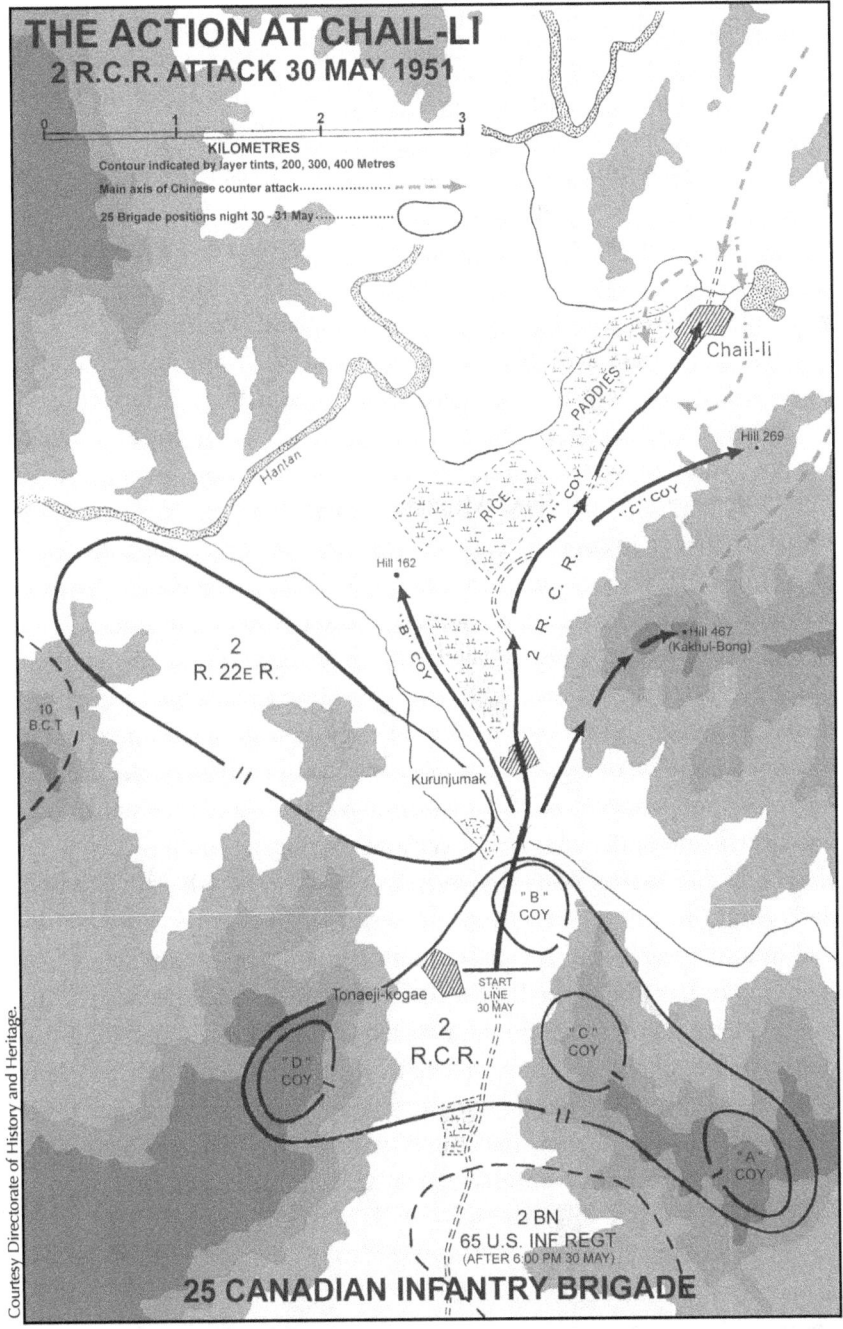

Despite the ferocity of the defence, "D" Coy clawed its way forward. By 1030 hours, "D" Coy reported they were almost at the objective, although enemy fire had not slackened. At that time, "A" Coy, which had entered Chail-Li, also came under attack. In fact, the Chinese were intently manoeuvring their troops in an attempt to isolate and cut-off "A" Coy. Chinese soldiers, dispersed in the rice paddies on either flank of the village and hidden in part by the mist and rain, opened an increasingly heavy fire on "A" Coy from as close as 25 metres away. Their deployment was initially overlooked by Major R.D. Medland, the OC of "A" Coy, because of the poor visibility caused by the driving rain storm but also because the troops he did see were wearing ponchos and looked very much like Canadian troops. He tried to contact "C" Coy on the wireless net but could not raise them. As such, he could not determine otherwise until they began to open fire.[30] At the same time, "B" and "C" Coys, who were busy trying to support the efforts of the other rifle companies were also under artillery and mortar fire. It seemed that the Chinese were now trying to isolate elements of the Battalion and destroy it piecemeal.

At 1116 hours, "D" Coy reported "they were advancing on their objective with but a short distance to go."[31] However, closing the last little distance seemed to be a peak to far. By early afternoon it seemed that a disaster was in the offing. "D" Coy was spread out on the Hill 467 feature and still under heavy fire. "A" Coy was increasingly under attack and all sub-units were under heavy artillery and mortar fire. Ominously, large numbers of Chinese troops were seen manoeuvring on the still exposed flanks of the battalion. The CO later assessed, "The enemy allowed tanks and infantry embussed in half-tracks to penetrate approximately 4,000 metres into their defences before they reacted in force." He added, "in two to three hours they counterattacked quite violently, attacking the objective frontally and from both flanks."[32] Exacerbating the problem was the fact that the RCR's flanking formations had not yet, as had been promised, closed up. The American 24th and 35th Infantry Regiments were still lagging well behind creating a 7,000 metre exposed gap on either flank.

By 1400 hours, the situation began to look grim and the CO began the dangerous job of disengaging his forces. But was it soon enough? At 1456 hours, "D" Coy reported, "the situation seemed impossible to escape from ... being overrun by hundreds of enemy."[33] Nonetheless, supported by tanks and "C" Coy they began their withdrawal down the hill. Through mutual support and protective artillery and tank fire, the Battalion worked its way back to safety. By 2000 hours, the entire unit was in a reserve defensive position, alert to the likelihood of a Chinese attack.

The battle had been a bloody one. In all, 2 RCR suffered six dead and 25 all ranks wounded. However, they had gained valuable experience. Moreover, they had learned first hand about their enemy. "The Chinese enemy proved to be stubborn and determined," wrote the CO. "He [the enemy] is skilful with respect to camouflage and siting of weapons [and] he is an excellent digger and appears to have good morale and discipline," added Keane.[34]

In the aftermath of the failed attack, 25 CIB held their position and then moved into Corps reserve on 1 June 1951. The brigade moved to area northwest of Uijongbu and spent a relatively peaceful three weeks. On 18 June, the unit found itself in the line once more near Chorwon, which represented the point of furthest UN penetration into North Korea. Despite the oppressive heat, the "Royals" placed great emphasis on active patrolling far beyond the forward defensive lines (FDLs). In the ensuing weeks the RCR played a deadly game of cat and mouse with the Chinese in the mountainous terrain that represented no man's land. Each side attempted to dominate the ground and inflict casualties on the opposing side.

At the end of the month the American government instructed General Matthew Ridgeway, who had replaced the sacked Douglas MacArthur, to invite the Chinese and North Koreans to discuss a ceasefire. The next day both sides agreed to meet on 8 July at a small village on the 38th Parallel called Kaesong. Unfortunately, nothing came of the talks except a short period of decreased activity. As a result of the parley, the UN forces halted offensive action and adopted a heavy program of patrolling throughout the summer.

On 17 July the "Royals" were relieved by a Turkish infantry battalion and the RCR then deployed to the Imjin River. Their stay here was short. Ten days later, they were again pulled from the line to join the First Commonwealth Division, which assumed operational control at noon the next day.[35]

The remainder of the summer epitomized conflict in general. "Fighting alternated between boredom and danger, intense physical effort and completely lazy days," wrote one chronicler.[36] The heavy patrolling continued with each side trying to dominate the ground. With the fall approaching and any hope of a lasting peace now but wishful thinking, the UN decided to advance once again. On 11 September, 2 RCR as part of the Commonwealth division, pushed permanently across to the north side of the Imjin River. The Chinese seemed to accept the loss of terrain and melted before the advance. The unit achieved its objective by 1930 hours and began to dig in and wire-in their position. The following days were spent on improving the defences and active patrolling. As always, enemy artillery and mortar fire plagued the "Royals" and created casualties. On 28 September, all three battalions of 25 CIB moved forward to new positions and dug in. However, they were not to stay here long. Another offensive was in the wind.

Five days later, on 3 October 1951, the commencement of Operation Commando saw the Commonwealth division push northwards once again. The new UN offensive, designed to put pressure on the Chinese to convince them to negotiate a lasting peace, comprised of a five division attack along the entire 60 kilometre frontage of I Corps. The First Commonwealth Division planned a 10 kilometre three phase advance. In essence, the division commander, Major-General A.J. H. Cassels, decided on a two brigade frontage assault with 29 British Commonwealth Infantry Brigade (BCIB) attacking the two mountains of Kowang-san (also known as "Little Gibraltar" and Hill 355) and Maryang-san (Hill 317), and 25 CIB assaulting the line of hills fronting the Sami-ch'on tributary in the south. Phase I, launched on D-day would see 29 BCIB capturing Hill 355; Phase II, 25 CIB capturing its line of hills, and Phase III, 29 BCIB pushing on to seize Hill 317, while 25 CIB completed their advance to their forward most objectives.

The offensive began on schedule, however, the distances to be travelled, the dense vegetation and rough terrain, as well as the enemy resistance thwarted the capture of Hill 355 on the first day. As a result, the Canadian advance was delayed by five hours, which allowed the Australians to capture Kowang-san. That freed up artillery assets to support the 25 CIB advance. Fortuitously, the loss of Hill 355 forced some of the Chinese forces that were positioned to repel the Canadian advance to withdraw from their well-prepared entrenchments. Consequently, The RCR met very little opposition and easily attained their objectives, Hills 159 and 175, which were halfway to the intended Jamestown Line position earmarked as the goal for Operation Commando. The PPCLI on their flank, however, did meet with some stiff resistance and were required to close with and destroy the enemy who refused to abandon their positions. The weaker than expected resistance allowed 25 CIB to advance to their final Jamestown Line objectives. Unfortunately, as the operation was

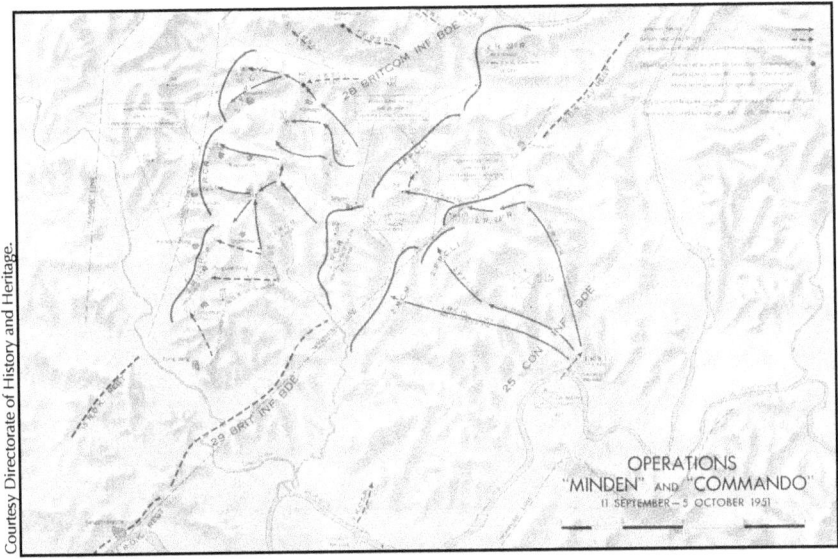

Operations Minden and Commando. This map also indicates the front line "Jamestown Line," the intermediate "Wyoming Line," and the depth "Kansas Line."

almost complete, in the early evening, "B" Coy, RCR, came under a heavy artillery bombardment that killed three men and wounded 10.

Nonetheless, by the end day, the Canadians attained their objectives, positions overlooking the Nabu-ri Valley, which represented no man's land between the UN forward positions and those of the Chinese. These positions represented roughly the ground the Canadians would hold for close to the next two years of fighting.

The Battalion now dug in once again, set about making their positions defensible, and settled in to a routine of patrolling, small scale skirmishing, repelling Chinese raids, and fighting the tedium of boredom. In the front lines, the soldiers slept "our clothes and boots on the outside of our sleeping bags on the ground inside the bunker," recalled Private Walter Rudolph.[37] Ammunition and grenades were close by — always ready in case of an enemy raid.

But the Chinese were not the only enemy that plagued them. "The rats in Korea," recalled one veteran, "were 2 to 3 times the size of rats we have in Canada." He explained, "the rats consistently bothered us ... they ate any food left open." Moreover, they crawled over soldiers while they slept and many of the troops were bitten.

Frequently, the tedium was broken by prisoners that were captured either through patrols, failed enemy attacks or simply through desertion.

A reverse slope RCR position overlooking the Nabu-ri Valley. This picture provides an idea of the underground existence experienced by the front line troops.

One prisoner captured on 14 October 1951, after a failed raid, provided a boost of morale for the "Royals." During questioning he stated that "the Chinese didn't want to fight, that Mao Tse Tung was Stalin's houseboy and that he was a 'Mother Fucker.'"[38]

The attritional warfare continued. The Chinese moved large numbers of heavy artillery pieces close to the front line and continually hammered the UN forward positions in conjunction with limited attacks by infantry. In return, the UN forces struck back, usually with sub-unit or smaller sized forces with limited objectives. At the end of the month, on 25 October 1951, UN command representatives and Chinese and North Korean delegates met at Panmunjom to resume peace talks, and the war entered its static phase. Political consideration, namely fear of provoking enemy retaliation, resulted in restrictions on offensive operations. In essence, nothing greater than a company-size raid was authorized. This became a hugely unpopular directive as it did not allow UN forces to disrupt Chinese intentions if a build-up of forces or material was detected before a suspected enemy offensive.

Nonetheless, small company sized raids were launched by the UN forces and 25 CIB. They in turn provoked enemy response. For The RCR

Private Johnny Decarie patches up a wounded Chinese soldier, 2 November 1951.

one such major test came on 2 November, when a Chinese battalion attacked "A" Coy's position. The "Royals" sensed trouble in the early afternoon when enemy infantry was seen massing across the valley. Friendly artillery began to pummel the obvious Chinese FUP, however, with little effect. The enemy simply moved to the rear slope and dead ground.

At 1800 hours, the Chinese artillery opened up and began to zero in on the RCR positions. The Chinese technique was not original, but it was effective. Enemy artillery would bombard the intended target and supporting positions to force the defenders to keep their heads down, while Chinese infantry would move forward to cut the wire or blow gaps in it with bangalore torpedoes. Once inside the wire the enemy would quickly try to storm into the trenches and firing pits.

At 2040 hours, the attack commenced. The Chinese battalion attacked with two companies, one conducting a frontal and the second approaching from the flank, with the third company in reserve. They were supported by a heavy weapons company that fired from a nearby hill. One official account revealed, "The enemy made two very determined assaults, wave after wave of Chinese storming the wire around the position. Throughout the assaults, despite enemy shell, mortar and small arms fire, Lieutenant [Edward] Mastronadi moved around his platoon encouraging his men to hold firm and at the same time securing information on the enemy's disposition in order to call down defensive fire tasks."[39] With bugles and whistles blowing the enemy attempted to penetrate between "A" and "C" Company but was repulsed.

The enemy continued to probe and press its attacks. Heavy and accurate enemy artillery and mortar fire continued to pound the position. Under cover of this hammering, the Chinese succeeded in blowing several holes in the defensive wire, and they now poured wave after wave of men through the gaps. In one section area, Private Rupert Bauer fought valiantly to keep the enemy from entering a gap in the wire in front of their section position. Firing his Bren gun non-stop it finally jammed. He quickly grabbed a Sten gun and without thought rushed closer to the hole in the wire and covered this entry point denying the enemy the ability to exploit the vulnerability.[40] Nonetheless, "at 0310 hrs 2 platoon 'A' Coy was attacked by large numbers of enemy," revealed the War Diary, "A fierce hand to hand battle raged with 2 platoon being compelled to withdraw to HQ area owing to overwhelming odds."[41] It was later learned that the platoon, during its eight hours of combat, had engaged and held up an entire Chinese battalion. In the process, it suffered 50 percent casualties.

The Canadian artillery quickly responded and concentrated fire on the abandoned positions. As morning dawned the Chinese attack dissipated and they melted away, leaving behind a number of dead, wounded, and prisoners. At 0630 hours, as friendly air strikes pummelled the Chinese forward positions, 3 Platoon moved forward and reoccupied the position abandoned earlier. Upon arrival, they found everything almost as it had been left, virtually untouched. In total they found 18

Private Bob McPherson reloads Bren gun magazines on 3 November 1951, the morning after the Chinese attacked "A" Coy.

enemy dead and captured three prisoners. RCR losses amounted to one killed and 14 wounded.

By the end of November, the First Commonwealth Division commander directed 25 CIB that "during the remainder of the armistice negotiations, every effort will be made to avoid casualties and to demonstrate our willingness to honour a cease fire." He elaborated that for the immediate future, the Commonwealth division was not to mount any offensive operations or raids, but was only to send out recce patrols and generally to "avoid engaging the enemy unless he threatened our positions by fire or movement."[42] As a result, a relative calm settled over the front.

The calm, however, was not to last long. The peace talks were making little to no progress. As the end of the year was approaching, the American command became concerned that the UN forces would lose their fighting edge. As a result, they directed that every patrol would make contact with the enemy. In fact the corps commander sent a message to his units

In the aftermath of a Chinese attack, members of 2 RCR search the ground near their position for enemy stragglers.

offering "a prize of $5.00 and an additional 5 days R&R leave to Japan … to the man who captured the first prisoner alive and in a condition to be interrogated." An additional bonus was thrown in. "The GOC," he informed all, "will also throw in a bottle of whisky."[43]

The impact on 25 CIB was minimal. They had always maintained a vigorous patrol schedule that saw each of the battalions sending out one to two patrols on a nightly basis. On 18 January 1952, 25 CIB was taken out of the line for the first time since September and assigned to divisional reserve where it was assigned the tasks of preparing defensive positions on the Wyoming and Kansas lines, as well as training. It remained in reserve for approximately six weeks.

Although in reserve, the harshness of the Korean winter quickly became apparent. Between November and March, because of the large variation in temperatures from one day to the next a damp cold persists, and conditions switch rapidly between thaw and freeze. One journalist explained, "the men's parkas, battledress and underwear became soaked and then frozen." He continued, "They crouched in a foot of ice water — blankets turned to sopping rags."[44] Furthermore, high winds and humidity caused the soldiers to often feel colder than the actual temperatures

"Royals" man a front line trench and bunker, March 1952.

suggested. These hardships would soon be in the past, however, for the "Royals" in 2 RCR were nearing the end of their Korean adventure.

On 10 March, 2 RCR returned to the front line for its last tour of duty. The first order of business was to improve the bunkers, which were too small for Canadian standards. "The English have a tendency to construct their bunkers as small as possible," wrote the war diarist, "the Canuck likes lots of room and comfort."[45] With reconstruction underway and the endless routine of sentry and patrols, the "Royals" once again faced the enemy in a "war of nerves."[46]

Though 2 RCR's time in Korea was almost up, and feelings were "running high with rotation coming up in April," according to the War Diary,[47] a relentless patrol schedule was maintained. The patrols brought the men into continuous contact with an equally tenacious enemy, causing many casualties in the run up to going home. "Patrols were terrifying," reminisced John Woods, "everyone was out there, North and South Koreans, Chinese and the Van Doos [R22R], none of whom spoke English." He added, "patrols were very intimate affairs."[48] Nonetheless, patrolling continued to the end. On 29 March 1952, 2 RCR made its last contact with the Chinese army when one of its ambush patrols captured

Members of "A" Coy, 2 RCR, are briefed in a crawl trench before conducting an operation, 20 March 1952.

a wounded prisoner. As April arrived, the 2 RCR veterans waited impatiently for their replacements. By mid-April the first elements of 1 RCR arrived and the relief in place began. By end of the month, 2 RCR was finally on its way home. For them, the war was over.

8
"Spit and Polish":
The Regulars in Korea, 1952–1953

As the 2nd Battalion, The RCR was completing its final engagement with the enemy, the advance elements of the 1st Battalion, "B" and "D" Coys, sailed out of Seattle aboard the USNS *Marine Phoenix* for Korea. They were followed the next day, 30 March 1952, by the remaining members of 1 RCR aboard the USNS *General William N. Black*. The incoming battalion rotated into the line and everyone understudied their counter part. On 16–17 April "A" and "D" Coys, 2 RCR, were relieved in place by "B" and "D" Coys, 1 RCR.[1] One member captured the moment:

> Thus after only nine days in Korea and but two in the line, 10 Platoon found itself at the forward most part of the battle line with nothing between us and the enemy but some unimpressive real estate, a small stream and a certain amount of barbed wire. The battered but still dangerous features known by their spot heights as Pt 116 and Pt 113 glowered at us with their faces scarred by UN explosives and Chinese digging.[2]

Two days later 1 RCR took over responsibilities for patrolling. Finally, on 25 April 1952, 1 RCR formally assumed control and responsibility of the area of operations.

The battalions were not the only entities to change over. Several days later, on 29 April, Brigadier Rockingham, the 25 CIB commander handed

Typical battalion echelon bivouac to the rear of the front line positions.

over command to Brigadier M.P. Bogert. In addition, at the beginning of May, General Matthew Ridgeway handed over his appointment as the UN supreme military commander in Korea to General Mark Clark.

The change in approach and attitude between the former Special Service volunteers and the newly arrived regular force was notable. Lieutenant-Colonel P.R. Bingham, who was wounded within days of arriving in theatre when he activated a trip wire during an inspection of his platoons on a training exercise, insisted on a high degree of "spit and polish."[3] In fact, on arrival Bingham announced, "A regular soldier should not only fight better than the non-regular, but should at all times conduct himself as a professional."[4] As a result, there was a greater emphasis on saluting in The RCR than in other units and the 1st Battalion, held regular formal mess dinners in the Officers' Mess every Wednesday. Moreover, Battalion officers were required to wear their No. 1 Dress (Blues) on these occasions. The official historian of the Canadian Forces in Korea remarked, "The attitude of 'spit and polish' the professionals brought with them to Korea was difficult to maintain in that country but ingenuity and perseverance overcame the difficulties." He added, they "took pride in immaculate lines, pressed uniforms and gleaming boots."[5]

Nonetheless, the Battalion quickly focused on learning the ropes. In the first few weeks patrol schedules ensured everyone was able to gain confidence and experience in operating in the new combat environment.

By late May, activity on both sides increased dramatically. Each night the Battalion had approximately 40 to 60 all ranks engaged in a myriad of standing, fighting, and reconnaissance patrols. The "Royals" also introduced the "jitters" patrol that was intended to keep the enemy in a state of anxiety. To achieve this, equipment such as bugles, whistles, tin-cans, and any other noise making instrument was employed.[6]

The Battalion's active patrol policy was in conformity with the 1st U.S. Corps HQ policy. Each forward battalion within the Commonwealth division was ordered to conduct one fighting patrol a week against enemy positions, and capture one prisoner every three days. The theory, as always, was easier than the practice. Although the units did their best — results were questionable. Moreover, the policy was costly as troops were forced to go deep into enemy territory to find their prey.

Patrols ranged from 20 men to entire companies and were supported by heavy supporting fire from tanks and artillery. Patrols passed through their own wire and defensive minefields, using existing gaps and crossed the floor of the valley and worked their way to the hills opposite them. Within 25 CIB, The RCR staged the most raids. In fact, the brigade commander ordered the Battalion "to cut down on patrols so other units can catch up."[7] The "Royals" concentrated on Hills 75 and 113, which lay

Chinese positions being hammered. This photograph shows the varied terrain that the "Royals" had to deal with.

across the valley of the Sami-ch'on tributary with Hill 166 immediately to the rear. In May, 1 RCR conducted seven large fighting patrols. The costliest occurred on the night of 22–23 May 1952, when five men were wounded and another killed.

Another fighting patrol, described by Major-General Cassels as a "specially daring raid against a strong enemy position" on Hill 113, which was more successful, occurred on 31 May.[8] The patrol was given a simple task — "kill or capture the enemy."

As the smoke from an air strike delivered by eight jet aircraft drifted lazily off the objective, the patrol left friendly lines and stealthily entered no man's land. The troops quickly crossed the valley floor and closed up on the burned-out village of Chinchon, which was approximately 300 metres from the forward enemy defences. Lieutenant A.A.S. Peterson, the patrol commander, then called in the fire plan. As artillery shells began to pummel Hill 113, Peterson led his men to the first line of trenches. These proved to be "deserted and in a state of disrepair."[9] The walls were broken in and there was brush in the trenches. At this location, Peterson left Sergeant H.J.D. Shore, seven men and a 2-inch mortar to form a firm base to provide security for the patrol's eventual withdrawal.

The patrol commander now called off the artillery fire, leaving only the tanks to continue to fire onto the objective. Under cover of this timed supporting fire program delivered by the tanks, the patrol then proceeded to the second line of trenches higher up the feature. These too were abandoned. Here, Peterson left Corporal Stinson and six men to clear the bunkers, while he pressed on with the remainder of his patrol to the crest of the hill.

Stinson and his group worked their way down the trench line clearing bunkers with phosphorous grenades. Each patrol member carried three high explosive (HE) grenades. Four soldiers were designated "bombers" and they carried 11 HE and five phosphorous grenades. At each bunker they yelled *"Chu-la"* (come out) before tossing in the grenades. All of a sudden, "one Chinaman appeared from a bunker with hands raised and said 'me officer.'"[10] He was subsequently taken prisoner, "subdued [hit on the head] and his head covered with a blanket."[11] However, things quickly heated up. Stinson's squad observed some enemy troops moving up the south side of Hill 113, defying the artillery, mortar, and machine gun fire pounding the objective area. As the enemy neared Stinson's location a gunfight broke out — grenades were thrown and small arms fire was exchanged. Private M.J. Fitzgerald, a Bren gunner opened fire and a number of enemy dropped but others tenaciously continued to crawl forward. Soon he was bombarded by a barrage of potato-masher type Chinese grenades. They were easy to see because of the flash and smoke. Nevertheless, one hit Fitzgerald on the head, bounced off, and, fortunately, burst harmlessly at his feet. Others failed to detonate.[12]

As the melee broke out Private J.M. McNeil, who was guarding the prisoner, was wounded in the arm. The Chinese prisoner quickly seized the opportunity and scrambled off but Private P. Mullet "stopped him with about 20 rounds."[13] Throughout the firefight the soldiers' cursed their Sten submachine guns as they repeatedly jammed when needed most.

Meanwhile, Peterson and the seven remaining soldiers worked their way along the trench on the crest of Hill 113, clearing the defences with phosphorous grenades. They quickly noted that there was a series of tunnels underneath the communication trench they were in, and they could actually see the enemy scurrying around below them. The discovery was no real surprise. By March 1952, intelligence on the Chinese tactics, techniques, and procedures had identified:

> The Chinese have shown themselves to be masters in the preparation of defensive works. The report noted that their defensive positions are a maze of bunkers, bays, weapon pits, storage and sleeping quarters. All these positions are connected by deep communication trenches. They made use of outposts located at the foot of occupied terrain features to warn of the approach of UN forces. Enemy held locations were a series of elaborately prepared defensive positions echeloned up the sides of the occupied terrain features and connected by communication trenches.[14]

The Chinese rapidly recovered from their initial surprise and the intense pounding they had taken by the supporting fire, emerging from bunkers and foxholes to approach from all directions. Chaotic fighting erupted as the enemy swarmed over the position. Peterson ordered Corporal Stinson's group to pull back to the firm base and withdrew his own group immediately as well. He did not hear Corporal Stinson's warning, "Don't come this way!" and so began to withdraw by the same route they had come. However, he quickly abandoned the idea when he was showered by grenades. Realizing that the enemy had weaseled their way between the elements of his patrol he now retreated straight down the feature.[15]

In the interim, Stinson's group came under increasing pressure. Additional Chinese reinforcements braved the cauldron of fire and advanced on the patrol over the open ground tossing grenades as they approached. As the fire fight intensified, at least four Chinese soldiers were killed, but two more of Stinson's men, and Stinson himself, were now wounded. Upon receiving the order to withdraw, Corporal Stinson led his group back down the crawl trench they had come up, however, not before searching the dead Chinese officer. Stinson personally covered the withdrawal and killed three enemy at a distance of 1.5 to 3 metres.

As the entire patrol was extricating themselves from the chaos they had created, Peterson called down another heavy artillery bombardment. The firm base also lent a hand to support the withdrawal. They pumped small arms and 2-inch mortar bombs (fired at low trajectory and close range) into the pursuing enemy. Under the curtain of fire, the patrol was able to break clean and make their way back to friendly lines.

Upon return, Corporal Stinson, who had just finished his 25th patrol, made no attempt to have his wounds dressed, in fact did not even disclose he was wounded, until he had finished his patrol debrief.[16] Based on the documentation gathered, the Chinese "officer" actually turned out to be Private Ho Chee Fah and no valuable information was retrieved.[17] Although no prisoners were taken, the patrol had met the other requirement. They counted five enemy killed and at least five wounded. Their own casualties amounted to four wounded.

Although the Battalion was heavily engaged on the front lines in their war of patrols, a secret mission soon took "B" Coy away from its front line tour. At 2300 hours, 22 May 1952, the sub-unit was pulled from its position. It was moved by truck and at 0700 hours the next morning dismounted and boarded a train for Pusan. "But up until now," noted the "B" Coy War Diarist, "our destination is unknown."[18] The following day the "Royals" arrived at the docks in Pusan and at 1830 hours that night boarded landing craft for the next leg of their journey. They finally arrived the next morning, 25 May, to find themselves on Koje-Do, a rocky, inhospitable island off the south coast of Korea near Pusan. It had been turned into a prisoner of war camp and by the end of 1951 housed approximately 130,000 North Korean and 20,000 Chinese prisoners.[19]

Unbeknownst to the "Royals," on 7 May the brewing cauldron in Koje-Do had exploded when the prisoners seized the camp commander,

"B" Coy Bren gunner guarding North Korean and Chinese prisoners on Koje-Do, 6 May 1952.

American Brigadier-General F.T. Dodd. Up to this point, prisoners were housed in compounds that held up to 5,000 inmates and were loosely guarded by American and South Korean guards. Not surprisingly, hard-core elements within the prisoner population began to organize resistance and rioting soon erupted. On 18 February 1952, the powder keg blew as an American battalion of soldiers entered a compound to restore order during a screening session.[20] Prisoners, armed with homemade weapons, attacked the soldiers, killing one and injuring 38. In response, the American troops opened fire inflicting 200 casualties. It became a propaganda nightmare.

In the aftermath, demonstrations of defiance increased within the compounds. However, under orders not to use force, American and South Korean guards simply formed an outer cordon of the compounds and left the prisoners within to rule themselves. And so, on 7 May, the commandant had entered a compound, against instruction and common sense, to speak to a delegation of prisoners. He was abruptly taken prisoner himself. In ensuing negotiations Dodd was released. The Americans wasted no time replacing him and eventually appointed the seasoned Brigadier-General

H.L. Boatner as commandant. The UN military command also directed the deployment of one British and one Canadian company to assist with the prison reform that was desperately needed.[21]

Major E.L. Cohen, the officer commanding "B" Coy, 1 RCR, agreed with the need for reform. He recalled upon arrival, "the cages resembled a midway." He explained, "hanging from the barbed wire were hundreds of cloth and paper signs, carrying insulting messages in English." Moreover, red flags flew from the tents within the compound. Cohen's impression was "that nothing much prevented a mass breakout ... the wire fences could have been pushed over without difficulty."[22]

The 1 RCR sub-unit, as well as "B" Coy, 1st Battalion, King's Own Shropshire Light Infantry, spent the next 10 days establishing their camp and preparing for their new duties. Training included lectures, demonstrations, and instruction on riot drill and the .30-calibre Browning machine gun. Then, on 4 June, came their turn. The Canadians and British took up guard duty over Compound 66, which held 3,200 North Korean prisoners, mainly officers. The "B" Coy War Diarist described their task:

> We occupied seven towers, placed at intervals about the Compound, with a Bren gunner on each of the towers' two platforms. Between these towers, there were sandbagged ground positions, seven in all, each containing a Bren gunner. There were three high barbed wire fences about [Compound] 66 and in between the outer two we had an 8-man perimeter guard, constantly patrolling and watching the POWs for unusual occurrences or disturbances.[23]

Eight days later the Commonwealth troops were ordered to move the prisoners from their compound to one of the new facilities built. The "Royals" were apprehensive. Only two days previously in a similar exercise, experienced American troops from the 187th (Airborne) Regimental Combat Team met furious resistance. The prisoners attacked the U.S. troops with spears, clubs, and homemade grenades. In the resulting melee 31 prisoners were killed and 111 wounded. Fortuitously, the next day, on 13 June, because of the "formal discipline" of the RCR troops and their British counterparts, the transfer was completed without incident, although the soldiers were required to line the entire route between the compounds, standing at the high port with bayonets fixed for three

"SPIT AND POLISH"

"B" Coy personnel manning a Compound 66 guard tower on Koje-Do.

hours. In the following weeks guard duty over other compounds was completed and on 8 July, "B" Coy was relieved by the American 92nd Military Police Battalion. By 14 July, they rejoined the Battalion. And so ended their part in what General Mark Clark described as the "biggest flap of the whole war."[24]

For the "Royals" not at Koje-Do, the war of patrols continued. On 21–22 June, "C" Coy, launched another noteworthy raid that proved costly. The losses totalled one killed and 22 wounded. The objective was once again Hill 113. Brigade assigned 1 RCR the mission of capturing five prisoners at which time the attacking force could leave immediately. Failing this, they were to seize and hold the feature for one hour.²⁵

At 0300 hours, 22 May 1952, "C" Coy left the relative safety of the Battalion position and moved by bounds to the ruins of Chinch'on, with 9 Platoon was left at the river to act as a firm base. As the remainder of the sub-unit moved to the base of the feature, the company commander called down additional supporting fire (i.e., two field regiments, two troops of tanks, a battery of 4.2-inch mortars, unit 81 mm mortars, and unit medium machine guns). As the main body reached the base of the hill, the firm base was brought forward to re-establish the firm base at that location. At this point the supporting fire was lifted to allow the assaulting force to begin the ascent. The tanks, however, maintained direct fire on the rows of communication trenches at the higher levels. As the fighting patrol advanced between the two lower rows of trenches a series of large detonations, believed to be anti-tank mines used in the anti-personnel role, ripped into their ranks. The forward observation officer (FOO), however, believing it to be friendly fire, cancelled the supporting tank fire.

The assaulting platoon, 7 Platoon, continued forward. As they reached the top of the hill, they came under heavy fire from enemy machine guns, burp guns, and grenades. One man was killed immediately, all three section commanders, the platoon commander, and four others were wounded. The platoon recoiled slightly and reorganized for a second assault. Once again they ran into a wall of fire at the cost of four more wounded.

The OC, Major Don Holmes, realized "one determined effort by either side would swing the balance." He was preparing to push 8 Platoon through 7 Platoon, when the ever present "friction of war" articulated by the great military strategist and theorist Von Clausewitz intervened. At this point someone, whose identity has never been established, shouted "get down" (apparently meaning stay low). However, the warning was taken as a directive to withdraw off the feature. "Consequently," lamented Holmes, "the attack, which might well have been successful, ended in a mad scramble down the hill."²⁶

At the end of June, 1 RCR was pulled from the front line positions on the Jamestown Line and moved into reserve in the Wyoming Line. For the next six weeks its main duty was providing work parties for the Kansas Line, which was the depth defensive position. "Wiring, wiring, wiring," lamented the War Diarist. If wiring was not a nuisance to many

Major Don Holmes inspects equipment before a night patrol by "C" Company, 1 RCR, 21 June 1952, in Korea.

of the soldiers the continuing emphasis on "spit and polish" and saluting probably was. "Vehicles are not clean enough," observed the CO during a number of his weekly CO's conferences. "Whenever a vehicle is stopped," he directed, "drivers will wipe off tac signs of dust."[27] Saluting also became an issue during many of these forums. "Saluting in vehicles is good but could be better," it was observed, "all people will salute including drivers."[28] Shortly thereafter another warning was given, "Saluting in vehicles must improve even more ... 100% is the only standard."[29] By end month, the standard had still not improved and additional admonitions on both cleanliness of coy tac signs and saluting were issued: "Drivers to be smartened up in saluting officers getting in and out of vehicles ... dress of drivers must improve ... saluting in "A" and "B" Ech is not up to standard of "F" Ech."[30]

To exacerbate the situation, on 27 July 1952, the monsoon like downpours broke the dry and dusty heat that had plagued the troops during May and June. The torrential rains now turned the dust into mud. Moreover, the Imjin River rose to a level 12 metres above the normal summer level. "For a time," wrote one regimental veteran, "it appeared

Corporal E.D. Fowler escorts Private Wang Teh Shen, a prisoner snatched on a daring patrol behind Chinese lines.

probable that it would be possible to bring the Canadian Navy upriver, to shell enemy positions."[31]

Fortuitously, the heavy rains stopped before the Battalion returned to front line duty on 10 August. However, they returned two weeks later with a fury. "To our disgust," noted the war diarist, "we find that many of the dug-outs are not as water repellent as could be wished." Days later, he added, "the rain is still coming down, and the place leaks like a sieve."[32] The heavy rains actually caused the collapse of a number of bunkers and dugouts, as well as the kitchen. In addition, the trenches themselves "are falling in right and left."[33] "C" Company was particularly hard hit. "This [24 August] was a bad night for the troops as most of them had no place to sleep and spent the night standing in the trenches … in the rain."[34] Between 18 and 25 August, over 150 bunkers within the brigade collapsed.[35] With bunkers and trenches collapsing, or at a minimum leaking, with up to two feet of water collecting in the trench line and dugouts, life in the front line was challenging, if not outright miserable.

As the rains subsided at the end of August, the enemy activity increased. During the brigade's previous tour on the Jamestown Line, the Chinese were not very active. Now they were. They moved into no man's land in strength. They attacked patrols, raided forward positions and increased their harassing fire. As the enemy activity increased the

"Royals" came under additional pressures. There were insufficient trained troops to keep the R22R up to strength. By the beginning of September it was 300 men short. As a result, on 6 September 1952, 1 RCR, which was already responsible for the most active part of the brigade's front was now assigned the largest battalion area. To cope with this added area, Bingham now had to create a fifth rifle company, which he did by skimming 98 all ranks from the other four rifle companies and Battalion HQ to create the ad hoc sub-unit. It was assigned the left most portion of the 1 RCR line.

As the fall progressed tensions along the Jamestown Line increased. The "Royals" continued with their active patrolling. On the night of 24 September one particular daring snatch patrol was conducted. Lieutenant H.R. Gardner and Corporal E.D. Fowler, stealthily infiltrated deep into a Chinese defensive position to their field kitchen area behind Hill 227. Once in position, they cut a signals wire and waited for an unsuspecting Chinese technician to come repair the line. They did not have long to wait. As the unsuspecting Private Wang Teh Shen began to fix the break, Gardner struck him with a blackjack while Fowler attempted to pin his arms. A furious struggle commenced with Shen shouting for help. After several minutes Shen submitted after he was threatened with a gun. However, just as the prisoner was being lifted to his feet, the first of the armed enemy response arrived. A hot pursuit was now undertaken as the "Royals" withdrew with their prisoner. Fortunately, Gardner had planned well, and a series of firm bases through which he could pass assisted his party, with prisoner in tow, in breaking clean of the enemy pursuit.[36] The War Diary graphically captured the safe arrival of the group: "the snatch patrol came in about 0730 hrs complete with a Chink prisoner — Cpl Fowler brought him in by the scruff of the neck."[37] The daring nature and success of the patrol was seen as "a feather in the cap of the Regiment."[38]

However, the Regiment would add yet another feather in its cap almost a month later. At the end of September, the "Royals" noted that "the front is continually being probed by small numbers of enemy with no damage being done."[39] At the time not much was thought of the activity. However, as events unfolded, a chilling foreboding struck the "Royals." By end March 1952, the First Commonwealth Division intelligence staff had developed a fairly comprehensive picture of Chinese tactics. Large scale attacks and battalion-size raids were generally preceded by a series of nightly probing attacks increasing in size each night. In addition, the actual attack was always preceded by artillery fire. The bombardments generally started hours prior to the actual assault working up to intense fire at H-Hour. The Chinese Army was known to attack through their own supporting fire. Large scale attacks were always accompanied by at least a battalion-size diversionary attack to a flank. Often tanks and self-propelled guns were used to support the attack by providing direct fire on bunkers and entrenchments. Directional tracer, flares, bugles, and whistles were all methods used to control and guide attacking enemy elements.

The attack on a given objective was always made by a direct assault on the feature itself with an effort at a simultaneous envelopment from two sides. The enemy was adept at leaving troops to contain and attack defended localities, while passing other troops between these strong points to attack positions in depth such as command posts and gun areas. The assaulting troops were invariably armed only with submachine guns and grenades. Bangalore torpedoes and home made devices were normally utilized by assaulting elements to remove defensive wire that was not destroyed by the artillery bombardment. In addition, the Chinese had stopped using mass attacks on a large front because of initial failures. They now concentrated on obtaining complete superiority at a given point, allowing them to concentrate their support weapons at the focal point of the attack.[40]

The "Royals" would soon experience this first hand. Unbeknownst to 1 RCR a tempest was brewing. Nonetheless, activity in the line continued. The War Diary captured the harsh reality:

> Patrol activity continued ... 6 Royals had accomplished what the remainder of the Div[ision] had been trying to do in capturing a prisoner. All ranks are very proud of Lt Gardner and his gallant men. Other patrols were of a less spectacular nature. There were short, sharp, bitter clashes by night where the courage and common sense of the patrol members triumphed over the enemy and the darkness. Each day ... has been a testing one for several members of this Battalion. Tests have been met.[41]

And so, 1 RCR continued its vigilance on Hill 355, labelled "Little Gibraltar" by the Americans because from the rear it bore a striking resemblance to the actual feature in the Mediterranean. To the north and west, however, its features were more gradual. It was the highest feature of the surrounding area. Five company positions secured Hill

355, also known as Kowang-San on Korean maps. Area I, which was on the southeast portion of the position was garrisoned by "E" Coy and faced the enemy positions on Hill 227. Area II was secured by "D" Coy. This critical piece of ground lay on the immediate opposite side of the saddle that ran between Hill 227 and Hill 355. In many ways, it was the doorway to "Little Gibraltar." Areas III and IV, manned by "A" and "C" Coy respectively, anchored the northern front of Hill 355, and Area V, was a reserve position manned by "B" Coy. The Battalion felt secure on Kowang-San. In fact, one "Royal" wrote, "D Coy is settled in and ready for whatever happens. We on 355 feel secure in the knowledge that no Chinks can sneak up on us."[42]

October began with a bang. Much in keeping with the Chinese offensive doctrine they began a systematic hammering of the Hill 355. On 1 October 1952, the Chinese fired nearly 1,000 rounds, primarily into Area II. The next day, the enemy dropped in another 600 rounds and succeeded in destroying the defences in the Vancouver Outpost, which was subsequently abandoned, as well as knocking out the tank in the southern platoon area. A similar intense bombardment occurred on the third day, after which firing slackened somewhat until 17 October when

View of Hill 355 ("Little Gibraltar").

the intensity of fire picked up once again. On 21 August, 1,600 rounds thundered into 1 RCR. The next day, "1 RCR received 2,426 rounds from the 'friendly' Chinamen … 18 tons of assorted misery," captured the War Diary.[43] In the interim, "B" Coy relieved "D" Coy in Area II, the hardest hit, after last light on 22 October.

The effect of the prolonged bombardment was clearly evident. Major Bob Richards, the officer commanding "D" Coy, spent 21 days under shell fire in crowded dugouts. "Its bunkeritis, that's what gets you," Richards observed. "Its knowing that you can't walk around or you'll get hit," he explained, "It gets so that even when there's almost no shelling at all you still get nervous." He added, "and, when they pour in 1,275 a day you've got a problem." Richards acknowledged, "The odd man breaks, and then you risk getting a run of it." He proudly noted, however, "They all were getting a bit starey-eyed toward the end, but they all came out with their weapons."[44] Lieutenant M.F. Goldie stated: "Life there is very primitive indeed. You can't move an eyebrow without being hit." He lamented, "You just lie all day with your face in the dirt."[45]

Privates Wilfred Main and Wilfred Mangeon were buried by explosions. They managed to make air holes to prevent smothering and then dug themselves out with their bare hands. Main lost his boots and manned an observation post for 48 hours in his stocking feet.[46]

"Casualties weren't so heavy though," reported Major Richards, "That was due to the discipline." He explained, "The only casualties were from direct hits on bunkers and trenches and you can't control that." He conceded, "But reactions got slower all the time. At the beginning you'd give an order and they'd jump to it. Later they got to looking for shelter on the way. They'd get there all right, but it would take longer."[47]

When "B" Coy arrived into the position they found the field defences very badly damaged and the greater part of the reserve ammunition, which was stored in the weapons pits, buried. In addition, the bunkers were caved in and the telephone lines cut. The fire continued throughout the day on the 23rd and into the night. "B" Coy stayed on alert after dark. Throughout, they could hear the detonation of heavy explosions, distinctly different from the incoming artillery and mortar shells. The soldiers knew the Chinese were blowing gaps in the wire, however, the intensity of the fire, prevented them from providing any form of response.

Throughout the day the bombardment had continued to wreak havoc on the company position. Bunkers, command posts and trenches collapsed. Ominously, during the day the enemy moved several self-

Private Heath Matthews awaits medical attention after a night patrol.

propelled guns and infantry guns forward. Around 1700 hours, the scale of the destruction led Lieutenant Gardner and Sergeant G.E.P. Enright to attempt to reorganize the men in their platoons, which now represented a collective strength of approximately 30 men.

At 1730 hours the firing almost completely ceased. "The silence was eerie," recalled Lieutenant Scotty Martin, "and somewhat unsettling after so many days of harassment."[48] The reprieve was not to last long. Approximately 45 minutes later the enemy hurled its most intense concentration of shells to date, focusing particularly at the left most platoon of "B" Coy and the right most platoon of "E" Coy. The Chinese had chosen the seam between the two sub-units for their break-in. As the bombardment reached its climax, the Chinese poured in shells and mortar rounds at a rate of 6,000 shells an hour for 30 minutes.[49] This effectively destroyed any remaining field defences. "At 1815 hours," Martin recalled, "Baker and Easy companies disappeared in clouds of smoke and dust."[50] Private Ted Zuber, who would go on to become a famous war artist, remembered, "the smoke was so thick you couldn't see anything, it burnt your lungs."[51] Lieutenant D.G. Loomis later wrote:

Its effect can hardly be described. It was shattering. I stopped counting the rounds about halfway through this bombardment — at 700 — and I only counted the orange flashes which I could see. Before it was over visibility was less than an arm's length due to the heavy pall of black fumes which caused everyone's eyes to water.[52]

The fire then lifted and shifted to the positions adjacent to "B" Coy. The sub-unit was now effectively cut off from the other positions as the enemy fire pummelled "A" and "E" Coys on the flanks for 45 minutes. The Chinese then launched an attack to take the 460-metre peak.

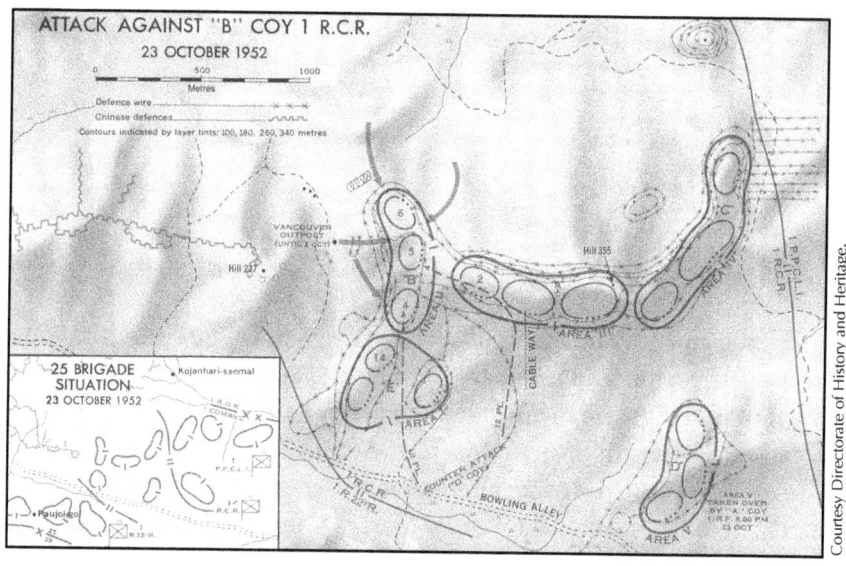

And so, as the bombardment continued on the flanks an enemy battalion swarmed over "B" Coy's shattered position. "At 1815 hrs," recorded the War Diary, "the tense words came to the CO, 'B' Coy was being overrun." It noted, "Heavy mortaring and shelling was followed by the enemy charging into "B" Coy position in the gathering dusk."[53] Private Arthur Alexander chillingly remembered, "The Chinese came in almost on top of the barrage screaming and firing their burp guns and throwing grenades."[54] The OC and his HQ, reported, "the sound of 'burp-guns,' horns bugles and whistles were heard even before the bombardment lifted."[55] Lieutenant Martin recalled, "Loud Chinese voices, whistles and bugles could be heard in Baker Company position only 50 yards away."[56]

Clearly, the Chinese attack was not unexpected, and a defensive fire plan had been organized. It was now executed. Artillery and 4.2-inch mortars thundered in assistance and hammered likely form-up points and approach routes. In addition, all possible Battalion HMGs, MMGs, and 81 mm and 60 mm mortars were called in for defensive fire (DF) tasks. As a result, a curtain of fire now rained down in front of "B" Coy and on to the approaches to the North of Hill 355. The "A" Coy War Diary recorded, "The enemy attacked 'B' Coy in estimated 2 Bn [battalion] strength, quickly overran 'B' Coy position and part of left hand Platoon 'A' Coy before being brought to a standstill."[57]

The battle for Area II had dissolved to desperate, savage close quarter, hand-to-hand combat. During the barrage Private Johnny Johnston crawled from foxhole to foxhole to repair weapons. He cleaned each part with gasoline and ensured they were ready when called upon. Later he calmly stripped two jammed Bren guns in the heat of the action and put them back in service. "He's the calmest man I've ever seen," praised his platoon commander, Lieutenant Edward Mastronardi after the battle.[58]

But he was not alone. Private Charles Morrison was rooted in his fighting trench when the Chinese hordes swarmed their position. He remained in place and fought desperately to enable his comrades to withdraw. "When last seen he was engaged in close combat with enemy."[59]

Sergeant Gerald Enright of 5 Platoon also displayed selflessness and courage. Ordered by his platoon commander to report their situation after all radio communications broke down, Enright fought his way through to "A" Coy's position under heavy fire. He reported the desperate plight of "B" Coy and then grabbed a radio and as much ammunition as he could carry and made his way back into the anvil of fire to assist his comrades beat back the seemingly endless tide of Chinese attackers.

Similarly, Lieutenant John Clark set a stirring example as he tenaciously held his position. Throughout he remained in the thick of the fighting. "He personally took an active part in the close fighting, throwing grenades and manning in turn a rifle, Bren, and Sten until each weapon's ammunition was expended."[60] When he realized that the remaining options were either annihilation or surrender, he reorganized the remainder of his platoon and successfully withdrew, carrying one of his wounded soldiers on his back, from their position to "A" Coy's entrenchments to continue on the fight.

"B" Coy by now was completely cut-off. Its neighbouring sub-unit, "E" Coy was the source of information for the Battalion HQ. Bingham

ESTABLISHING A LEGACY

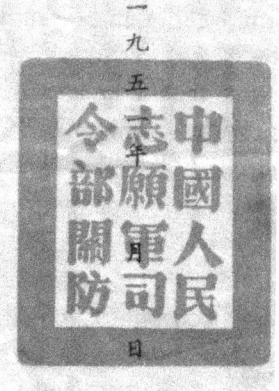

SAFE CONDUCT PASS

투항안전증

THE CHINESE PEOPLE'S
VOLUNTEER'S HEADQUARTERS

ORDER

The *BEARER*, regardless of his nationality or rank, will be duly accepted and escorted to a rear People's Volunteer Garrison or POW Camp; and on arrival will be guaranteed in accordance with our policy of leniency to prisoners of war, the following four great affirmations:

1. Security of life.
2. Retention of all personal belongings.
3. Freedom from maltreatment or abuse.
4. Medical care for the wounded.

THE CHINESE PEOPLE'S VOLUNTEER'S HEADQUARTERS

Chinese Safe Conduct Pass (front and back).

was on leave, so the fight was now in the hands of the acting CO, Major Francis Klenavic. Observation was obscured by the smoke and dust of the raging firefight.

The first clear information occurred at 1836 hours, when the 4 Platoon Commander arrived to Battalion HQ and reported that his platoon had been overrun. At this time it was impossible to contact the left most platoon of "A" Coy and it was presumed that they too had been overwhelmed. "D" Coy, in the unit's depth position, was warned off at 1850 hours to put in a counterattack at 1900 hours. At 1910 hours, OC "A" Coy called in a close-in DF. To this point the extent of the enemy attack or penetration had not been determined. It was not until later, that it became clear the Chinese had merely conducted a diversionary attack against "A" Coy's position.

At 1916 hours, OC "E" Coy deployed a small patrol to investigate the status of "B" Coy. They determined that the Chinese now possessed Area II. "A" and "C" Coy Coys continued to report movement directly to the front of their positions and continued to call in "danger close" artillery shoots. At 1943 hours, OC "B" Coy reported that he, 5 Platoon Commander, and 12 men had reached the left platoon of "A" Coy. He grimly reported that no friendly troops remained in action in the former "B" Coy area. As a result, Area II was now swathed with fire.

Plans were now consolidated for the counterattack to regain the lost position. By 2045 hours, all was set. A relieving force from "A" Coy, took over "D" Coy's position and all supporting tank and air assets were coordinated. The plan entailed a complex pincer movement with one platoon attacking from behind "E" Coy's position, while another platoon (a diversion) would attack through "A" Coy.

As the final preparations were made for the counterattack, Battalion HQ could still not determine the intent of the enemy. The weight of the attack, and the enemy's continuing activity to the west and north of Hill 355 reinforced the belief that this was just Phase 1 of a larger attack. At 2110 hours, a sudden increase in enemy artillery and mortar fire on "E" Coy seemed to indicate an impending assault.

In response, all available artillery and mortar assets fired an impressive response. Area II and all approaches to Hill 355 were now covered in a blanket of fire. It appeared that the speed and weight of the response fire took the steam out of the enemy's advance. Chinese supporting fire faltered, slackened, and then tapered off to harassing fire for the remainder of the engagement.

By 0105 hours, 24 October, "D" Coy was poised to launch the counterattack. Seven minutes of artillery fire preceded the assault. 10 Platoon assaulted from the left and into the extreme most position of Area II. They encountered no opposition. At the same time 12 Platoon attacked from "A" Coy's position on the right and occupied the centre position in Area II. Once again, they too met no opposition. The enemy had melted away. By 0331 both assaulting platoons linked up and the situation was restored.[61] "D" Coy then cleared out the rubble and made the position "fightable." The grim task of evacuating the dead and the wounded then commenced.

In the end, the battle cost the Battalion 18 killed, 35 wounded, and 14 taken prisoner. "The Regimental Banner," captured the War Diary proudly, "atop 355 is shot and shelled — but it still flys."[62]

On 1 November 1952, the Regiment was relieved by the 1st Battalion, Royal Australian Regiment. Its tenure on Hill 355 was long and costly. The Battalion now moved into divisional reserve. By the end of the month, 25 CIB was returned to the front but 1 RCR remained in a supporting role. Its remaining time in Korea was relatively quiet. It supported 25 CIB operations, manned the "Hook" for roughly a 30 day period in December and January, and conducted the normal heavy regimen of patrols. The Battalion's departure finally came on 30 March when it sailed from Pusan to Kure, Japan. Finally, on 9 April, 1 RCR boarded the USNS *Marine Lynx* and sailed for home.

The 1st Battalion was replaced by the 3rd Battalion, The RCR (3 RCR), which had been warned off for Korea on 23 September 1952. It had completed its training and embarked on the USNS *General C.C. Ballou* in Seattle, on 27 February 1953. Through various stops, ships, and trains, 3 RCR found themselves in Tokchon, from where they moved by road to the divisional rear area near Kuam-ni. Here, on 31 March, they were given a demonstration of an attack, after which time they officially became the Regiment's third unit to serve in Korea, although its Regimental flag had already been flying for six days. 1 RCR was more than anxious to pass on the torch when the first members of 3 RCR had arrived.

The latest rotation of "Royals" did not have long to wait before moving to the front lines. On 6 April 1953, 25 CIB returned to the line, this time under the leadership of Brigadier J.V. Allard. The RCR moved into brigade reserve near the junction of the Sami-ch'on and Imjin Rivers. Approximately two weeks later, 3 RCR relieved 1 R22R in the front line positions to allow the French Canadians to conduct their rotation with their 3rd Battalion. The remainder of the month was relatively quiet. However, things were about to change.

The ground to the front of the Commonwealth division was challenging. The CO, Lieutenant-Colonel K.L. Campbell, explained, "The terrain was made up of steep sided hills joined by steep-sided ridges and separated by valley varying from narrow bush choked ravines to wide flat bottomed valleys floored with paddy."[63] This made covering the normal 2,300–3,700 metre battalion frontage by small arms fire difficult. Moreover, the slopes of the hills were covered in brush and long grass that gave good cover for an approach. This was the daunting terrain that faced 3 RCR, as it manned its position on Hill 187.

The nature of the ground the Battalion was responsible for resulted in "platoon positions on the more prominent hills loosely grouped into coy localities suited to the ground pattern."[64] "A" Coy was on the high ground; "D" Coy on the ridge to the southwest; "C" Coy held the western half of the ridge running west from Hill 187, while platoons from "B" Coy were distributed between the two ridges to the south. Because of the amount and type of terrain to be covered, the platoon positions within each of the localities, as well as between localities, were well dispersed. As a result, these distances negated effective mutual support by rifle or light machine guns from one position to the next.

Fortuitously, the static nature of the war allowed for mortars and artillery to register many targets. As a result, all the dead ground, FUPs, and lines of approach were ranged-in and marked as DFs. This was important since the defences themselves were run-down. The CO complained:

> When 3 RCR moved into its sector, the position was badly run down. The wiring was insufficient. The trenches were not deep enough. There were gaps in the communication trenches. The fire bays were of a poor design and had no adequate overhead cover. The bunkers were too high, too lightly timbered and had too little overhead cover. They were also too far removed from the fighting positions.[65]

To add to the problem, the "Royals" were frustrated in their attempts at improving the position. Each night they were only able to repair the damage that was done during the day by enemy shelling. The Chinese had developed an accurate picture of the RCR position and could deliver fire with some precision. The static position of the front, active and aggressive patrolling by the Chinese, clear observation from their positions on Hill 166, the obvious signs of RCR ongoing improvements to their position (namely the spoil from digging), all provided the enemy with a clear picture of the RCR layout. The Chinese would soon put this to good use.

In addition, when the neophyte 3rd Battalion arrived to take over the front line, they found no man's land dominated by the enemy. They developed a progressive patrolling program to acclimatize the unit to the terrain and enemy tactics so that they could wrest control of the valley away from the Chinese. However, before the plan could be finalized the enemy struck.

Very little warned 3 RCR of the impending attack, other than reports of increased patrols on the front and north flank of "C" Coy. These were largely ignored by the chain of command as the overcharged imagination of green troops. However, other signs also provided some indication. Although there was no increase in the volume of enemy fire, most of the incoming rounds were focused on "C" Coy. In addition, it appeared that enemy patrols began focusing on the wire in front of "C" Coy.

For these reasons, a standing and fighting patrol were deployed on the night of 2 May 1953, to deal with the Chinese incursions. Contact was made and a heavy fire fight ensued. What at first was assessed as two opposing patrols bumping in the dark soon became tragically inaccurate. The Chinese element was just the screen for a larger raid. The Chinese assault was divided into five groups. The first element, was the counter-patrol force of three patrols to screen their larger assaulting force. The next group consisted of section groups responsible for creating gaps in the wire. They were followed by three groups of 15 men each, charged with destroying bunkers and clearing trenches. Behind them came two platoon size "snatch" groups. Finally, a company strength group was held in reserve to reinforce the assault or exploit success.

As the patrols exchanged fire, the Chinese who had by now created the necessary gaps in the wire, called down a tremendous concentration of fire on the objective. As the "Royals" hunkered down to ride out the storm, the enemy assault forces rushed in, oblivious to their own bombardment. As the fire lifted to the rear the assault force began throwing grenades and destroying the field defences. At the same time, the "snatch" parties began grabbing prisoners.

Initially, the intensity of fire and the suddenness of the enemy allowed the Chinese to maintain momentum. However, quickly the "Royals,"

"SPIT AND POLISH"

Chinese positions under artillery fire. This picture captures the steep terrain with its heavy foliage and covered approaches.

relatively safe in their bunkers, called in artillery on their own position. Second-Lieutenant E.H. Hollyer "saw a wave of from 50 to 60 Chinese coming up the hill, throwing grenades." As soon as the enemy entered the communication trenches the platoon commander called for the defensive fire to be switched onto his own position.[66] "The Chinese were overrunning 7 Pl and the SOS task was fired in this area," recorded the War Diary at 0010 hours, "2/Lt Hollyer called for VT as the enemy were in large numbers and were over-running 7 Pl and approaching 5 Pl."[67] Quickly, proximity fused artillery shells (or better known as air burst) showered "C" Coy's position with lethal shards of molten metal and shrapnel.

The initiative now began to shift. The enemy objective was a magnet for fire from artillery, mortar, tank, and machine guns. Furthermore, brigade HQ directed that all guns in range assist the beleaguered RCR company by firing on enemy approaches, likely FUPs, and resupply routes. The combined fire cut a swath through the Chinese ranks. "The enemy sustained heavy casualties, the trenches being literally filled with them," recalled Second-Lieutenant Hollyer, "they were rolling their dead and wounded over the lip of the hill where litter bearers were hauling them away."[68]

Nonetheless, the remaining elements of "C" Coy under tremendous pressure from the enemy withdrew from the position. The CO alerted the R22R to send forward a company to relieve one of his depth sub-units, namely "D" Coy, so that he could use it to launch a counter attack. However, it soon became apparent that the Chinese were in the process of withdrawing. As such, an 11-man fighting patrol was sent to reoccupy the former "C" Coy position. Initially, they were repulsed by heavy mortar fire, but shortly after first light on 3 May, were able to complete the task.

Evacuation of a "Royal" in a Sikorsky S-51 helicopter to No. 8055 MASH, U.S. Army.

Paul E. Tomelin, Library and Archives Canada PA-128851.

The attack had been a costly one. The tally was grim. The "Royals" lost 26 killed, 27 wounded, and seven taken prisoner.[69] "The last thing I did on Hill 187 was cry," acknowledged Ed Nieckarz, "I counted only 11 people walking off the hill from our platoon and I wondered where in Hell everyone else was."[70]

This attack, however, represented the last major engagement for the Canadian infantry in Korea. The Chinese focused their attention for the remainder of the war on American and South Korean positions. Aside from patrolling and operational moves to conduct reliefs in the line, there were no events of note. On 27 July 1953, an armistice was signed, bringing an ended to "a static campaign, fought in a primitive country."[71] The demarcation line became the existing battle line. The "Royals" remained in Korea until 27 March 1954, when they finally set sail for home.

On that note, the first 70 years of The Royal Canadian Regiment ended. For that entire time, Canada's oldest infantry regiment faithfully carried out its responsibility to the nation. Never did it falter or fail the Canadian people. From its inaugural battle experience in the North-West Rebellion, through its ordeal in South Africa at the turn of the Century where it set a name and reputation for not only itself, but the nation at large, through the crucible of two world wars, and a scant five years later Korea; the Regiment set a legacy of duty and honour — always For Country.

APPENDIX A
Key Events Timeline

1883

21 December: General Order No. 26 was issued authorizing the formation of three schools of infantry ("A" Coy — Fredericton, New Brunswick; "B" Coy — St. Jean, Quebec; and "C" Coy — Toronto, Ontario), formed into one corps, known as the Infantry School Corps. The commandants were "A" Coy, Lieutenant-Colonel G.J. Maunsell; "B" Coy, Lieutenant-Colonel G. d'Orsonnens; and "C" Coy, Lieutenant-Colonel W.D. Otter.

1884

7 January: Thomas MacKenzie was the first to enrol as a recruit in the Infantry School Corps.

April: "A" Coy, "B" Coy and "C" Coy inaugurated the first course of infantry training for officers and men of the militia.

1885

27 March: Lieutenant-Colonel R.B. Denison, deputy adjutant general at Toronto, received orders to call out "C" Coy, along with 250 volunteers from the 10th Royal Grenadiers and the Queen's Own Rifles, to be prepared to move west on short notice in response to the North West Rebellion.

27 March: 90 all ranks from "C" Coy, the Infantry School Corps departed Toronto on trains to participate in quelling the North-West Rebellion.

7 April: "C" Coy and attached volunteers arrived in Winnipeg via the C.P.R.

8 April: "C" Coy set out to Qu'Appelle, where Canadian government forces were assembling to counter the rebels.

24 April: Lieutenant-Colonel Otter's column, including half of "C" Coy under Lieutenant R.L. Wadmore, marched unopposed into Battleford.

24 April: Members of "C" Coy, the Infantry School Corps under the command of Major Henry Smith participated in the battle of Fish Creek.

24 April: Private Arthur J. Watson, "C" Coy, Infantry School Corps was killed in action during the battle of Fish Creek. He became the first "Royal Canadian" killed on active service.

2 May: Members of "C" Coy, the Infantry School Corps under the command of Lieutenant Wadmore participated in the battle of Cut Knife Creek.

7 May: Major Smith and his "C" Coy was ordered to board the steamer S.S. *Northcote* to assist in the attack on Batoche.

9 May: Major-General Frederick Dobson Middleton's column attacked Batoche. "C" Coy, on board the S.S. *Northcote* participated in the attack by creating a diversion. Damage to the steamer took them out of action for the remainder of the battle. They returned to Batoche three days later.

October: "C" Coy, which formed part of the garrison at Battleford until this point, relinquished the post in full to the NWMP.

1887

18 August: The government authorized the formation of "D" Coy in London, Ontario. Lieutenant-Colonel H. Smith was in command. Although authorized, the Coy was not actually formed until early in 1888.

APPENDIX A

1892

24 May: The government of the Dominion of Canada granted the Infantry School regimental status; accordingly, it became the Canadian Regiment of Infantry.

1893

24 May: On Queen Victoria's birthday, The Regiment was granted a royal prefix, thus becoming The Royal Regiment of Canadian Infantry (RRCI). The Regiment was also permitted to wear the imperial cipher, V.R.I. ("Victoria Regina Imperatrix" — latin for "Victoria, Queen and Empress")

29 November: Regimental Order No. 1, RRCI, announced the appointments of Regimental sergeant-major, quartermaster-sergeant, orderly-room sergeant, sergeant-bugler and hospital sergeant would be made by headquarters. Individuals would be selected based on efficiency and would be drawn from the entire Regiment.

November: The GOC the Canadian militia ordered that Company band organizations be discontinued.

1894

General Order No. 83 directed that the Coys would be re-designated: London, No. 1; Toronto, No. 2; St. Jean, No. 3; and Fredericton, No. 4.

August: All four Coys concentrated for the first time at the Engineer's Camp at Lévis, Quebec, for six weeks of battalion training.

1896

5 September: Lieutenant-Colonel Maunsell became the first commanding officer of The RRCI.

1898

21 March: An Order-in-Council established that "a Field Force composed of volunteers from the permanent troops of the Dominion should be dispatched to Fort Selkirk."

3 May: Members of the RRCI moved to Ottawa to participate in the Yukon Field Force. Lieutenant-Colonel T.D.B. Evans, Royal Canadian Dragoons, was in command, with Major D.D. Young, RRCI, acting as second-in-command.

6 May: The Yukon Field Force departed Ottawa by rail for Vancouver.

16 May: The Regiment arrived at Fort Wrangel, Alaska aboard the *Islander*.

21 May: The Regiment arrived at Glenora, BC aboard the *Stikine Chief* and the *Strathcona*.

15 July: Lieutenant-Colonel Otter assumed command of the Regiment, succeeding Lieutenant-Colonel Maunsell.

11 September: The Yukon Field Force arrived in Fort Selkirk.

1 October: A detachment of 2 officers and 50 men from the Yukon Field Force were sent to Dawson as reinforcements for the NWMP.

1899

31 March: The Regiment was renamed The Royal Canadian Regiment of Infantry (often incorrectly abbreviated to the Royal Canadian Regiment). Lieutenant-Colonel Otter was the CO.

4 July: Regimental Orders announced the second concentration of battalion training at Rockcliff Camp, Ottawa.

July: The Yukon Field Force was reduced by half.

1 August: The first Honorary Colonelcy was established. The appointment was filled by Field Marshal Viscount Wolseley.

APPENDIX A

3 September: The Regimental Depot and Coy was established at Quebec City, Quebec.

28 September: Lieutenant-Colonel L. Buchan assumed command of The Regiment, succeeding Lieutenant-Colonel Otter.

14 October: The Canadian government agreed to send a military contingent to South Africa.

18 October: The prime minister and his cabinet approved the establishment and deployment of a regiment of infantry, namely the 2nd (Special Service) Battalion, The Royal Canadian Regiment (RCR) — 1,000 strong commanded by Lieutenant-Colonel Otter.

23 October: Orders were issued to concentrate the eight companies that will make up the Battalion, which were raised throughout Canada, in Quebec City.

27 October: The 2nd (Special Service) Battalion was formed and the officers gazetted.

30 October: The 2nd Battalion boarded the S.S. *Sardinian,* at Quebec City, for the deployment to South Africa.

30 November: The 2nd Battalion arrived at Cape Town, South Africa, and moved to Green Point Common.

3 December: The 2nd Battalion stopped at De Aar.

7 December: The 2nd Battalion deployed to the Orange River.

10 December: The 2nd Battalion relieved the Royal Munster Fusiliers as part of the garrison of Belmont.

1900

January: The 2nd Battalion was bivouacked in the area of Belmont.

1 January: "C" Coy, 2nd Battalion, The RCR, as part of a flying column under the command of Belmont Camp commandant, Lieutenant-Colonel Pilcher, assisted in the attack on the Sunnyside kopjes, and subsequently the town of Douglas, South Africa.

8 January: The pared down Yukon Field Force was renamed the Yukon Garrison.

12 February: The 2nd Battalion moved out of Belmont to Gras Pan, to join the 19th Brigade under Major-General Horrace Smith-Dorrien

13–18 February: The 19th Brigade moved to Paardeberg Drift via Ram-Dam, Waterval, Reit Drift, Wegdraai, Jacobsdal, and Klip Drift.

18 February: The 2nd Battalion crossed the Modder River and was engaged in combat for the first time as a battalion. The engagement started at 0930 hours and continued until nightfall. This was the start of the nine-day battle of Paardeberg.

21–23 February: The 2nd Battalion, as part of 19th Brigade manned a series of kopjes west of Artillery Hill, South Africa, to oppose a Boer relieving force attempting to break through British lines to Cronje's defensive position.

26 February: The 2nd Battalion relieved the Duke of Cornwall's Light Infantry from entrenchments 600 metres from the Boer position at Paardeberg Drift.

27 February: At 0200 hours, the 2nd Battalion conducted a night attack on the Boer lines. Although the attack was unsuccessful, causing most of the force to withdraw, "G" and "H" Coys remained on the battlefield and dug in close to the Boer position. When dawn arrived, the Boers realized they were outflanked and surrendered, ending the Battle of Paardeberg with the capitulation of General Cronje and his army.

7 March: 19th Brigade was engaged at Poplar Grove, South Africa. The 2nd Battalion was in reserve but during the action was attached to the Highland brigade where it was tasked to seize a series of kopjes.

15 March: The 2nd Battalion, as part of the 9th Division, entered Bloemfontein, the capital of the Orange Free State captured without opposition two days earlier.

25 March: In Canada, the 3rd (Special Service) Battalion, under the command of Lieutenant-Colonel B.H. Vidal, assumed garrison duties at the Halifax Citadel.

APPENDIX A

31 March: The 2nd Battalion occupied Boesman Kop with half its strength, and the remainder was engaged near Waterval Drift, along the Modder River.

5 April: The 2nd Battalion moved against some resistance to occupy positions Leeuw Kop, southeast of Bloemfontein.

21 April: The 19th Brigade relieved the 18th Brigade at Springfield.

25 April: The 19th Brigade was engaged at Israels Poort at that time Lieutenant-Colonel Otter was wounded. Lieutenant-Colonel Buchan assumed temporary command of the 2nd Battalion.

26 April: The 2nd Battalion was sent to Thaba Mountain, to hold it in the event of attack.

28 April: The 2nd Battalion was engaged at Eden Mountain.

30 April: The 19th Brigade assaulted Thaba Mountain.

10 May: The 2nd Battalion was engaged in the area of the Zand River.

14–24 May: The 2nd Battalion, encountered little resistance and marches from Kroonspruit, by way of Lindley, Witpoort, Elands Spruit and Prospect, to Vredefort Station.

26 May: The 2nd Battalion was the first infantry battalion to cross into the Transvaal. Lieutenant-Colonel Otter reassumes command of the Battalion.

29 May: The 2nd Battalion was engaged at Doorn Kop.

May: The Yukon Garrison moved from Fort Selkirk to Dawson.

3 June: The 2nd Brigade was engaged at 'Six-Mile Spruit' — the Battalion was held in reserve at Schwartz Kopjes.

5 June: The 2nd Battalion led 19th Brigade, which was the lead formation of General Sir Ian Hamilton's column, into Pretoria.

8 June: The 19th Brigade took up positions on the British line of communication.

13 June-2 August: The 2nd Battalion occupied Springs.

25 June: The last 100 soldiers of the Yukon Garrison (formerly the Yukon Field Force) was withdrawn from the Klondike.

1 July: Lieutenant-Colonel G.R. White assumed command of the 3rd (Special Service) Battalion, succeeding Lieutenant-Colonel Vidal.

3 July: Members of the Yukon Garrison arrived in Vancouver in the S.S. *Amur* from Skagway.

3 August: The 2nd Battalion arrived at Wolvehoek, to join General C.P. Ridley's column, to participate in the Vredefort operation.

17 August: After two cancelled missions, the 2nd Battalion camped at Tweefontein.

24–26 September: Sixteen officers and 230 other ranks of the 2nd Battalion concentrated in Pretoria, and, in accordance with their attestation agreements, moved to Cape Town to board the S.S. *Idaho* for Halifax.

8 October: The remaining members of the 2nd Battalion in South Africa concentrated at Silverton.

24 October: The 2nd Battalion was relieved by a detachment of the West Riding Regiment, and moved to Pretoria to participate in the ceremony annexing the Transvaal the following day.

7 November: The 2nd Battalion arrived in Cape Town and boarded the *Hawarden Castle* for England.

29 November: The 2nd Battalion arrived at Southampton and proceeded directly to London, England.

30 November: The 2nd Battalion paraded at Windsor Castle and was inspected by Queen Victoria.

12 December: After various tours in England, the 2nd Battalion departed Liverpool on the *Lake Champlain* for the return trip to Canada.

23 December: Upon their arrival in Halifax, the troops were discharged and the

2nd Special Service Battalion was disbanded.

1901

22 January: Queen Victoria died after 64 years on the throne — 1837–1901.

1 April: Regimental HQ was effectively transferred from Wolseley Barracks, London to Stanley Barracks, Toronto, in conjunction with Lieutenant-Colonel Buchan's command appointment of No. 2 Depot.

11 October: King's and Regimental Colours were presented in Toronto, for services rendered in the North West Rebellion and in South Africa, by His Royal Highness, during the Canadian visit of the Duke and Duchess of Cornwall and York. There was a five-year lapse before the Regiment actually took possession of the Colours because of corrections that were required. As a result, they were sent back to England and not returned until 1906.

2 December: The Regiment was officially renamed The Royal Canadian Regiment, with Lieutenant-Colonel Buchan commanding.

1902

31 May: The war in South Africa was formally ended.

29 September: The 3rd (Special Service) Battalion was relieved by the British 5th Battalion, Royal Garrison Regiment.

1 October: General Order No. 107 disbanded the 3rd (Special Service) Battalion.

30 October: Regimental Orders specified that as of 31 May 1895, the Queen had extended to warrant officers, NCOs and men of the Canadian Forces, the right to win the Meritorious Service Medal, the Medal for Distinguished Conduct in the Field, and the Long Service and Good Conduct Medal.

1903

24 June: The first of the medals mentioned 30 October 1902 were awarded.

1904

16 February: Brevet/Lieutenant-Colonel D.D. Young assumed temporary command of The Regiment, succeeding Lieutenant-Colonel Buchan.

23 July: The Regiment was administered by militia headquarters.

November: On behalf of H.M. (His Majesty) King Edward VII, the governor general of Canada, His Excellency the Earl of Minto, presented banners in recognition of service during the South African War by the 2nd Special Service Battalion, the Royal Canadian Field Artillery, and the Royal Canadian Garrison Artillery.

1905

May: Upon the announcement of the impending withdrawal of the British garrison in Halifax, The Regiment was reorganized on a 10 Coy basis to fill the new task.

25 May: The relief garrison, under Lieutenant-Colonel Wadmore, arrived in Halifax to assume duties at the Citadel.

May: It was around the time of the move to the Halifax garrison that the regimental march, known as "The RCR March," was first used.

15 September: Lieutenant-Colonel Wadmore assumed command of The Regiment (taking the responsibility away from militia headquarters).

1907

The Regiment was redistributed, and alphabetical designations were once again assigned: Regimental HQ, Halifax, NS; "A"-"F" Coys, Halifax; "G" Coy, Quebec, QC; "H" Coy, Fredericton, NB; "I" Coy, Toronto, ON; "K" Coy, London.

1908

July: The Regiment participated in the Tercentenary celebrations at Quebec.

1909

5 July: The Regiment was called in to aid civil power when a strike broke out at Dominion Coal Company in Cape Breton.

1910

4 March: The Dominion Coal strike ended and the Regiment returned to Halifax.

6 May: H.M. King Edward VII died at Buckingham Palace. H.M. King George V assumed the throne.

12 July: "A" and "B" Coys were called out when a strike broke out at the Springhill Mines, Nova Scotia.

1 September: Lieutenant-Colonel S.J.A. Denison assumed command of The Regiment, succeeding Lieutenant-Colonel Wadmore.

1911

Major A.O. Fages, 50 other ranks and the band, represented The Regiment at the coronation of H.M. King George V.

1912

August: After the Regiment provided a guard of honour for H.R.H. (His Royal Highness) the Duke of Connaught, eight coys and the band concentrated at Petawawa for summer training.

1913

The Regiment's authorized strength was reduced from 961 to 954 all ranks.

1 January: Promoted to lieutenant-colonel, Fages assumed command of The Regiment, succeeding Lieutenant-Colonel Denison.

10 July: The Regiment provided a guard of honour for General Sir Ian Hamilton, inspector-general of Overseas Forces of the British Army.

1914

30 July: Regiment began preparations, in the event of war.

4 August: Great Britain declared that a state of war existed with Germany, as of 2300 hours. As a result, Canada was automatically at war as well. Orders for "mobilization at war stage" then came into effect and the Regiment took up a defensive posture in Halifax and the Maritimes in accordance with national defence plans.

11 August: The Regiment received authorization to expand, which eventually added four provisional companies (No. 1-4) to the order of battle.

30 August: Field Marshal H.R.H. the Duke of Connaught inspected the Regiment in Halifax.

11 September: The Regiment, with a strength of about 938 all ranks, sailed for duty in Bermuda aboard the S.S. *Canada*.

14 September: The Regiment disembarked at Hamilton, Bermuda, and relieved the British 2nd Battalion, Lincolnshire Regiment.

28 September: The Regiment conducted a guard of honour 100 men strong for His Excellency Sir G. Bullock, governor of Bermuda on the occasion of the opening of the Colonial House of Legislature in Hamilton.

1 October: The Regiment was reorganized on an eight company basis: "A" and "C" Coys became the new "A" Coy; "B" and "D" became "B" Coy; "E" and "F" became "C" Coy; "G" and "H" became "D" Coy; "I" and "K" became "E" Coy; Provisional Coys No. 1 and 2 became "F" Coy; No. 3 became "G" Coy; and No. 4 became "H" Coy.

13 October: Field Marshal H.R.H. the Duke of Connaught was appointed honorary colonel of the Regiment, succeeding Field Marshal Lord Wolseley.

1915

1 January: Lieutenant-Colonel A.E. Carpenter assumed command of The Regiment, succeeding Lieutenant-Colonel Fages.

1 February: The Regiment was reorganized on a four Coy basis, each with four platoons: "A" and "E" Coys became "A" Coy; "B" and "G" became "B" Coy; "D" and "H" became "C" Coy; and "C" and "F" Coys became "D" Coy.

13 August: The Regiment was relieved of duty in Bermuda by the 38th Battalion, CEF, and boarded the SS *Caledonian* for return to Canada.

26 August: The Regiment, aboard the S.S. *Caledonian,* set sail to join the CEF in Europe.

6 September: After disembarking at Plymouth, England, The Regiment arrived in Shorncliffe at Quested Farm Camp where it began training for service in France.

14 September: The Regiment received supplies for service in France, including trading the "R.C.R." shoulder flash for one that read "V.R.I.;" at this time a Reserve Battalion was created consisting of 500 men. It later functioned as a depot for The RCR and the PPCLI. The depot was later broken up and The Regiment was reinforced by other Canadian reserve battalions from England.

1 November: An advance party of The RCR arrived in France, and proceeded to Rest Camp No. 5. Meanwhile, back in Shorncliffe, the main body of The RCR marched to Folkestone where it embarked for the crossing to France.

3 November: The advance party of The RCR was joined by the main body of The Regiment at Pont de Briques.

6 November: The Regiment (36 officers and 1,006 other ranks) was inspected and welcomed into the Canadian Corps by Lieutenant-General Sir E.A.H. Alderson at Seely Château.

10–15 November: The Regiment moved to Aldershot Huts, then into the trenches at Ploegsteert, for training with the 1st Canadian Division.

19 November: The Regiment moved forward into the Corps Reserve billets at La Clytte, where it relieved the Canadian Cavalry Brigade.

28 November: Sergeant D. Carrol of "D" Coy was the first member of the Regiment killed in action by the enemy.

14 December: Orders announced the formation of the Canadian Corps Troops Infantry Brigade, under the command of Lieutenant-Colonel A.H. MacDonell. It was charged with the defence of Kemmel Hill.

16 December: The Canadian Corps Troops Infantry Brigade was disbanded. Field Marshal Sir John French, commander-in-chief is replaced by General Sir Douglas Haig.

19 December: A German gas attack in the Ypres Salient resulted in the Regiment experiencing gas exposure for the first time when wind blew gas into its billets at La Clytte.

20 December: It was announced that the battalions of the former Canadian Corps Troops Infantry Brigade will reform into the 7th Canadian Infantry Brigade, under the command of Brigadier-General A.C. Macdonell, D.S.O.; the brigade was the senior brigade of the 3rd Canadian Division under Major-General M.S. Mercer.

22 December: The 7th Canadian Infantry Brigade was officially established.

1916

7–8 January: The Regiment took over brigade reserve billets at Tea Farm and moved into the trenches — C3 to D2 — in the line.

12 January: The Regiment was relieved by the 49th Battalion and moved into Dranoutre, in reserve.

January-February: The Regiment rotated between billets and front line duty. Steel helmets were issued to the Regiment for the first time.

17 February: Brigadier-General A.C. Macdonell was wounded. Temporary command of the brigade was taken by Lieutenant-Colonel A.H. MacDonell. Major E.K. Eaton took temporary command of the Regiment.

March: The 7th Brigade Machine-Gun Corps was raised by Major H.T. Cock (RCR).

APPENDIX A

7 March: The Regiment was in divisional reserve at Locre.

8–20 March: The Regiment rested at Mont des Cats. During this period Lieutenant-Colonel A.H. MacDonell reassumed command of the Regiment. There was also an outbreak of scarlet fever and measles.

20 March: The Regiment moved into the Ypres salient.

25 March: The Regiment took up in front line positions at Maple Copse.

29 March: The Regiment was relieved by the 60th Battalion and returned to Ypres and Camp "C."

5 April: The Regiment relieved the 4th Canadian Mounted Rifles at Belgian Château and Zillebeke Dugouts.

13–24 April: The Regiment moved into the Sanctuary Wood sector. During this period Lieutenant-Colonel A.H. MacDonell left the Regiment and was succeeded temporarily by Major Eaton.

20 April: Lieutenant-Colonel Hill assumed command of the Regiment, succeeding Lieutenant-Colonel Macdonell.

24 April: After moving in to rest in Camp "E," The Regiment suffered 3 killed, 7 mortally injured, and 24 wounded during an aerial attack.

7 May: The Regiment relieved the 42nd Battalion at Maple Copse.

16 May: The Regiment was relieved by the 60th Battalion and moved into divisional reserve at Camp "A."

23 May: The Regiment relieved the 49th Battalion at Belgian Chateau and Zillebeke Bund.

28 May: Lieutenant-General, the Honorable Sir Julian Byng, K.C.B., K.C.M.G., M.V.O. assumed command of the Canadian Corps, succeeding Lieutenant-General, Alderson, K.C.B.

31 May: The Regiment relieved the 42nd Battalion astride the Menin Road, in the Hooge sector.

2 June: The Canadian front suffered a severe bombardment, such as many had not seen since the beginning of hostilities, this being a precursor to an attack by the Germans.

6 June: The Regiment was relieved by the 28th CIB, and moved into Camp "B," by way of Ypres.

7–21 June: The Regiment rested in the area of Steenvoorde.

13 June: The 1st Canadian Division counterattacked and pushed the Germans back to the original positions (i.e., as at the start of the 2 June German offensive).

21 June: The Regiment relieved the 2nd Battalion, Irish Guards, at the front.

27 June: The Regiment was relieved by the PPCLI and moved back to Ypres.

30 June-10 July: The Regiment was at Camp "B" and conducted training and various other activities.

1 July: The Battle of the Somme began.

10 July: The Regiment was once again on the front line in the Ypres Salient.

19 July: The Regiment was relieved by the 1st CMR and moved back to Camp "A."

23 July: The Regiment moved to Steenvoorde.

27 July: The Regiment was inspected by the Canadian Corps commander, Lieutenant-General Byng.

31 July-1 August: The Regiment relieved the 4th CMR in Camp B, then moved to relieve the 5th CMR at Ypres.

24 August: The Regiment moved into billets in the area of Cassel, via Abeele, to prepare for the participation of the Canadian Corps in the Battles of the Somme.

7–13 September: The Regiment moved towards the Brickfields at Albert, where preparations were made for a renewal of the Battle of the Somme.

15 September: The 7th Brigade — including the Regiment — is ordered to Usna Hill. The Regiment advanced to reserve positions between Courcelette and Pozières.

16 September: The Regiment attacked Zollern Graben.

17–23 September: The Regiment moved back to Tara Hill, after heavy casualties and then proceeded back to the billets at the Brickfields.

2 October: The Regiment relieved the 5th CMR.

8 October: The Regiment relieved the 42nd Battalion at the front line and then proceeded to attack Regina Trench.

9 October: After an advance, The Regiment was forced back, and suffered heavy casualties. It was forced to return to Tara Hill.

10–29 October: The Regiment moved to relieve the 2nd/17th Battalion, London Regiment in reserve at Neuville St. Vaast via Warloy, La Vicogne, Prouville, Villers l'Hôpital, Brunville, Pénin, and Cambligneul. On 29 October, they relieved the 49th Battalion in the La Folie Sector of the front. Captain H.M. Logan is temporarily second-in-command.

November: The Regiment rotated in and out of the front. Major M.M.L. Garon became second in command, and temporary regimental commander on 27 November.

December: The Regiment rotated in and out of the front lines.

1917

January: The Regiment rotated in and out of the front lines.

22 January: Major C.R.E. Willets, in command, issued an Operational Order outlining a raid to be carried out north of Watling Crater.

23 January: A party of 27, all ranks, met with success in carrying out the raid called for by Major Willets. The Germans tried, with no success, to retaliate.

12 February: The Regiment was relieved at the front by the 24th Battalion of the

2nd Canadian Division, and withdrew to reserve positions at Mont St. Eloy.

13 February-21 March: The Regiment was at Bruay conducting various training. Coys were also reorganized into three platoons, with the platoons being further reorganized into sections of specialists. The Regiment was also specifically preparing for the attack against Vimy Ridge scheduled for early April.

14 February: The Regiment was inspected on the Bruay-Divion Road by Field Marshal Sir Douglas Haig, the commander-in-chief.

9 March: The Regiment was inspected by the Right Honourable Sir Robert Borden, the prime minister of Canada.

21 March: "C" and "D" Coys moved from Bruay to La Motte.

22 March: "C" Coy moved in to relieve the right Coy of the 58th Battalion at the front, the point from which The Regiment was to mount its part of the Vimy attack.

23 March: The second section of The Regiment moved into La Motte camp, and "D" Coy relieved "C" Coy.

1 April: Forward sections of The Regiment were relieved by parts of the 60th and 43rd Battalions, and moved into Villers-au-Bois.

2-7 April: The Regiment was planning and preparing for the attack on Vimy Ridge.

7 April: "A" and "B" Coys and a platoon of "D" Coy moved to Grange Tunnel.

8 April: The Regiment moved into the jumping off positions at the front.

9 April: The Regiment participated in the Canadian Corps attack against Vimy Ridge. The assault began at 0530 hours.

11 April: The Regiment was relieved by the 58th Battalion and moved back to Villers Camp.

16-18 April: The Regiment moved forward to the Quarries Line, then to shelters to the rear of Fort George.

APPENDIX A

24 April: The Regiment relieved the 1 CMR at La Folie Area and became brigade reserve.

30 April–1 May: The Regiment was relieved by the 58th Battalion and moved to the Quarries Line, then to Villers-au-Bois.

7–21 May: The Regiment was concentrated in Grange Tunnel, from which it carried out various construction duties and patrolling.

21 May–06 June: The Regiment was at Villers-au-Bois rehearsing for a raid on the German front in the Avion area. This action was to be carried out by the 7th CIB along with the 4th Canadian Division.

6 June: Lieutenant-General Byng was promoted to general and appointed commander of the British 3rd Army. Accordingly, Sir Arthur Currie was promoted lieutenant-general and appointed commander of the Canadian Corps.

7 June: The Regiment moved forward to the Quarries Line to prepare for the attack.

8 June: The Regiment participated in the successful raid on the Germans in the Avion area.

9 June–2 July: The Regiment was in the 3rd Line of the Vimy defences before moving into the area of the Grange Tunnel.

2–11 July: The Regiment relieved the 58th Battalion on the front in the Avion sector.

11–19 July: The Regiment moved into the Château de la Haie area. During this period Major-General A.C. Macdonell succeeded Lieutenant-General Currie in the command of 1st Canadian Division, and was succeeded in the command of 7th Brigade by Brigadier-General H.M. Dyer, D.S.O.

19–25 July: The Regiment was in the Souchez Valley undergoing training and participating in work parties.

25 July–19 August: The Regiment moved into Lapugnoy, by way of Villers-au-Bois, Château de la Haie, and Coupigny, for training.

ESTABLISHING A LEGACY

7 August: The Regiment was visited by Lieutenant-General Currie who also inspected the Battalion's administrative organization.

15 August: The Canadian Corps, in its first action under the command of Lieutenant-General Currie, attacked and captured Hill 70 in the Lens area.

21–26 August: The Regiment relieved the 22nd and 25th Battalions in the front line at Hill 70.

26 August-4 September: The Regiment returned to the rear as brigade reserve.

4–18 September: The Regiment was training in the area of Villers-au-Bois. Temporary command of the Regiment was assumed by Major A.E. Willoughby.

18–24 September: The Regiment was on the front lines in the Mericourt sector.

29 September-5 October: The Regiment was on the front, after moving from Neuville St. Vaast to relieve the PPCLI.

6–16 October: The Regiment moved, by way of Écurie and La Belle Épine, to Bailleul.

16–23 October: The Regiment was in Padelles. While here, it was announced that Major Willets was to succeed Lieutenant-Colonel Hill in command of the Regiment.

22 October: The Regiment was inspected by Field Marshal H.R.H. the Duke of Connaught near the village of Barre.

23–29 October: The Regiment was at Wieltje, where is suffered casualties when providing support to the 8th and 9th Brigades during the first phase of the Battle of Passchendaele.

29 October: The Regiment moved forward to Abraham Heights, to take over support positions.

30 October: The second phase of the Battle of Passchendaele began.

5 November: The Regiment concentrated at Watou. The Regiment suffered casualties in the order of 11 officers and 247 other ranks.

6 November: The third phase of the Battle of Passchendaele began.

14–18 November: The Regiment was at the front, on the Passchendaele-Westroosebeke Road. When the four day tour ended, the casualty list for Passchendaele rose to 14 officers and 375 other ranks.

20 November-21 December: The Regiment was at Rely for training.

17 December: The Regimental Colours were buried in the debris after the Halifax Explosion. They were recovered several days later and taken to a safe location.

23 December: The Regiment moved into Souchez.

29 December: The Regiment relieved the PPCLI on the front, north of the Souchez River.

1918

4 January: The Regiment was relieved, and moved into Liévin.

10 January: The Regiment relieved the PPCLI north of the Souchez River.

19 January-21 February: The Regiment moved to Suburban Camp, Bois des Alleux.

1 March: A portion of the Regiment moved to Cellars Camp, Neuville St. Vaast.

6 March: The Regiment moved over Vimy Ridge to relieve the 43rd Battalion in the Avion sector of the front.

12–31 March: The Regiment moved between the reserve trenches on the Lens-Arras Road and the Avion sector of the front.

April: The Regiment rotated between duty on the front line and in reserve.

May: The Regiment was quartered in Cambligneul, Lières, and Bourecq and conducted training.

1–25 June: The Regiment was at Bourecq and conducted various training exercises.

28 June: The Regiment moved into the Neuville Vitasse sector to relieve the 29th Battalion of the 2nd Canadian Division.

4 July: Now a lieutenant-colonel, Willets, D.S.O., assumed command of the Regiment, succeeding Lieutenant-Colonel Hill.

6–14 July: The Regiment was at Wailly Huts.

14–25 July: The Regiment was on the front, in support positions in the Neuville Vitasse sector.

27–30 July: The Regiment was at Wanquetin. Major Willoughby assumed temporary command.

8 August: The Regiment participated in the Battle of Amiens.

9 August: The Regiment moved forward to an area southwest of Beaucourt, in the second stage of the battle.

14–15 August: The Regiment recaptured Parvillers.

15 August: The Regiment moved back to Le Quesnel Wood.

16–19 August: The Regiment moved back to Valley Wood.

18 August: The 7th Brigade was inspected by the Premier of France (M. Clemenceau), Field Marshal Haig and General Sir Henry Rawlinson.

19 August: The Regiment was visited by Lieutenant-General Currie in Valley Wood.

26 August: 7th Brigade , including The RCR, participated in an attack on Arras.

28 August: When the 3rd Division was relieved, the Regiment's casualties totalled 196.

2 September: The Regiment moved through Arras to positions on the front.

19–26 September: The Regiment was at Bernville.

27 September: The Regiment moved into Quéant.

APPENDIX A

28 September: The Regiment attacked the Marcoing Line. Major C.B. Topp, of the 42nd Battalion assumed temporary command when Lieutenant-Colonel Willets was severely wounded.

29 September: Captain C.L. Wood assumed temporary command of the Regiment from Major Topp.

30 September: The Regiment launched an attack from positions west of the Cambrai-Douai road.

1 October: Lieutenant M.F. Gregg was awarded the Victoria Cross, the first member of The Regiment to be awarded this decoration for his actions during the attack on the Marcoing Line.

1–10 October: The Regiment was in Quarry Wood.

8 October: Lieutenant-Colonel G.W. MacLeod assumed command of The Regiment from Captain Wood.

15 October: Members of the Regiment attended the funeral in Quéant of Major-General L.J. Lipsett, C.B., C.M.G., former GOC 3rd Division, who was killed by a sniper. Major-General Lipsett is succeeded by Major-General F.O.W. Loomis, C.B., C.M.G., D.S.O.

22 October: The Regiment moved forward through the Forêt de Raismes.

30 October: The Regiment moved to Raismes and Vicoigne.

6 November: The Regiment moved to Valenciennes and Onnaing.

7 November: The Regiment moved out of Onnaing in support of the PPCLI by way of Quiévrechain to Quiévrain.

9 November: The Regiment moved to Boussu.

10 November: The Regiment was ordered to continue on to the attack on Mons. Lieutenant D.D. Shields and four other ranks of "B" Coy were the last members killed in the war.

11 November: No. 5 Platoon, "B" Coy enterd the town and was greeted by some of the town's officials. The platoon commander, Lieutenant W.M. King, was the first Allied officer to reach the centre of town. At 0830 hours, the Regiment received the message that hostilities would cease at 1100 hours.

11 November–11 December: The Regiment remained in Mons and participated in various honours and services.

15–20 December: The Regiment was billeted at Bourgeois-sous-Rixensart.

31 December: The Regiment celebrated the New Year at Renaux, where the first formal mess dinner in many months was held.

1919

January: The Regiment was billeted in Estaimbourg.

29 January: Lieutenant-Colonel Hill assumed command of The Regiment, succeeding Lieutenant-Colonel MacLeod.

1–3 February: The Regiment moved to Le Havre and the Canadian Embarkation Camp.

6 February: The Regiment boarded the S.S. *Mona Lisa* to cross the Channel.

7 February: The Regiment arrived in Weymouth and headed for Bramshott Camp.

1 March: The Regiment boarded the S.S. *Adriatic* at Liverpool, for their return to Canada.

9 March: The Regiment arrived in Halifax, NS, to an enthusiastic welcome from the city, and after a march through the city, the CEF battalion of The RCR was disbanded.

3 April: Daily Order No. 1 issued, marking the return of the Regiment to duty in the Permanent Force.

October: "D" Coy was sent to Montreal to establish a Regimental Station, as the entire Regiment was still stationed in Halifax.

11 November: "D" Coy, under Captain W.J. Home, participated in the first ceremonies marking Armistice Day.

H.M. King George V granted the Regiment permission to wear Queen Victoria's cipher V.R.I. ("Victoria Regina Imperatrix" — latin for "Victoria, Queen and Empress") in perpetuity. This was done in memory of Queen Victoria and the Regiment's exemplary service in the First World War.

1920

8 January: Regimental HQ was moved to Montreal, to the Peel Street Barracks.

3 June: The Regiment was concentrated at Valcartier Camp to continue its training and reorganization.

20 September: Regimental HQ along with "C" and "D" Coys move to Rosedale Barracks, Toronto. Near this time, the nucleus of the newly formed "B" Coy moved to Stanley Barracks, Toronto.

7 December: Regimental HQ along with "C" Coy moved to Tecumseh Barracks, in London.

21 December: The Montreal Station, in the Prince of Wales Barracks is established by "D" Coy.

1922

27 February: Formal trooping of the South African Banner in London.

1924

July: The *Connecting File*, which began as a mimeographed sheet after the war, develops into a monthly magazine. It became a quarterly magazine in 1925.

15 October: Lieutenant-Colonel Seeley Smith assumed command of the Regiment, succeeding Lieutenant-Colonel Hill.

Regimental Coy locations: HQ, London; "A" Coy, Halifax; "B" Coy, Toronto; "C" Coy, London; and "D" Coy, Montreal.

ESTABLISHING A LEGACY

25 October: "D" Coy moved to the Infantry Barracks at St. Jean, QC, from the Prince of Wales Barracks, Montreal.

1925

December: H.M. King George V, approved the affiliation of the Gloucestershire Regiment of the British Army with The RCR.

1926

The RCR Old Comrades Association was organized by Lieutenant-Colonel C.H. Hill

1927

11 November: The Regiment participated in memorial services at Arlington Cemetery, Washington, D.C.

Lieutenant-Colonel Smith received permission, on behalf of the Regiment, from NDHQ to change the crown of the cipher from the inappropriate Hanoverian type to that actually used at the time of Queen Victoria.

1928

6 February: The Regiment participated in services at St. Paul's Cathedral, London, in memory of Field Marshal Haig, who had died in January.

1929

General Order No. 110 awarded Battle Honours for services during First World War to The Regiment and other forces.

4 April: General Otter is invited to become colonel-in-chief of the Regiment.

7 May: General Otter, K.C.B., C.V.O., Honorary colonel and former CO of The Regiment, died.

21 September: Lieutenant-Colonel R.J.S. Langford assumed command of the Regiment, succeeding Lieutenant-Colonel Smith.

1 October: Major-General S.J.A. Denison became honorary colonel of The Regiment.

1931

4 April: The Regiment provided a guard of honour for the new governor general of Canada, His Excellency the Earl of Bessborough and Lady Bessborough.

17 December: "A" Coy moved from the Citadel in Halifax to Wellington Barracks, marking the first time since 1778, the Citadel was without a Canadian or British garrison.

1932

26 May: The Regiment was presented with new Colours by His Excellency the Earl of Bessborough, including Honours won up to, and including the First World War. The old Colours were deposited in Cronyn Memorial Church.

1933

The Regiment received a banner from H.M. King George V commemorating the Expeditionary Force's contribution in First World War, that was placed in St. Mark's Church, Halifax.

8–11 September: Fiftieth anniversary celebrations of the Regiment's establishment were conducted in London, Ontario. The Regimental Colours were trooped at Wolseley Barracks, to end the celebrations.

30 November: General Currie, G.C.M.G., K.C.B., died in Montreal.

1935

15 May: Lieutenant-Colonel M.K. Greene assumed command of the Regiment, succeeding Lieutenant-Colonel Langford.

ESTABLISHING A LEGACY

1936

20 January: H.M. King George V died at Sandringham, and the Regiment participated in the service in Victoria Park, London, United Kingdom.

26 August: The Vimy Memorial was unveiled by H.M. King Edward VIII.

The Canadian Armoured Fighting Vehicle School was established at London, Ontario, under the control of The RCR.

10 December: Edward VIII abdicated the throne of England.

1937

May: The Regiment participated in the coronation ceremony of H.M. King George VI.

8 November: Major-General Denison, honorary colonel, died and was succeeded by Major-General The Hon. A.H. MacDonell.

1938

1 November: Lieutenant-Colonel K.M. Holloway assumed command of the Regiment, succeeding Lieutenant-Colonel Greene.

1939

7 June: The Regiment provided a guard for the King and Queen when they visited London, Ontario, during their Canadian tour.

24–31 August: All leave was cancelled. A state of national emergency existed.

1 September: National headquarters ordered "M"-day — mobilization for war commenced.

7 September: All companies of the Regiment were ordered to recruit to wartime strength.

10 September: Canada officially declared war on Germany.

15 November: The Regiment was concentrated at Valcartier, QC.

26 November: Lieutenant-Colonel V. Hodson assumed command of the Regiment, succeeding Lieutenant-Colonel Holloway.

17 December: The Regiment departed Camp Valcartier for Halifax.

19 December: The Regiment embarked on the S.S. *Almanzora* for overseas duty.

22 December: The Regiment aboard the S.S. *Almanzora* actually set sail for England.

30 December: The Regiment disembarked in Gourock, Scotland and proceeded to Aldershot, England.

1940

24 January: The Regiment provided an Honour Guard of 100 men, under the command of Major T. Eric Snow, on the occasion of the King's visit to Aldershot.

24 May: The Regiment embarked upon the S.S. *Canterbury* at Dover, its destination was Calais to act as the lead unit of 1 CIB, which was the lead for the 1st Canadian Division, which was tasked with protecting the lines of communication of the British Expeditionary Force in France. They disembarked later the same day without ever leaving port. The mission was cancelled because of the chaos on the continent.

8 June: The Regiment was reviewed by the King and Queen.

14 June: The main body of the Regiment embarked at Plymouth on the S.S. *El Mansour* en route to Brest, as part of a last ditch effort to save France.

17 June: The Regiment, and other forces, returned to Plymouth, England, after much confusion on the continent.

18 June-July: The Regiment was at Aldershot where it reorganized.

July-September: The Regiment was stationed at Charlwood, Surrey.

25 August: The Regiment suffered its first casualty to enemy action when a bomb was dropped by an enemy fighter aircraft killing Private G.E. Dowell and Private W. McAllister.

9 September: The Regiment was put on one hour notice when the German invasion seemed imminent.

October-November: The Regiment was stationed at Reigate-Redhill, Surrey. During this time the wearing of the Regimental flash became regulation for all serving members.

21 October: Major Snow assumed command of the Regiment, succeeding Lieutenant-Colonel Hodson.

December: The Regiment was moved to Brighton and was responsible for coastal defence against enemy landings.

1 December: Lieutenant-Colonel M.K. Green reassumed command of the Regiment, succeeding Major Snow.

31 December: The Regiment was involved in the Canadian Corps Exercise (Ex) Fox.

1941

2 January: The Regiment provided a Guard of Honour for a memorial service at Pitts Cottage in Westerham. Attendees included the Duke of Devonshire; Canadian cabinet ministers J.L. Ralston and C.D. Howe; Canadian High Commissioner Vincent Massey; and generals Crerar, McNaughton, Pearkes, and Odlum.

14 January: The Regiment participated in Ex Ordex, meant to practice the response to an enemy landing in England.

15 January: The Regiment's cross-country team won the divisional competition.

April: The Regiment moved to summer billets in the Chipstead area.

APPENDIX A

12 April: The Regimental cross-country team won the Canadian Army finals.

16 May: The U.S. ambassador to the United Kingdom, accompanied by General McNaughton and General Pearkes, visited the Regiment.

22 May: The Regiment defended its locality against a simulated airborne attack during Ex Parex.

27 May: The Regiment was in the Tonbridge area, on Ex Brenda.

6 June: The Regiment was in the area of Chichester on Ex Waterloo.

11 July: The Regiment acted as enemy force for Ex Parex.

15 July: Lieutenant-Colonel Snow reassumed command of the Regiment, succeeding Lieutenant-Colonel Greene.

20 July: The Regiment moved to Bisley for field firing.

24 July: The Regiment, along with the 48th Highlanders, participated in an attack exercise at Gatwick airport.

August: The Regiment participated in Exs Albert and Roft.

7 September: "D" Coy was presented the Championship Banner, as most efficient company. The King also proclaimed this day a Special Day of Prayer to commemorate the Battle of Britain.

September: The Regiment was involved in Ex Bumper — the largest manoeuvres ever held in Britain.

21 October: The Regiment participated on Ex Plunger.

4 November: The Regiment participated on Ex Gildex.

20 November: The Regiment relieved the South Wales Borderers at Selsey during Ex Scram.

November-December: The Regiment was posted to Selsey Bill, Sussex, on coastal defence duty.

ESTABLISHING A LEGACY

1942

3 January: The Regiment began training exercises in the Bognor Regis area, England.

16 January: Field Marshal H.R.H. the Duke of Connaught, The Regiment's first colonel-in-chief, died.

2 February: The Canadian Fusiliers, City of London, Regiment was activated as a full-time battalion, mainly to serve in Kiska.

March: The Regiment participated on Exs Donald, Duck, and, later, Mickey and Mouse.

April-August: The Regiment moved into summer quarters at Arundel Park, Sussex.

6–8 April: The Regiment conducted defensive Exs Robin I and Robin II.

22–23 April: The Regiment participated in Ex Beaver II, which was offensive in nature.

May: The Regiment participated in the 11-day Ex Tiger, in which soldiers marched 170 miles.

5–8 August: The Regiment arrived at Waldron Down, Possingworth Camp, after having spent three days on Ex Independence.

2 September: The Regiment participated in Ex Breaststroke.

1 October: The Regiment participated in Ex Harvest.

11–12 October: The Regiment participated in Ex Breaststroke II.

November: The Regiment was involved in various activities, indoor training and short courses.

17 December: At Duke's Camp, Inverary, the Regiment began training with landing craft and practised establishing bridgeheads on hostile shores.

25 December: The Regiment was involved in Ex Noel I.

27 December: The Regiment was involved in Ex Noel II.

31 December: The Regiment returned to Possingworth Camp, by way of Greenock.

1943

16 January: The rifle companies conducted infantry-armour cooperation training at Possingworth Park, England.

January: The Regiment replaced the metal "RCR" badge with "CANADA."

January: The Battalion converted to a new war establishment of three rifle Coys. "D" Coy was redistributed throughout the other companies.

9 February: The Regiment marched to Angmering, by way of Brighton.

12 February: The Regiment was once again at Possingworth Park, and subsequently was sent to the Eastbourne area to relieve the PPCLI.

3 March: Lieutenant-Colonel R.M. Crowe assumed command of the Regiment, succeeding Lieutenant-Colonel Snow.

10 March: The Regiment participated in Ex Spartan in the area of Angmering.

30 March: The Regiment practiced water crossings at the Adur and Arun rivers.

12 April: The Regiment moved out of Possingworth, to relieve the Seaforth Highlanders at Eastbourne.

30 April: The Regiment was once again at Duke's Camp, Inverary.

2 May: The Regiment conducted landing exercises.

7–8 May: The Regiment deployed to Cumnock, Ayrshire.

19 May: The Regiment participated in an amphibious exercise — Ex Wetshod, off the Isle of Aran.

22 May: The Regiment returned to Cumnock.

May: The Regiment prepared for its deployment to the "front," although not yet aware where exactly they were going.

May: "D" Coy (the fourth rifle coy) of the Regiment was reactivated.

13 June: The Regiment deployed from Cumnock to Falsane to board the Dutch ship *Marnix Van St. Aldegonde*.

18 June: While heading downriver, the Regiment participated in Ex Stymie I, as a dress rehearsal for the coming invasion.

22 June: A second dress rehearsal was conducted.

29 June: While at sea, as part of the Eighth Army, members of the Regiment learned that they were en route to the Mediterranean for a large-scale combined operation.

9 July: The invasion fleet converged and orders for Operation Husky, the invasion of Sicily) were given.

10 July: Operation Husky commenced. The Regiment deployed on the right flank of 1 CIB and was responsible for clearing Roger Green Beach, destroying a coast defence battery, and, on order, capturing the Pachino airfield. Privates Butler and Hefford were the first to be killed in battle during the war.

11 July: The Regiment as part of the invasion force fought their way inland towards Rossolini.

12 July: The Regiment advanced to Giarratana, where General Bernard Montgomery visited 1 CIB the next day.

16 July: The Regiment reached Caltagirone.

18–19 July: The Regiment arrived at Valguarnera, where they came to the assistance of the Hastings and Prince Edward Regiment (H&PER).

21–24 July: The Regiment was engaged at Assoro.

24 July: The CO, Lieutenant-Colonel Crowe was killed in the attack on Agira. Acting Lieutenant-Colonel T.M. Powers assumed command.

APPENDIX A

24–25 July: The Regiment was engaged along the Leonforte-Agira road, at Nissoria, and ultimately moved into the town of Agira.

26 July: The Regiment relieved the PPCLI to the northeast of Leonforte.

30 July: The Regiment joined with the 231 (Malta) Brigade in the assault on the town of Regalbuto.

1 August: The Regiment moved to Regalbuto, along the Regalbuto-Cantenanuova road.

2–4 August: "D" Coy was ordered to cross the Cerementario gorge and occupy the high ground. Subsequently, "A" and "B" Coys were to seize Tower Hill, while "C" Coy was held in reserve.

4 August: The Regiment occupied Monte San Giorgio.

5 August: The Regiment moved through Regalbuto to Carcaci, two miles east of Adrano.

10 August: The Regiment, as part of 5th British Division, was placed under command of the 13th Corps.

12 August: The Regiment moved into the Militello area for a rest and training.

13 August: Lieutenant-Colonel D.C. Spry assumed command of the Regiment, succeeding Acting Lieutenant-Colonel Powers.

22 August: Lieutenant-General Andrew G.L. McNaughton, the commander of the Canadian Army Overseas visited the Battalion in Millitello.

26 August: The officers of The RCR were briefed on Operation Baytown the intended landing at Calabria on the Italian mainland.

27 August: The RCR won the 1 CIB sports day.

2 September: Commander 1 CIB, Brigadier H.D. Graham, inspected the Battalion before the invasion of Italy.

3 September: The Regiment embarked at Santa Teresa di Riva, Sicily and landed at a beach near Reggio Di Calabria, on the Italian mainland.

7 September: The Regiment moved into Gambarie.

8 September: Italy surrendered, however, the Germans quickly occupied the country.

9 September: The Regiment boarded buses and moved to an assembly area to the north of Locri.

10 September: The Regiment arrived at the bivouac area, east of Catanzaro, where the 1st Canadian Division was concentrating before moving northward.

11 September: The Regiment passed Catanzaro and continued on to Petrona.

12 September: GOC 1 Cdn Div, Major-General Guy G. Simonds visited the Battalion and gave a detailed explanation of the situation in Italy and the attitude to be taken towards the Italians.

16 September: The Regiment boarded transport for Potenza and bivouacked en route at Terranova.

18–26 September: The Regiment was at Montalbano.

27 September: The Regiment moved to Gravina.

29 September: "B" Coy, as part of the advance guard of 1 CIB was ordered to advance towards Campobasso.

30 September: The Regiment main body left Gravina for Foggia.

1 October: "B" Coy as part of the 1 CIB Vanguard Force attacked Motta. The assault failed and the task of capturing Motta was passed to The RCR. A daylight attack failed, however, the town was captured after a sharp bombardment and a subsequent night attack.

3 October: The Regiment seized Motta Ridge.

4 October: The Regiment was engaged at San Marco. As a result, the Germans were driven out by dawn the following day.

5 October: The Regiment moved into position in preparation for an attack on Campobasso.

APPENDIX A

6–12 October: The Regiment was engaged at Hill 400.

14 October: The Regiment seized Campobasso, assisted by the landing of a British Special Service Brigade at Termoli. Campobasso, renamed Maple Leaf City became the new leave centre.

20 October: "B" Coy captured the town of Busso.

21 October: "D" Coy seized Oratino.

24 October: The Regiment crossed the Biferno River, with orders to clear the Castropignano area.

25 October: "D" Coy seized Castropignano, which was deserted.

1–2 November: "A" Coy relieved the H&PER at Molise and Frosolone and "D" Coy occupied Duronia.

5 November: The Regiment was now concentrated at Duronia for a period of rest.

24 November: The MND, Colonel the Honourable J.L. Ralston visited the Regiment in Duronia. He was accompanied by Lieutenant-General Harry D.G. Crerar, Major-General Chris Vokes, and Brigadier Howard Graham.

30 November: The Regiment was transferred to 5th Corps, under Lieutenant-General Charles Allfrey.

1 December: The Regiment pulled out of Duronia.

2 December: The Regiment arrived at the staging area northwest of Termoli.

3 December: The Regiment crossed the Sangro River.

4 December: The Regiment marched through Fossacesia and Rocca to a point just beyond San Vito Chieteno.

5 December: The Regiment moved into San Vito Chieteno.

5–6 December: The 1st Canadian Division battle of the Moro River commenced.

8 December: The Regiment attacked San Leonardo after the failed Seaforth Highlander of Canada assault several days earlier. The RCR was stopped due to heavy machine-gun and artillery fire, as well as enemy tanks.

9 December: The Regiment was ordered to move forward to San Leonardo to link up with 2 CIB, who had seized the town. Just as the Regiment began its deployment, a strong German counterattack split the forward elements of the Battalion. "B" and "C" Coy already en route continued on to San Leonardo, while "A" Coy and the Regimental command group withdrew to the original river crossing. Lieutenant Mitch Sterlin's platoon did not receive the order and was left in their fortified stone house to fight off repeated German attacks, earning the moniker "Sterlin's Castle." They withdrew that night and joined the remainder of the Regiment.

10 December: The Regiment was ordered to consolidate on the south bank of the Moro River to cover the gap between San Leonardo and the H&PER bridgehead. At 1800 hours, they were ordered to cross the river and hold a position on the track between San Leonardo and the H&PER bridgehead.

16 December: Lieutenant-Colonel Spry was appointed acting brigade commander during the absence of Brigadier-General Graham who was ill. Major W.W. Mathers took temporary command of the Regiment.

17 December: The Regiment moved through San Leonardo to the west of the town in preparation to for an attack on the Ortona-Orsogna crossroads.

18 December: The Regiment attacked to the east of Villa Grande, under the code name Orange Blossom. This attack was the second phase (following an attack by the 48th Highlanders) of 1 Cdn Div attempt to break through to Ortona. An inaccurate artillery barrage left the enemy untouched and the Regiment's two leading companies ("C" and "D") were virtually annihilated. Major I.A. Hodson, the deputy commanding officer, assumed command of the Regiment because Major Mathers had been shot in the arm by a sniper.

19 December: The attack on the crossroads was renewed. This time, with "B" Coy leading, behind an effective artillery barrage, and supported by tanks, the attack was successful. Major Hodson, who was severely ill with jaundice and malaria, turned over command to Major A.S.A. Galloway.

23 December: "Buckforce" consisting of 9 and 16 platoons, supported by six mortar detachments, was conducted as a feint attack to fool the enemy into

APPENDIX A

believing an attack was taking place on a broad front in an effort to support of 1 CIB operations designed to relieve pressure at Ortona.

24–25 December: The Regiment was now deployed as part of a 1 CIB three battalion succession of attacks to hook around the west and north of Ortona and cut off its defenders. A confused battle raged for two days.

26 December: General Sir Oliver Leese, the former commander of 30 Corps took over the Eighth Army when General Montgomery was recalled to England to prepare for the Normandy invasion.

28 December: The Germans withdrew from Ortona.

30 December: 1 CIB was pulled from the line. The Regiment took up positions astride the Villa Grande road.

1944

1 January: General Montgomery passed command of the British Eighth Army to General Leese.

1–13 January: The Regiment was bivouacked in the area north of the Villa Grande-Ortona crossroads.

5 January: The corps commander, Major-General Crerar, accompanied by Brigadier Spry inspected the Regiment.

6 January: Lieutenant-Colonel Mathers returned and reassumed command of the Regiment.

13 January: The Regiment moved into the San Nicol area and relieved the 5th Royal West Kents of the 8th Indian Division.

20 January: Major Galloway, took temporary command of the Regiment during the hospitalization of Lieutenant-Colonel Mathers.

26 January: A platoon from "A" Coy was unsuccessful in its attempt to occupy a former enemy position labelled "Bluebell," which was a cluster of houses, in no man's land. The Germans had cleverly allowed a patrol to enter the area unopposed, but when the Regiment attempted to occupy it in strength they were engaged by heavy machine-gun fire that forced them to abort the attempt.

1 February: Two war correspondents arrived in the unit lines to interview the Regimental pioneers.

10–11 February: The Carlton and York Regiment of 3 CIB relieved The RCR in San Nicola and San Tommaso. The Regiment then moved into a rest area south of San Vito.

13 February: A Church of England service and later a Roman Catholic Mass were conducted in the rest area. At 1200 hours, Lieutenant-General Crerar, the 1 Cdn Corps commander arrived to confer with the CO.

14 February: The divisional band played two concerts for the soldiers of The RCR in their rest area. During the day, work parties were busy improving the coastal road.

17 February: Large parties of "Royals" of all ranks were sent into San Vito to see the ENSA show (entertainment for soldiers).

21 February: A Regimental dinner was held in San Vito at The Sword and Drum, an officers club created by 1 Cdn Div. Present were the CO and all Regimental officers, as well as Major-General Vokes, the divisional commander and Brigadier Spry, the 1 CIB commander.

27 February: The Regiment moved through Ortona in relief of the Seaforth Highlanders in the coastal sector north of the seaport.

2 March: At a Divisional investiture at San Vito, members of the Regiment were presented with decorations won during the Sicilian/Italian campaign.

4–5 March: The Regiment was relieved by the 48th Highlanders, but remained north of Ortona in reserve.

9 March: The Regiment relieved the H&PER north of San Nicola.

20 March: The Regiment was relieved by the 48th Highlanders, and withdrew to become the brigade reserve.

22 March: Hot baths at a mobile shower room were made available in Ortona. In addition, a wet canteen and an entertainment show were laid on for the troops.

APPENDIX A

28 March: The Regiment relieved the H&PER in the coastal sector.

7 April: Lieutenant-General C.W. Alfrey, Commander 5 Corps visited RHQ. He and seven officers stayed with the Regiment for a few days to get a situational awareness of the front.

11 April: Lieutenant-Colonel Mathers resumed command of the Regiment. The RCRs were also relieved by the 48th Highlanders.

17 April: Lieutenant-Colonel Mathers and all company commanders attended a divisional conference in San Vito at which time Major-General Vokes briefed on upcoming operations.

19 April: A carefully planned raid against German positions, code named Operation Carnival, was conducted by "C" Coy as cover for the impending relief in place. Intense enemy fire necessitated the raiding force withdraw after a prolonged firefight.

21 April: The Regiment was relieved by the 2/4th Gurkhas. The Regiment then moved to Ortona where it embossed in motor transport and moved to the brigade assembly area.

22 April: The Regiment redeployed to Oratino area, north of Campobasso where it conducted training in preparation for upcoming operations.

29 April: Battle Dress was replaced by bush shirts, slacks, and summer underwear.

30 April: The Regiment left the Oratino area and arrived the same day in the area of Gottfreda, south of Lucera. They conducted "marrying up" exercises with "C" Squadron, 142nd Royal Tank Regiment for two days.

4 May: The Regiment moved through Benvento to billet east of Caserta.

5 May: The Regiment arrived in Limatola, on the Volturno River, inland from Naples and south of the Cassino battlefield. Here it conducted assault boat training.

11 May: At 2300 hours, the attack on the Gustav Line and the drive to Rome began once again — The Regiment remained in Reserve at Limatola.

12 May: The CO and all company commanders attended a conference on the deliberate break-in battle. At 1630 hours, the Battalion was assembled and a message from General Alexander, GOC 15 Army Group, announcing the new offensive launched the previous day, was read to the troops. In addition, Major-General Vokes was formally introduced to all officers of The RCR.

14 May: The Regiment moved to Canadian Corps area, southwest of Casino.

15 May: The Regiment moved up to the front in preparation of joining the Liri Valley battle.

16 May: The Regiment advanced to contact parallel to the Liri River and conducted an unsuccessful battalion assault on Point 59. However, the Germans withdrew from the position under the cover of darkness.

17 May: The Regiment resumed the advance towards the Hitler Line.

18 May: The Regiment dug in close to the forward defensive line of the German Hitler Line.

20 May: General Leese directed the Canadian Corps to attack and break through the Hitler Line defences.

23 May: The RCR seized Postion 106.

24 May: At first light "C" Coy and the scout platoon cleared the town of Pontecorvo.

24–30 May: The Regiment rested at a bivouac west of Pontecorvo.

31 May: The Regiment occupied positions on Highway 6, west of Frosinone.

1 June: The Regiment advanced to Ferentino and found it lightly held by the enemy. Lieutenant-Colonel Mathers was transferred to command the Canadian training battalion at Avellino. He was replaced by Lieutenant-Colonel J.W. Ritchie.

2 June: The Regiment occupied Ferentino.

3 June: The Regiment seized the town of Agnani.

APPENDIX A

4 June: Rome was liberated by the 5th Army. The RCR conducted a Church of England Church Parade in Anagni, which was followed by a march through town. A battalion of 600 partisans joined the parade and march past.

June: Operation Overlord, the invasion of Europe was launched. Allied forces landed in Normandy, France.

9 June-26 July: The Regiment was at rest and training in the Piedmonts d'Alife area.

10 June: Major-General Vokes, commander of the 1st Canadian Division, addressed the Regiment.

14 June: The Drums were re-established.

21 June: 1 CIB sports day at Telesi. The RCR win the tug of war competition. The Regimental Drums played two selections during the competition.

23 June: 1 Cdn Div sports day at Telesi. The Regimental Drums conduct a concert.

25 June: Ex Derby focusing on infantry/tank cooperation was conducted.

27 June: The Regimental Drum band returned from a leave to Rome and claimed they were the first Allied Military band to play in St. Peter's Square.

3 July: Major-General Vokes inspected the Regiment. A regimental dinner was held that night.

6 July: Parade and ceremonial inspection by Brigadier Spry in Piedmonte.

14-15 July: The Regiment participated in Ex Vulcan, which focused on an assault river crossing and the establishment of a bridgehead.

26 July: The Regiment arrived in the staging area north of Valmontane, under the strictest security measures.

27 July: The Regiment deployed to a staging area near Spoleto, by way of Rome, Narni, and Terni.

2 August: The RCR arrived at Castiglione di Lago, on Lake Trasimino and continued on Castilina in Chianti, south of Florence.

6 August: The Regiment moved into Florence, and relieved the 1st Scots Guards on the south bank of the Arno River.

9 August: The Regiment moved back to the staging area north of Siena, after being relieved by the 1st Royal Fusiliers of the 17th Indian Brigade.

10 August: The Regiment deployed once again.

18 August: The Regiment arrived at a staging area north of Jesi near Ancona.

22 August: The Regiment moved into the area south of Orciano.

23 August: The Regiment moved into the area of Montemaggiore, behind the Metauro River.

25–26 August: The Regiment led the 1 CIB assault across the Metauro River and seized Saltara.

26 August: The "Royals" were surprised by a visit from British Prime Minister Winston Churchill and the supreme Allied commander in Italy, General Alexander.

28 August: The Regiment was in reserve at San Vito.

29 August-02 September: The Regiment was at rest in the area of Villa Grande.

3 September: The Regiment established a bridgehead across the Conca River and led the advance towards Misano Ridge, which represented the next German defensive line before Rimini.

4–6 September: The Regiment was embroiled in a vicious set of battles on Misano Ridge.

8 September: The Regiment rested Gradara, southwest of Riccione.

10 September: Padre Wilkes held a memorial service for those who had fallen in the previous battles.

14 September: The Regiment moved south of Riccione, Major A.S.A. Galloway took command of the Regiment for the ensuing battle as the brigade commander ordered all COs to be LoB for the initial engagement.

APPENDIX A

15–19 September: The Regiment participated in the battle for the Rimini airfield. On 16 September Lieutenant-Colonel Ritchie reassumed command.

20 September: Padre Wilkes was posted out of the Regiment. He was later replaced by Captain Rokeby-Thomas.

23 September-10 October: The Regiment was at rest in the area north of Riccione.

29 September: The MND, Colonel J.L. Ralston visited the Regiment.

10 October: The Regiment moved to Sant'Arcangelo, west of Rimini, then continued on the cover a gap in the Canadian lines in the area of Gambettola.

13–14 October: The Regiment is engaged in the area of Gambettola and Emilian Way.

15 October: The Regiment advanced towards the Pisciatello River.

16 October: The Regiment controlled the eastern bank of the Pisciatello River.

18 October: The attacked across the Pisciatello River.

19 October: The Regiment was relieved and moved back into the area of Sant'Arcangelo.

1–28 November: The Regiment returned to its former billets north of Riccione for rest and further training (e.g., assault river crossings and range work).

17 November: A regimental mess dinner was held. The chief guest was Lieutenant-General Charles Foulkes the new 1 Cdn Corps Commander.

29 November-01 December: The Regiment moved into the area of the Montone River.

3 December: The Regiment was poised to cross the Lamone River.

5 December: The Regiment successfully establishes a bridgehead across the Lamone River. By 0700 hours a German counterattack annihilated "B" Coy and shortly thereafter "C" Coy. By 1200 hours the bridgehead was withdrawn.

6 December: The Regiment reorganized. "A" and "D" Coys remained intact, though understrength. "B" and "C" Coys combined into one weak company and a new fourth company, "X" Coy, was generated by using Scout Platoon, personnel from Support Coy and "B" Ech.

9 December: Lieutenant-Colonel W.W. Reid assumed command of the Regiment, succeeding Lieutenant-Colonel Ritchie who had been sacked for the Lamone River failure.

11 December: The Regiment crossed the Lamone River, which had been breached by 3 CIB and advanced towards the Fosso Vecchio.

12 December: The Regiment crossed the Naviglio River.

14 December: The Regiment was relieved by the West Nova Scotia Regiment on the south bank of the Fosso Vecchio.

18 December: The Regiment, along with the H&PER and the 48th Highlanders, attacked the Fosso Vecchio. The attack was unsuccessful.

21 December: The Germans withdrew to the flood banks of the Senio River and The Regiment advanced to a point just short of the enemy's forward defensive line.

22 December: The Regiment was relieved by the Seaforth Highlanders.

1945

3 January: "C" Coy was re-established and "X" Coy was disbanded. The Regiment moves to Villanova, northeast of Bagnacavallo.

10 January: The Regiment relieved the Royal 22nd Regiment south of Bagnacavallo.

28 January: The Regiment as part of 1 CIB was pulled back to the area of Russi.

3 February: The Regiment moved to the north of Mezzano, near the Senio River.

13 February: It was announced that 1 Canadian Corps would soon rejoin the

First Canadian Army in North-West Europe. As a result, the Canadian Corps HQ left the Italian Front.

23–24 February: The Regiment was relieved and moved south to Cesenatico, south of Ravenna.

25 February: The Regiment continued to Grottomare, north of the Solarian Way.

28–29 February: The Regiment moved to Harrod's Camp, north of Leghorn, by way of Foligno and Pontassieve, ending its involvement in the Italian campaign.

7 March: The Regiment was loaded aboard Liberty ships in Leghorn harbour. The ships sailed the next day.

9 March: The first elements of the Regiment landed at Marseilles, France at 1700 hours.

10 March: The Regiment was at a staging area north of Marseilles.

11–16 March: The Regiment was en route to Schilde, Belgium.

22 March: "The Drums" participated in the Change of Guard and Retreat ceremonies at First Canadian Army Headquarters in Holland.

31 March: Buglers left to participate in the Battle of Vimy Ridge memorial service. Included are two soldiers whose fathers had fought in the battle.

3 April: The Regiment moved across the German border into the staging area in the Reichswald forest.

9 April: The Regiment moved into the concentration area northeast of Zutphen, behind the Ijssel River.

12 April: After the establishment of a bridgehead by the PPCLI and the Seaforth Highlanders, the Regiment crossed the Ijssel and continued to the west, north and southwest.

13 April: "B" and "C" Coys advanced almost halfway to Apeldoorn, Holland. "A" and "D" Coys advanced towards the Zutphen-Apeldoorn canal.

13 April: Arnhem was captured by 1st Canadian Corps, with assistance from

49th British Division and elements of 5th Canadian Armoured Division.

14 April: Dutch underground informed the Allies that the Germans were evacuating Apeldoorn, resulting in a push to reach the town, but after several casualties, the operation is abandoned.

15 April: The Regiment prepared to attack Apeldoorn, with "B" and "C" Coys in the lead.

17 April: The Germans withdrew from Apeldoorn and "C" and "A" Coys move into the town unopposed.

18 April: The Regiment moved into the area of Garderen.

4 May: The Germans in northwest Germany, Holland, Denmark, and the Frisian Islands accepted unconditional surrender, to go into effect at 0800 hours 5 May 1945.

6 May: The Regiment came under the command of 2 CIB.

8 May: The Regiment as part of 2 CIB deployed to the Ijmuiden Fortress.

8–18 May: The Regiment secured the Ijmuiden Fortress and disarmed German forces.

15 May: Lieutenant-General Foulkes inspected the Regiment.

21 May: A composite company under command of Lieutenant-Colonel Reid, participated in a victory parade at The Hague.

25 May: Lieutenant-General Foulkes, Major-Generals Murchie and Foster, and Brigadiers Kitching and Bogart visited the Regiment.

4 June: Lieutenant-Colonel Reid passed command to Major Darton, since he was returning to Canada to command a second battalion of The RCR designated for service in the Pacific theatre.

9 June: Major F.G.C. Darton assumed command of the Regiment, succeeding Lieutenant-Colonel Reid.

20 June: The Regiment moved east to Soest, Holland.

APPENDIX A

17 July: Lieutenant-General Foulkes relinquished command of 1 Cdn Corps to return to Canada, to serve as chief of the general staff.

1 August: A second battalion of The RCR was formed at Barriefield, Ontario known officially as 1 Bn (RCR), 1st Canadian Infantry Regiment, 6th Canadian Division. It was organized along American lines for employment in the Pacific. Lieutenant-Colonel Reid assumed command.

19 August: The Regiment participated in a service in honour of the Allied victory.

2 September: The Regiment moved to Ostend, where it boarded the *Princess Josephine Charlotte* to make the crossing to Dover.

6 September: The Regiment was given 10 days embarkation leave.

24 September: The Regiment sets sail from Southampton, aboard the *Nieuw Amsterdam,* for Canada.

27 September: With the defeat of Japan (officially 2 September) there was no longer a need for the 6th Canadian Division. As a result, 1 Bn (RCR) stationed in Barriefield was redesignated the 2 Bn, RCR (2 RCR).

29 September: The Regiment reached Halifax.

1 October: The Regiment arrived at London, Ontario, and is granted a 30-day leave.

23 October: Lieutenant-Colonel J.M. Houghton assumed command of 2 RCR, succeeding Lieutenant-Colonel Reid.

November: 2 RCR moved from Barriefield to Brockville Military Camp, taking over the camp formerly used by the officer training cadre. The Battalion had shrunk to approximately 400 all ranks as a result of discharges and industrial and farm leaves.

21 December: A Colour guard retrieved the Kings and Regimental Colours from London and delivered them to Brockville.

1946

1 January: Colonel Snow issued Circular Letter No. 9 that explained that that letter was to be the last to be sent as the *Connecting File* would once again be published.

January: The first issue of the *Connecting File* since 1939 is published. The Regiment is now consolidated in Brockville. The Battalion's strength is now up to 800 all ranks.

January: Interim Force personnel were assigned to "A" and "B" Coys.

9 January: The Regiment provides a guard of honour for the visit of General Dwight D. Eisenhower to Ottawa.

May: "C" and "D" Coys were activated with a restricted establishment.

1 March: The RCR Bugle Band was re-established. It had a strength of 29 men. It consisted of six snare drums, two tenor drums, one base drum, one pair cymbals and 18 buglers.

11 March: A guard of honour of 30 soldiers was chosen to be part of a composite guard of honour for the opening of Parliament on 14 March.

12 April: The Regiment provided a guard for the arrival of the new governor general, His Excellency Field Marshal Viscount Alexander of Tunis at Union Station in Ottawa.

13 May: The Regiment provided a guard of honour for the governor general on the occasion of the opening of the War Art Gallery of the National Museum in Ottawa.

27 May: With a strength of 519 personnel, the Regiment deployed to Camp Petawawa for the next five months for training.

July: The strength of the Regiment was 300. The remaining personnel are to form the nucleus of The RCR. The Bugle Band was disbanded.

6 August: The Regiment provided a guard of honour for the governor general's visit to Kingston. Lieutenant-Colonel Houghton was presented with the Order of the British Empire.

APPENDIX A

27 August: The Regiment provided a guard of honour for Field Marshal Viscount Montgomery of Alamein.

1 October: 2 RCR was redesignated as The Royal Canadian Regiment. Lieutenant-Colonel Houghton is in command.

21 October: The Regiment returned to Brockville after five months of training in Camp Petawawa.

1947

15 February: The RCR Bugle Band was once again recreated. By April the band was 20 strong.

7 November: The RCR Depot and The RCR Ladies Auxiliary presented a silver memorial to the fallen comrades of Second World War to the Regiment in Brockville.

1948

9 January: The Canadian SAS Company was officially established. The organization was an integral part of the Joint Air School, Rivers, and had a strength of 125 all ranks. The company itself consisted of a platoon from each of the Active Force infantry regiments (RCR, PPCLI, and R22R). The Cdn SAS Coy was disbanded in 1949, upon the completion of parachute/air transportability training by the third and final Active Force infantry unit (R22R).

27 May to 1 June: The Regiment moved from Brockville to Petawawa for its summer training camp. The move was a combination of marching and motor transport.

28 July: NDHQ authorized the commencement of airborne/air-transported training for the three Active Force Infantry Regiments. This was the conceptual beginning of the Mobile Striking Force (MSF). Together, the three (RCR, PPCLI, and R22R) infantry battalions were loosely described as an Airborne Brigade.

December: The RCR platoon, Cdn SAS Coy, was employed as instructional cadre from December 1948 to February 1949 in the Parachute Training Wing of the JAS.

15 December: Lieutenant-Colonel P.R. Bingham assumed command of The Regiment, succeeding Lieutenant-Colonel Houghton, who was posted to Camp Borden to command the Royal Canadian School of Infantry.

1949

January-May: Two platoons of "Royals," part of Canadian Cadre No. 3, were attached to the U.S. Marine Corps for a period of five months to undergo amphibious training.

February: The custom of marching the Colours to the church on the nearest Sunday to Paardeberg Day was resurrected.

1 May: The RCR was officially transformed into an airborne unit. This entailed the parachute training of one rifle company and selected elements of Battalion HQ, Support, and Headquarters Companies.

2 May: 1 RCR began basic air-transportability training. Each week a group of 32 all ranks was dispatched to the CJATC. Each serial was given two weeks of advanced air portability training followed by a four week parachutist course.

18 June: A 100-man guard of honour participated in the Bicentennial celebration of the city of Halifax.

16 July: A 100-man guard of honour was mounted in Brockville on the occasion of the Centennial celebration of the City of Brockville. The guard was inspected by Governor General Alexander.

12 August: The Regiment assisted the Ontario Provincial Police and Brockville police in the recapture three escaped prisoners from the town jail.

8 November: The Regiment moved to CFB Petawawa.

29 November: The camp fire brigade assisted the Brockville City Fire Department fight a fire that broke out in a large business block in the centre of the business district.

December: "D" Coy was reconstituted as a "young soldier company" where new recruits were posted.

1950

January: "B" Coy deployed to Fort Churchill for pre-Arctic indoctrination and participation in Ex Sundog.

Late March: Approximately 75 percent of 1 RCR was trained as military parachutists.

May: The RCR, as an entire battalion, paraded for the first time in the maroon beret.

25 June: North Korea invaded South Korea initiating the Korean War. The United States rallied other countries, including Canada and Great Britain, to endorse the use of force again the communist aggression.

July: The RCR officially became an Airborne Infantry Battalion under authority Army Establishment E/RCIC/2/3.

17 July-04 August: The Regiment conducted Ex Beaver Dam in Algonquin Park to practice jungle fighting. During the exercise "D" Coy provided a 50-man escort for the funeral of former Prime Minister W.L.M. King.

7 August: Prime Minister St. Laurent announced that Canada will send a brigade consisting of the 2nd Battalions of each of the three Regular Army regiments to Korea.

9 August: 1 RCR was formed from the existing battalion. Lieutenant-Colonel P.R. Bingham remained in command.

17 August: 2 RCR was formed from special enlistments. Lieutenant-Colonel R.A. Keane assumed command.

18 October: 2 RCR was presented with its Regimental Banner officially assuming the status of an independent battalion. This was the largest parade in the history of the Regiment.

November: 3 RCR began to form at Fort Lewis, Washington.

3 November: 1 RCR provided a 75-man guard of honour for the Right Honourable Mr. Shinwell, the British secretary of war, and Mr Fockema-Andrea, secretary of state for war for the Netherlands.

16 November: 2 RCR departed for Fort Lewis, Washington.

20 November: 2 RCR arrived at Fort Lewis for preparatory training before deploying to Korea.

27–28 November: Continuation parachute training for "C" Coy. A large scale 1 RCR parachute training exercise, Ex Pinetree, was cancelled.

1951

10 January: 3 RCR officially became an independent battalion at Fort Lewis, Washington. Lieutenant-Colonel K.L. Campbell assumed command. By 15 January its strength was 40 officers and 702 men.

25 January-20 February: "C" Coy participated in Ex Sundog II, a sub-unit MSF exercise in Fort Churchill, Manitoba with the aim of comparing the relative efficiency of parachute assault in the Arctic with a coordinated attack by an air-transported force.

8–9 February: 58 paratroopers of "C" Coy, 1 RCR, jumped onto a tented camp on DZ (drop zone) Proctor Field, Shilo, Manitoba, to practice "smothering tactics." An additional 15 paratroopers made an afternoon jump.

9 February: Ex Sundog II. Another 58 1 RCR paratroopers retried the "smothering" tactics with dismal results. High winds scattered the jumpers over the area 2,500 yards in length by 2,000 yards in width. The nearest jumper landed 700 yards away from the enemy positions.

22 February: Ex Sundog II. 114 paratroopers from "C" Coy, 1 RCR, dropped near Churchill in the Nualla Area to conduct an attack on an enemy position. The DZ was reported cleared in 12 minutes.

21 February: 2 RCR received confirmation that it would be sent to Korea.

3 March: The RCR Band was deployed to Fort Lewis, Washington.

15 March: By this date "B," "C," and "D" Coys 3 RCR were disbanded because of large drafts of soldiers being sent to fill vacancies within 2 RCR and 25 Brigade. The Battalion now resembled a company.

APPENDIX A

1 April: 3 RCR was tasked as part of 25 CIB Replacement Group and was moved back to Canada to train.

20 April: 2 RCR boarded the USNS *General Edwin E. Patrick* bound for Korea.

April: One platoon of 1 RCR paratroops was dropped onto DZ Clement, Camp Petawawa as part of Ex Longstick to practice RV drills and attacks against a defended position.

May: Continuation parachute training conducted by 1 RCR at Rockcliffe, Ottawa, and DZ Clement, Camp Petawawa.

5 May: Ex Old Comrade. Thirty-nine paratroops from 1 RCR jumped in London, Ontario.

4 May: 2 RCR arrived in Pusan Harbour.

5 May: 2 RCR joined 25 CIB in Korea.

7 May: 3 RCR deployed from Fort Lewis to Camp Wainwright for training.

9 May: Continuation parachute training conducted by 1 RCR at DZ Clement, Camp Petawawa.

9 May: 3 RCR arrived in Camp Wainwright. The reinforcement drafts were separated immediately and prepared for Korea. They deployed on 3 June.

11 May: 2 RCR conducted Ex Charleyhorse. Coys practiced attacks on the highest hill in the vicinity of their bivouac.

16 May: 2 RCR moved towards the front, in the area of the Han River.

17 May: Continuation parachute training conducted by 1 RCR at Rockcliffe, Ottawa, and DZ Clement, Camp Petawawa.

22 May: Major-General A.J.H. Cassels, commander of the Commonwealth division accompanied by Brigadier Rockingham, 25 CIB commander, visited 2 RCR.

24 May: 2 RCR came under the command of 25th U.S. Infantry Division, and was ordered to relieved the Turkish Brigade at Sunar-ri, in the P'och'on valley, north of Kwang'ju.

25 May: The Battalion fought its first action in the area of the P'och'on valley, while clearing the slopes of the mountain. The Regiment's first casualty of the campaign was Private. J.C. Beaudry.

28 May: 2 RCR reached the 38th Parallel.

30 May: The Battalion fought its first decisive battle in the area of Kakhul-bong (Hill 467) and the village of Chail-li.

1–18 June: 25 CIB was relieved by the 65th U.S. Regimental Combat Team, and was under the command of 3rd U.S. Division. The brigade was at rest northwest of Uijonbu.

18 June-17 July: 2 RCR was engaged in the area of Chor'won and Hill 730.

30 June: The American government instructed General M. Ridgeway to invite the Chinese and North Koreans to discuss a ceasefire. The next day both sides agreed to meet on 8 July at a small village on the 38th Parallel called Kaesong.

July: Ex Iron Eagle. The (RCR) Regimental NCO course participated in a night jump onto DZ Clement, Camp Petawawa. Upon landing, a three-mile compass march was conducted.

5 July: Twenty 1 RCR paratroops conducted continuation training at Ipperwash, Ontario.

12 July: 1 RCR conducted its first water drop into the Ottawa River. The CO, Lieutenant-Colonel Bingham, was the first of 10 jumpers to hit the water. An additional 60 paratroopers jumped onto DZ Clement as part of a firepower demonstration. An additional 46 completed a continuation parachute descent.

18 July: 2 RCR relieved an infantry unit from the 28th British Commonwealth Infantry Brigade in the Imjin River area.

26 July: 10 members from 1 RCR conducted a water jump into the Ottawa River. Captain J. R. MacDougall made the descent with a 58 (Radio) set. This was the first time an attempt was made to jump into the water while carrying equipment.

28 July: The First Commonwealth Division under command Major-General Cassels assumed operational control of 25 CIB at noon.

APPENDIX A

29 July: "C" Coy, 3 RCR was reconstituted in Wainwright.

August: A total of 370 1 RCR paratroopers completed a continuation parachute descent during the month.

9 August: 10 members from 1 RCR conducted water jumps into the Ottawa River. Another 71 paratroopers underwent continuation training on DZ Clement.

13–15 August: 2 RCR conducted Operation Dirk, a battalion-sized two-day patrol north of the Imjin River.

22 August-10 September: 1 RCR Battalion conducted Ex Chipmunk, a unit level exercise that covered offensive and defensive operations in the Petawawa training area.

11 September: 2 RCR participated in Operation Diggin — a relief in place of the Royal Australian Regiment on the north side of the Imjin River.

15 September: Fifty 1 RCR paratroopers conducted a parachute descent at Malton, Ontario as the feature attraction of the National Air Show, and 3 RCR departed Camp Wainwright.

18 September: 3 RCR returned to Camp Petawawa.

3–5 October: Operation Commando commenced. This was a five division attack along the entire 60 kilometre frontage of I Corps.

7 October: Corps Commander, Lieutenant-General James Van Fleet, visited 2 RCR's battle position.

10 October: 3 RCR was in Ottawa for the visit of H.R.H. Princess Elizabeth and Prince Philip, the Duke of Edinburgh.

2–3 November: The Chinese launched a battalion attack against "A" Coy, 2 RCR. By 0630 hours, 3 November the "Royals" recaptured 2 Platoon's position, which had been overrun by the enemy.

1952

2 January: Lieutenant-Colonel G.C. Corbould assumed command of 2 RCR, succeeding Lieutenant-Colonel Keane.

January: "A" Coy, 1 RCR was participating in Arctic Exercise Pole Star II in Churchill.

18 January: 2 RCR was part of 25 CIB was moved out of the line into divisional reserve.

28 January: The Regiment formed a 2 RCR detachment to serve as a parachute company under Major R. Cole.

29 January: "A" Coy, 2 RCR was designated as the Parachute Company, as part of the MSF requirement. It was stationed in Petawawa.

31 January: Brigadier Milton F. Gregg became the Regimental honorary colonel.

February: A new unit was formed in Camp Petawawa known as Petawawa Detachment 2 RCR. It was the reinforced parachute company left behind by 1 RCR, which was preparing to deploy to Korea. This detachment was to be the nucleus of a reformed 2 RCR parachute battalion.

15 February: The Regiment participated in a memorial service for King George VI.

29 February: 2 RCR conducted Ex Limber, a combined arms assault river crossing exercise.

29 March: "B" and "D" Coys, 1 RCR sailed out of Seattle aboard the USNS *Marine Phoenix* for Korea. They were followed the next day by the remaining members of 1 RCR aboard the USNS *General William N. Black*.

10 March-23 April: 2 RCR rotated into the Jamestown Line for its last tour duty of front line duty in Korea. By 1000 hours, 10 March, they had completed the relief in place with the 1st Battalion, Royal Leicestershire Regiment.

10 April: The first elements of 1 RCR, "B" and "D" Coys, arrived in Inchon, Korea.

11 April: "B" and "D" Coys, 1 RCR, joined 2 RCR in the Kansas Line.

14 April: Lieutenant-Colonel Bingham, CO 1 RCR, was wounded when he triggered a trip wire during an inspection of platoon positions during a training exercise. Major F. Klenavic, the DCO, assumed temporary command.

15 April: Divisional boundaries were redrawn. The Canadian sector ran along the eastern edge of the Sami-ch'on Valley and in the area of the river.

16–17 April: "B" and "D" Coys, 1 RCR assumed control when they officially relieved two "A" and "D" Coys, 2 RCR in the Kansas Line.

25 April: 1 RCR formally replaced 2 RCR and assumed responsibility for the area of operations.

27 April: Brigadier-General M.P. Bogert succeeded Brigadier-General Rockingham as commander 25 CIB.

30 April: 3 RCR returned to Wainwright for the summer to participate in training and field exercises.

End-April: Petawawa Detachment 2 RCR, reinforced by returning veterans who had volunteered for parachute duty, was renamed "A" Coy, 2 RCR.

4 May: The first draft of 2 RCR sailed from Kure, Japan aboard the USNS *Pvt. Sadao S. Munemori* for Vancouver, BC.

5 May: RCR paratroopers dropped on Crumlin Airport, London, Ontario, as part of the "Old Comrades Reunion."

12 May: The second draft of 2 RCR sailed from Yokohama, Japan aboard the USNS *General Simon B. Buckner* for home.

18 May: The first draft of 2 RCR arrived in Vancouver where it was greeted by thousands of people. After a short parade through the city, the "Royals" boarded special trains and departed on 60 days leave.

22 May: The second draft of 2 RCR arrived in Seattle, Washington, and boarded trains for leave.

22 May: "B" Coy, 1 RCR was pulled from its front line position and deployed to a secret location.

25 May: "B" Coy, 1 RCR arrived at Koje-Do, and was tasked with guard duty for a PoW compound holding approximately 150,000 prisoners.

28 May: 52 members of "A" Coy, 2 RCR participate in Ex Deer Fly I in Fort Churchill, Manitoba. This was a summer Arctic indoctrination exercise.

End-May: 2 RCR commenced reorganizing as a parachute battalion.

June: 1 RCR manned the defences of the Jamestown line.

4 June: "B" Coy assumed guard duties at the Koje-Do PoW compound.

16 June: Fifty members of "B" Coy, 1 RCR conducted a guard of honour for Governor General, Field Marshal Alexander's visit to Koje-Do.

18 June: "B" Coy, 1 RCR, provided the escort to transfer 6,300 prisoners from Compound 602 to Compound 66 in Koje-Do.

30 June: 1 RCR was relieved by the 3rd Royal Australian Regiment and moved into reserve at the Wyoming line.

9 July: 1 RCR moved back to a depth position in the Kansas line.

10 July: "B" Coy, 1 RCR was relieved at Koje-Do by the American 92nd Military Police Battalion.

14 July: "B" Coy rejoined the Battalion.

August: 85 jumpers from "A" Coy, 2 RCR conducted a parachute jump in St. Thomas, Ontario.

10 August: 1 RCR returned to front line duty taking up a position in the Jamestown Line.

3 September: National headquarters announced that 3 RCR will relieve 1 RCR in the spring of 1953, in Korea.

6 September: Commander 25 CIB directed 1 RCR to form a fifth rifle company

APPENDIX A

"E" Coy, to take over a portion of R22R's position since they experienced significant personnel shortages.

12 September: Major-General M.M. Alston-Roberts-West, the new Commonwealth division commander visited the Battalion.

15 September: 50 RCR paratroopers conducted a parachute descent at the Malton Airport, Ontario, as part of the National Air Show

5 October: The lead elements of 3 RCR returned to Camp Petawawa from Camp Wainwright.

23–24 October: The Chinese assault Hill 355. "B" Coy was overrun, but timely counterattacks by "C" Coy, recaptured the position by 0400 hours.

1 November: The Regiment was relieved at Hill 355 ("Little Gibraltar"/Kowang-San) by the 1st Royal Australian Regiment. "E" Coy was disbanded.

29 November: 1 RCR, as part of 25 CIB, moved back to the front line astride Sami-ch'on.

3 December: 1 RCR provided 30 men for a Commonwealth guard of honour for the visit of President-elect Dwight Eisenhower.

28 December: 1 RCR relieved 1 PPCLI on the "Hook."

1953

9 January: Para Wing, 2 RCR, was established in a "H" Hut in London.

12 January: 2 RCR departed Camp Petawawa for London.

28 January: 1 RCR was relieved by a battalion of 2nd U.S. Division, and proceeded into army reserve.

10 February: 2 RCR supported by 1st Light Battery (Paratroop), Royal Canadian Artillery, participated in Ex ASDZ I. They were tasked to secure Rivers airfield.

February-March: 1 RCR was in depth conducting rest, training and various other activities.

1 March: 3 RCR arrived in Seattle, Washington. It boarded the USNS *General C.C. Ballou.*

19 March: The Regimental Depot was created as a result of a reorganization.

25 March: 3 RCR relieved 1 RCR in Korea.

30 March: 1 RCR conducted a ceremony at the United Nations cemetery in Pusan, to honour fallen comrades.

1 April: The Canadian Infantry Battalions each received 100 South Korean soldiers, under Katcoms (Korean Augmentation to Commonwealth Forces) to augment their strengths.

9 April: 1 RCR, aboard the USNS *Marine Lynx,* sailed for Seattle, Washington.

19 April: 3 RCR relieved the R22R on Hill 187 in the central sector of the Jamestown Line front.

21 April: Brigadier J.V. Allard, C.B.E., D.S.O., E.D., assumes command of 25th Canadian Infantry Brigade.

23 April: 1 RCR arrived in Seattle, where members boarded trains for Canada.

27 April: 1 RCR arrived in Ottawa, where it was granted the Freedom of the City. With ceremony, the Colours are returned.

2 May: The Chinese attacked 3 RCR on Hill 187 inflicting heavy casualties. This was the last major engagement of the war for the "Royals."

May: 3 RCR remained on the front.

7 June: The PPCLI relieved 3 RCR who moved back into reserve for training and sports.

15 June: The RCR Depot was formed. Major E.L. Cohen assumed command.

21 July: Corporal J.A. Ferlatte and three Katcoms are the last Regimental casualties of the war.

APPENDIX A

27 July: The Korean War ended. The armistice was signed at 1000 hours and the ceasefire took at 2200 hours that night

27 July: Mr. R.W. Mayhew, Canadian ambassador to Japan, visited 3 RCR.

31 July: Major F. Klenavic assumed command of 1 RCR, succeeding Lieutenant-Colonel Bingham.

24 August: 1 RCR relieved 2 RCR of the MSF tasking (because of 2 RCR's rotation to Germany).

25 September: 1 RCR conducted continuation parachute drops in Petawawa to begin its "long uphill climb to a parachute unit." Between 25 September and 6 November, the unit made 233 jumps.

17 October: 2 RCR advance party arrived in Holland and departed for Soest Station by train where it arrived the following day and was met by Brigadier W.A.B. Anderson. The advance party settled in Camp C-5.

8 November: 2 RCR main body arrived in Soest. They were stationed at Fort York.

9 November: Lieutenant-General Simonds, the CGS visited 2 RCR in Soest.

9 November: 1 RCR provided a guard of honour for the visit of President Dwight D. Eisenhower to Ottawa.

22 November: 2 RCR rear party arrived in Europe.

8 December: Field Marshal H.R.H. Prince Philip became colonel-in-chief of The Regiment.

27 December: Lieutenant-General T.R. McCoy assumed command of 1 RCR, succeeding Major Klenavic.

December: A reorganization of the CF was in formulation under which the third battalions of each of the infantry regiments would be cut and reconstituted as battalions in Canadian Guards Brigade.

APPENDIX B
Key Appointments

Colonels-in-Chief

FM HRH The Duke of Connaught: 4 April 1929 — 6 January 1941
FM HRH The Prince Philip, Duke of Edinburgh: 8 December 1953 — Present

Honorary Colonels

FM The Hon Viscount Wolseley of Cairo: 1 July 1899 — 25 March 1913
FM HRH The Duke of Connaught: 13 October 1914 — 4 April 1929
Gen Sir William G. Otter (Not Gazetted): 4 April 1929 — 7 May 1929
MGen S.J.A. Denison: 1 October 1929 — 8 November 1937
MGen The Hon A.H. MacDonell: 8 November 1937 — 12 November 1939
Brig The Hon M.F. Gregg: 31 January 1952 — 31 January 1958

Honorary Lieutenant-Colonels

Col C.H. Hill: 13 November 1939 — 19 April 1946

Commandants

Infantry School Corps: designated 1883
Canadian Regiment of Infantry: designated 1892
Royal Regiment of Canadian Infantry: designated 1893
LCol G.J. Maunsell (A Coy): 1883 — 1896
LCol G. d'Orsonnens (B Coy): 1883 — 1896

LCol W.D. Otter (C Coy): 1883 — 1896
LCol H. Smith (D Coy): 1887 — 1896

Commanding Officers

Royal Regiment of Canadian Infantry

LCol G.J. Maunsell: 5 September 1896 — 15 July 1898
LCol W.D. Otter: 15 July 1898 — 28 February 1899

Royal Canadian Regiment of Infantry (designated 1899)

LCol W.D. Otter: 1 March 1899 — 28 September 1899
LCol L. Buchan: 28 September 1899 — 25 March 1901

2nd (Special Service) Battalion, Royal Canadian Regiment of Infantry (formed 1899 — disbanded 1900)

LCol W.D. Otter: 29 September 1899 — 25 April 1900
LCol L. Buchan: 25 April 1900 — 26 May 1900
LCol W.D. Otter: 26 May 1900 — 23 December 1900

3rd (Special Service) Battalion, Royal Canadian Regiment of Infantry (formed 1990 — disbanded 1902)

LCol B.H. Vidal: 10 April 1900 — 1 July 1900
LCol G.R. White: 1 July 1900 — 1 October 1902

The Royal Canadian Regiment (designated 1901)

LCol L. Buchan: 25 March 1901 — 16 February 1904
Temporary — B/LCol D.D. Young: 16 February 1904 — 23 July 1904
Administered by Militia Headquarters: 23 July 1904 — 15 September 1905
LCol R.L. Wadmore: 15 September 1905 — 1 September 1910
LCol S.J.A. Denison: 1 September 1910 — 1 January 1913
LCol A.O. Fages: 1 January 1913 — 1 January 1915
LCol A.E. Carpenter: 1 January 1915 — 6 September 1915
LCol A.H. MacDonell: 6 September 1915 — 16 April 1916
LCol C.H. Hill: 20 April 1916 — 4 July 1918
LCol C.R.E. Willets: 4 July 1918 — 28 September 1918

Temporary — Capt C.L. Wood: 29 September 1918 — 8 October 1918
LCol G.W. MacLeod: 8 October 1918 — 29 January 1919
LCol C.H. Hill: 29 January 1919 — 15 October 1924
LCol E.A. Seeley Smith: 15 October 1924 — 21 September 1929
LCol R.J.S. Langford: 21 September 1929 — 15 May 1935
LCol M.K. Greene: 15 May 1935 — 31 October 1938
LCol K.M. Holloway: 1 November 1938 — 25 November 1939
LCol V. Hodson: 26 November 1939 — 21 October 1940
Maj T.E.D'O. Snow: 21 October 1940 — 30 November 1940
LCol M.K. Greene: 1 December 1940 — 15 July 1941
LCol T.E.D'O. Snow: 15 July 1941 — 24 February 1943
LCol R.M. Crowe: 3 March 1943 — 24 July 1943
A/LCol T.M. Powers: 25 July 1943 — 12 August 1943
LCol D.C. Spry: 13 August 1943 — 17 December 1943
A/LCol A.S.A. Galloway: 18 December 1943 — 5 January 1944
LCol W.W. Mathers: 6 January 1944 — 1 June 1944
LCol J.W. Ritchie: 2 June 1944 — 8 December 1944
LCol W.W. Reid: 9 December 1944 — 8 June 1945
Maj F.G.C. Darton: 9 June 1945 — 1 October 1945

1st Battalion, 1st Regiment, 6 Cdn Inf Div
(formed 1 August 45 — redesignated 27 September 45)

LCol W.W. Reid: 1 August 1945 — 27 September 1945

2nd Battalion The Royal Canadian Regiment
(designated 27 September 45 — redesignated 1 October 46)

LCol W.W. Reid: 27 September 1945 — 23 October 1945
LCol J.M. Houghton: 23 October 1945 — 1 October 1946

The Royal Canadian Regiment
(designated 1 October 46 — redesignated 9 August 50)

LCol J.M. Houghton: 1 October 1946 — 15 December 1948
LCol P.R. Bingham: 15 December 1948 — 9 August 1950

1st Battalion, The Royal Canadian Regiment

LCol P.R. Bingham: 9 August 1950 — 31 July 1953
Maj F. Klenavic: 31 July 1953 — 27 December 1953

LCol T.R. McCoy: 27 December 1953 — 4 October 1957

2nd Battalion The Royal Canadian Regiment

LCol R.A. Keane: 17 August 1950 — 2 January 1952
LCol G.C. Corbould: 2 January 1952 — 31 August 1957

3rd Battalion The Royal Canadian Regiment
(Formed 10 January 51 — disbanded 21 July 54)

LCol K.L. Campbell: 10 January 1951 — 21 July 1954

The Royal Canadian Regiment Depot
(formed 19 March 1953 — disbanded 8 December 1968)

Maj E.L. Cohen: 15 June 1953 — 9 September 1956

Home Station Commanders

LCol P.R. Bingham (Camp Petawawa): 25 February 1952 — 1 July 1953
Maj F. Klenavic: 1 July 1953 — 9 October 1953
LCol G.C. Corbould (Wolseley Barracks): 9 October 1953 — 27 December 1953
LCol T.R. McCoy: 27 December 1953 — 2 November 1955

Regimental Sergeants-Major

Infantry School Corps

CSM Thomas McKenzie (A Coy): June 1884 — 1892
Sgt Maj Spackman (C Coy): 1885 —

Canadian Regiment of Infantry

CSM Thomas McKenzie: 1892 — 1893

Royal Regiment of Canadian Infantry

CSM Thomas McKenzie: 1893 — 1 December 1895
Sgt Maj A.J. Fowlie (A Coy): 1 December 1895 — 25 March 1901

APPENDIX B

Royal Canadian Regiment of Infantry

Sgt Maj A.J. Fowlie: 1899 — 1900

2nd (Special Service) Battalion, Royal Canadian Regiment of Infantry

Sgt Maj D. Borland: 1899 — 1900

3rd (Special Service) Battalion, Royal Canadian Regiment of Infantry

Sgt Maj W.P. Butcher: 1 April 1900 — 1 October 1902

The Royal Canadian Regiment

Sgt Maj A.J. Fowlie: 25 March 1901 — 1903
Sgt Maj J.B. Munro: 1903
Sgt Maj R. Cumming: 1903
Sgt Maj H.T. Brewer: 1907
Sgt Maj Utton: 1911
Sgt Maj J. Dymond: 1911
Sgt Maj E.H. Price: 1911
Sgt Maj A.A. Turner: August 1914 — 19 November 1914
Sgt Maj J.S. Legge: 19 November 1914 — 1 November 1915
Sgt Maj H. Phillips: 1 November 1915
Sgt Maj H. Beard: 1915
A/RSM H. Longergan: 1916
RSM W.R. Roberts: 1917 — 31 July 1924
RSM John Wyatt: 1918
WO I F. Davis: 12 May 1934–12 July 1938
RSM John Wyatt: 20 June 1935
RSM H.M. Bevis: 1936
RSM J.H. Adams: 1939
RSM F.G.C. Darton: 1939 — 30 November 1940
RSM A.C. McKenzie: 1 December 1940 — 1942
RSM A.C. McDonnell: 1942 — 5 January 1944
RSM V.G. Lewington: 5 January 1944 — 1 July 1944
RSM D.P. Duffey: 1 July 1944 — January 1945
RSM J.L. Goodridge: January 1945 — June 1945
RSM J.A. Fischer: June 1945 — December 1945
RSM J.L. Goodridge: December 1945 — 1950

1st Battalion, The Royal Canadian Regiment

WO1 F.A. Burns: 1950 — 1954

2nd Battalion, The Royal Canadian Regiment

WO1 J.J.T. McManus: 9 August 1950 — 26 August 1953

3rd Battalion, The Royal Canadian Regiment

WO1 J.M. MacKay: September 1951 — March 1954

The Royal Canadian Regiment Depot

WO1 E. Tracz: 15 August 1953 — 6 January 1954

The Royal Canadian Regiment Band

Bandmasters

Station Bands

Sgt C. Hyes (Fredericton): 1884 — 1888
B/WO1 R. Fisher (London): 1888 — 1891

Regimental Band
Capt M. Ryan: 21 June 1905 — 26 August 1916
Lt H.G. Jones: 26 August 1916 — November 1919
Capt M. Ryan: November 1919 — 22 January 1924
Capt L.K. Harrison: July 1924 — September 1939

Bandmasters/Directors of Music

Lt J. Proderick: 1940 — April 1945
WO1 B. Bacah: April 1945 — 1946
Lt D.B. Armstrong: 1946 — November 1953

APPENDIX C
Battle Honours

Note: Entries in italics are honours emblazoned on the Regimental Colours.

Northwest Canada

1. *Saskatchewan*

2. *North-West Canada, 1885*

South Africa

3. *Paardeberg*

4. *South Africa, 1899–1900*

First World War

5. *Ypres, 1915*

6. Gravenstafel

7. St. Julien

8. Festubert, 1915

9. *Mount Sorrel*

10. *Somme, 1916*

11. Pozieres

12. Flers-Courcelette

13. *Ancré Heights*

14. Arras, 1917

15. *Vimy, 1917*

16. Arieux

17. Scarpe, 1917

18. *Hill 70*

19. *Ypres, 1917*

20. *Passchendaele*

21. *Amiens*

22. Arras, 1918

23. Scarpe, 1918

24. Droucourt-Queant

25. *Hindenburg Line*

26. Canal du Nord

27. Cambrai, 1918

28. *Pursuit to Mons*

29. France and Flanders, 1915–1918

APPENDIX C

Second World War

30. *Landing in Sicily*

31. Valguarnera

32. Agira

33. Adrano

34. Regalbuto

35. Sicily, 1943

36. Landing at Reggio

37. *Motta Montecorvino*

38. Campobosso

39. Torella

40. *San Leonardo*

41. The Gully

42. *Ortona*

43. Cassino II

44. Gustav Line

45. Liri Valley

46. *Hitler Line*

47. *Gothic Line*

48. *Lamone Crossing*

49. Misano Ridge

50. *Rimini Line*

51. San Martino-San Lorenzo

52. Pisciatello

53. Fosso Vecchio

54. *Italy, 1943–1945*

55. Apeldoorn

56. *North-West Europe, 1945*

Korea

57. *Korea, 1951–1953*

NOTES

Introduction

1. John A. Lynn, *Battle: A History of Combat and Culture* (Boulder, CO: Westview, 2003), 156.

2. Captain J.A. Johnston, "A Year with the Royal Canadian Regiment," *The Connecting File*, Winter 1950–1951, 54.

3. Arthur Bryant, "The Fate of the Regiment," *The Connecting File*, April 1948, 19.

4. Editorial, *The Connecting File*, Fall-Winter 1953–1954, 5.

5. Note that in this volume, up until 1945, the terms *battalion* and *regiment* are used interchangeably because The RCR consisted of only a single battalion.

6. The first RCR regimental history is R.C. Fetherstonhaugh, *The Royal Canadian Regiment, 1883–1933* (Fredericton, NB: The RCR, 1936). The second is G.R. Stevens, *The Royal Canadian Regiment: Volume Two — 1933–1966* (London, ON: London Printing Co., 1967). Part 2, Volume 3, to be released by 2010, is entitled *From The Cold War into the New Millennium: The History of the Royal Canadian Regiment 1954–2008*.

ESTABLISHING A LEGACY

Chapter 1: A Pressing Need

1. The country was divided into nine military districts with headquarters at London (No. 1), Toronto (No. 2), Kingston (No. 3), Brockville (No. 4), Montreal (No. 5 for English units and No. 6 for French units), Quebec City (No. 7), No. 8 (responsible for New Brunswick), and No. 9 (responsible for Nova Scotia).

2. The Red River Rebellion began in October 1869 when the Métis, who had not been consulted, feared for their property rights, and became enraged at their treatment they received from surveyors sent to implement the transfer of Prince Rupert's Land from the Hudson's Bay Company to the Canadian government, formed a provisional government of their own. It ended in 1870, with the arrival of British forces and Canadian militia sent to impose the rule of law.

   The Fenian raids were organized by Irish-Americans who wished to help Ireland secure its independence from Britain by attacking Britain's North American colonies. The first raid occurred in New Brunswick in April 1866; the next on the Niagara frontier in June; a third at Missisquoi the same month; and two over the Quebec border in 1870. In sum, they posed little real threat. However, they did persuade New Brunswick to join Confederation and they perpetuated the militia myth.

3. Quoted in Ken Bell and C.P. Stacey, *100 Years: The Royal Canadian Regiment 1883–1983* (Don Mills, ON: Collier Macmillan, 1983), 14.

4. R.C. Fetherstonhaugh, *The Royal Canadian Regiment, 1883–1933* (Fredericton, NB: The RCR, 1936), 8.

5. Quoted in Desmond Morton, *The Last War Drum* (Toronto: Hakkert, 1972), 3.

6. Of the militia component — 3,000 were drawn from eastern Canada; 1,200 from Manitoba and 800 from the Northwest. The actual force consisted of approximately 4,400 infantry, 650 cavalry/mounted troops, 300 artillery, and 550 NWMP. It also included about 2,000 transport auxiliaries. Major-General Middleton, the force commander, was a veteran of combat in New Zealand and India. He was twice recommended for the Victoria Cross (VC) during the Indian Mutiny. He was also a former commandant of the Royal Military College at Sandhurst.

7. Letter, Captain R.L. Wadmore (C Coy) to his wife, 7 April 1885. Library and Archives Canada [henceforth LAC], Manuscript Group [henceforth MG] 29, Series E81, File R, Lyndhurst Wadmore Fonds — Scrapbook.

8. The Royal Canadian Regiment Museum Archives [henceforth RCR Archives], Series 1 — North-West Rebellion, Vol. 1, File 7, "The Rebellion and its Fomenters," *The New Brunswick Reporter*, Saturday, 23 May 1885, Vol. 41, No. 41, 2.

9. Major-General T.B. Strange was a retired British artillery officer who saw service in India during the Indian Mutiny in 1857. Upon return to Canada, he was given command of one of the two permanent artillery batteries established in 1871. He had retired in 1882 and returned to service three years later to command one of the columns.

10. RCR Archives, Series 1 — North-West Rebellion, Vol. 1, File 3, Letter, Major W.M. Gartshoe to his wife, 13 April 1885.

11. The Frog Lake Massacre was perpetrated by Big Bear's Cree warriors on 1 April 1885. In total they killed nine settlers and took several hostages.

12. Much to the benefit of Middleton and his troops — Riel actually undermined his rebellion by hindering his very capable military commander. He continually refused to allow Dumont to attack the inexperienced militiamen at night or to wage a guerrilla style war (i.e., raids and ambushes) that would arguably have had a catastrophic effect on the raw inexperienced soldiers. Continual skirmishing would have also created time delays and greater logistic problems for the government troops (i.e., ammunition, supplies, and casualties).

13. Quoted in Morton, *The Last War Drum,"* 62.

14. RCR Archives, Series 1 — North-West Rebellion, Vol. 1, File 10, "Report of Maj Gen F Middleton — 1 May 1885, Fish Creek," Extracts from Militia Orders.

15. *Ibid.*

16. C.P. Mulvaney, *The North-West Rebellion* (Toronto: A.H. Hovey & Co., 1885), 145.

17. Middleton's forces suffered 50 casualties, 10 dead and 40 wounded — a casualty rate of approximately 15 percent. Dumont's forces suffered 11 dead and 18 wounded. RCR Archives, Series 1 — North-West Rebellion, Vol. 1, File 10, "Report of Maj Gen F Middleton — 1 May 1885, Fish Creek," Extracts from Militia Orders.

18. RCR Archives, Series 1 — North-West Rebellion, Vol. 1, File 10, "Lt Col W.D. Otter's Report to Maj Gen F. Middleton … Engagement with Chief Poundmaker and his Band, 2 May 1885," Extracted from General Order (GO) 13, dated 8 July 1885.

19. Diary, Lieutenant Richard Cassel, in R.C. Macleod, ed., *Reminiscences of a Bungle by One of the Bunglers — and Two Other Northwest Rebellion Diaries* (Edmonton, AB: University of Alberta Press, 1983), 153. Another contemporary account stated, "in five minutes after the first shot was fired, Colonel Otter's force was completely surrounded and being fired on from all sides. It was evident he had run into a trap. The situation began to look desperate." Mulvaney, 163.

20. RCR Archives, Series 1 — North-West Rebellion, Vol. 1, File 10, "Lt Col W.D. Otter's Report to Maj Gen F. Middleton … Engagement with Chief Poundmaker and His Band, 2 May 1885." Extract from GO 13, dated 8 July 1885.

21. During the course of the battle the carriage on both NWMP 7-pound cannons broke rendering them almost useless. The artillery pieces were later withdrawn by jerry-rigging carriages that could haul them away.

22. Quoted in Bob Beal and Rod Macleod, *Prairie Fire. The 1885 North-West Rebellion* (Toronto: McClelland and Stewart, 1994), 251.

23. Quoted in Beal and Macleod, *Prairie Fire*, 251. One participant revealed, "They are the beau ideal of skirmishers, expose themselves but little and move with marvelous quickness." Diary, Lieutenant Richard Cassels in R.C. McLeod, ed., *Reminiscences of a Bungle by One of the Bunglers — and Two Other Northwest Rebellion Diaries* (Edmonton, AB: University of Alberta Press, 1983), 157.

24. Historians have almost universally agreed that the battle was a defeat for the government forces. Moreover, most judged it to be ill-judged and totally unnecessary. Battleford was safe and Poundmaker made little effort to actively enter into hostilities with the government.

25. Mulvaney, 113.

26. See RCR Archives, Series 1 — North-West Rebellion, Vol. 1, File 10, "Report to Maj Gen F Middleton from Maj H Smith, ISC — Batoche." Extract from GO 24, dated 30 Oct 1885.

27. Quoted in Jack Granatstein, *Canada's Army* (Toronto: University of Toronto Press, 2002), 31.

28. Quoted in Ian McCulloch, "Yukon Field Force 1898–1900," *The Beaver*, Vol. 77, No. 5, October-November 1997, 4.

29. See Canada, *House of Commons Debates* [henceforth *Debates*], 8 February 1898, 187–189 and 222–223.

30. Letter, T.D.B. Evans to Lady Aberdeen, 1 September 1898. LAC, MG 26 G, Laurier Fonds, Vol. 85, Yukon Affairs, Microfilm C-759.

31. Department of Militia and Defence for the Dominion of Canada. *Report for the Year Ended December 1898* (Ottawa: Queen's Printer, 1899); and *Debates*, 4 May 1898, 4795–4798.

32. Quoted in Brereton Greenhous, ed., *Guarding the Goldfields. The Story of the Yukon Field Force* (Toronto: Dundurn Press, 1987), 23.

33. More than half the force came from the RCRI. The remainder was drawn from the Royal Canadian Artillery (RCA) and the Royal Canadian Dragoons (RCD). There were also six women who accompanied the Force — four members of the Victorian Order of Nurses, a reporter for the Toronto *Globe*, and the wife of the NWMP inspector in Dawson. Volunteers were induced to join by the fact that all would receive double pay. This was quickly a mute point since prices in the Klondike were so exorbitant that the cost of living soon cancelled out the increase in pay.

34. *Debates*, 8 February 1898, 222.

35. Although the force was required to steam in U.S. territorial waters (i.e., the Stikine River), a treaty was in place that granted Canada free navigational access to the river.

36. The 60 tons of supplies included: 300 rounds of ammunition for each

rifle, 25,000 rounds for the Maxim machine gun, and 200 rounds for the two 7-pounder cannons. Ration staples included 40,000 kilograms of tinned meats, 20,000 kilograms of "hard tack" biscuits, and 63,000 kilograms of flour.

37. Quoted in Greenhous, 49.

38. Letter Evans to Lady Aberdeen, quoted in McCulloch, 7. Rations were another concern by all. Lester noted, "Everyone is complaining of not getting full rations. All we had for supper tonight was two small buns about the size of a Boston cracker and a couple of spoonfuls of apples." LAC, MG 29, Edward Lester fonds, Accession E105, File No. 2 — Lester, Edward Lester's Diary [henceforth Lester's Diary], 4. However, once they reached Lake Teslin the problem resolved itself because there was an ample supply of fish.

39. Quoted in Greenhous, 49.

40. Lester's Diary, 28. Pain is always relative. A few months later Lester complained of a new menace. "We are terribly tormented by a species of small black fly," he wrote, "of which there are millions; they are worse than the mosquitoes & more venomous." *Ibid.*, 82.

41. Faith Fenton Dispatches, in Greenhous, 107.

42. Georgia Powell's Dispatch, in Greenhous, 125.

43. Lester's Diary, 32 and 49. Georgia Powell wrote: "From mountain to swamp and bog — bogs into whose cold, damp, mossy depths we would sink to our knees, and under which the ice still remains, swamps where we trampled down bushes and shrubs to make footing for ourselves, and where the mules stick many times, often as many as twenty all down at once, sometimes having to be unpacked to be taken out our baggage dumped in the mud, and where the mosquitoes held high revelry." Powell Dispatch in Greenhous, 124.

44. Lester's Diary, 51 and 70.

45. *Ibid.*, 53.

46. Quoted in Greenhous, 22.

47. See for example, Letter, "Faced Mutiny and Starvation," from Captain C. St. A. Pearse to friends, 27 November 1898. LAC, Sir Edward Thomas Henry Hutton fonds, [henceforth Hutton Papers], Microfilm C-1218.

48. Quoted in Canada, *The "Force" in the Yukon* (Ottawa: Minister of Supply and Services Canada, 1979), 14.

49. Quoted in McCullough, 11.

50. The reduction of the Yukon Field Force included the dispatch of Lieutenant-Colonel Evans. He was replaced by Major T.D. R. Hemming of the RCRI. The force itself was renamed the Yukon Garrison and the headquarters was moved from Selkirk to Dawson. The remainder of the troops left in June 1900.

51. LAC, Hutton Papers, Microfilm C-1218, Letter, Hutton to Evans, 8 February 1899.

Chapter 2: Making Canada Proud

1. The British held the colonies of Cape Colony and Natal on the South African coasts. The Boer territories of Transvaal and the Orange Free State were distinctly anti-British. The discovery and exploitation of large gold deposits spurred the growth of in power and prestige of the two breakaway republics. The economic bonanza attracted non-Boer residents (Uitlanders), specifically English subjects from the British coastal colonies of Cape Colony and Natal. The practice of the Boer republics was not to grant non-residents equal status. In fact, the Uitlanders bore the burden of taxation and had no political rights whatsoever. This perceived exploitation soon generated resentment and pleas to the British government by their "loyal" subjects for assistance. See Thomas Pakenham, *The Boer War* (New York: Random House, 1979), chapters 5 to 9. The most comprehensive, and arguably best work on the Canadian participation in the conflict is Carman Miller, *Painting the Map Red: Canada and the South African War 1899–1902* (Ottawa: The Canadian War Museum, 1993). See also Brian A. Reid, *Our Little Army in the Field: The Canadians in South Africa* (St. Catharines, ON: Vanwell, 1996).

2. The pro-war element was not a monolithic group of imperialists. It was a mélange of English Canadians, especially from Ontario and the English-speaking parts of Quebec. There was also the anti-war faction. The largest

group was the French Canadians. They perceived no Canadian interest at stake in far away Transvaal or the Orange Free State. More important, war could lead to the hated and feared conscription. There were also the economic arguments against involvement. Troops cost money, which could be better spent on national development and improving the infrastructure in Quebec. But the French Canadians were not the only anti-war voice. The inability to see any vital Canadian security or other interest involved was the main reason others were against Canadian involvement. By this time significant Irish and German immigrant communities spread through out the country — there was no enthusiasm from them largely on the grounds that it was nothing more than another example of British subjugation. Furthermore, many in labour circles felt war would be too disruptive to agriculture and emerging industry. There were also pacifists like the Doukhobors and Mennonite communities, as well as the national Women's Christian Temperance Union (WCTU).See C.P. Stacey, *Canada and the Age of Conflict, Vol. 1*, 57–68; Gwynne Dyer and Tina Viljoen, *The Defence of Canada* (Toronto: McClelland & Stewart, 1990), 157–163; Miller, 16–50; and Carl Berger, *The Sense of Power: Studies in the Ideas of Canadian Imperialism 1867–1914* (Toronto: University of Toronto Press, 1970), 131–147.

3. Hutton went so far as to write to the colonial secretary, and state: "Having perhaps better cause to know this intense feeling of military enthusiasm and deep rooted loyalty than most Canadians I especially warned the Minister of Militia and several others of the Cabinet of the consequences of any hesitation upon their part to offer troops." Letter, Hutton to Chamberlain, 2 November 1899. See also letter to Lord Wolseley, 2 November 1899. LAC, MG 21, Add. Mss., Hutton Papers, Microfilm C-1219.

In Canadian military circles, the GOC, Major-General Hutton, was quietly working up hopes by letting the militia know that he had a well-organized plan for an expeditionary force and that supportive individuals were to be in it. The imperialist press, such as the *Montreal Star* published by the jingoist Hugh Graham was also constantly beating the "commitment drum" harder and harder. On 3 October 1899, the *Canadian Military Gazette* (the widely distributed newspaper of the Canadian militia) published details of Hutton's secret plan adding confidently that the government was likely to send the force. Conveniently and simultaneously, a Colonial Office circular arrived in Canada thanking the dominion for offering troops — which of course it had not. It too found its way into the public domain. Evidence pointed to Hutton's behind the scenes manipulations. If so, it was a clear challenge to cabinet authority. Eventually, when enough facts accumulated, the government insisted that the British recall the abrasive GOC. However, the damage had been done and Laurier was cornered into supporting the war effort with a Canadian contribution. See Desmond Morton, *The Canadian: General Sir William Otter* (Toronto: A.M. Hakkert Ltd., 1974), 160–164; Stacey, *Canada and the Age of Conflict*, Vol. 1, 57–70; Morton, *A Military History of Canada* (Toronto: McClelland & Stewart, 1992), 113–115; and "Canadian Troops for Transvaal," *The Canadian Military Gazette*, Vol. 14, No. 19, 3 October 1899, 11.

4. See *Debates*, Vol. 61, 24 March 1902, 1685; LAC, Record Group [henceforth RG] 24, Vol. 1850, File G.A.Q. 13-39 (7-13), "The South African War, 1899–1902. Considerations Leading Up to Decision to Provide a Contingent," 263; RCR Archives, Series 3 Boer War 1899-1900, Vol. 2, File 5, "1,000 Men will form the Canadian Force," *Quebec Chronicle*, 14 October 1899; and "Canada's Field Force for the Transvaal," *The Canadian Military Gazette*, Vol. 14, No. 20, 17 October 1899, 11.

5. *Debates*, Vol. 61, 24 March 1902, 1685; "The South African War, 1899–1902. Considerations Leading Up to Decision to Provide a Contingent," 263; "Canada's Field Force for the Transvaal," *The Canadian Military Gazette*, Vol. 14, No. 20, 17 October 1899, 11.

6. Joseph Schull, *Laurier — The First Canadian* (Toronto: Macmillan of Canada, 1965), 381.

7. Department of Militia and Defence, *Supplementary Report — Organization, Equipment, Despatch and Service of the Canadian Contingents During the War in South Africa 1899-1900* (Ottawa: S.E. Dawson, Queen's Printer, 1901), 1–3. See also Stacey, *Canada and the Age of Conflict*, Vol. 1, 60–66; Sanford Evans, *The Canadian Contingents* (Toronto: Publishers' Syndicate Ltd, 1901), 54 and 73.

8. "The South African War, 1899–1902. Considerations Leading Up to Decision to Provide a Contingent," 264–265.

9. Ironically, after the hard political fight to send the first contingent, within the next two weeks, on 1 November 1899, the government offered a second contingent, consisting of artillery and mounted infantry. The British did not respond immediately to the offer. Two days later, they politely declined. The political criterion of a unified front was already achieved. As such, they were reluctant to take on the costly burden of more "ineffective" colonial

troops. However, the disastrous turn of events in-theatre soon had them clamouring for more colonial contributions. As a result the Canadian government dispatched the second contingent, which consisted of a brigade (three batteries) of artillery and two mounted infantry battalions, called 1 and 2 Canadian Mounted Rifles (CMR). 1 CMR was later renamed The Royal Canadian Dragoons in August 1900. 2 CMR, that was based largely on the North-West Mounted Police was then renamed 1 CMR. Unlike the first contingent the second contingent was actually a coalition of three smaller units that were given different tasks and attached to various different British formations. In total, the second contingent numbered approximately 1,289 men. It also represented the last official Canadian contribution to the war. Although other Canadians served, they were not raised as Canadian contingents. Rather, they were volunteers to formations raised by the British, such as the South African Constabulary, or privately raised units such as Lord Strathcona's Horse. In the end, 8,372 Canadians served during the Boer War from 1899–1902. Of this number 224 were killed (89 in action and 135 from disease) and 252 were wounded. See "Considerations Leading Up to Decision to Provide a Contingent," 270; and Granatstein, *Canada's Army*, 45.

10. Department of Militia and Defence, *Supplementary Report ... 1901*, 8.

11. Report A, Otter to Adjutant General, 26 January 1901, in Department of Militia and Defence, *Supplementary Report ... 1901*, 11.

12. LAC, MG 30, Series E-231, File — typescript of letters and biographical sketch Ramsay fonds, Letter, Ramsay to sister, 22 November 1899.

13. LAC, MG 29, Acession E-59, File 1 — Bennett, S.A. Correspondence 1899, Letter, Bennett to his Mother, 8 November 1899.

14. *Ibid.*, 11.

15. The British Army and Modern Conceptions of War," *Royal United Services Institute (RUSI)*, Vol. 60, No. 40, September 1911, 1181. See also Sanford Evans, *The Canadian Contingents* (Toronto: The Publishers' Syndicate Ltd., 1901), 36.

16. For a detailed account of the British military failure see Bernd Horn, "Lost Opportunity: The Boer War Experience and its Influence on British and Canadian Military Thought," in Bernd Horn, ed., *Forging a Nation: Perspectives on the Canadian Military Experience* (St. Catharines, ON:

Vanwell, 2002), 81–106. In brief, the British problems had many causes: A traditional, conservative, arguably anti-intellectual officer corps that placed greater emphasis on courage and dash than on tactical acumen and the study of modern war; the failure to understand the advances in technology and their impact on combat; overconfidence bred from a litany of wars against poorly armed tribesmen; an overall absence of initiative and innovative thought at all levels; and the failure to practice the most rudimentary fieldcraft skills such as using camouflage, seeking cover, and conducting detailed reconnaissance before an attack. See also: "Military Criticism," *The Army and Navy Gazette*, Vol. 61, No. 2105, 26 May 1900, 503 and "Some Lessons of the War," No. 2106, 532; "The War Summary," *Globe and Mail*, 27 December 1899, Vol. 55, No. 15,555, 1.

17. David Throup, ed., *British Documents on Foreign Affairs: Reports and Papers from the Foreign Office Confidential Print*. Part I, Series G, Africa, 1885–1914. Vol. 8 Anglo-Boer War I: From Eve of War to Capture of Johannesburg, 1899–1900 (Bethesda, MD: University of Publications of America, 1995), 235.

18. *Ibid.*, 239

19. Winston S. Churchill, *The Boer War — London to Ladysmith via Pretoria, Ian Hamilton's March* (London: Leo Cooper, 1989), 31–32.

20. Report A, Otter to Adjutant General, 26 January 1901, in Department of Militia and Defence, *Supplementary Report ... 1901*, 11.

21. En route, on arrival at Orange River the Battalion disembarked to allow the Gordon Highlanders to take over the train and proceed to the front. Lord Methuen, who was at the Modder River was in desperate need of reinforcements. The British command, not surprisingly, decided on regular British troops instead of colonials and therefore, chose the Highlanders over The RCR. This proved to be a fortuitous decision. The Highlanders were decimated at the debacle at Magersfontein on 11 December. In addition, while awaiting transport to Belmont, "C" Coy built a long loading platform that won the Canadians great praise from the British command.

22. LAC, RG 9, II-A3, Vol. 32, Microfilm T-10404, "South Africa War Records Reports, RCRI, January-June 1900" [henceforth RCR South Africa War Reports], 25 January 1900.

23. LAC, MG 30, Series E-231, File — typescript of letters and biographical sketch Ramsay fonds, Letter, Ramsay to sister, 22 November 1899. He further described, "Each man has one blanket and his great coat and just rolls himself in the former and lays on the ground with his feet towards the pole of the tent, and uses his haversack for a pillow."

24. Stanley McKeown Brown, *With the Royal Canadians* (Toronto: The Publishers' Syndicate Ltd., 1900), 104. Brown was a war correspondent.

25. LAC, MG 29, E-76, Jesse C. Biggs Fonds, RCR, Letter, Jesse Biggs to Aunt, 29 December 1899.

26. "RCR South Africa War Reports," 3 February 1900.

27. LAC, MG 29, Acession E-59, File 1 — Bennett, S.A. Correspondence 1899, Letter, Bennett to his Mother, 13 December 1899.

28. *Ibid.*, 30 December 1899.

29. LAC, MG 29, E-93, J.A. Perkins Fonds, RCR, Letter, J.A. Perkins to mother, 2 January 1900.

30. "Letters from the Regiment in South Africa," The RCR, *Connecting File*, January 1937, Vol. 16, No. 4, 6.

31. RCR Archives, Series 3 Boer War 1899–1900, Vol. 2, File 17, "An Echo of the South African War," Recollections of J.W. Jeffery.

32. Kopjes are large masses of igneous rock, flat-topped or sharp pointed, from 200 to 800 feet high. They provided great points of observation and fire. "I tell you what they have is hard country for our troops to fight in," wrote one participant, "These kopjes (rocky hills) are regular fortresses. You would wonder how our troops could get up them in a fight." Another soldier asserted, "Almost every one of them is a natural fortress." LAC, MG 29, E-101, Jos. Wm. Jeffery Fonds, RCR, Letter, J. William Jeffery to friends, 18 January 1900; and LAC, MG 29, E-93, J.A. Perkins Fonds, RCR, Letter, J.A. Perkins to mother, 26 January 1900.

33. Miller, 79–80.

34. "RCR South Africa War Reports," 6 February 1900.

35. "RCR South Africa War Reports," 11 February 1900.

36. 19th Brigade was composed of the 1st Battalion, Duke of Cornwall's Light Infantry; 2nd Battalion King's Own Shropshire Light Infantry; 1st Battalion Gordon Highlanders; and the 2nd Battalion RCR.

37. Lord Robert's army also included 5,000 native drivers and 25,000 animals.

38. "South African Letter from Our Own Correspondent," near Paardeberg Drift, 25 February 1900, The *Canadian Military Gazette*, Vol. 15, No. 7, 3 April 1900, 7.

39. LAC, John Kennedy Hill Fonds, Microfilm M-300, Lance-Corporal J. Kennedy Hill Diary, South Africa, 1899–1900 [henceforth Kennedy Hill Diary].

40. RCR Archives, Series 3 Boer War 1899–1900, Vol. 2, File 15, "Diary of Private F.H. Dunham, South African Campaign" [henceforth Dunham's Diary] Part III, Paardeberg. Also available from LAC, MG 29, Accession E-89, File 4, "Diaries of Pte F.H. Dunham South African Campaign, 1899–1900," Typescript of original diary.

41. Dunham's Diary.

42. Kennedy Hill Diary. See also LAC, MG 30, Series E 397, File Correspondence, Letter, J. Cooper Mason to Father, 21 February 1900; and *Ibid.*, Letter, Mason to Mother 27 February 1900.

43. See "RCR South Africa War Reports," 23 February 1900.

44. Dunham's Diary.

45. W. Hart-McHarg, *From Quebec to Pretoria with the Royal Canadian Regiment* (Toronto: William Briggs, 1902), 108.

46. LAC, MG 30, E-369, File no. 1, Diary of Pte W.J. Green, Diary of Captain W.J. Green, 19 February 1900.

47. "South African Letter," 7.

48. "RCR South Africa War Reports," 23 February 1900.

49. "RCR South Africa War Reports," 23 February 1900.

50. See LAC, RG 9, 11-A-3, Vol. 34, Microfilm T-10405, "RCR South Africa War Reports," 26 February 1900; "South African Diary, 2nd Bn (SS) Royal Canadian Regiment, Otter's Diary" [henceforth Otter's Diary], 19 February 1900; and Miller, 92–97. The actual time of the charge varies by different accounts anywhere from 1630 hours to 1730 hours. The official Bn war report gives both 1730 and 1715 hours (i.e., difference between the 23 and 26 February reports). Otter wrote in his diary, "The greatest possible steadiness was shown by the men."

51. Dunham Diary.

52. LAC, MG 30, E-372, file — Robert Gordon Stewart fonds, Letter, reproduced in a contemporary clipping, by Reverend O'Leary, RC Chaplain to The RCR, at Paardeberg.

53. Colonel Lawrence Buchan, "With the Infantry in South Africa," a lecture delivered at the Canadian Military Institute, 3 February 1902, 7.

54. LAC, MG 30, Series E 397, File Correspondence, Letter, J. Cooper Mason to Father, 21 February 1900; and *Ibid.*, Letter, Mason to Mother 27 February 1900. He later added, "It is not my place to criticize, but for any sane person to think a body of men could dash across 700 yards of open ground in face of a concealed enemy, is to me a mystery."

55. RCR Archives, Series 3 Boer War 1899–1900, Vol. 2, Charles Henry Tweddell Diary — E Coy 2 RCR Boer War.

56. "South African Letter," 7.

57. Dunham Diary.

58. Kennedy Hill Diary. See also "RCR South Africa War Reports," 23 February 1900. The official Battalion Report states the fire was "most deadly and impossible to advance against."

59. Letter, J. Cooper Mason to Father, 21 February 1900; and Dunham Diary.

60. See Kennedy Hill Diary and Miller, 98–101. Smith-Dorrien was not culpable — it was Lord Kitchener who had ordered the attack.

61. To avoid confusion the number is given in yards instead of metres to parallel the description given in the eyewitness accounts. However, for the purest, a yard equals 0.9144 metres . See Report A, Appendix A1, Otter to Adjutant General, 26 January 1901, in Department of Militia and Defence, *Supplementary Report … 1901*, 42–44 for Otter's account of the day's events.

62. Dunham Diary.

63. Letter, Thompson to his brother, quoted in Cameron Pulsifer, "Richard Rowland Thompson and his Queen's Scarf. An Historical Investigation," *Canadian Military History, Vol.* 6, No. 1, Spring 1997, 78.

64. LAC, MG 29, Acession E-59, File 2 — Bennett, S.A. Correspondence 1900, Letter, Bennett to his Mother, 23 February 1900. Another soldier wrote home, "Fighting is all right to read about in papers and books perhaps, but as for actually experiencing it and going through the life that leads to it, is a far different thing. As for myself, I have had quite enough of the fighting part of it and the Canadians of the first contingent seem unanimous in saying they want no more fighting." LAC, MG 29, E-101, Jos. Wm. Jeffery Fonds, RCR, Letter, J. William Jeffery to friends, 18 March 1900.

65. Report A, Otter to Adjutant General, 26 January 1901, in Department of Militia and Defence, *Supplementary Report … 1901*, 18.

66. RCR Archives, Series 3 Boer War 1899–1900, Vol. 1, File 56, "Wrote on a Rock," 27 March 1900, clipping from an unknown newspaper.

67. Dunham Diary.

68. See Otter's Diary, 26–28 February 1900; and Report A, Appendix A3, Otter to Adjutant General, 26 January 1901, in Department of Militia and Defence, *Supplementary Report … 1901*, 46–47 for Otter's account of the attack. See also "RCR South Africa War Reports," 2 March 1900.

69. Buchan, "With the Infantry," 9.

70. Dunham Diary, Letter sent from Paardeberg Drift, 3 March 1900.

71. RCR Archives, Series 3 Boer War 1899–1900, Vol. 2, File 16, Recollections of the Boer War by Gerald Carogan, June 1902.

ESTABLISHING A LEGACY

72. LAC, MG 29, E-93, J.A. Perkins Fonds, RCR, Letter, J.A. Perkins to mother, "Modder's Drift," no date.

73. LAC, MG 29, E-101, Jos. Wm. Jeffery Fonds, RCR, Letter, J. William Jeffery to friends, 18 March 1900.

74. Brown, 217. Buchan described the opening volley as, "when, of a sudden, something coming very near the popular conception of Hades opened up in front of us." Buchan, "With the Infantry," 9.

75. Report A, Appendix A3, Otter to Adjutant General, 26 January 1901, in Department of Militia and Defence, *Supplementary Report ... 1901*, 46.

76. *Ibid.* Gerald Carogan recalled, "Someone shouts retire ... hundreds of Boer jump up some 80 yards in front firing as fast as they can load — men are falling in heaps every where — broken spirited — broken hearted — all that is left of them — those that went into that charge with a smile on their face and a cheer on their lips watch them now as they stumble back recognizing every foot of the way a comrade dead or dying, who a few short moments ago was full of life — still the awful carnage goes on, and as I stumble blindly back the bullets falling like rain...." RCR Archives, Series 3 Boer War 1899–1900, Vol. 2, File 16, Recollections of the Boer War by Gerald Carogan, June 1902.

77. Dunham Diary.

78. "[T]he poor fellow just died as I grabbed him," wrote Thompson to his brother. See Letter, Thompson to his brother, quoted in Pulsifer, 78. The original scarf is held by the Canadian War Museum.

79. Report A, Appendix A3, Otter to Adjutant General, 26 January 1901, in Department of Militia and Defence, *Supplementary Report ... 1901*, 47.

80. John Marteinson, *We Stand on Guard* (Toronto: Ovale, 1992), 63; and Miller, 109. The performance of the Canadians, and all colonials in fact, in South Africa created at the time a re-examination of the age-old prejudice against colonial military competence. In many ways the pendulum now seemed to swing to the other extreme. The influential British *Army and Navy Gazette* commented on the effectiveness of "a few really skilled riflemen of good physique, like the colonials." In fact, it went so far as to say, "The rough-riders of our colonies are the only men who can meet the Boer on equal

terms and beat him." See Editor, "Some Lessons of the War," *The Army and Navy Gazette*, Vol. 61, No. 2106, 532; and "Army Notes," *The Army and Navy Gazette*, Vol. 61, No. 2088, 27 January 1900, 79. Winston Churchill "judged a militia army not very much less competent than a standing army." See Tuvia Ben-Moshe, *Churchill Strategy and History* (Boulder, CO: Lynne Rienner Publications, 1992), 10. Field Marshal Lord Wolseley believed that the colonials would have stood up against European regulars. "The colonial contingents," he believed, "would have fought anybody." But he quickly added, "I would not extend that same expression of opinion to the very large bodies of men we sent out from here [England]." The commissioners from the Elgin Commission of Enquiry, established to examine the conduct of the war, themselves described the colonies as "half soldiers by their upbringing." Quoted in Preston, 266–267 The Canadians themselves began to realize that they easily matched the courage and effectiveness of those that they had formerly so highly esteemed. Lieutenant Morrison observed, "And it must be said that Canada's soldiers compare favorably with the 'regulars.'" What they lacked in drill, they more than made up for in "physique" and "in spirit and dash and a certain air of self-reliant readiness to hold their own." See Morrison, 20. See also "South African Letter," *Canadian Military Gazette*, 20 February 1900, 7. Others echoed those same sentiments. "The Imperial soldier is not taught to think," criticized Stanley Brown, a journalist. "The Canadians were different," he added, "and therein lay the secret of their success, when they had to, on almost a moment's notice take the field and compete with some of the best regiments in the British army." Brown concluded, "that is where the soldier who could think and did think, and who could rely, to a small extent at least, on his own resources, was able to take his place along with the British man of the line, and not only equal but surpass in nearly every way the average Tommy." Brown, 136–137. Private Arthur Bennett wrote, "I don't want to hear you talk of the British Regulars any more, for they for the most part are of the most untidy crowd I have every seen.... The spirit of most of the Imperials seems to be not to fight, they would much rather not go into action at all. LAC, MG 29, Acession E-59, File 2 — Bennett, S.A. Correspondence 1900, Letter, Bennett to his Mother, 12 January 1900.

81. Brown, 138.

82. "Gen. Cronje's Surrender," *Globe and Mail*, 27 February 2000, 1; and Report A, Otter to Adjutant General, 26 January 1901, in Department of Militia and Defence, *Supplementary Report ... 1901*, 33–35. Private Bennett wrote, "The Canadians made such a name for themselves at Paardeberg that everyone in

Cape Town was anxious to get a Canadian Badge, and paid high prices for them." LAC, MG 29, Acession E-59, File 2 — Bennett, S.A. Correspondence 1900, Letter, Bennett to his Mother, 11 June February 1900.

83. Quoted in Robert Page, *The Boer War and Canadian Imperialism* (Ottawa: Canadian Historical Association, 1987), 14; and C.P. Stacey, "Canada and the South African War, Part IV," *The Canadian Army Journal*, Vol. 4, No. 5, October 1950, 10.

84. Report A, Otter to Adjutant General, 26 January 1901, in Department of Militia and Defence, *Supplementary Report ... 1901*, 34.

85. *Ibid.*, 18.

86. Hart-McHarg, 147.

87. LAC, MG 29, E-101, Jos. Wm. Jeffery Fonds, RCR, Letter, J. William Jeffery to friends, 18 March 1900.

88. LAC, MG 29, Accession E-59, File 2 — Bennett, S.A. Correspondence 1900, Letter, Bennett to his Mother, 16 March 1900.

89. Directorate of History and Heritage [henceforth DHH], File 77/559, "Diary of J.A. Perkins from January 31st 1900 Until Arriving in Canada in November," 24–26 February 1900 [henceforth Perkins Diary].

90. LAC, MG 29, E-76, Jesse C. Biggs Fonds, RCR, Letter, Jesse Biggs to Aunt, 16 March.

91. Letter, Bennett to his Mother, 16 March 1900.

92. LAC, MG 29, E-89, F.H. Dunham Fonds, RCR, Diaries of Pte. F.H. Dunham, South African Campaign, 1899–1900, 1 January 1900.

93. T.G. Marquis, *Canada's Sons on Kopje and Veldt: A Historical Account of the Canadian Contingents* (Toronto: The Canada's Sons Publishing Co., 1900), 218.

94. DHH, File 145.2R13 (D8), A.S. McCormick, M.D., "The 'Royal Canadians' in South Africa, 1899–1902," 4. McCormick wrote: "If we find water we fill or bottles by brushing away the slime from a frog pool or filling them from

a pool dirty and stirred up by animals." "The Contrast," *The Connecting File*, April 1948, 24.

95. See Reid, 69; Fetherstonhaugh, 121; "South-African Letter," *Canadian Military Gazette*, 3 April 1900, 7; Page, 14; and Miller, 119.

96. Quoted in Morton, *The Canadian*, 203.

97. Perkins Diary, 24 February 1900.

98. Newspaper clipping, no date, no publication. LAC, MG 29, E-93, File 7 — Clippings.

99. Morton, *The Canadian*, 203; and Miller, 84 and 119.

100. Reid, 70.

101. Private Dunham recorded in his diary, "Hundreds of men to my knowledge were lying in the worst stages of typhoid with only a blanket and a thin waterproof between their aching bodies and the hard ground, with no milk & hardly any medicine, without beds, stretchers, mattresses, without pillows, without linen of any kind, without a single nurse amongst them, with only a few ordinary privates to act as orderlies, rough & untrained to nursing." Dunham's Diary, Comments on the Campaign. See also Hart-McHarg, 156–158; Morton, *The Canadian*, 210–212; Fetherstonhaugh, 122; and Miller, 83 & 120–121. The outcry in England and Canada as a result of the reports eventually led to a Royal Commission to investigate the matter. Overall the problems encountered were attributed to the harsh environment and exigencies of the campaign.

102. *Debates*, 6 June 1900, 6790; Miller, 119; and "Considerations Leading Up to Decision to Provide a Contingent," 272. The issue was brought before Parliament by a MP as a result of an article in the *Military Gazette* that stated: "Evidence is forthcoming, however, which goes to prove that the question of the comfort and good health, and even the lives, of our troops in South Africa has been sacrificed to consideration which we can only say call for strict investigation."

103. See Otter's Diary, 25 April 1900; "RCR South Africa War Reports," 28 April 1900; and Report A, Appendix A4, Otter to Adjutant General, 26 January 1901, in Department of Militia and Defence, *Supplementary Report … 1901*, 48–49.

ESTABLISHING A LEGACY

104. Hart-McHarg, 172.

105. Report A, Otter to Adjutant General, 26 January 1901, in Department of Militia and Defence, *Supplementary Report ... 1901*, 36.

106. See Otter's Diary, 16 June — 1 August 1900.

107. Report A, Otter to Adjutant General, 26 January 1901, in Department of Militia and Defence, *Supplementary Report ... 1901*, 25.

108. Report A, Otter to Adjutant General, 26 January 1901, in Department of Militia and Defence, *Supplementary Report ... 1901*, 25, 27–30. See also LAC, RG 9, II-A-3, Vol. 32, "Reports — 2 S.S. Bn" for the time period in question.

109. Quoted in "Considerations Leading Up to Decision to Provide a Contingent," 275.

110. McCormick, 8.

111. Brown, 291. A veteran revealed, "you could feel your head swelling as the truth gradually dawned on you that the term 'colonial,' instead of being the designation of a people 'a little lower than the angels' was in future to be synonymous in the military Valhalla with that of Mars himself." Lieutenant E.W.B. Morrison, *With the Guns in South Africa* (Hamilton, ON: Spectator Printing Company, Ltd., 1901), 293.

112. LAC, MG 30, E-399, File MacDonell, A.H., Menus N.D. 1900–1909, *Daily News* correspondent.

113. Miller, 98.

114. See Bernd Horn and Ronald G. Haycock, "The Primacy of National Command and Control: Boer War Lessons Learned," in Bernd Horn, ed., *The Canadian Way of War: Serving the National Interest* (Toronto: Dundurn Press, 2006); and Horn, "Lost Opportunity," 81–106.

Chapter 3: Service and Suffering

1. "Royal Canadians" and the more contemporary "Royals" will be used interchangeably throughout the volume.

NOTES

2. See Fetherstonhaugh, 181–183. "A" and "B" Coys were called out to aid the civil power again on 12 July 1910 when a strike broke out at Springhill Mines in Nova Scotia.

3. See Colonel G.W.L. Nicholson, *The Official History of the Canadian Army in the First World War: Canadian Expeditionary Force 1914–1919* (Ottawa: Queen's Printer, 1962), 6–24.

4. See Jean-Pierre Gagnon, "Canadian Soldiers in Bermuda During World War One," *Histoire Sociale-Social History*, Vol. 23, No. 45, May 1990, 10.

5. See Canada, "Royal Canadian Regiment, Nominal Roll of All Ranks Serving in Bermuda, *Militia Orders*, 1915.

6. The Regiment consisted of 10 companies, "A" to "K" (with no "J" Coy). Another four provisional companies were established in response to the 11 August 1914 authorization from militia headquarters to expand.

7. LAC, RG 24, Vol. 6407, File AHQ-44-2-20, "Abridged Annual Report upon The Royal Canadian Regiment inspected at Halifax, N.S. 23rd August 1915."

8. LAC, Canadian Broadcasting Corporation, Radio: Flanders Fields, interview 402, Interview, W.J. Howe, RCR by CBC, January 1963.

9. The 7th Canadian Infantry Brigade was designated the senior brigade of the soon to be formed 3rd Canadian Infantry Division of the Canadian Corps.

10. LAC, A. Green Fonds, MG 30, E440, File 12, WWI Correspondence, 1916–1917, Letter, Anson to Mother, France, 2 November 1916.

11. Quoted in Fetherstonhaugh, 221.

12. "Ex Serjeant [sic] Freeland's Diary," The RCR, *Connecting File*, January 1938, Vol. 17, No. 1, 14.

13. RCR Museum Archives, War Diary. Royal Canadian Regiment — 3rd Canadian Division [henceforth RCR War Diary] from 1st May to 31st May, 1916. Vol. 7, War Diary entry, 30 May 1916. It added, "wounded cannot be taken out of front line or Reserve line in the daytime."

14. RCR Museum Archives, RCR War Diary, 2 June 1916. The quiet interlude was to ensure the German artillery did not interfere with their wire cutting parties who were preparing gaps in the Canadian wire that their troops would use to attack the following day.

15. Interview, Mr. Dean, RCR by CBC, 31 October 1963. LAC, Canadian Broadcasting Corporation, Radio: Flanders Fields, interview 403.

16. The 4th Mounted Rifles suffered 89 percent casualties. Of 702 all ranks, only 76 came through unscathed. A German participant wrote: "the whole enemy position was a cloud of dust and dirt, into which timber, tree trunks, weapons and equipment were continually hurled up, and occasionally human bodies." Nicholson, 148–149.

17. See Nicholson, 148; and Fetherstonhaugh, 228.

18. RCR Museum Archives, RCR War Diary, War Diary Entry, 2 June 1916. Nicholson writes that the attack commenced shortly after 1300 hours.

19. *Ibid.*

20. *Ibid.*

21. During this attack the Germans blew four mines that had been laid previously but had not been detonated. The delay was fortuitous because The RCR had been standing over the mines the day before. The explosion created a large gap that threatened the Canadian Corps. The Germans easily captured Hooge but were halted from further penetration by the flanking 60th British Brigade. In addition, as the Germans advanced up Menin Road, it was the Lewis guns of The RCR, which had not been able to withdraw from the position with the remainder of The Regiment, as well as The Regiment's section of the 7th Brigade Machine Gun Company, who were key in stopping any further penetration.

22. The Somme battles of 1916 caused great controversy because of their cost in human lives and the apparent callousness and lack of tactical acumen of the generals. Commander-in-Chief, Field Marshal Sir Douglas Haig insisted the Allies had been successful and claimed the battles were essential to first, relieve the pressure off the French at Verdun; second, prevent the transfer of German troops to other fronts; and third, attrite the German Army, which, it was argued, could not mobilize as many resources as the Allies.

The Somme battles cost a total of about 1,200,000 men (each side losing approximately 600,000).

23. RCR Museum Archives, RCR War Diary, 1st September to 30th September, 1916, Vol. 11, Appendix 6A, Lieutenant-Colonel C.H. Hill, "The Royal Canadian Regiment. Narrative of Events. 15th, 16th & 17th September 1916."

24. LAC, RG 9, Historical Records, RCR, III-D-1, Vol. 4706, Quoted in Letter and attached file, Adjutant-General, Canadians to Officer I/C Canadian War Records, "The History of the Royal Canadian Regiment" [henceforth "Canadian War Records — Regimental History"], 19 March 1918.

25. *Ibid.* As of 10 September 1916, an order from corps HQ directed that "In all operations not more than 20 officers per battalion, including headquarters, are to accompany the battalions on the attack. Remainder to include due proportion of all ranks. 15% of senior NCOs also to remain behind." This "left out of battle" (LoB) policy was to ensure there was a suitable cadre of survivors to rebuild a unit after an attack.

26. RCR Museum Archives, RCR War Diary, From 1st October to 31st October 1916, Appendix 3 and 4, "Narrative of Operations of the Royal Canadian Regiment, 7th, 8th, and 9th October 1916," 3.

27. *Ibid.*, 3.

28. RCR Archives, Series 5, First World War, 1914–1918, Vol. 3, File 42, "Extract from Daily Orders, 7th Canadian Inf Bgde."

29. "Canadian War Records — Regimental History," 4–5.

30. RCR Archives, Series 5, First World War, 1914–1918, Vol. 3, File 49, "Honours and Awards, CEF, The Royal Canadian Regiment."

31. RCR Archives, Series 5, First World War, 1914–1918, Vol. 3, File 42, "Extract from Daily Orders, 7th Canadian Inf Bgde."

32. Fetherstonhaugh, 259.

33. LAC, A. Green Fonds, MG 30, E440, File 12, WWI Correspondence, 1916–1917, Letter, Anson to Mother, France, 7 November 1916.

34. LAC, Canadian Broadcasting Corporation, Radio: Flanders Fields, interview 402, Interview, W.J. Howe, RCR by CBC, January 1963.

35. Nicholson, 249.

36. The resulting density was one heavy gun for every 18 metres and one field gun for every nine metres. See Colonel C.P. Stacey, *Introduction to the Study of Military History*, 6th edition (Ottawa: Directorate of History, n.d.), 92.

37. Granatstein, 113.

38. Nicholson, 251.

39. RCR Museum Archives, RCR War Diary, 1st April to 30th April, 1917, Appendix 2, "Summary of Operations of The Royal Canadian Regiment," 13 April 1917.

40. RCR Archives, Series 5, First World War, 1914–1918, Vol. 3, File 19, Robert England, "Recollections of a Nonagenarian of Service in The Royal Canadian Regiment, 1916–1919."

41. *Ibid.*

42. RCR Archives, Series 5, First World War, 1914–1918, Vol. 3, File 43, "Narrative of Operations Leading Up To, and the Part Actually Played by the 7th Canadian Infantry Brigade in the Attack and Capture of Vimy Ridge, 9 April 1917."

43. RCR Archives, Series 5, First World War, 1914–1918, Vol. 3, File 49, "Honours and Awards, CEF, The Royal Canadian Regiment."

44. RCR Archives, Series 5, First World War, 1914–1918, Vol. 3, File 43, "Narrative of Operations Leading Up to, and the Part Actually Played by the 7th Canadian Infantry Brigade in the Attack and Capture of Vimy Ridge, 9 April 1917."

45. See Stacey, *Introduction to the Study of Military History*, 96; and Granatstein, *Canada's Army*, 113.

46. Fetherstonhaugh, 282–283.

47. See RCR Museum Archives, RCR War Diary, 1st June to 30th June, 1917, Appendix 4, "Summary of Operations of The Royal Canadian Regiment."

48. For his efforts on the raid, Lieutenant Gregg was awarded the Military Cross.

49. Nicholson reported that 7th Brigade claimed to have killed 560 Germans and reported only 335 casualties of their own — 38 being fatal. See Nicholson, 281.

50. See Nicholson, 281; and Fetherstonhaugh, 288 and 291.

51. LAC, Canadian Broadcasting Corporation, Radio: Flanders Fields, interview 405–406, Interview, D.D. Spencer, RCR by CBC, 7 September 1963.

52. Currie was appointed commander of the Canadian Corps on 6 June 1917.

53. See RCR Museum Archives, RCR War Diary, 1st October to 31th October 1917, Appendix 11, "Summary of Operations of The Royal Canadian Regiment," 29 October — 4 November 1917.

54. The casualty toll for the Canadian Corps was 15,654. See Granatstein, *Canada's Army*, 123–124; and Fetherstonhaugh, 306.

55. LAC, Canadian Broadcasting Corporation, Radio: Flanders Fields, interview 402, Interview, W.J. Howe, RCR by CBC, January 1963.

56. See RCR Museum Archives, RCR War Diary, 1st August to 31th August 1918, Appendix 3, "Narrative of Operation — 8 August 1918."

57. "7th Cdn. Inf. Bde. Report on Operations undertaken South-East of Amiens 8–16 August 1918, Appendix 8 to Brigade War Diary," quoted in Nicholson, 400. See also James McWilliams and R. James Steel, *Amiens — Dawn of Victory* (Toronto: Dundurn Press, 2001), 139.

58. See RCR Museum Archives, RCR War Diary, 1st August to 31th August 1918, Appendix 8, "Narrative of Operation — 14/15 August 1918."

59. The VC citation for Gregg run in *The London Gazette*, 6 January 1919 read: "For most conspicuous bravery and initiative during operations near Cambrai, 27th September to 1st October 1918. On 28th September, when the advance of the brigade was held up by fire from both flanks and by

thick uncut wire, he crawled forward alone and explored the wire until he found a small gap, through which he subsequently led his men, and forced an entry into the enemy trench. The enemy counter-attacked in force, and, through lack of bombs, the situation became critical. Although wounded, Lt. Gregg returned alone under terrific fire and collected a further supply. Then rejoining his party, which by this time was much reduced in numbers, and, in spite of a second wound, he reorganized his men and led them with the greatest determination against the enemy trenches, which he finally cleared. He personally killed or wounded 11 of the enemy and took 25 prisoners, in addition to 12 machine guns captured in this trench. Remaining with his company in spite of wounds, he again on the 30th September led his men in attack until severely wounded. The outstanding valour of this officer saved many casualties and enabled the advance to continue." Milton Gregg eventually achieved the rank of brigadier. From 1947–1957, he held successively the ministerial portfolios of Fisheries, Veterans Affairs, and Labour.

60. Fetherstonhaugh, 362.

61. A controversy later erupted over which unit actually entered the city first as the RHC contested that they in fact were the first to enter and sign the book — Lieutenant Biggar of the RHC stating that he signed further down the page to allow space for appropriate text to be added later. However, an inquiry in 1923, which actually solicited evidence from the mayor himself, determined that Lieutenant King and The RCR were in fact the first to enter the heart of the city and sign the book. See LAC, RG 24, C-b-e, Vol. 1822, GAQ-5-34, "First to Enter Mons"/"RCR into Mons."

62. Canada, *Canada in the First World War and the Road to Vimy Ridge* (Ottawa: Veterans Affairs, 1992), 16; and LAC, RG 150, Vol. 504, "Casualties Recapitulation, France and Belgium."

Chapter 4: "Fighting Men from Canada"

1. The PPCLI was charged with infantry duties in Western Canada and the R22R was tasked with similar responsibilities in the city and fortress of Quebec.

2. See Major Burns, "1932 Prize Essay — Protection of the Rearward Services and Headquarters in Modern War," *Canadian Defence Quarterly* (*CDQ*), Vol. 10, No. 3, April 1933, 296–305; and Major E.L.M. Burns, "A

Step Towards Modernization," *CDQ*, Vol. 12, No.3, April 1935, 298. Burns ominously added, "A 2 1/2 mile an hour soldier in a 60 mile an hour age is an anachronism. And nothing can be so costly as a military anachronism." Burns finished his career as a lieutenant-general.

3. The school also had two obsolete Vickers Mark VI tanks. It received 14 more in August 1939.

4. G.R. Stevens, *The Royal Canadian Regiment: Volume Two 1933–1966* (London, ON: London Printing Co., 1967), 10.

5. LAC, RG 24, Series C-1, File 3276, Microfilm C-5061, Canada. *Report of the Annual Inspection for the Fiscal Year 1932–33* (Ottawa: Department of National Defence, 1932), 15.

6. LAC, RG 24, Series C-1, File 3276, Microfilm C-5061, Canada. *Report of the Annual Inspection for the Fiscal Year 1934–35* (Ottawa: Department of National Defence, 1934), 15.

7. LAC, RG 24, Series C-1, File 3276, Microfilm C-5061, Canada. *Report of the Annual Inspection for the Fiscal Year 1938–38 [sic]* (Ottawa: Department of National Defence, 1938), 15.

8. Brigadier Moogk quoted in Stevens, 11.

9. RCR Museum Archives, War Diary entry, Highlights and Appendices, Serial 4, 24–31 August 1939. *Ibid.*, War Diary RCR, Sep-Dec 1939, Highlights and Appendices. The entry for 1 September read, "Orders were received by telephone at about 1430 hours to mobilize for C.E.F." RCR Museum Archives, War Diary RCR, Vol. 1, 1 September 39 to 31 December 39, War Diary entry, 1 September 1939.

10. Interview with Lieutenant-Colonel Tom Burnett, 2 February 2005.

11. 1 CIB consisted of The RCR, the Hasting and Prince Edward Regiment and the 48th Highlanders.

12. LAC, MG 30, Series E563, Vol. 2, File 2-8, Daniel Charles Spry Fonds, Letter, Spry to Bonzo, 12 December 1939.

13. Interview, Tom H. Burnett, 2 February 2004.

14. *Ibid.*

15. Strome Galloway, *55 Axis* (Montreal: Provincial Publishing Co., 1946), 30.

16. See Stevens, 22.

17. RCR Museum Archives, RCR War Diary, Volume 2, 1 January 40 to 30 June 40, War Diary entry, 24 May 1940.

18. The German victory was somewhat deceptive. Its success owed as much to their innovative doctrine and tactics as it did to the Allied unpreparedness. Quite simply, the modern German mechanized spearhead was largely a facade. Nearly 80 percent of the German Army for both the French and Russian campaigns remained a foot and horse-drawn army. See Williamson Murray and Allan R. Millett, eds., *Military Innovation in the Interwar Period* (New York: Cambridge University Press, 1996); John A. English, *On Infantry* (Westport, CT: Praeger, 1984), 47–85; Len Deighton, *Blood, Tears, and Folly* (London: Pimlico, 1995), 160–204; and Len Deighton, *Blitzkrieg* (Edison, NJ: Castle Books, 2000).

19. Fifty-three thousand French troops were evacuated 3–4 June, after the withdrawal of the British forces was complete on 2 June. The British Admiralty estimated that approximately 338,226 men were evacuated between 26 May and 3 June. The British left behind 2,000 guns, 60,000 trucks, 76,000 tons of ammunition, and 600,000 tons of fuel and supplies. Cesare Salmaggi and Alfredo Pallavisini, *2194 Days of War* (New York: Gallery Books, 1988), 4 June 1940; and I.C.R. Dear, ed., *The Oxford Companion to World War II* (Oxford: Oxford University Press, 1995), 312–313. Another account gives the losses as 475 tanks, 38,000 vehicles, 12,000 motorcycles, 8,000 telephones, 1,855 wireless sets, 7,000 tonnes of ammunition, 90,000 rifles, 1,000 heavy guns, 2,000 tractors, 8,000 Bren guns, and 400 anti-tank guns. On 6 June the War Cabinet was informed that there were fewer than 600,000 rifles and only 12,000 Bren guns in the whole of the United Kingdom. John Parker, *Commandos: The Inside Story of Britain's Most Elite Fighting Force* (London: Headline Book Publishing, 2000), 15. Yet another source gives the losses as: stores and equipment for 500,000 men, about 100 tanks, 2,000 other vehicles, 600 guns, and large stocks of ammunition. A.J. Barker, *Dunkirk: The Great Escape* (London: J.M. Dent & Sons Ltd., 1977), 224. A major problem with determining numbers is the actual categorization of equipments.

20. John Swettenham, *McNaughton, Volume 2* (Toronto: The Ryerson Press Toronto, 1969), 117–119. See also C.P. Stacey, *Six Years of War: The Army in Canada, Britain and the Pacific, Volume 1* (Ottawa: Queen's Printer, 1966), 287–295. One junior NCO in England at the time, recalled the period as one of constant alarms and drills. He stated, "you were never sure if it was an exercise or the real thing." He concluded, "they never failed to scare the hell out of us!" Interview with R.B. Firlotte, 20 November 1998.

21. Galloway, *55 Axis*, 40.

22. *Ibid.*, 40.

23. RCR Museum Archives, RCR War Diary, Vol. 4, 1 May 41 to 30 May 41, War Diary entry, 30 May 1941. The following month he reiterated, "Morale is quite good in spite of the continued inaction of a definite fighting nature." War Diary entry, 30 June 1941.

24. DHH, File 171.009 (D187), Special War Course — Battle Drill Training, 24 August 1942–17 March 1943, Memorandum (explaining the Battle Drill), Colonel R.G. Whitelaw, office of the chief of the general staff to the general officers in command of the Atlantic and Pacific commands and the district officers commanding, Ottawa, 18 May 1942.

25. Of the 4,963 Canadians who participated, 907 were killed and 1,946 became prisoners. Almost half of the force never even made it to shore. See Brian Villa, *Unauthorized Action: Mountbatten and the Dieppe Raid* (Toronto: University of Oxford Press, 1989).

26. RCR Museum Archives, RCR War Diary, Vol. 4, 1 June 43 to 30 June 43, War Diary entry, 29 June 1943. RCR War Diary.

27. *Ibid.* Galloway wrote of the change brought forth by vigourous PT and the construction of "a heart-breaking but body-building assault course," on which were taught "all angles of the new 'battle drill' which included the firing of small arms, mortars, and the throwing of grenades by the battalion instructors as the troops "ran the gauntlet." Galloway, *55 Axis*, 55.

28. RCR Museum Archives, War Diary RCR Depot, 1 August 1943 — 31 August 1943, Letter, Crowe to Colonel W. Neilson, At Sea, 1943.

29. RCR Museum Archives, War Diary RCR Depot, 1 August 43 — 31 August

43, "The Royal Canadian Regiment (Overseas) Bulletin, Somewhere at sea, July 8 1942."

30. RCR Museum Archives, RCR War Diary, Vol. 9, 1 July 43 to 31 December 43, War Diary entry, 1 July 1943.

31. *Ibid.*

32. Galloway, *55 Axis*, 70. The War Diary supports this statement. It reveals, "Training continued to-day, now concentrated almost solely on putting people into the picture, so that not a bren-gunner, not a rifleman in the Bn will have the slightest doubt as to what to expect or what to do." RCR Museum Archives, RCR War Diary, 1 July 43 to 31 July 43, War Diary entry, 7 July 1943.

33. D = model year; U = amphibian; K = all-wheel drive; W = dual rear axles. The vehicle was developed from vehicles used for rescue purposes in the Florida swamps.

34. Major R.G. Liddell, "The Assault on the Beaches of Pachino, Sicily," *The Connecting File*, April 1946, 24-4.

35. There are some minor variances in times, actions, narratives, and interpretations between the myriad of literature that covers the early hours of The Regiment's part in the invasion of Sicily. This account uses the Regimental War Diary as the basis of timings and actions.

36. Liddell, "The Assault," 24-5.

37. RCR Museum Archives, Letter, Tommy Powers to Colonel Snow, Sicily 8 August 1943.

38. George Burrows, interview with author, 26 July 2005.

39. RCR Museum Archives, RCR War Diary, Vol. 9, 1 July 43 to 31 December 43, War Diary entry, 10 July 1943.

40. RCR Museum Archives, Letter, Tommy Powers to Colonel Snow, Sicily 8 August 1943.

41. George Burrows, interview with author, 26 July 2005. He added that the

troops started filling their canteens with wine since they knew that was pure but were never sure if wells had been poisoned or not.

42. Interview, Ian Hodson by Edward Park, 19 November 2005.

43. Galloway, *55 Axis*, 73.

44. RCR Museum Archives, Letter, Liddell to Bonner, 16 December 1943.

45. RCR Museum Archives, Letter, Tommy Powers to Colonel Snow, Sicily 8 August 1943.

46. George Burrows, interview with author, 26 July 2005.

47. RCR Museum Archives, RCR War Diary, Vol. 9, 1 July 43 to 31 December 43, War Diary entry, 12 July 1943.

48. RCR Museum Archives, RCR War Diary, Vol. 9, 1 July 43 to 31 December 43, War Diary entry, 14 July 1943. The war diary assessment is borne out by other memoirs and accounts. It seems "Monty" was popular with the troops and held their confidence.

49. RCR Museum Archives, RCR War Diary, Vol. 9, 1 July 43 to 31 December 43, War Diary entry, 13 July 1943.

50. RCR Museum Archives, RCR War Diary, Vol. 9, 1 July 43 to 31 December 43, "Summary of Events, 18 July 1943."

51. Captain R.A. Couche, "The Charge of the Royal Canadian Regiment at Valguarnera," *The Connecting File*, July 1946, 36–1.

52. RCR Museum Archives, RCR War Diary, Vol. 9, 1 July 43 to 31 December 43, War Diary entry, 18 July 1943.

53. *Ibid.*

54. RCR Museum Archives, RCR War Diary, Vol. 9, 1 July 43 to 31 December 43, War Diary entry, 20 July 1943.

55. RCR Museum Archives, RCR War Diary, Vol. 9, 1 July 43 to 31 December 43, War Diary entry, 21 July 1943.

ESTABLISHING A LEGACY

56. Interview, Ian Hodson by Edward Park, 19 November 2005.

57. Major C.H. Lithgow, "The Battle of Nissoria, 24 July 1943," *The Connecting File*, 17.

58. RCR Museum Archives, RCR War Diary, Vol. 9, 1 July 1943 to 31 December 1943, War Diary entry, 24 July 1943.

59. Crowe, Cummings, and Turner were later found dead. Burton was missing and was presumed wounded and captured.

60. RCR Museum Archives, RCR War Diary, Vol. 9, 1 July 1943 to 31 December 1943, War Diary entry, 21 July 1943.

61. RCR Museum Archives, Letter, Tommy Powers to Colonel Snow, Sicily 8 August 1943.

62. One platoon from "A" Coy actually infiltrated into Regalbuto, which was still held by at least 400 Germans. Lieutenant M.C.D. Bowman gathered much useful information and he was awarded the Military Cross for his daring. However, the action cost 13 men missing, presumed captured.

63. See RCR Museum Archives, RCR War Diary, Vol. 9, 1 July 1943 to 31 December 1943, War Diary entry, 2 August 1943; and Major A.S.A. Galloway, "A Brief History of The Royal Canadian Regiment from the Outbreak of World War II to the Cessation of Hostilities," *Connecting File*, January 1946, 3–4.

64. RCR Museum Archives, Letter, Liddell to Bonner, 16 December 1943.

65. George Burrows, interview with author, 26 July 2005.

Chapter 5: No Soft Underbelly

1. The Germans suffered 11,600 casualties in Sicily. Conversely, the Allies, who engaged approximately 12 divisions, suffered 19,000 casualties, the Canadians losing 2,310 consisting of 562 killed, 1,664 wounded, and 84 prisoners of war. J.L. Granatstein, *Canada's Army* (Toronto: U of T Press, 2002), 227. The RCR casualties were approximately 102 in total (32 killed, 70 wounded or missing). Strome Galloway, *Bravely into Battle* (Toronto: Stoddart, 1988), 148.

2. RCR Museum Archives, RCR War Diary, Vol. 9, 1 July 1943 to 31 December 1943, War Diary entry, 26 August 1943.

3. *Ibid.*

4. RCR Museum Archives, RCR War Diary, Vol. 9, 1 July 1943 to 31 December 1943, War Diary entry, 3 September 1943.

5. Galloway, *Bravely into Battle*, 147.

6. Strome Galloway, *Some Died at Ortona: The Royal Canadian Regiment in Action in Italy 1943, a Diary by Strome Galloway* (London: RCR Association, 1983), 120.

7. RCR Museum Archives, RCR War Diary, Vol. 9, 1 July 1943 to 31 December 1943, War Diary entry, 8 September 1943.

8. The German reaction was predictably swift. Because the resident 14th Panzer Corps was in the process of taking over Italian defensive positions the initial response was ad hoc and piecemeal. However, the Germans fought a skilful battle and were able to contain the Allies in a shallow beachhead. By 12 September the Germans were able to build up their forces faster than the Allies and threatened the entire landing. Drastic measures including the addition of thousands of reinforcements, two additional battleships and air support from the entire Mediterranean strategic air force turned the tide. By 16 September the Germans began to withdraw to Naples.

9. Galloway, *Some Died at Ortona*, 128. He was referring to three shots he fired into the ground to scare away peasants who were crowding around his company lines near Catanzaro.

10. RCR Museum Archives, RCR War Diary, Vol. 9, 1 July 1943 to 31 December 1943, War Diary entry, 1 October 1943.

11. *Ibid.*

12. *Ibid.* See Strome Galloway, "The Road to Campobasso," *The Connecting File*, January 1946, 30–35, for his detailed account of the action. He was OC "B" Coy at the time.

13. RCR Museum Archives, War Diary, RCR Depot, 1 October to 31 October 1943, Annex 1, William Stewart, "RCR's Led Drive into Italian Hills," unidentified newspaper clipping.

14. At the time Private Douglas was seriously wounded and could not be evacuated from Motta. As a result, he and Corporal Hinton, who himself was slightly wounded yet volunteered to stay with Douglas, remained in the town during the bombardment. Both survived.

15. George Burrows, interview with author, 26 July 2005.

16. DHH, File 145.2R13.011 (D2), "Account by Lt. Col D.C. Spry, Officer Commanding Royal Canadian Regiment," given to Capt. Hughes at Duronia on 27 Nov 1943.

17. Stewart, "RCR's Led Drive into Italian Hills."

18. RCR Museum Archives, RCR War Diary, Vol. 9, 1 July 1943 to 31 December 1943, War Diary entry, 2 October 1943.

19. William Stewart, "Londoners Took Part in Difficult Advance," clipping, unknown newspaper, 10 October 1943.

20. DHH, File 145.2R13.011 (D2), "Account by Lt. Col D.C. Spry, Officer Commanding Royal Canadian Regiment," given to Captain Hughes at Duronia on 27 Nov 1943.

21. *Ibid.*, 2–3 October 1943.

22. DHH, File 145.2R13.011 (D2), "Account by Lt. Col D.C. Spry, Officer Commanding Royal Canadian Regiment," given to Captain Hughes at Duronia on 27 November 1943.

23. *Ibid.*, 4 October 1943.

24. *Ibid*, 27 November 1943.

25. RCR Museum Archives, Series 7, World War II, 1939–1945, Vol. 7, File 25, J.P. Gore, "RCR Fought 26 Battles in Italy and Holland, Retreated but Once," *The Free Press*, 2 October 1945.

26. Quoted in Daniel G. Dancocks, *The D-Day Dodgers* (Toronto: McClelland & Stewart, 1991), 137.

27. G.K. Wright, "The Road to Campobasso — and Beyond," October 11 — November 2, 1943, *The Connecting File*, April 1947, 24.

28. *Ibid.*, 25.

29. Despite the bloodless capture of the town, the commander of the 26th Panzer Grenadier Division advised his corps commander that he had abandoned Campobasso "after severe fighting."

30. Wright, 26.

31. RCR Museum Archives, Letter, R.G. Liddell to Major H.V. Bonner, 16 December 1943.

32. Wright, 26.

33. RCR Museum Archives, RCR War Diary, Vol. 9, 1 July 1943 to 31 December 1943, War Diary entry, 28 October 1943.

34. RCR Museum Archives, Series 7, World War II, 1939–1945, Vol. 10, File 7, "Canadians in Italy Fight Mud, Huns Too," clipping, unknown newspaper, 11 October 1943.

35. The "Winter Line" refers to the German network of defences that included the Bernhard Line stretching across central Italy from the east coast to the central Apennines, where it linked up with the Gustav Line, which extended to the Tyrrhenian Sea.

36. Reproduced in Galloway, *Some Died at Ortona*, 165.

37. *Ibid.*, 169. S-Mines was the English expression for *Schuminen* or "shoe" anti-personal mine, which was a little wooden box that when stepped on exploded showering the unlucky individual with metal pellets.

38. Major-General Guy G. Simonds was transferred to take command of the 5th Canadian Armoured Division.

39. RCR Museum Archives, RCR War Diary, Vol. 9, 1 July 1943 to 31 December

1943, War Diary entry, 8 December 1943.

40. Quoted in Mark Zuehlke, *Ortona: Canada's Epic Second World War Battle* (Toronto: Stoddart, 1999), 123; and; Dancocks, 159. Comfort also wrote: "Everywhere destruction and disintegrations: shattered buildings, mutilated trees, a spectral landscape of heaped-up fleshless bones, jostled by concussion and blast in a hideous monotonous danse macabre."

41. RCR Museum Archives, War Diary, RCR Depot, 1 January 1944 to 31 January 1944, Letter, Major W.W. Mathers to H.V. Bonner, 16 December 1943.

42. Galloway's description as he watched "A" Coy advance. Galloway, *55 Axis*, 108.

43. Galloway, *Some Died at Ortona*, 176.

44. See RCR Museum Archives, RCR War Diary, Vol. 9, 1 July 1943 to 31 December 1943, "B" Coy Narrative, 8 December 1943, to IO.

45. RCR Museum Archives, RCR War Diary, Vol. 9, 1 July 1943 to 31 December 1943, War Diary entry, 9 December 1943.

46. DHH, File 145.2R13.011 (D3), "Account by Lt. Col D.C. Spry, R.C.R.," 4 January 44.

47. Quoted in Zuehlke, 133.

48. RCR Museum Archives, RCR War Diary, Vol. 9, 1 July 1943 to 31 December 1943, War Diary entry, 12 December 1943.

49. RCR Museum Archives, RCR War Diary, Vol. 9, 1 July 1943 to 31 December 1943, War Diary entry, 14 December 1943.

50. Zuehlke, 226.

51. Divisional artillery commander, Brigadier Bruce Matthews, was concerned about the second phase of the operation because of the innumerable challenges — no pre-registration, inaccurate maps, rough terrain, as well as unsecured and undefined start lines. It was also later discovered that a 500-metre error existed on three of the map sheets, which had British grids superimposed on them. See Dancocks, 173.

52. RCR Museum Archives, RCR War Diary, Vol. 9, 1 July 1943 to 31 December 1943, War Diary entry, 18 December 1943.

53. RCR Museum Archives, Series 7, World War II, 1939–1945, Vol. 7, File 25, J.P. Gore, "RCR Fought 26 Battles in Italy and Holland, Retreated but Once," *The Free Press*, 2 October 1945.

54. Galloway, *55 Axis*, 111.

55. Major W.W. Mathers, "Arielli Front — Italy," *The Connecting File*, January 1949, 33.

56. RCR Museum Archives, RCR War Diary, Vol. 9, 1 July 1943 to 31 December 1943, War Diary entry, 18 December 1943.

57. *Ibid.*

58. Mathers, "Arielli Front," 33.

59. No company was greater than 65 men. "C" and "D" Coys, as well as 4 Platoon were combined to form one composite "C" Coy. "D" Coy would be reformed later once reinforcements arrived.

60. RCR Museum Archives, RCR War Diary, Vol. 9, 1 July 1943 to 31 December 1943, War Diary entry, 19 December 1943.

61. *Ibid.*, 20 December 1943.

62. This toast is shared every year at the Regimental Birthday mess dinner in the traditional fashion.

63. RCR Museum Archives, Series 7, World War II, 1939–1945, Vol. 10, File 7, Douglas Amaron, "Strange Stories Told of Battle for Ortona," clipping, unknown newspaper, 10 January 1944.

64. Farley Mowat, *The Regiment* (Toronto: McClelland & Stewart, 1981), 157.

65. Galloway, *55 Axis*, 118.

66. The cost of the eight-kilometre advance from the Moro River to the northern outskirts of Ortona to 1 Canadian Division and the 1st Armoured

Brigade was 2,339 men.

67. RCR Museum Archives, Series 7, World War II, 1939–1945, Vol. 7, File 25, J.P.Gore, "RCR Fought 26 Battles in Italy and Holland, Retreated but Once," *The Free Press*, 2 October 1945.

Chapter 6: The Final Stretch

1. Strome Galloway, *55 Axis* (Montreal: Provincial Publishing Co., 1946), 123.

2. Quoted in Daniel G. Dancocks, *The D-Day Dodgers* (Toronto: McClelland & Stewart, 1991), 214.

3. Strome Galloway, *Bravely into Battle* (Toronto: Stoddart, 1988), 174. Crerar arrived in the Mediterranean theatre as the commander of the newly created 1st Canadian Corps in October 1943. The change in tone was felt immediately. Major-General Chris Vokes, commander of 1st Canadian Division lamented, "life became a sort of administrative hell on earth." Quoted in Dancocks, 204. All soldiers in the corps grumbled as the easygoing manner and glamour of the Eighth Army gave way to the petty spit and polish of Crerar's new reign.

4. Peter Stursberg, Reporter CBC, Italian Front, 22 March 1944. LAC, Audio Reel C-10106, 1967–0032 CBC, audio track 72:50–76:50.

5. RCR Museum Archives, RCR War Diary, Vol. 10, 1 January to 30 June 44, War Diary entry, 10 March 1944.

6. *Ibid.*

7. Galloway, *Bravely into Battle*, 175.

8. Galloway, *55 Axis*, 123.

9. RCR Museum Archives, Series 7, World War II, 1939–1945, Vol. 10, File 7, Louis V. Hunter, "Canadian Patrols Out Nightly in Italy," *Free Press*, 4 November 1943.

10. RCR Museum Archives, RCR War Diary, Vol. 10, 1 January to 30 June 1944, War Diary entry, 15 January 1944. An entry on 1 March 1944 showed the

continuing effort. "As soon as dusk fell," it recorded, "our patrols became active." *Ibid.*, 1 March 1944. The same was again reported nine days later: "As soon as darkness fell our patrols became active." *Ibid.*, 10 and 12 March 1944.

11. Strome Galloway, *Sicily to the Siegfried Line: Being Some Random Memories and a Diary of 1944–45* (Kitchener, ON: Arnold Press, nd), 12.

12. Quoted in Dancocks, 215. He assessed it as "stupidity."

13. Galloway, *Bravely into Battle*, 177.

14. Major W.W. Mathers, "Arielli Front — Italy," *The Connecting File*, January 1948, 34.

15. These attacks were designed as holding actions to keep the Germans from transferring forces from the Adriatic to the Tyrrhenian Sea coast where the Allies attempted a landing at Anzio on 22 January 1944, to break the stalemate on the western flank of the Italian campaign.

16. Galloway, *55 Axis*, 129.

17. *Ibid.*, 129.

18. RCR Museum Archives, RCR War Diary, Vol. 10A, 1 January to 30 June 44, No. 4, The RCR, Training Memorandum No. 1/44, 12 February 1944.

19. RCR Museum Archives, RCR War Diary, Vol. 10A, 1 January to 30 June 44, No. 2, The RCR Training Directive No. 1 of 1944. The Training directive, signed by the acting CO, Major Galloway, emphasized that it was "the responsibility of every officer, NCO and man to put everything he has got into this period of training. Old Hands must be especially charged with this, and Coy Comd will have a talk with all pre-Moro members of the Regiment on their responsibilities at this time. This training period is a challenge to every one of us to rebuild in the splendid foundations of the Past, a fighting battalion that is second to none. Men Die, Wars End, But the Regiment Lives on!"

20. Galloway, *55 Axis*, 134.

21. RCR Museum Archives, RCR War Diary, Vol. 10A, 1 January to 30 June 44, War Diary entry, 24 January 1944.

22. See note 8, chapter 5. On 22 January 1944, two Allied corps were landed at Anzio, approximately 35 kilometres south of Rome. However, the landing was quickly pinned down by the Germans and required emergency reinforcement to prevent it from being destroyed altogether. "We hoped to land a wild cat that would tear out the bowels of the Boche," complained Winston Churchill, "instead we have stranded a vast whale with its tail flopping about in the water!" Quoted in Dancocks, 229.

23. Quoted in Dancocks, 241.

24. RCR Museum Archives, Series 7, World War II, 1939–1945, Vol. 10, File 28, LGen E.L.M. Burns, "The Set-Piece Attack — Lessons from the Breakthrough of the Hitler Line," 6 July 1944.

25. RCR Museum Archives, Series 7, World War II, 1939–1945, Vol. 9, File 14, "1 Canadian Infantry Brigade in the Liri Valley Battle by Commander 1 Canadian Infantry Brigade."

26. G.K. Wright, "Hitler Line — Phase 1," *The Connecting File*, July 1948, 30.

27. *Ibid.*, 30.

28. RCR Museum Archives, RCR War Diary, Vol. 10A, 1 January to 30 June 44, War Diary entry, 16 May 1944.

29. Wright, 31.

30. War Diary entry, 16 May 1944.

31. Wright, 31.

32. War Diary entry, 16 May 1944; and Wright, 31.

33. RCR Museum Archives, RCR War Diary, Vol. 10B, 1 January to 30 June 44, No. 2, War Diary entry, 16 May 1944. "Battle Narrative — The RCR, 15 May to 24 May 1944," puts the casualties at 12 killed and 25 wounded.

34. RCR Museum Archives, Series 7, Second World War, 1939–1945, Vol. 9, File 14, "The Adolf Hitler Line," 1. Annex to "1 Canadian Infantry Brigade in the Liri Valley Battle by Commander 1 Canadian Infantry Brigade."

35. "Battle Narrative — The RCR, 15 May to 24 May 1944."

36. W.M. Rich, "Hitler Line — Phase II," *Connecting File*, July 1948, 34.

37. "The Adolf Hitler Line," 2.

38. War Diary entry, 23 May 1944.

39. Rich, 34.

40. Galloway, *55 Axis*, 140.

41. RCR Museum Archives, RCR War Diary, Vol. 10A, 1 January to 30 June 44, War Diary entry, 3 June 1944.

42. George Burrows, interview with author, 26 July 2005.

43. RCR Museum Archives, RCR War Diary, Vol. 11 A, No. 2, 1 July to 31 December 44. RCR Museum Archives, War Diary entry, 6 August 1944.

44. War Diary entry, 8 August 1944.

45. *Ibid.*

46. War Diary entry, 25 August 1944.

47. *Ibid.*

48. Quoted in Dancocks, 323.

49. Galloway, *55 Axis*, 155–156.

50. RCR Museum Archives, RCR War Diary, Vol. 11 A, No. 2, 1 July to 31 December 44, War Diary entry, 3 September 1944.

51. War Diary entry, 4 September 1944.

52. *Ibid.*

53. War Diary entry, 5 September 1944.

54. War Diary entry, 6 September 1944.

55. Lieutenant-Colonel G.W.L. Nicholson, *Official History of the Canadian Army in the Second World War: The Canadians in Italy, 1943–1945* (Ottawa: The Queen's Printer, 1956), 543.

56. War Diary entry, 16 September 1944.

57. Galloway, *55 Axis*, 162.

58. RCR Museum Archives, Series 7, Second World War, 1939–1945, Vol. 10, File 7, Major Bert S. Wemp, "Fast as Huns Replaced RCR's Mow Them Down in Fierce Rimini Battle," clipping, unknown newspaper, unknown date.

59. War Diary entry, 17 September 1944.

60. Galloway, *Sicily to the Siegfried Line*, 22.

61. G.R. Stevens, *The Royal Canadian Regiment: Volume Two 1933–1966* (London, ON: London Printing Co., 1967), 160.

62. RCR Museum Archives, RCR War Diary, Vol. 11 A, No. 2, 1 July to 31 December 44, War Diary entry, 18 October 1944.

63. Galloway, *55 Axis*, 173.

64. Stevens, 167.

65. Nicholson, 612–613.

66. Quoted in Dancocks, 390.

67. J.L. Granatstein, *Canada's Army* (Toronto: University of Toronto Press, 2002), 283.

68. RCR Museum Archives, RCR War Diary, Vol. 11 A, No. 2, 1 July to 31 December 44, War Diary entry, 4 December 1944.

69. Quoted in Dancocks, 391.

70. *Ibid.*

71. War Diary entry, 4 December 1944.

72. DHH, File 145.2R13.011 (D1) Docket II, "Account by Maj JM Houghton, OC 'A' Coy RCR, of the Lamone R BrHead Night 4/5 Dec. Given to Hist Offr 1 Cdn Inf Div 30 Jan 45."

73. War Diary entry, 5 December 1944.

74. *Ibid.*

75. *Ibid.*

76. *Ibid.*

77. *Ibid.*

78. *Ibid.*

79. *Ibid.* The Olafson assault bridges were later blown by RCR Pioneers, who conducted the risky task under enemy fire. Higher headquarters feared that the enemy would use the bridges to attack the weakened 1 CIB units.

80. DHH, File 145.2R13.011 (D1) Docket II, "Account by Maj JM Houghton, OC 'A' Coy RCR, of the Lamone R BrHead Night 4/5 Dec. Given to Hist Offr 1 Cdn Inf Div 30 Jan 45."

81. *Ibid.*

82. Farley Mowat, *The Regiment* (Toronto: McClelland & Stewart, 1981), 282.

83. Galloway, *Bravely into Battle*, 230.

84. War Diary entry 26 December 1944. See also Galloway, *Sicily to the Siegfried Line*, 58.

85. RCR Museum Archives, RCR War Diary, Vol. 11C, No. 1, 1 July to 31 December 44, "Personal Message from the Corps Commander," Italy, Christmas Day, 1944.

86. Galloway, *Sicily to the Siegfried Line*, 71.

ESTABLISHING A LEGACY

87. RCR Museum Archives, RCR War Diary, Vol. 12, No. 1, 1 January to 30 June 45, War Diary entry, 16 February 1945.

88. RCR Museum Archives, RCR War Diary, Vol. 12, No. 1, 1 January to 30 June 45, War Diary entry, 14 April 1945.

89. RCR Museum Archives, RCR War Diary, Vol. 12, No. 1, 1 January to 30 June 45, War Diary entry, 4 May 1945.

90. The 1 CIB HQ had been tasked to go to Berlin to represent the Canadian Army with three battalions. The 48th Highlanders were transferred under command 3 CIB.

91. RCR Museum, "VE Day" Newspaper clipping, Album "1990s & Misc 4163.1966/69."

92. War Diary entry, 8 May 1945.

93. Ten battle honours were emblazoned on the Colours (i.e., Landing in Sicily, Motta, Montecorvino, San Leonardo, Ortona, Hitler Line, Gothic Line, Lamone Crossing, Riini Line, Italy 1943–1945, and North-West Europe 1945). The other 17 are: Valguarnera, Agira, Adrano, Regalbuto, Gustav Line, Liri Valley, Nisano Ridge, San Martino-San Lorenzo, Pisciatello, Fosso Vecchio and Apeldoorn.

94. RCR Museum, VE Day" Newspaper clipping, Album "1990s & Misc 4163.1966/69."

Chapter 7: A Return to Combat

1. Lieutenant-Colonel W. W. Reid, "Foreword," *The Connecting File*, January 1946, 3. This was the first *Connecting File* published since 1939.

2. Desmond Morton, *A Military History of Canada* (Toronto: McClelland & Stewart, 3rd Ed, 1992), 225.

3. Canada, *Debates*, 19 August 1946, 5059.

4. Canada, *DND Report 1946* (Ottawa: Department of National Defence, 1946), 27.

5. *Debates*, 9 July 1947, 5327. Claxton became MND on 12 December 1946. Prime Minister W.L.M. King directed Claxton to slash defence spending. Claxton's task was to ensure "the utmost economy consistent with security should be effected in the Defence Department." He realized that "the most important question in defence planning after the war was: how much should be spent on defence?" The military's lack of priority in the government's agenda soon became apparent. Claxton's official biographer recorded that the minister's "effort to define a realistic role for the military clashed with the prime minister's desire virtually to eliminate defence spending." Claxton's success in reducing military expenditures prompted King to joyously remark in his diary, "Claxton has done wonderful work in compelling the defence forces to cut down different establishments, effecting a savings of something like $100,000,000." *Debates*, 9 July 1947, 5327. Claxton became MND on 12 December 1946. See also Canada, *Canada's Defence* (Ottawa: DND, 1947), 17; David Bercuson, *True Patriot: The Life of Brooke Claxton* (Toronto: University of Toronto Press, 1993), 164–166; *Debates*, 13 February 1947, 394 and 9 July 1947, 5327; and J.W. Pickersgill and D.F. Forster, *The Mackenzie King Record, Vol. 4* (Toronto: University of Toronto, 1960), 9–10.

6. G.R. Stevens, *The Royal Canadian Regiment: Volume Two 1933–1966* (London, ON: London Printing Co., 1967), 200. The Army was capped at a total strength of 27,000. See J.L. Granatstein, *Canada's Army* (Toronto: University of Toronto Press, 2002), 316.

7. To avoid confusion, the designations of the period are as follows: *Airborne* is used "for those troops, units and their equipment which form part of airborne formations and for which specific airborne war establishments exist. They are composed, equipped, and trained primarily for the purpose of operating by air and of making assault landings. They include parachute and air landing troops. *Air-transportable* designates those units, other than those of airborne formations which can be transported by air and employed in a tactical role. They may be part of a light division already specially equipped for movement by air in transport aircraft or they may be part of any other formation whose equipment as been exchanged or modified as necessary for a particular operation and for an approach by air instead of by land or sea." Canada, Army, Directorate of Military Training, *Military Science Part I and II, 1948–1949*, 97.

8. DHH, File 112.3M2 (D369), "Command, Mobile Striking Force," 21 October 1948; and George Kitching, *Mud and Green Fields: The Memoirs*

of *Major-General George Kitching* (St. Catharines, ON: Vanwell Publishing Ltd., 1986), 248.

9. The name change occurred officially 1 April 1949, although in practice many in NDHQ and JAS itself used the new title long before. Its role was to conduct: research in air-portability of Army personnel and equipment; user trials of equipment, especially under cold weather conditions; limited development and assessment of airborne equipment; training of paratroop volunteers; training in air-portability of personnel and equipment; training in maintenance of air; advanced training of Glider pilots in exercises with troops; training in some of the uses of light aircraft. DHH, File 168.009 (D45), "The Organization of an Army Air Centre In Canada," 29 November and 27 December 1945; DND Report 1949, 13; and *War Diary — JAS/CJATC*, 5 March and 1 April 1949 respectively.

10. LAC, RG 24, Reel C-8255, File HQS 88–60–2, "SAS Company," 30 October 1947, 4 and "Requested Amendment to Interim Plan — SAR," 11 September 1947. See also DHH, Files 145.4 (D2) and 112.3H1.003 (D5).

11. In late October 1947, once the government had given approval for the creation of the sub-unit, aim began to morph. An Army report blatantly highlighted the true intention of the organization, "The formation of a SAS Company is in line with British Army Air Group post war plans; whereby the SAS is being retained as a small group integrated within the Airborne Division. This provision is to keep the techniques employed by SAS persons during the war alive in the peacetime army." LAC, RG 24, Reel C-8255, File HQS 88–60–2, "SAS Company," 30 October 1947 (Air S94).

12. Selection standards included the requirements to be: a bachelor; in superb physical condition; demonstrate initiative, self-reliance, and control; immensely quick in thought and action; have a strong sense of discipline; and an original approach. Canadian Airborne Museum, Research Papers on Canadian Airborne Organizations, Part 1, 1.C, Document 1 — "Canadian Special Air Service Company," 1. See Bernd Horn, "A Military Enigma: The Canadian Special Air Service Company, 1948–49," *Canadian Military History*, Vol. 10, No. 1, Winter 2001, 21–30 for more information on the SAS Coy.

13. Its full responsibilities, in priority, were:

   a) Provide a tactical parachute company for airborne training.

This company is to form the nucleus for expansion for the training of the three infantry battalions as parachute battalions;

b) Provide a formed body of troops to participate in tactical exercises and demonstrations for courses at the CJATC and service units throughout the country;

c) Preserve and advance the techniques of SAS [commando] operations developed during WW II 1939–1945;

d) Provide when required parachutists to back-up the RCAF [Royal Canadian Air Force] organizations as detailed in the Interim Plan for air Search and Rescue; and

e) Aid Civil Authorities in fighting forest fires and assisting in national catastrophes when authorized by Defence Headquarters.

See LAC, RG 24, Reel C-8255, File HQS 88-60-2, "SAS Terms of Reference," 16 April 1948; "Duties of the SAS Coy," 29 January 1948; SAS Coy-Air Training Directive," December 1948; and "Aviation Teamwork in Canada," *Military Review*, Vol. 28, No. 5, August 1948, 96–97.

14. LAC, RG 24, Vol. 2371, File HQ-88-33, Army / Air Training of Airborne Infantry, Vol. 1, "Training of the PPCLI for the Airborne/Air-transported Operations," 28 July 1948. See Bernd Horn, *Bastard Sons: An Examination of the Canadian Airborne Experience 1942–1995* (St. Catharines, ON: Vanwell, 2001) for a detailed account of Canada's airborne history.

15. DHH, File 112.3M2 (D369), "Brigade Headquarters — Army Component — Mobile Striking Force," 29 April 1949; and "Operational Requirement of Airborne Forces for the Defence of Canada," 29 November 1948. The commitment prior to 1 May 1949 was for the availability of one battalion combat team capable of responding within two months of an enemy lodgement, two battalion combat teams within four months and a brigade with six months. Throughout this period the military was incapable of meeting these demands.

16. DHH, 112.3M2 (D369), "Operational Requirement of Airborne Forces for the Defence of Canada," 29 November 1948.

17. "Editorials," *The Connecting File*, Summer 1950, 4. The Regiment moved into Victoria Barracks, which was a converted hospital building.

18. When the Japanese surrendered in 1945, the United States occupied the southern half of Korea and the Soviet Union moved into the northern half. The 38th Parallel was used as a boundary. The intent was a temporary occupation pending steps to establish a unified independent country. However, as the Cold War developed the divided country became part of the growing conflict between former allies. The Americans created a democratic state under Syngman Rhee. On 10 May 1948 elections were held in South Korea and on 15 August the Republic of Korea was established and subsequently recognized by the UN General Assembly. The Soviet Union immediately countered and established an armed Communist state, the Democratic People's Republic of Korea" under the control of wartime guerrilla leader Kim Il Sung. Moreover, by December they announced that they had withdrawn all their forces from the peninsula and thus, forced the Americans to do the same. Shortly thereafter trouble began to brew as North Korean patrols began to penetrate into South Korea. With the withdrawal of the Americans, the ROK army, armed with only small arms and mortars, was left to face a hostile well-armed neighbour.

19. *Debates*, 12 February 1951, 260. The government program called for an armed force of 115,000 men and an expenditure of $5 billion. See also *House of Commons Debates Official Report — The Defence Programme*, 5 February 1951, 1–7; *Canada's Defence Programme 1951–52*, 5–10.

20. Canada, *House of Commons Debates Official Report — The Defence Programme*, "Speech by the Hon. Brooke Claxton, MND," 5 February 1951, 3–7.

21. "Editorial," *The Connecting File*, Winter 1950–1951, 7.

22. C.H.L. "The Second Battalion," *The Connecting File*, Winter 1950–1951, 57.

23. RCR Museum Archives, War Diary, 2 RCR 1 May 51- 31 May 51, War Diary entry, 5 May 1951.

24. 25 CIB comprised of: Three infantry battalions, one regiment of artillery, a field ambulance unit, a transport company, an infantry workshop, and two field-repair detachments. It had an authorized strength of 4,960 all ranks and a reinforcement pool of 2,105 all ranks. David Bercuson, *Blood on the Hills* (Toronto: University of Toronto Press, 1999), 40.

25. William Johnston, *A War of Patrols* (Vancouver: University of British Columbia Press, 2003), 37.

26. 2 PPCLI, as part of the British 27th Infantry Brigade was tasked with protecting the withdrawal of the 6th ROK Division, which had been battered by the Chinese offensive, through the Kap'yong Valley. On the night of 24–25 April 1951, the advancing Chinese attacked the hill top defences of the PPCLI and the Royal Australian Regiment. The Australians were forced to withdraw, but the PPCLI held their positions at great cost and stopped the enemy advance. They were awarded a U.S. presidential unit citation.

27. War Diary entry, 27 May 1951.

28. War Diary entry, 30 May 1951.

29. Interview with author, 3 August 2007.

30. "The Attack on Chail-Li," *Remembering the Forgotten War: Korea 1950–1953* (Kemptville, ON: Veterans Publications, May 1997), 23.

31. War Diary entry, 30 May 1951.

32. RCR Museum Archives, Series 9, Korean War, 1950–1953, Vol. 13, File 44, Lieutenant-Colonel R.A. Keane, "Report on Operations in Korea 25 May — 5 June 51," 12 June 1951, 3.

33. War Diary entry, 30 May 1951.

34. Keane, "Report on Operations in Korea 25 May — 5 June 51," 12 June 1951, 2.

35. The division was composed of 25 CIB, 28 BCIB, made up of Australian, British and New Zealand troops, and 29 British Infantry Brigade.

36. "2nd Bn. The Royal Canadian Regiment," *The Connecting File,* Fall-Winter 1951–1952, 12.

37. Private Walter S.C. Rudoph ("D" Coy, 2 RCR), "Canadians in the Korean War 1951–1953," *Pro Patria*, Issue 85, October 2003, 42.

38. Prisoners of war (PoW) often passed on incredible information. For instance, one PoW reported that he was told by his CO that a "Monkey Division" had arrived from China. Apparently, the leaders down to company level were Chinese troops but below this level all were monkeys. The PoW related,

"Monkeys were well trained so that they followed orders strictly. Only those who were always with the monkeys could give commands. Monkeys were trained mainly for guerrilla tactics and could throw hand grenades and fire a pistol." RCR Museum Archives, War Diary, 2 RCR 1 October 1951 to 31 October 1951, War Diary entry, 14 October 1951; *Ibid.*, ISUM (intelligence summary) No. 18, dated 19 Oct 1951.

39. RCR Museum Archives, RCR Korea Awards & Citations, "Award of Military Cross to 2B 4391 Lieutenant Edward John Mastronardi, Royal Canadian Infantry Corps."

40. RCR Museum Archives, RCR Korea Awards & Citations, "Award of the Distinguished Conduct Medal to F.800160 Private Rupert Edward Bauer, Royal Canadian Infantry Corps."

41. RCR Museum Archives, War Diary, 2 RCR 1 November 1951 to 30 November 1951, War Diary entry, 3 November 1951.

42. Quoted in Johnston, 227.

43. RCR Museum Archives, War Diary, 2 RCR 1 February 1952 to 29 February 1952, War Diary entry, 12 February 1952.

44. Quoted in John Melady, *Korea: Canada's Forgotten War* (Toronto: Macmillan, 1983), 67.

45. RCR Museum Archives, War Diary, 2 RCR 1 March 1952- 31 March 1952, War Diary entry, 10 March 1952.

46. *Ibid.*

47. RCR Museum Archives, War Diary, 2 RCR 1 March 1952- 31 March 1952, War Diary entry, 31 March 1952.

48. Interview with author, 27 June 2007.

Chapter 8: "Spit and Polish"

1. The actual dates are difficult to discern as there are many conflicting accounts and references. The dates used in Volume 2 of the Regimental

History by Stevens have been incorporated.

2. RCR Museum Archives, Appendix M, War Diary, 1 RCR 1 April 1952- 30 April 1952, "Life in the Outpost."

3. On 14 April 1952, Bingham was inspecting platoon positions during an exercise when he tripped a booby trap and received shrapnel wounds. He was evacuated to Japan for treatment but returned to duty in theatre 2 May.

4. DHH, File 145.2 R13.013 (D4), "Activities of 1st BN, The Royal Canadian Regiment, January-April 1952. Account of Interview Given by Lt-Col P.R. Bingham C.O. 1 Bn R.C.R. in Paekhang-myon Area, on 14 May 52."

5. Lieutenant-Colonel Herbert Fairlie Wood, *Strange Battleground: Official History of the Canadian Army in Korea* (Ottawa: Queen's Printer, 1966), 184.

6. "Battalion Notes," *The Connecting File*, Spring-Summer 1952, 31.

7. RCR Museum Archives, Appendix C, War Diary, 1 RCR 1 June 1952 to 30 June 1952. RCR, "Commanding Officer's Conference," 080930 June 1952.

8. Wood, 189.

9. RCR Museum Archives, Appendix X, War Diary, 1 RCR 1 June 1952- 30 June 1952, "Preliminary Report on 1 RCR Fighting Patrol, Night 31 May / 1 June 52."

10. *Ibid.*

11. *Ibid.*; and DHH, File 145.2R13.013 (D6), "RCR Fighting Patrol on Point 113, 31 May 52. Account of Interview with 14 participants, by Major F.G.B. Maskell and Capt F.R. McGuire, in Paekhang-myon Area on 5 June 52."

12. "RCR Fighting Patrol on Point 113, 31 May 52."

13. "RCR Fighting Patrol on Point 113, 31 May 52," Appendix B, "Further Information Supplied by NCO IC No. 2 Section."

14. RCR Museum Archives, War Diary, 2 RCR 1 Mar 1952- 31 Mar 1952, "Intelligence Brief (based on info available up to 25 Mar 52) Prepared by: General Staff (Intelligence) HQ 1 Commonwealth Division), 12.

15. "RCR Fighting Patrol on Point 113, 31 May 52."

16. RCR Museum Archives, RCR Korea Awards & Citations, "Award of Military Medal to SG 9631 Corporal Arthur Irvine Stinson, Royal Canadian Infantry Corps."

17. "Preliminary Report on 1 RCR Fighting Patrol, Night 31 May/1 June 52."

18. RCR Museum Archives, War Diary entry, 23 May 1952. War Diary of "B" Coy [1 RCR], May 1 1952 to May 30 1952.

19. Wood, 190.

20. The prisoner population was screened to identify and release South Koreans that were inadvertently part of the prisoner population. By the end of 1951, 38,000 South Koreans were released as civilians.

21. The order actually came from the Commonwealth division based on a telegram from the commander in chief of British Commonwealth Forces Korea on 21 June 1952 that stated additional troops (other than American) would be requested. The next day a warning order was received from Eighth Army through 1 U.S. Corps HQ. As a result, at 1530 hours, 22 May 1952, Brigadier Bogert ordered "B" Coy, 1 RCR to Koje-Do. He immediately informed Lieutenant-General Simonds, who notified General Charles Foulkes, who in turn informed the MND. The news was not well received. The news of the rioting and subsequent killings did not play well at home and now Canada was potentially embroiled in this political hot potato. To exacerbate the issue, Canada had not been consulted in advance. An immediate attempt was made, through the Canadian ambassador in Washington and the U.S. secretary of state, to have the order countermanded. See DHH, File 681.013 (D11), "Commonwealth Participation on Koje;" and Wood, 193.

22. DHH, File 410B25.013(D20), "Interview with Major E.L. Cohen, RCR, Friday 16 Nov 62 subject: Koje Island."

23. DHH, File 410B25.013(D20), After Action Report written by Major E.L. Cohen, "B Company, 1st Battalion, The Royal Canadian Regiment, In the Field, August 52."

24. Quoted in Wood, 191.

25. DHH, File 410B25.013(D31), "'C' Coy 1 RCR Raid on PT 113 (21/22 Jun 52) — Account of Interview Major D.E. Holmes to Capt F.R. McGuire (Hist Offr 25 Cdn Inf Bde), Paekhang-Myon Area, 8 Jul 52."

26. *Ibid.*

27. RCR Museum Archives, Appendix C, War Diary, 1 RCR 1 June 1952- 30 June 1952, "Commanding Officer Conference, 161500 June 52."

28. RCR Museum Archives, Appendix C, War Diary, 1 RCR 1 June 1952- 30 June 1952, "Commanding Officer Conference, 080930 June 52."

29. RCR Museum Archives, Appendix C, War Diary, 1 RCR 1 June 1952- 30 June 1952, "Commanding Officer Conference, 161500 June 52." Anti-Tank platoon was credited with having the "best record of saluting."

30. RCR Museum Archives, Appendix C, War Diary, 1 RCR 1 June 1952- 30 June 1952, "Commanding Officer Conference, 230930 June 52." Things did not improve. In July the CO directed, "Saluting in vehs [vehicles] must improve. Existing conditions is deteriorating. All personnel will salute." RCR Museum Archives, Appendix C, War Diary, 1 RCR 1 July 1952- 31 June 1952, "Commanding Officer Conference, 101900 July 52."

31. "Battalion Notes," *The Connecting File*, Vol. 24, No. 1, Spring-Summer 1952, 33.

32. RCR Museum Archives, War Diary entry, 24 and 26 August 1952. War Diary of "D" Coy [1 RCR], 1 August 1952 — 31 August 1952.

33. RCR Museum Archives, War Diary of "B" Coy [1 RCR], 1 August 1952 — 31 August 1952, War Diary entry, 25 August 1952.

34. RCR Museum Archives, War Diary of "C" Coy [1 RCR], 1 August 1952 — 31 August 1952, War Diary entry, 24 August 1952.

35. Wood, 203.

36. DHH, File 410B25.013 (D17), "1 RCR Fighting Patrol, 1 Offr and 5 OR, 24 September 52 — Debriefing."

37. RCR Museum Archives, War Diary of "C" Coy [1 RCR], 1 September 1952

— 30 September 1952, War Diary entry, 24 September 1952.

38. RCR Museum Archives, War Diary, 1 RCR, 1 September 1952 — 30 September 1952, War Diary entry, 24 September 1952.

39. RCR Museum Archives, War Diary, 1 RCR, 1 September 1952 — 30 September 1952, War Diary entry, 30 September 1952.

40. RCR Museum Archives, War Diary, 2 RCR 1 March 52- 31 March 52, "Intelligence Brief (based on info available up to 25 Mar 52) Prepared by: General Staff (Intelligence) HQ 1 Commonwealth Division), 7.

41. RCR Museum Archives, War Diary, 1 RCR, 1 September 1952 — 30 September 1952, War Diary entry, 30 September 1952.

42. RCR Museum Archives, War Diary of "D" Coy [1 RCR], 1 August 1952 — 31 August 1952, War Diary entry, 12 August 1952.

43. RCR Museum Archives, War Diary, 1 RCR, 1 October 1952 — 30 October 1952, War Diary entry, 22 October 1952.

44. RCR Museum, Album Miscellaneous RCR Clippings, Bill Boss, "Reactions of Men Under Fire for 21 Days Are Described," Unidentified newspaper clipping.

45. *Ibid.*

46. RCR Museum, Album Miscellaneous RCR Clippings, Bill Boss, "Canadians Get Buried, Shelled, but they carry on," Unidentified newspaper clipping.

47. Boss, "Reactions of Men Under Fire for 21 Days Are Described."

48. J.W. Martin, "The Short, Valiant Life of Easy Company," *Remembering the Forgotten War: Korea 1950-1953* (Kemptville, ON: Veterans Publications, May 1997), 35.

49. RCR Museum, Album Miscellaneous RCR Clippings, Bill Boss, "Colonel Says Sound Basic Training Essential Requirement of Troops," Unidentified newspaper clipping.

50. Martin, 35.

51. Interview with author, 30 July 2007.

52. Quoted in Wood, 208.

53. RCR Museum Archives, War Diary, 1 RCR, 1 October 1952 — 30 October 1952, War Diary entry, 23 October 1952.

54. RCR Museum, Album Miscellaneous RCR Clippings, William Drylie, "RCR's Princess Pats Beat Back 1,000 Reds in Hand-to-Hand Fight," Unidentified newspaper clipping.

55. RCR Museum Archives, Series 9, Korean War, 1950–1953, Vol. 13, File 25, "Report B Coy's Part in Action Night 23/24 Oct," Appendix A, to "Report on 1 RCR Action Night 23/24 Oct 52," 25 November 1952.

56. Martin, 36.

57. RCR Museum Archives, War Diary of "A" Coy, (1 RCR), 1 October 1952 — 30 October 1952, War Diary entry, 23 October 1952.

58. RCR Museum, Album Miscellaneous RCR Clippings, "Shelled Four Days 100 RCR's Cut 1,000 Chinese to Ribbons," newspaper clipping.

59. RCR Museum Archives, RCR Korea Awards & Citations, "Award of Mention-In-Dispatches (Posthumous) to SB 10793 Private Charles Joseph Morrison, 1st Battalion, The Royal Canadian Regiment."

60. RCR Museum Archives, RCR Korea Awards & Citations, "Award of Military Cross to ZB 4331 Lieutenant John Clark, 1st Battalion, The Royal Canadian Regiment."

61. RCR Museum Archives, Series 9, Korean War, 1950–1953, Vol. 13, File 25, "Report on 1 RCR Action Night 23/24 October 52," 25 November 1952; and DHH, File 410B25.013 (D24), "The Attack on 'Little Gibraltar' (Pt 355), 23 October 52." As a result of much of the reserve ammunition being buried during the preparatory bombardment, a new ammo scale was implemented. Bren gunners now carried a minimum of six magazines; Riflemen carried four Bren magazines and 50 rounds of .303 ammo; Sten gunners carried no fewer than six Sten and two Bren magazines; and all ranks carried two grenades.

62. RCR Museum Archives, War Diary, 1 RCR, 1 October 1952 — 30 October 1952, War Diary entry, 22 October 1952.

63. DHH, File 145.2R13019(D1), 7, "Summary of Experiences Korean Campaign — 25 March 53 — Armistice — 25 March 54, LT-COL K.L. Campbell OBE, CD," 25 March 1954.

64. Ibid., 7.

65. Quoted in Wood, 231.

66. "Enemy Activity Against 7 PL, 3 RCR, 2 and 3 May 53" — Account of Interview with Second Lieutenant EH Hollyer, Paekhang-Myon Area, 6 May 53.

67. RCR Museum Archives, War Diary, 1 RCR, 1 May 1953 — 31 May 1953, War Diary entry, 3 May 1953.

68. Quoted in Wood, 235.

69. Ibid., 236.

70. "Attack on Hill 187," *Remembering the Forgotten War: Korea 1950–1953* (Kemptville, ON: Veterans Publications, May 1997), 42.

71. DHH, File 145.2R13019(D1), 1, "Summary of Experiences Korean Campaign — 25 March 53 — Armistice — 25 March 54, LT-COL K.L. Campbell OBE, CD," 25 March 54.

GLOSSARY

BCIB	British Commonwealth Infantry Brigade
Bde	Brigade
BGen	Brigadier-General
BHQ	Battalion Headquarters
Bn	Battalion
Brig	Brigadier
BSP	Basic Security Plan
Capt	Captain
CASF	Canadian Army Special Force
CBC	Canadian Broadcasting Corporation
Cdn	Canadian
Cdn SAS Coy	Canadian Special Air Service Company
CEF	Canadian Expeditionary Force
CIB	Canadian Infantry Brigade
CGS	Chief of the General Staff
CJATC	Canadian Joint Air Training Centre
CMR	Canadian Mounted Rifles
CO	Commanding Officer
Comd	Commander
Coy	Company
Cpl	Corporal
DCO	Deputy Commanding Officer

DF	Defensive Fire
DHH	Directorate of History and Heritage
Div	Division
DND	Department of National Defence
DUKW	D=model year; U=amphibian; K=all wheel drive; W=dual rear axles
DZ	Drop Zone
Ex	Exercise
FDL	Forward Defensive Lines
FOO	Forward Observation Officer
FM	Field Marshal
FUPs	Form Up Points
Gen	General
GO	General Order
GOC	General Officer Commanding
H&PER	Hastings and Prince Edward Regiment
HBC	Hudson's Bay Company
HE	High Explosives
HMG	Heavy Machine Guns
HQ	Headquarters
ISUM	Intelligence Summary
JAS	Joint Air School
LAC	Library and Archives Canada
LCol	Lieutenant-Colonel
LGen	Lieutenant-General
LMG	Light Machine Gun
LoB	Left out of Battle
LSI	Landing Ship Infantry
LST	Landing Ship Tank
Lt	Lieutenant
Maj	Major

MG	Machine Gun
MGen	Major-General
mm	millimetre
MMG	Medium Machine Gun
MND	Minister of National Defence
MSF	Mobile Striking Force
NATO	North Atlantic Treaty Organisation
NCO	Non-Commissioned Officer
NDHQ	National Defence Headquarters
NKPA	North Korea People's Army
NWMP	North-West Mounted Police
OC	Officer Commanding
PIAT	Projectile, Infantry, Anti-Tank
Pl	Platoon
PoW	Prisoner of War
PPCLI	Princess Patricia's Canadian Light Infantry
Pte	Private
QOR of C	Queen's Own Rifles of Canada
R22R	Royal 22nd Regiment
RCD	Royal Canadian Dragoons
RCR	Royal Canadian Regiment
RCRI	Royal Canadian Regiment of Infantry
RE	Royal Engineers
Recce	Reconnaissance
RHC	Royal Highlanders of Canada
RHQ	Regimental Headquarters
RN	Royal Navy
ROK	Republic of Korea
RRCI	Royal Regiment of Canadian Infantry
RSO	Regimental Standing Orders
Sqn	Squadron
Sgt	Sergeant
S.S.	Steamship

U.K.	United Kingdom
UN	United Nations
U.S.	United States
USNS	United States Navy Ship
VC	Victoria Cross
VRI	*Victoria Regina Imperatrix* (Victoria, Queen and Empress)
VT	Variable Time
WWI	First World War
WWII	Second World War
2IC	Second-in-Command

SELECTED BIBLIOGRAPHY

Beal, Bob, and Rod Macleod. *Prairie Fire: The 1885 North-West Rebellion.* Toronto: McClelland & Stewart, 1994.

Bell, Ken, and C.P. Stacey. *100 Years: The Royal Canadian Regiment 1883–1983.* Don Mills, ON: Collier Macmillan, 1983.

Bercuson, David J. *Blood on the Hills: The Canadian Army in the Korean War.* Toronto: University of Toronto Press, 1999.

Berton, Pierre. *Vimy.* Toronto: McClelland & Stewart, 1986.

Bland, Douglas. *Canada's National Defence, Vol. 1: Defence Policy.* Kingston, ON: Queen's School of Policy Studies, 1997.

Currie, Lieutenant-General Sir A.W. *Canadian Corps Operations During the Year 1918.* Ottawa: Department of Militia and Defence, 1919.

Dancocks, Daniel G. *The D-Day Dodgers: The Canadians in Italy, 1943–1945.* Toronto: McClelland & Stewart, 1991.

——. *Spearhead to Victory: Canada and the Great War.* Edmonton, AB: 1987.

Department of Militia and Defence. *Supplementary Report — Organization, Equipment, Despatch and Service of the Canadian Contingents During the War in South Africa 1899-1900.* Ottawa: S.E. Dawson, Queen's Printer, 1901.

Douglas, W.A.B., and Brereton Greenhous. *Out of the Shadows: Canada in the Second World War.* Toronto: Dundurn Press, 1995.

Evans, Sanford. *The Canadian Contingents.* Toronto: Publishers' Syndicate Ltd, 1901.

Fetherstonhaugh, R.C. *The Royal Canadian Regiment, 1883-1933.* Fredericton, NB: The RCR, 1936.

Galloway, Strome. *Bravely into Battle.* Toronto: Stoddart, 1988.

____. *Sicily to the Siegfried Line.* Kitchener, ON: Arnold Press, n.d.

____. *Some Died at Ortona: The Royal Canadian Regiment in Action in Italy 1943.* London, ON: The RCR, 1983.

____. *"55 Axis" with The Royal Canadian Regiment, 1939-1945.* Montreal: Provincial Publishing Co., 1946.

Granatstein, J.L. *Canada's Army.* Toronto: University of Toronto Press, 2002.

Granatstein, J.L., and Desmond Morton. *Canada and the Two World Wars.* Toronto: Key Porter Books, 2003.

Goodspeed, D.J., ed. *The Armed Forces of Canada, 1867-1967: A Century of Achievement.* Ottawa: Canadian Forces Headquarters, 1967.

Greenhous, Brereton, ed. *Guarding the Goldfields: The Story of the Yukon Field Force.* Toronto: Dundurn Press, 1987.

Harris, Stephen J. *Canadian Brass.* Toronto: University of Toronto Press, 1988.

Hart-McHarg, W. *From Quebec to Pretoria with The Royal Canadian Regiment*. Toronto: William Briggs, 1902.

Haycock, Ronald G. *Sam Hughes*. Waterloo, ON: Wilfrid Laurier Press, 1986.

Horn, Bernd. *Bastard Sons: The Canadian Airborne Experience, 1942–1995*. St. Catharines, ON: Vanwell Publishers, 2001.

____, ed. *The Canadian Way of War: Serving the National Interest*. Toronto: Dundurn Press, 2006.

____, ed. *Forging a Nation: Perspectives on the Canadian Military Experience*. St. Catharines, ON: Vanwell Publishers, 2002.

Horn, Bernd, and Stephen J. Harris, eds. *Warrior Chiefs: Perspectives on Senior Canadian Military Leaders*. Toronto: Dundurn Press, 2001.

Johnston, William. *A War of Patrols: Canadian Army Operations in Korea*. Vancouver: University of British Columbia Press, 2003.

Melady, John. *Korea: Canada's Forgotten War*. Toronto: MacMillan, 1983.

Maloney, Sean M. *Canada and UN Peacekeeping: Cold War by Other Means 1945–1970*. St. Catharines, ON: Vanwell, 2002.

____. *War Without Battles: Canada's NATO Brigade in Germany 1951–1993*. Whitby, ON: McGraw-Hill Ryerson Limited, 1997.

Marquis, T.G. *Canada's Sons on Kopje and Veldt: A Historical Account of the Canadian Contingents*. Toronto: The Canada's Sons Publishing Co., 1900.

McLeod, R.C., ed. *Reminiscences of a Bungle by One of the Bunglers — and Two Other Northwest Rebellion Diaries*. Edmonton, AB: University of Alberta Press, 1983.

McWilliams, James, and R. James Steel. *Amiens: Dawn of Victory*. Toronto: Dundurn, 2001.

Middlemiss, D.W., and J.J. Sokolsky. *Canadian Defence: Decisions and Determinants*. Toronto: Harcourt Brace Jovanovich, 1989.

Miller, Carman. *Painting the Map Red: Canada and the South African War 1899-1902*. Ottawa: The Canadian War Museum, 1993.

Morton, Desmond. *The Canadian: General Sir William Otter*. Toronto: A.M. Hakkert Ltd., 1974.

———. *The Last War Drum*. Toronto: Hakkert, 1972.

———. *A Military History of Canada*. Toronto: McClelland & Stewart, 1992.

———. *A Peculiar Kind of Politics: Canada's Overseas Ministry in the First World War*. Toronto: University of Toronto Press, 1982.

———. *When Your Number Is Up: The Canadian Soldier in the First World War*. Toronto: Random House, 1993.

Morton, Desmond, and Jack Granatstein. *Marching to Armageddon*. Toronto: Lester & Orpen Dennys, 1989.

Mulvaney, C.P. *The North-West Rebellion*. Toronto: A.H. Hovey & Co., 1885.

Nicholson, Lieutenant-Colonel G.W.L. *Official History of the Canadian Army in the First World War: Canadian Expeditionary Force, 1914-1919*. Ottawa: Queen's Printer, 1964.

———. *Official History of the Canadian Army in the Second World War: The Canadians in Italy, 1943-1945*. Ottawa: Queen's Printer, 1966.

Rawling, Bill. *Surviving Trench Warfare: Technology and the Canadian Corps, 1914--1918*. Toronto: University of Toronto Press, 1992.

Reid, Brian A. *Our Little Army in the Field: The Canadians in South* Africa. St. Catharines, ON: Vanwell, 1996.

Stacey, C.P. *Canada and the Age of Conflict: A History of Canadian External Policies,* Vol. 1, 1867–1921. Toronto: Macmillan, 1977.

———. *Six Years of War: The Army in Canada, Britain, and the Pacific.* Ottawa: Department of National Defence, 1955.

Stanley, G.F.G. *Canada's Soldiers: The Military History of an Unmilitary People.* Toronto: Macmillan, 1960.

Steele, Captain Harwood. *The Canadians in France 1915–1916.* London, Eng.: T. Fisher Unwin Ltd., 1920.

Stevens, G.R. *The Royal Canadian Regiment: Volume Two 1933–1966.* London, ON: London Printing Co., 1967.

Wood, Lieutenant-Colonel Herbert Fairlie. *Strange Battleground: The Operations in Korea and Their Effects on the Defence Policy of Canada.* Ottawa: Queen's Printer, 1966.

Zuehlke, Mark. *Ortona.* Toronto: Stoddart, 1999.

ABOUT THE AUTHOR

Colonel Bernd Horn was born in Montreal on 9 October 1959. He attended the University of Waterloo where he obtained an honours bachelor of arts degree in political science. He entered the Canadian Forces by joining the militia in 1981, enrolling in the Highland Fusiliers of Canada. Upon graduation from university in 1983, he transferred to the regular force and received his Regimental affiliation with The Royal Canadian Regiment.

From 1983 to 1987, Colonel Horn was assigned to 1 RCR, where he held various positions, including platoon commander; officer commanding reconnaissance platoon; and executive assistant to the deputy chief of staff, United Nations Force in Cyprus. He attended the Continuous French Language School in Victoria, British Columbia, in 1987 and was subsequently posted to the Canadian Forces Officer Candidate School in Chilliwack, British Columbia, in 1988, where he held the positions of platoon commander/instructor and school adjutant.

Colonel Horn attended the Canadian Land Forces Command and Staff College in 1991 and returned to 1 RCR as the second-in-command of Administration Company upon completion. In the summer of 1992, he was appointed officer commanding Bravo Company and in September of that year took his sub-unit to the former Yugoslavia on the first deployment of Operation Cavalier as part of the 2 RCR Battle Group.

In July 1993, Colonel Horn was posted to the Canadian Airborne Regiment as the officer commanding 3 Commando. Following attendance at the Canadian Forces Command and Staff College in Toronto from 1995 to 1996, he became the staff officer to the director general strategic planning in National Defence Headquarters (NDHQ).

Colonel Horn received his master in war studies in June 1997. He was also awarded the Governor General's Gold Medal for academic achievement for his work. That summer he was posted to the Royal Military College in Kingston and commenced his PhD program in war studies. He graduated in May 2000 and earned the Barry D. Hunt Memorial Award, which is given to the graduate student of highest academic standing in the departments of history and war studies.

In June 1999, before completing his PhD studies, Colonel Horn was selected as the chief of staff to Lieutenant-General R.A. Dallaire and the OPD 2020 Officership Project in NDHQ. The following summer, he was posted back to the Royal Military College as an assistant professor of history, as well as the special assistant to the principal.

From June 2001 until March 2003, Colonel Horn was the commanding officer of the First Battalion, The Royal Canadian Regiment in Petawawa, Ontario. During this time, in May 2002, he was inducted by the governor general of Canada as an Officer of the Order of Military Merit. Following command, he completed a one-year tour as the deputy director of the Army's Directorate of Land Strategic Concepts in Kingston, before promotion in June 2004. He was subsequently appointed the director of the Canadian Forces Leadership Institute. In April 2007, he became the deputy commander of the Canadian Special Operations Forces Command.

INDEX

Active Militia (*see also* Permanent Force), 16, 111
Adrano, 134, 289, 327, 372
Agira, 128–32, 288–89, 327, 372
Albergo da Gambarie, 141
Aldershot, 114, 267, 283
Alderson, Lieutentant-General E.A.H., 77, 267, 269
Aldworth, Lieutenant-Colonel William, 58–59
Alexander, General Sir Harold, 154, 174–75, 184, 244, 296, 298, 304, 306, 314
"All Canadian Trail," 32
Allard, Brigadier J.V., 248, 316
Almanzora, S.S., 113, 283
Amiens, 99, 101, 276, 326, 353, 392
Anglian, S.S., 37
Anschluss, 112
Anzio, 174, 180, 367–68
Apeldoorn, 198–99, 301–02
Arielli River, 166, 168, 169, 171
Arras, 88, 101–02, 275–76, 326
Assoro, 127–28, 288
Augusta, 119
Australia, 63
Austria, 112
Austro-Hungarian Empire, 75

Bagnacavallo, 193, 300
Barossa Barracks, 114
Barriefield, 200, 205, 303

Basic Security Plan (BSP), 207–08
Batoche, 19–21, 25–27, 256
Batteries, 16, 125, 175, 331, 338
Battle Drill, 53, 113, 117, 189, 357
Battle of Britain, 116, 285
Battleford, 19–21, 23–25, 29, 256, 332
Belgium, 5, 81, 88, 96, 198, 301, 354
Bennett, Arthur, 46, 50, 65–66, 345
Bermuda, 75–77, 266–67
Biferno River, 152, 291
Big Bear, 19–20, 23, 29, 331
Bingham, Lieutenant-Colonel P.R., 128, 208, 228, 239, 245, 306–07, 310, 313, 317, 379
Black Week, 46–47, 53
Bloemfontein, 54, 65, 67, 260–61
Boer War (*see also* South African War), 13, 72, 335, 337–44, 346, 348
Boers, 41, 46, 48–49, 51–54, 57, 59–65, 69, 260
Boesman Kop, 67, 261
Bogert, Brigadier M.P., 228, 313, 380
Borden (*see also* Camp Borden, Canadian Forces Base Borden), 111–12, 306
Borden, Sir Frederick, 37
Borden, Right Honourable Sir Robert, 272
Boulogne, 115
Bourlon Wood, 103
Britain (*see also* England, Great Britain), 41–43, 48, 67, 71, 75–76, 112, 116–17, 285, 307, 330, 356–57, 393

British, 13, 15–16, 18, 33, 41–48, 51–54, 57, 59, 61–71, 73, 75, 88–89, 92, 95, 99, 103, 115–16, 118–19, 134, 139, 142, 154, 174, 184, 190, 192, 207, 218, 234, 260–61, 263–64, 266, 273, 280–81, 283, 289, 291, 298, 302, 304, 307, 310, 330–31, 335, 339, 344–45, 350, 356, 364, 374, 377, 380
British Army — Formations and Units
  1st Battalion, King's Own Shropshire Light Infantry, 234
  2nd Battalion, King's Own Shropshire Light Infantry, 341
  1st Battalion, Leinster Regiment, 70
  3rd British Division, 116
  4th British Division, 190
  4th Indian Division, 190
  5th British Corps, 139, 289
  8th (Eighth) Army, 119–121, 154–55, 174–75, 192–93, 288, 293, 366, 380
  10th Royal Grenadiers, 19, 255
  12th Royal Tank Regiment, 186
  13th Corps, 139, 289
  15th Army Group, 174
  19th Brigade, 54, 60, 67–68, 260–61, 341
  28th British Commonwealth Infantry Brigade (BCIB), 310, 377
  29th British Commonwealth Infantry Brigade (BCIB), 218
  30 Corps, 293
  51st Highland Division, 119
  52nd (Lowland) Divisions, 116
  142nd Royal Tank Regiment (*see also* Suffolk Tanks), 173, 295
  231 (Malta) Brigade, 132, 139, 289
British Columbia, 45, 395
Brockville, 205–06, 208, 303–06, 330
Bruay, 88, 272
Buchan, Lieutenant-Colonel Lawrence, 61, 68, 259, 261, 263–64, 320, 342–44
Burdett, Tom, 114, 167
Burns, Lieutenant D., 186
Burns, Lieutenant-General E.L.M., 110, 179, 355
Burrows, George, 122–24, 145, 181, 358–60, 362, 369
Busso, 151, 291

Byng, General Sir Julian H.G., 81, 88, 269–70, 273

Cabinet, 16, 42, 44, 259, 284, 336, 356
Calais, 115, 283
Calder, Brigadier Allan, 193
Caledonian, S.S., 77, 267
Calgary, 20, 143
Cambrai, 101–02, 104, 277, 326, 353
Camp Borden, 111–12, 306
Camp Petawawa, 208, 304–05, 309–12, 315, 322
Campbell, Lieutenant-Colonel K.L., 249, 308, 322, 384
Campeau, Lieutenant L.H., 195
Campobasso, 142, 149–51, 290–91, 295, 363
Canada — Formations and Units (*see also* specific regiments)
  1st Armoured Brigade, 156
  1st Battalion, The RCR (1 RCR), 211, 226–28, 230, 234, 236–37, 239–40, 242, 248, 306–17, 321, 324, 380, 395–96
  1st Canadian Army, 190, 200
  1st Canadian Corps, 175, 183, 197, 301, 366
  1st Canadian Infantry Brigade (1 CIB), 113, 115, 121, 124, 126, 131, 134, 139–40, 142–44, 146, 150, 152, 162, 166, 168, 171, 175, 179–80, 184–85, 188, 190, 193, 196, 198, 200, 283, 288–90, 293–94, 297–98, 300, 355, 371–72
  1st Canadian Infantry Division (1st Division), 79
  1st Canadian Infantry Regiment, 200, 303
  2nd Battalion, The Royal Canadian Regiment (2 RCR), 44–45, 70–71, 201, 205, 211–14, 217, 224–27, 234, 236–37, 259–62, 303, 305, 307–15, 317, 321–22, 324, 341–42, 396
  2nd Canadian Infantry Brigade (2 CIB), 128–29, 131, 159, 162, 166, 180, 200, 292, 302
  2nd Canadian Infantry Division (2nd Division), 77, 79
  3rd Battalion, The RCR (3 RCR), 70–71, 211, 248–50, 307–09, 311,

INDEX

313-17, 322, 324
3rd Canadian Infantry Brigade (3 CIB), 139-40, 148, 162, 180, 184, 188, 192-93, 196, 199, 294, 300, 372
3rd Canadian Infantry Division (3rd Division), 79, 349
4th Canadian Infantry Division (4th Division), 91-93, 96, 100, 103
5th Canadian Armoured Division, 171, 302, 363
6th Canadian Division, 200, 303
7th Canadian Infantry Brigade (7th Brigade), 79, 85, 268, 349
8th Canadian Infantry Brigade (8th Brigade), 80, 101
11th Canadian Armoured (Ontario) Regiment, 166
14th (Calgary) Tank Regiment, 143
25th Canadian Infantry Brigade (25 CIB), 212-14, 217-18, 220, 223-24, 227, 229, 248, 309-10, 312-16, 376-77
42nd Battalion (see also RHC), 82, 86, 93, 97, 102, 104-06, 269, 271, 277, 354
48th Highlanders, 127-28, 131, 146, 150, 152, 156, 162-63, 166-68, 178-80, 183, 185, 188, 198-200, 285, 292, 294-95, 300, 355, 372
49th Battalion, 82, 84, 93, 97, 102, 268-69, 271
58th Battalion, 92, 102, 272-73
90th Winnipeg Battalion of Rifles, 22
Canadian Armoured Fighting School, 111
Canadian Army Special Force (CASF), 211-12
Canadian Corps, 77, 81, 84-86, 88-89, 92, 95-96, 98-99, 101-02, 105, 170, 175, 183, 192, 267-70, 272-74, 284, 296, 300-01, 349-50, 353
Canadian Expeditionary Force (CEF), 77, 109, 116, 267, 278
Canadian Forces Base
  Borden, 111-12, 306
  Petawawa, 208-09, 211, 265, 304-06, 309-13, 315, 317, 322, 396
Canadian Joint Air Training Centre (CJATC), 207, 306, 374-75
Canadian Pacific Railway (CPR), 19
Canadian Regiment of Infantry, 29-30,

257, 319, 322
Canadian Special Air Service Company (Cdn SAS Coy), 207, 305
Canal du Nord, 102-03, 326
Canterbury, S.S., 115, 283
Cape Breton, 74, 265
Cape Colony, 54, 335
Cape Town, 46-48, 70, 259, 262, 346
Carden-Lloyd Machine Gun Carriers, 111
Carleton and York Regiment, 166, 171
Carogan, Gerald, 61, 344
Caron, Adolphe, 16
Casa Berardi, 163
Cassels, Major-General A.J.H., 218, 230, 309-10, 332
Castropignano, 152, 291
Catanian Plain, 119
Chail-Li, 214, 216, 310, 377
Chamberlain, Joseph, 42-43, 47-48
Chilkoot Pass, 32
China, 212, 377
Chinch'on, 236
Churchill, Winston, 48, 116, 118, 184, 209, 298
Civil Power, 17, 74, 109-10, 265, 349
Clark, Lieutenant John, 245
Clark, Lieutenant-General Mark, 142, 154, 228, 235
Clark's Crossing, 20
Claxton, Brooke, 206, 213, 373
Cohen, Major E.L., 234, 316, 322
Cold War, 7-8, 326
Colenso, 46, 48
Collver, Claude, 91
Colville, General Sir Henry, 63
Comfort, Charles, 158, 364
Companies (Coy — see also Infantry School Corps)
  "A" Coy, 45, 94, 97, 100-01, 103-05, 123, 127, 133, 144-45, 147, 150, 152, 158-60, 164, 167-68, 176-78, 181, 183-88, 191, 194-97, 199-200, 214, 216, 221, 223, 245, 247-49, 255, 266-67, 279, 281, 291-93, 302, 311-14, 360, 364
  "B" Coy, 45, 94, 97, 100-01, 103-04, 106, 121-22, 126, 129, 131, 139, 141-45, 147, 150, 152, 158-60, 162, 164, 167-68, 171, 176-77, 180, 184,

399

187, 191, 193–95, 197–99, 206, 214, 216, 219, 232–35, 241–45, 247, 249, 255, 265–67, 272, 277, 279, 289–92, 299, 304, 307, 314–15, 349, 361, 364, 380
"C" Coy, 19–20, 22, 25–29, 45, 51–52, 57, 85, 89, 97, 100–01, 103–04, 122, 139, 145, 147–48, 150, 152, 159–60, 164, 168, 176, 178, 181, 184–86, 190–91, 193–96, 198–200, 214, 235–36, 241, 247, 249–52, 255–56, 259, 266–67, 272, 279, 289, 292, 296, 299–302, 308, 311, 315, 339, 365
"D" Coy, 29, 45, 49, 59, 89, 97, 101–05, 109, 122–23, 126, 129–32, 144, 147, 150, 152, 155, 158–60, 164, 176–77, 180, 184, 186–88, 191, 194, 196–97, 214, 216, 227, 241–42, 247–49, 252, 256, 266–68, 272, 278–80, 285, 287–89, 291, 301, 304, 306–08, 312–13, 365
"E" Coy, 45, 57, 241, 243–45, 247, 266–67, 315
"F" Coy, 45, 264, 266–67
"G" Coy, 45, 264, 266
"H" Coy, 45, 63, 260, 264, 266
Tactical HQ, 176–77, 186, 195, 197
Compound 66, 234–35, 314
Conca River, 185, 298
Confederation, 16, 330
Constantine, Superintendent Charles, 30
Cornwalls (*see also* Duke of Cornwall's Light Infantry), 57–58, 60
Convent Hill, 184
Courcelette, 82–83, 271, 326
Crerar, Lieutenant-General Harry, 170–71, 284, 291, 293–94, 366
Cronje, General Piet, 54, 59–60, 64–65, 260
Crowe, Lieutenant-Colonel R.M, 120, 124, 126, 129–31, 287–88, 321, 360
Crozier, Superintendent L.N.F., 17–18
Cummings, Corporal, 131, 360
Currie, Lieutenant-General Sir Arthur, 96–97, 273–74, 276, 281, 353
Cut Knife Creek, 24, 26, 256
Czechoslovakia, 112, 209

Dawson, 30, 37–39, 258, 261, 333, 335

Deadman, Lance-Corporal R.E., 177
DeWet, General, 69
Dieppe, 118
Dill, General Sir John, 115
Dillon, Captain R.M., 124
Dominion Coal Company, 74, 265
Dornier Feature, 186–87
Douai Plain, 86
Douglas, 51–52, 260
Duke of Cornwall's Light Infantry (*see also* Cornwalls), 57, 260, 341
DUKW, 121
Dunham, Private F., 55–56, 58–59, 61–62, 66, 347
Dumont, Gabriel, 21, 331–32
Duronia, 152–54, 291
Dyea, 32

Earl of Minto, 42, 264
Eden Mountain, 68, 261
Eighth Army, 119–21, 154–55, 174–75, 192–93, 288, 293, 366, 380
England (*see also* Britain, Great Britain), 42, 48, 70, 75, 77, 106, 111–14, 116–18, 122, 135, 137, 174, 201, 262–63, 267, 282–84, 286–87, 293, 345, 347, 357
Enright, Sergeant Gerald, 243, 245
Evans, Lieutenant-Colonel T.D.B., 30, 32, 34, 36, 39, 258, 335

Fabeck Graben, 82
Fages, Lieutenant-Colonel Alfred Octave, 76, 265, 267, 320
Fenian Raids, 16, 330
Fenton, Faith, 35, 334
First Commonwealth Division, 217–18, 223, 239, 310
Fish Creek, 21–23, 25, 256, 331–32
Flanders, 8, 95, 170, 326
Florence, 183, 297–98
Foggia Plain, 142
Foglia River, 183–85
Fontaine-Notre-Dame, 103
Fort Lewis, 211–12, 307–09
Fort Pitt, 19–20
Fort Selkirk, 30, 33–34, 37–38, 258, 261
Fortore River, 148
Fosso Vecchio, 197, 300, 272

Foulkes, Captain (later Lieutenant-General) Charles, 12, 112, 197, 299, 302–03, 380
Fowler, Corporal E.D., 238–39
France, 75, 77, 83, 114–16, 170, 198, 267, 276, 283, 297, 301, 326
Franz Ferdinand, Archduke, 75
Fredericton, 16, 255, 257, 264, 324
Freeland, Sergeant, 80
Frenchman's Butte, 29

Galloway, Major Strome, 12, 114, 116, 121, 123, 140–42, 147, 155, 163, 165, 167–72, 181, 185, 188, 190, 197–98, 292–93, 298, 321, 357, 364, 367
Gardner, Lieutenant H.R., 10, 239–40, 243
Gaston, Charles, 85–86
General C.C. Ballou, USNS, 248, 316
General Order
　No. 26, 16, 255
　No. 83, 257
　No. 107, 263
　No. 110, 280
General William N. Black, USNS, 227, 312
German Air Force, 116
German Army (*see also* specific regiments)
　1st German Parachute Division, 146, 186
　12th (Twelfth) Army, 198
　90th Light Division, 156
　90th Panzer Grenadier Division, 156
　114th Jäger Division, 194
　356th Infantry Division, 195
Germany, 75, 112, 117–18, 198, 200, 266, 283, 302, 317
Giarratana, 124, 288
Gildone, 150
Glenora, 32, 258
Gold Rush, 30
Gordon Highlanders, 52, 61, 63, 339, 341
Gothic Line, 181, 183–85, 327, 372
Gourock, Scotland, 114, 283
Graham, Brigadier Howard D., 139, 144, 152–53, 162–63, 289, 291
Grange Tunnel, 89, 272–73
Gras-Pan, 54
Great Britain (*see also* Britain, England), 116, 266, 307

Greek Brigade, 188
Gregg, Lieutenant Milton, 94–95, 99, 103–04, 106, 277, 312, 319, 353–54
Gully, The, 162, 165–66, 327
Gustav Line, 174–75, 178, 295, 327, 363, 372

Haig, Field Marshal Sir Douglas, 95, 268, 272, 276, 280
Halifax, 15–16, 70, 73–74, 76–77, 109, 113, 201, 262, 264–66, 278–79, 281, 283, 303, 306, 349
Halifax Citadel, 70–71, 260
Halifax Explosion, 275
Hamilton, General Sir Ian, 68, 261
Hart, Major-General Fitzroy, 69
Hart-McHarg, Sergeant W., 57, 65, 68
Hastings and Prince Edward Regiment (H&PER), 123, 127–29, 131, 146, 150, 152, 156, 160, 162, 166–68, 171, 179–80, 183, 188, 190–91, 193, 195–96, 199–200, 288, 291–92, 294–95, 300, 306
Hawarden Castle, 70, 262
Heidelberg Trench, 100
Hill 70, 88, 95, 274, 326
Hill 113, 230–31, 236
Hill 135, 86
Hill 145, 86, 91–92
Hill 187, 249, 252, 316
Hill 227, 239, 241
Hill 355 (*see also* Kowang-san, "Little Gibraltar"), 218, 240–41, 245, 247–48, 315
Hill 467 (*see also* Kakhul-bong), 214, 216, 310
Hitler, Adolf, 112, 148, 166, 174
Hitler Line, 174–76, 178–80, 296, 327, 368, 372
Hodson, Major Ian A., 123, 128, 164–65, 292
Holland, 198, 200, 301–02, 317
Hollyer, Second-Lieutenant E.H., 251
Holmes, Major Don, 236–37
Hooge, 80–81, 269, 350
Hudson's Bay Company (HBC), 33, 330
Hughes, Sam, 75
Hunt, Lieutenant J.R., 120
Husky (*see also* Operation Husky), 119, 288

Hutton, Major-General Edward T.H., 39, 41–42, 335, 336

Ijssel River, 198, 301
Imjin River, 213, 217–18, 237, 248, 310–11
Infantry School Corps, 17–18, 22, 25, 29, 255–56, 319, 322
Israels Poort, 67, 261
Italy, 121, 135, 137, 139–44, 148, 154, 168, 172, 174, 181, 184, 198, 203, 289–90, 298, 328, 363, 365, 372

Jacobsdal, 54, 260
Jamestown Line, 218–19, 236, 238–39, 312, 314, 316
Jeffery, Private William, 62, 65, 340
Jelsi, 150
Joice, Lieutenant J.E., 193–94

Kaesong, 217, 310
Kakhul-bong, 214, 310
Kansas Line, 219, 236, 313
Kap'yong, 213, 377
Keane, Lieutenant-Colonel Robert A., 214, 217, 307, 312, 322
Kennedy Hill, Lance-Corporal John, 55–56, 341
Kimberley, 54
King, Lieutenant W.M., 106, 277, 354
King's Own Shropshire Light Infantry (Shropshires), 57, 61–63
Kingston, 16, 45, 304, 330
Kitchener, Lord, 58, 342
Klenavic, Major Francis, 247, 313, 317, 321–22
Klip Drift, 54, 260
Klondike, 32, 35, 262, 333
Koje-Do, 232–33, 235, 314, 380
Korea, 7, 205, 209, 211–13, 217, 219, 225, 227–28, 232, 237, 248, 252–53, 307–09, 312, 314, 316, 328, 376
Kowang-san (*see also* Hill 355, "Little Gibraltar"), 218

La Folie Wood, 91
La Torre, 156
Ladysmith, 54, 339
Lake Champlain, 70, 262
Lake Superior, 19

Lamone River, 192–93, 196, 299–300
Laurier, Wilfrid, 41–44, 64, 337
Leonforte, 128–29, 289
Le Quesnel Wood, 101, 276
Lens, 98, 274–75
Lester, Private Edward, 35, 334
Lévis, Quebec, 29, 257
Liberal Party, 42
Liddell, Major R.G., 121–22, 124, 135, 158, 358
Liri River, 175–76, 178, 296
Liri Valley, 174–75, 296, 327, 372
Lithgow, Major C.H., 129, 208, 360
Little Gibraltar (*see also* Hill 355, Kowang-san), 218, 240–41, 315, 383
London, England, 112, 175, 205, 262, 280, 282
London, Ontario, 29, 45, 47, 70, 73, 109–10, 202, 205, 256–57, 263–64, 271, 279, 281–82, 286, 303, 309, 313, 315, 324
Loomis, Lieutenant D.G., 243, 277
Loyal Edmonton Regiment, 166, 171, 185, 191
Luce River, 100
Ludendorff, General Erich von, 100

MacArthur, General Douglas, 210, 212, 217
MacDonald, Sir John A., 154
Macdonell, Brigadier-General A.C., 85–86, 268–69, 273
Magersfontein, 46, 48, 339
Manitoba, 16, 45, 208, 308, 314, 330
Marano River, 188, 190
Marcoing Line, 103–04, 277
Marecchia River, 190
Marine Phoenix, USNS, 227, 312
Marnix Van St. Aldegonde, 118, 288
Mason, Lieutenant J.C., 58–59
Mastronadi, Lieutenant Edward, 222
Mathers, Lieutenant-Colonel/Major W., 158, 163–64, 176, 180, 292–93, 295–96, 321
Maucini, 121–22
Maunsell, Lieutenant-Colonel George J., 30, 255, 257–58, 319–20
McCormick, A.S., 66, 346
McMahon, Corporal N.J., 189

McNaughton, Lieutenant-General A.G.L., 115–16, 134, 284–85
Meadows, Lance Sergeant, 193–94
Medland, Major R.D., 216
Metauro River, 183, 190, 298
Métis, 17, 19, 21–22, 27–28, 330
Middleton, Major-General Frederick, 18–23, 25, 27–29, 256, 330–32
Miles, Lieutenant Leonard, 177
Military Districts, 16, 330
Militia, 15–20, 29–30, 32, 37, 39, 41, 43, 46, 71, 73–75, 109–11, 255, 257, 264, 330, 336, 345, 349
Militia Act, 16, 71, 76
Militia Headquarters (Ottawa), 17, 29, 74, 111, 264, 320, 349
Militello in Val Di Catania, 135, 289
Milner, Alfred Lord, 47
Misano Ridge, 185, 298, 327
Mobile Striking Force (MSF), 208, 305, 308, 312, 317
Modder River, 54–55, 64, 260–61, 339
Modica, 124
Mons, 105–06, 277–78, 326
Monteciccardo, 184
Montgomery, Field Marshal Sir Bernard Law, 124, 125, 154–55, 198, 288, 293, 305, 359
Montreal, 16, 45, 109, 278–81, 330
Moro River, 156, 158–60, 162, 169, 291–92, 365
Motta, 143–46, 153, 327, 362, 372
Motta Ridge, 146, 290
Mount Etna, 134
Munich Agreement, 112

Nabu-ri Valley, 219–20
Naples, 142, 149, 295, 361
Natal, 48, 54, 335
National Defence Headquarters (NDHQ), 207, 280, 305, 374
New Brunswick, 45, 255, 330–31
New Zealand, 63, 330, 377
Niagara-on-the-Lake, 112
Nissoria, 128–31, 289
Non-Permanent Active Militia (*see also* Militia), 111
Northcote, 25–28, 256
North Atlantic Treaty Organisation (NATO), 209, 211
North Korean People's Army (NKPA), 209, 212
North Saskatchewan River, 19, 29
North-West Europe, 200, 203, 301, 328, 372
North-West Mounted Police (NWMP), 17–18, 21, 23, 30, 38–39, 256, 258, 330, 332–33, 338
North-West Rebellion, 13, 17–18, 29, 53, 253, 256, 331–33
Norway, 114
Nova Scotia, 45, 73–74, 109, 265, 300, 330, 349

Ogilvie, William, 39
O'Leary, Reverend, 58
Operation Baytown, 135, 137, 139
Operation Commando, 218, 311
Operation Husky, 119, 288
Orange Free State, 41, 47, 65, 260, 335–36
Oratino, 151, 173, 291, 295
Ortona, 154, 156, 162–63, 165–66, 168–69, 172–73, 292–95, 327, 365, 372
Ortona-Orsogna Crossroads, 156, 162, 165, 292
Ottawa, 17–19, 21, 30, 32, 45, 59, 74, 111–12, 208, 258, 304, 309–11, 316–17
Otter, Lieutenant-Colonel W.D., 18, 20–21, 23–25, 27, 29, 43–44, 46, 48–49, 51–53, 58–60, 62–65, 68–70, 255–56, 258–59, 261, 280, 319–20, 332, 342

Pachino, 119, 121–22, 139, 168, 288
Panmunjom, 220
Passchendaele, 8, 95–96, 98, 274–75, 326
Paardeberg, 13, 63–64, 71, 260, 325, 342, 345
Paardeberg Day, 306
Paardeberg Drift, 54–56, 60, 63–64, 71, 260, 341, 343
Parvillers, 100, 276
Pelves, 102
Perkins, J.A., 51, 65–66
Permanent Force (*see also* Active Militia), 15–17, 32, 44, 73, 75, 109–12, 206–07, 278
Pesaro, 183
Pescara, 154, 166

Petawawa (*see also* Canadian Forces Base [CFB] Petawawa), 208–09, 211, 265, 304–06, 309–13, 315, 317, 322
Peterson, Lieutenant A.A.S., 230–32
"Phoney War," 142
Piedmonte, 181, 297
Pilcher, Lieutenant-Colonel Thomas, 51–52, 259
"Pimple," The, 92
Pisciatello River, 191, 299
Point 59, 177–78, 296
Point 106, 179–80
Point 167, 139
Point 761, 152
Poland, 112, 114
Pontecorvo, 175–76, 179–81, 296
Pope, Major Billy, 120, 127
Poplar Grove, 64, 260
Poundmaker, 19–21, 23–25, 29, 332
Powell, Georgia, 35
Powers, Major T.M., 131, 135, 288–89, 321
Pretoria, 64, 67–69, 261–62
Prince Edward Island, 45
Princess Louise Dragoon Guards, 143
Princess Patricia's Canadian Light Infantry (PPCLI), 80–82, 97, 101–02, 104–05, 109, 131, 156, 190, 198, 206, 208, 212–13, 218, 267, 270, 274–75, 277, 287, 289, 301, 305, 315–16, 354, 377
Princip, Gavrilo, 75
Pusan, 211–12, 232, 248, 309, 316

Qualye, Lieutenant Jim, 161
Qu'appelle, 20
Quebec, 29, 42, 45, 73, 75, 109, 255, 257, 259, 264, 330, 335–36
Quebec City, 16, 45, 73, 109, 259, 264, 330, 336, 354
Queen's Own Rifles of Canada, 19
Queen's Scarf, 343
Quested Farm Camp, 77, 267

Ragusa, 124
Ramsay, Frederick, 46, 49
Red River Rebellion, 16–17, 330
Reid, Lieutenant-Colonel W.W., 196, 206, 300, 302–03, 321
Regalbuto, 132–34, 289, 327, 360, 372
Reggio Di Calabria, 139–42, 289, 327

Regina Trench, 83–85, 271
Regular Force (*see also* Permanent Force), 15, 29, 41, 111, 228
Republic of Korea (ROK), 209, 376–77
Rhineland, 112
Riccione, 185, 187–88, 190, 192, 298–99
Rich, Lieutenant W., 181
Ridgeway, General Matthew, 217, 228, 310
Riel, Louis, 17–19, 21, 28, 331
Rimini, 181, 183, 188–90, 298–99, 328
Rimini Airfield, 188–90, 299
Ritchie, Lieutenant-Colonel J.W., 186, 193, 196, 296, 299–300, 321
Roberts, Field Marshal Lord, 64, 70–71
Roccaspromonte, 152
Rockingham, Brigadier J.M., 213–14, 227, 309, 313
Rolph, Captain Frank, 189
Rome, 148, 154, 175, 181, 295, 297, 368
Rossolini, 123, 288
Royal Air Force, 139
Royal Australian Regiment (1st Battalion), 248
Royal Canadian Dragoons (RCD), 32, 258, 333, 338
Royal Canadian Regiment (RCR), 7–8, 13–14, 17, 30, 34, 39, 44, 63, 65, 152, 172, 253, 258–59, 263, 305, 320–24, 329
Royal Canadian Regiment of Infantry (RCRI), 258, 320, 323, 333, 335
Royal Highlanders of Canada (RHC — *see also* 42nd Battalion), 82
Royal Navy (RN), 139
Royal Regiment of Canadian Infantry (RRCI), 28–29, 32, 257–58, 319–20, 322
Royal 22nd Regiment (R22R), 109, 191, 196, 206, 225, 239, 248, 252, 300, 305, 315–16, 354
Royal Winnipeg Rifles, 22

Salerno, 142
Saltara, 183–84, 298
San Fortunato, 189–90
San Leonardo, 156, 158–60, 162–63, 292, 327, 372
San Lorenzo, 188, 328, 372
San Lorenzo-in-Strada, 187

INDEX

San Marco, 146, 148, 290
San Martino, 188, 190, 328, 372
San Nicola, 166, 169, 171, 294
San Stefano, 141
San Tommaso, 166, 294
San Vito, 155, 171, 184, 291, 294–95, 298
Sangro River, 149, 154–55, 291
Sant'Arcangelo, 191
Santerno, 192–93
Sardinian, S.S., 45–47, 259
Saskatchewan Light Infantry, 168
Scotland, 114, 283
Seaforth Highlanders of Canada, 156, 185
Senio River, 193, 197, 300
Sensée River, 103
Serbia, 75
Sicily, 119–20, 123, 127, 134–35, 137, 139–40, 202, 288–89, 327, 372
Sifton, Clifton, 30
Simonds, Major-General G.G., 129, 131, 133, 139, 290, 317, 363, 380
Siracusa, 119
Skagway, 32, 262
Slags Kraal, 65
"Slaughterhouse Hill," 160, 162
Smith, Brigadier Desmond, 193
Smith, Major Henry, 25, 27
Smith, Captain J.B., 187
Smith-Dorrien, Major-General Horrace, 54, 59, 65–68, 71, 260, 342
Snell, Lieutenant Wilf, 200, 203
Somme, 81–82, 86, 270, 326, 350–51
South Africa, 41–42, 44–47, 52, 63–65, 70, 259, 262–63, 325, 344, 347
South African War (*see also* Boer War), 70, 264
South Korea (*see also* Korea), 209, 307, 376
Soviet Union, 209, 376
Springfield, 67, 261
Springs, 68–69, 262
Spry, Lieutenant-Colonel Daniel, 114, 135, 141, 144, 146–48, 159–60, 162–63, 166, 168, 289, 292–94, 297, 321
St. Jean, 109, 255, 257, 280
Steele, Sam, 38, 393
Sterlin, Lieutenant Mitch, 159–61, 292
Sterlin's Castle, 161, 292
Stikine River, 32, 333

Stikine Route, 32
Stinson, Corporal, 230–32
Stormberg, 46–48
Straits of Messina, 139
Strange, Major-General Thomas, 20, 29, 331, 365
Suffolk Tanks (*see also* 142nd Royal Tank Regiment), 173
Sunnyside Kopje, 51
Swift Current, 20, 23

Telegraph Creek, 32–33
Teslin Lake, 33, 36
Teslin Trail, 32, 34
Thaba Mountain, 68, 261
38th Parallel, 212–13, 217, 310, 376
Thompson, Private Richard Rowland, 59, 63, 344
Thorne, Major Eric, 194
Three Rivers Armoured Regiment, 124
Tollo Road, 166
Topp, Major C.B., 104, 277
Toronto, 16, 19, 22, 28, 45, 52, 73, 109, 255–57, 263–64, 279, 330
Transvaal, 8, 41, 61, 261–62, 335
Tugela River, 48
Turner, Private Fred, 130–31, 360

Uitlanders, 41, 335
United States Fifth Army, 174, 193
United States of America (U.S.), 32, 118, 307, 376
Usna Hill, 82, 271

Valcartier, 75, 113, 279, 283
Valguarnera, 125–26, 288, 327, 372
Vancouver, 32, 160, 241, 258, 262, 313
Vian, Rear-Admiral Sir Philip, 119
Victoria, Queen, 29, 63, 70, 257, 262–63, 279–80
Victoria Cross (VC), 63, 99, 104, 106, 277, 330, 353
Vidal, Lieutenant-Colonel B.H., 70, 260, 320
Villa Grande, 163, 298
Villa Rogatti, 156
Vimy Ridge, 86, 88–90, 92–93, 98, 272, 275, 301
Vizzini, 125

Vokes, Major-General Chris, 128, 156, 162, 166, 179–80, 190, 291, 294–97, 366
Volturno River, 154, 173, 295

Wadmore, Lyndhurst, 19, 26, 74, 256, 264–65, 320
Walsh, Major J.M., 30
War of 1812, 15
War Office (U.K.), 44
Waterval Drift, 67, 261
White Pass, 32
Wilkinson, Captain J.H.R., 195
Windsor Castle, 70, 262
Winnipeg, 18–19, 22, 256

Wood, Captain C.L., 277, 321
Wright, G.K., 149, 176
Wyoming Line, 219, 236

Yalu River, 212–13
Young, Major D., 37, 258, 264, 320
Young Men's Christian Association (YMCA), 51
Yukon, 6, 30, 32–34, 37
Yukon Field Force, 30, 32–34, 37–39, 41, 258, 260, 262, 335
Yukon Garrison, 260–62, 335
Ypres, 8, 77, 79–81, 95, 268–70, 325–26

Zollern Graben, 82, 271

www.ingramcontent.com/pod-product-compliance
Lightning Source LLC
Chambersburg PA
CBHW052054300426
44117CB00013B/2126